Correction Terms

• To help you learn to use the material of this course for your own writing, your instructor will probably ask you to write and revise at least one essay a week. When you turn in an essay, your instructor will read it and write notes in the margins telling you how to strengthen it. These notes will use the terms on this page. Each term is printed in a black band at the right-hand edges of the pages covering that material, in the same position it has on this page. When you receive a corrected essay, find each term on this list and then look for the black band on the corresponding pages of the book. On those pages, you will find clearly labeled examples of faulty writing and correct revisions, followed by a brief correction comment in bold type. You can quickly figure out what the weakness is and how it can be corrected. Then return to your essay, find a weakness of this type, and correct it in the same way. The correction terms are meaningful in themselves, and soon you will find yourself understanding them without referring to the text.

pages 287–294	**abstract**
236–242	**article**
260–265	**capital**
209–216	**comma 1, 2, & 3**
217–225	**comma 4**
191–201	**comparison**
42–46	**conclusion**
243–249	**contraction**
326–334	**direct/indirect**
24–34	**evidence needed**
83–91	**fragment**
335–343	**idiom**
35–41	**introduction**
302–308	**mixed structure**
318–325	**modification**
177–183	**modifier ending**
185–190	**modifier form**
356–367	**monotonous**
309–317	**parallel**
146–158	**past verb**
102–109	**plural**
250–259	**possessive**
135–145	**present verb**
123–132	**pronoun form**
110–115	**pronoun number**
116–122	**pronoun person**
228–235	**punctuation**
295–301	**reference**
92–101	**run-together**
266–278	**spelling**
14–23	**support**
167–174	**tense shift**
5–13	**thesis**
159–166	**verb combination**
202–208	**word form**
344–355	**wordy**
279–286	**wrong word**

The Basic Writing Book

JOYCE STITH

California State University at Hayward

Little, Brown and Company BOSTON TORONTO

Acknowledgments

Sherwood Anderson. Excerpt from "I'm a Fool" by Sherwood Anderson, published in *The Dial,* February 1922. Reprinted by permission of Harold Ober Associates Incorporated. Copyright 1922 by Dial Publishing Company, Inc. Renewed 1949 by Eleanor Copenhaver Anderson.

Leonard Cohen. "Go By Brooks" from *The Spice-Box of Earth* by Leonard Cohen. Published in 1965 by The Viking Press, Inc. Reprinted by permission of Viking Penguin Inc. and McClelland and Stewart Limited.

John Galsworthy. "Japanese Quince" from John Galsworthy, *A Motley.* Copyright 1910 by Charles Scribner's Sons; copyright renewed. (New York: Charles Scribner's Sons, 1910.) Reprinted with the permission of Charles Scribner's Sons.

Jane Jacobs. Excerpt from *The Death and Life of Great American Cities* by Jane Jacobs. Copyright © 1961 by Jane Jacobs. Reprinted by permission of Random House, Inc.

Oxford Advanced Learner's Dictionary of Current English. 12 entries from the 3rd (1974) edition, © Oxford University Press 1974. Reprinted by permission of Oxford University Press.

Bernard Shaw. Extracts from *Arms and the Man* and *Man and Superman* by Bernard Shaw reprinted by permission of The Society of Authors on behalf of the Bernard Shaw Estate.

William Strunk, Jr. and E. B. White. Excerpts from *The Elements of Style,* Third Edition, by William Strunk, Jr. and E. B. White (Copyright © 1979 by Macmillan Publishing Co., Inc.). Reprinted by permission of Macmillan Publishing Co., Inc.

James Thurber and E. B. White. Excerpt from *Is Sex Necessary?* (New York: Harper & Row, 1929). Reprinted by permission.

E. B. White. Excerpt from "The Faith of a Writer: Remarks by E. B. White upon Receiving the 1971 National Medal for Literature," *Publishers Weekly,* December 6, 1971. Reprinted by permission of E. B. White.

E. B. White. Excerpt from "The Winter of the Great Snows" (p. 54) in *Essays of E. B. White.* Copyright © 1971 by E. B. White. This essay first appeared in *The New Yorker.* Reprinted by permission of Harper & Row, Publishers, Inc.

Work by these students is included with their permission:

Hassan Al-Bourainain. Essays on memories of Jabail and on women's role in Saudi Arabia, © 1982 by Hassan Al-Bourainain.

Bruce Thomas Allen. Essay comparing two baseball players, © 1982 by Bruce Thomas Allen.

Betzaida Barela. "Serenades," © 1982 by Betzaida Barela.

Gordon Black. Essays on the fun of driving and on mopeds, © 1982 by Gordon Black.

Chang Bao-ho. "The Trip to Chen De," © 1982 by Chang Bao-ho.

Gwynn Corley, Essay on Karate, © 1982 by Gwynn Corley.

Katherine Dukes. Essay on lending money, paragraph on her mother's spirit, © 1982 by Katherine Dukes.

Farida Gulshad. "Raja, the Grasshopper Who Loved to Drink Tea," © 1982 by Farida Gulshad.

Dan Huber. Essay on the importance of eating breakfast, © 1982 by Dan Huber.

Deborah L. Johnson. Essay on high-heeled shoes, © 1982 by Deborah L. Johnson.

Pamela Kaye Jones. "Washington, D.C.," © 1982 by Pamela Kaye Jones.

Torri K. Jones. Essay on her mother, © 1982 by Torri K. Jones.

Catherine Leung. "At Last, a Cheap French Restaurant," "My Neighborhood," and "My Plan for the Summer," © 1982 by Catherine Leung.

Tonianne Marquez. "The Things That Make Me Laugh," © 1982 by Tonianne Marquez.

Denise Michel. Essay on visiting grandparents in Iowa, © 1982 by Denise Michel.

David Montez. Essay on neighborhood pollution, © 1982 by David Montez.

Dahlia M. Moodie. Essay on her kitchen, © 1982 by Dahlia M. Moodie.

Thu Nguyen. Essay on mother, © 1982 by Thu Nguyen.

Stan Pisle. "Tragedy or Triumph?" © 1982 by Stan Pisle.

Paul R. Pomeroy. Essay on pit bulls, © 1982 by Paul R. Pomeroy.

Cheryl Simpson. Essays on her first date and on childlessness, © 1982 by Cheryl Simpson.

Roger Smith. Essay on his dog, Shep, © 1982 by Roger Smith.

Thalia McNeil Smith. Essay on her elementary school, © 1982 by Thalia McNeil Smith.

Stephen Stolp. Essay on a shoe box, © 1982 by Stephen Stolp.

James Vaughan. Essay comparing boxing and karate, © 1982 by James Vaughan.

John W. Vertrees. Essay on junk food, © 1982 by John W. Vertrees.

Preface

• *The Basic Writing Book* grew out of the basic writing program at California State University at Hayward because no available text included all the materials the teachers used each term. Because our students are beginning writers, we wanted a text with a little material on organization, simple treatment of all the common sentence problems, lots of good writing and proofreading exercises, and typical student essays to criticize and correct. Because our students begin writing early in the term when most of the course content has not yet been introduced, we also wanted a book that could serve as a reference tool so that students could eliminate from their essays weaknesses that had not yet been covered in class. In other words, we wanted a text that combined elements of the rhetoric, the grammar, the workbook, the reader, and the handbook, but none existed. This book evolved to fill that gap.

This textbook is designed for the basic writing course that covers all skills required for and all aspects of beginning essay writing. Starting with essay organization including thesis, outline, body paragraphs, introduction, and conclusion, the text then covers identification of subjects, verbs, and clauses and correction of run-together sentences and fragments. From there I turn to sentence consistency including detailed work on correct use of pronouns, verbs, and modifiers. Next I cover the four basic comma rules, semicolons, and colons. The chapter on word correctness covers articles, contractions, possessives, capitals, and spelling. The last third of the book is devoted to refinement of diction and syntax: precise and concrete word choice, careful use of pronouns and modifiers, consistent and parallel structures, direct and indirect speech, and idiom. The last chapter treats refinement of sentences in context and covers concise wording and sentence variety.

The Basic Writing Book was written for today's basic writing students, people with limited vocabularies and reading skills and little or no background in writing or grammar. Some speak English as a second language; others speak a nonstandard dialect from which many of the distinctions of standard English have been dropped. This book is designed to give these people, as quickly as possible, the writing skills necessary for success in college. It covers the most common weaknesses of beginning writers, treats only those patterns which cause student errors, and includes no more grammar than is necessary for correct writing.

This book is based on the conviction that people can learn a skill only by practicing it, so each unit includes a brief explanation followed by many exercises. The explanations are simple and straightforward, expressed whenever possible in common-sense language, and amply illustrated by clearly labeled examples of faulty and correctly revised forms. Each explanation ends with a brief correction comment for quick reference.

The exercise sections in each chapter begin with sentence-length writing assignments designed to establish the skill in the student's writing behavior. These are followed by correct and incorrect sentences so the student can learn to distinguish faulty forms and correct them. Beginning with simple sentences, these proofreading exercises progress to more difficult ones and end with a student-written paragraph. Next, each set of exercises contains a longer passage. Those in the first seven chapters are typical student essays containing weaknesses of all types so students can review some skills and preview others. Because the last three chapters emphasize writing refinement more than correctness, they contain professionally written passages for analysis and emulation. Every third set of exercises includes essay-writing assignments and others contain paragraph-writing assignments. Each unit ends with two sets of moderately difficult exercises for independent study, answers to which are at the back of the book.

Student writing improves most quickly if students write frequently, receive specific criticism, and then eliminate their weaknesses. Because they will frequently make errors that have not yet been covered in class, this text is also set up as a reference tool. In addition to positive comments, the teacher or reader can suggest corrections by writing notes in the margins such as "fragment," "improve the parallel," or "wrong pronoun form," using the correction terms listed on page i. Each term is printed on tabs in the margins of the pages covering the weakness, so the student can turn directly from each note to the relevant pages of the book. Each tabbed unit includes an explanation, plenty of examples, and a correction comment in boldface type. The student can read the correction comment to learn what to do, the examples to learn how to do it, and the explanation itself if necessary. Each unit can be understood independently, without referring to other units. After consulting the text, the student can return to the essay, find a similar weakness, and make the required correction. Soon the student will respond directly to the reader's note without referring to the text.

This book grows out of years of study and diverse experiences teaching and supervising basic writing. As a graduate student at the University of California at Santa Barbara I studied methods of teaching writing and student-taught basic writing to freshmen in the Educational Opportunity Program. In 1972 I joined the English faculty of Kent State University, where I taught both basic and college-level freshman English and coordinated the Learning Improvement Program at the Tuscarawas Campus. There I developed programs for pre-college testing and placement and for individualized instruction of remedial writing. In 1977 I accepted my present position in the English Department of California State University at Hayward where I have developed and coordinate the basic writing program, working closely with the American Language Program, the Learning Center, and the Intercultural Education and Resource Center. Perhaps most important, each week of the last eight academic years I have read an average of sixty essays by beginning writers.

Many people contributed to this book. I want to thank the people at Little Brown, especially Don Palm, who introduced me to Little Brown, Molly Faulkner, who cheerfully and capably transformed my ideas into reality, and David W. Lynch, who shepherded the book through production. I also want to thank Kim Flachmann (California State University-Bakersfield), C. Jeriel Howard (Northeastern Illinois University), Cecilia Macheski (LaGuardia Community College), and Jean Wyrick (Colorado State University) for their many valuable suggestions and welcome support, and Professor Richard S. Beal of Boston University, for his high standards and frank criticism.

I want to thank my colleagues in the English Department at California State University at Hayward, especially the chair, Jim Murphy, for their most generous assistance and support. I am also grateful to all the typists who helped me with the manuscript—Claire Browne, Milly Flemming, Sheila Mahoney, Kathlyn Peterson, Gwen Underwood, and above all my assistant Joan Ferguson for her patience, intelligence, and good sense. I am also indebted to the teachers and tutors in the basic writing program, who spent many hours with early drafts of this book and made many valuable suggestions. Most of all I want to thank my students, who taught me what to say, who wrote much of the material of this book, and who tolerated the inconveniences of a textbook in manuscript. Their diligence and eagerness to learn inspired and sustained me.

I am especially indebted to the following students who most generously allowed their essays to be used in this text:

Hassan Al-Bouainain	Deborah Lynn Johnson	Thu Nguyen
Bruce Allen	Pamela Jones	Stan Pisle
Betzaida Barela	Torri Jones	Paul Pomeroy
Gordon Black	Catherine Leung	Cheryl Simpson
Chang Bao-Ho	Toni Marquez	Roger Smith
Gwynn Corley	Thalia McNeil	Stephen Stolp
Katherine Dukes	Denise Michel	James Vaughn
Farida Gulshad	David Montez	John Vertrees
Dan Huber	Dahlia Moodie	

To the Student

• *The Basic Writing Book* is designed to teach you, as quickly, efficiently, and painlessly as possible, the writing skills required for success in college. Because you will often be required to demonstrate your knowledge of course material by writing essays and essay exams, your grades in college will depend directly on your ability to write effectively. This book begins by showing you how to organize your material into a convincing essay that makes a point and backs it up with a watertight argument. This format can be adapted to any college writing assignment. Then it takes up the language of the business and academic worlds.

People change their language as they move from one situation to another. You probably speak several forms of English, for example: one with your mother, another with your friends, yet another with your English teacher, and so on. Language that is correct in one place may be inappropriate and therefore cause confusion in another place. If you suddenly started speaking to your friends in the same language that you use with your English teacher, they would be surprised, and that surprise would prevent them from really paying attention to the ideas you were trying to express. Inappropriate language calls attention to the words; appropriate language calls attention to the ideas.

This text is designed to teach standard English, the language that is used in the business and academic worlds. Standard English is not "better" than other forms of English, it's just appropriate and therefore correct in these worlds. In fact, it is inferior to some forms of English because it's less colorful, but at the same time it is superior to most other forms, because it's logically tighter and more rigorous. When we label a group of words "incorrect" or "faulty," these words may be "incorrect" only in a setting where standard English is spoken and "correct" in other situations.

Contents

The Structures 1

1 • Building the Essay 1

From Subject to Thesis 5
  Exercises 10;   Independent Study 13

Building an Outline 14
  Exercises 16;   Independent Study 22

Writing Body Paragraphs 24
  Exercises 27;   Independent Study 32

Writing Introductions 35
  Exercises 38;   Independent Study 40

Writing Conclusions 42
  Exercises 43;   Independent Study 45

2 • Identifying Subjects and Verbs 47

The Elements 47
  Exercises 50;   Independent Study 53

Combinations 54
  Exercises 54;   Independent Study 58

Some Important Distinctions 60
  Exercises 62;   Independent Study 65

3 • Understanding Sentences 66

Connecting Clauses 66
  Exercises 69;   Independent Study 73

Inserting Clauses 75
  Exercises 76;   Independent Study 81

The Conventions 83

4 • Separating the Sentences 83

Sentence Fragments 83

Exercises 85; Independent Study 90

Run-Together Sentences 92

Exercises 96; Independent Study 100

5 • Matching the Parts 102

Nouns 102

Exercises 104; Independent Study 108

Pronouns: Number 110

Exercises 112; Independent Study 115

Pronouns: Person 116

Exercises 117; Independent Study 121

Pronouns: Form 123

With More than One Person 123

Exercises 124

"Who" and "Whom" 126

Exercises 127

With "than" and "as" 130

Exercises 130

Noun and Pronoun Review 133

Verbs: Present Tense 135

Exercises 139; Independent Study 145

Verbs: Past Tenses 146

Exercises 150; Independent Study 158

Verbs: Combinations 159

Exercises 162; Independent Study 166

Verbs: Tense Shifts 167

Exercises 169; Independent Study 173

Verb Review 175

Modifiers: Past Participles as Modifiers 177

Exercises 178; Independent Study 182

Modifiers: Adjectives and Adverbs 184

Exercises 186; Independent Study 189

Modifiers: Comparisons 191

Exercises 194; Independent Study 200

Wrong Word Form 202

Exercises 203; Independent Study 207

6 • Punctuating Correctly 209

Comma Rules 1, 2, and 3 209
Exercises 211;   Independent Study 215

Comma Rule 4 217
Exercises 219;   Independent Study 224

Comma Review 226

Semicolons and Colons 228
Exercises 230;   Independent Study 234

7 • Polishing the Words 236

Articles 236
Exercises 238;   Independent Study 242

Contractions 243
Exercises 245;   Independent Study 248

Possessives 250
Exercises 252;   Independent Study 258

Capitals 260
Exercises 261;   Independent Study 265

Spelling 266
Exercises 273;   Independent Study 278

Strong Writing 279

8 • Good Materials 279

Exact Words 279
Exercises 281;   Independent Study 286

Concrete Subjects and Verbs 287
Exercises 289;   Independent Study 293

9 • Careful Assembly 295

Vague Pronoun Reference 295
Exercises 297;   Independent Study 300

Mixed Constructions 302
Exercises 304;   Independent Study 308

Parallel Structure 309
Exercises 310;   Independent Study 316

Dangling and Misplaced Modifiers 318
Exercises 319;   Independent Study 325

Direct and Indirect Speech 326
Exercises 329;   Independent Study 334

Idiom **335**

Exercises 337;   Independent Study 342

10 • Distinctive Designs **344**

Concise Wording 344

Exercises 348;   Independent Study 354

Sentence Variety 356

Exercises 361;   Independent Study 365

Independent Study Answers **368**

Index **389**

Lists of the most common English prepositions, linking verbs, helping verbs, connecting words, and clause punctuation are inside the back cover

The Basic Writing Book

The Structures

1. Building the Essay

• Greg's heart pounded as he read the essay question on his urban studies midterm: "Is San Francisco prepared for a major earthquake?" He knew all about San Francisco and its historic earthquakes. He immediately started writing and described the intensity, the destruction, and the aftermath of several earthquakes, devoting most of his attention to the big one of 1906. He was able to include fascinating details and anecdotes from a book he had finished reading only the night before the exam. He was still excited when he turned in his essay and hurried out to celebrate his triumph.

His pride changed to horror when he got his exam back at the next class meeting. He had received an F.

Greg's problem is a common one. Many people think college essays and examinations demand that students write down all the facts they know on a subject. More than memory, however, a college essay requires careful thought and planning. It is first a place for people to show how well they can use the material they have learned.

An essay should prove the truth of a clearly stated idea, judgment, or opinion. Greg wrote a lot of facts, but he didn't answer the question he was asked. He should have decided whether or not San Francisco is prepared for a major earthquake, clearly stated his opinion, and built a logical argument to prove it. He should have supported that argument with carefully selected and phrased facts and details. Successful writers do not show all they know but select from that knowledge the best possible evidence to prove a point. They know many facts, but, more important, they understand the material well enough to use it, and they know how to express their knowledge in writing as effectively as possible.

Most good essays are variations on a very simple format that can be adapted to present watertight arguments on a wide range of writing assignments. Figure 1 presents that format in a diagram of a six-hundred-word essay; Figure 2 shows the skeleton, the basic outline of an essay written on Greg's essay question; and Figure 3 shows that outline fleshed out with evidence into a convincing essay.

Figure 1

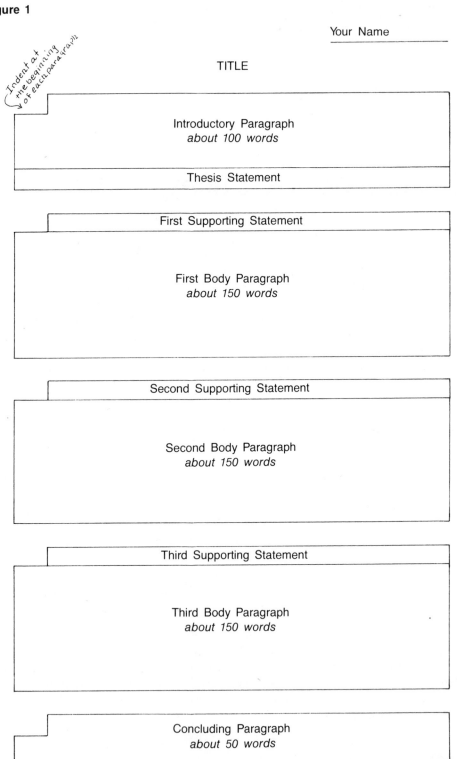

Your Name _____

Indent at the beginning of each paragraph

TITLE

Introductory Paragraph
about 100 words

Thesis Statement

First Supporting Statement

First Body Paragraph
about 150 words

Second Supporting Statement

Second Body Paragraph
about 150 words

Third Supporting Statement

Third Body Paragraph
about 150 words

Concluding Paragraph
about 50 words

Figure 2

Thesis

San Francisco is not prepared for a major earthquake.

Support

1. The leaders have no way to communicate.

Supports — support or prove the thesis.

Support

2. Many of the buildings are not sound enough.

Support

3. The citizens are not prepared.

Figure 3

TRAGEDY OR TRIUMPH?

Introduction — it interests the reader in the subject and presents the thesis

In its fairytale setting on a hilly peninsula between the Pacific Ocean and the San Francisco Bay, San Francisco has prospered. It has tall, sleek skyscrapers, thousands of fine restaurants, and a thriving tourist industry. Residents and visitors alike enjoy the exhibits, architecture, and landscaping of San Francisco's unique museums as well as the rich cultural contributions of the city's many colorful ethnic communities. However, sometimes a cloud passes over the city, and fear constricts its people's hearts. San Francisco faces the prospect of a major earthquake in the near future, and the city is not adequately prepared. ← Thesis

Body paragraph #1

In the event of a mammoth earthquake, the community leaders would have no direct method of communicating. The city would lose electricity, and the telephone system would fail or be jammed by frantic callers. Debris would block the streets and prohibit conventional travel between city offices. The mayor, the police and fire chiefs, and the director of city services would need non-land-tied methods of communicating. Budget cuts have delayed the purchase of two-way radios necessary to prevent destruction that could cost more in life and property than the quake itself. Fires, not the quake itself, caused the major damage of the 1906 quake. City leaders cannot organize emergency operations if they can't communicate. — Support #1

Body paragraph #2

These details prove their support

Many of San Francisco's buildings are not structurally sound enough to withstand a great quake. These buildings would create major problems for the city after a large earthquake. Several police and fire stations have masonry exteriors which would fall, blocking access to the stations and severely inhibiting the use of emergency police and fire vehicles. Many homes in San Francisco are built with their frames resting unattached to their foundations. The rolling motions of an earthquake can rock a house right off its foundation and cause severe property damage. This problem can be alleviated by sinking anchored bolts through the frames into the foundations of these houses, thereby attaching the house to the foundation. Easy and inexpensive as this modification is to carry out, many homes still remain unprotected. — Support #2

Body paragraph #3

Many of San Francisco's citizens themselves are not prepared for a major earthquake. Many people do not realize that an earthquake could leave them stranded at work or school. They have not made physical provisions for eating and sleeping away from home, and many families are not psychologically prepared for the fact that some family members might be unable to reach home either in person or by telephone. People do not have the basic knowledge of first aid which would save countless lives, and many don't even know how to turn off the main gas line to their houses. They have no back-up methods of cooking, obtaining fresh water, or extinguishing a small fire before it becomes a big problem. If people were stripped of all their modern conveniences, they would be lost, cold and hungry, and totally unprepared for the problems that faced them. — Support #3

These supports prove the thesis

Science tells us a great quake in the San Francisco area is inevitable. We can ignore that fact and be defeated, or we can accept the challenge and organize for victory. Many thousands of lives are at stake; we cannot just continue to hope we will all be on vacation when the next major earthquake strikes.

Conclusion — It gives the importance of the thesis in today's world and relates the thesis to the future with recommendations or predictions.

FROM SUBJECT TO THESIS

Sometimes you'll be asked to write an essay in response to a question. Then you must answer the question and prove that your answer is right. More often, however, you'll be asked to write an essay on a general subject.

Don't misunderstand. Your instructors do not really mean that you should write about those general subjects. Instead they want you to write on very narrow topics that fall within those general subjects. Good essays on the subject of music might be on such topics as a one-night career as a professional dancer, special effects at an Earth, Wind, and Fire concert, or guitar playing as a route to social success—not on music in general. Therefore you must begin your essay by finding your topic within the assigned subject.

You can write good essays only on topics that you know about, are interested in, can think of facts about, and have ideas on. Answering the following questions will help you narrow your subject into such topics. When an instructor assigns an essay subject, ask yourself the following questions about it and jot down your answers according to the procedure suggested below.

1. What parts of the subject have I had experience with? Use a separate sheet of paper for each part. For example, if your instructor assigned the subject "high school," you might end up with six parts and therefore six pieces of paper, one with each of these headings:

graduation activities   proms

cheerleading   track

sexism   the moral majority

2. What aspects of each part am I interested in? What did I notice? Space your answers out on the page. Your prom page might have these words on it:

bands   photographers

expense   drinking

chaperones   discrimination

3. Who was involved? Jot down names around the words they relate to. Around "chaperones" you might write

Mrs. Seeley   Mr. Drew

Mr. Benton   Margaret Hansen

Coach Watson   Dr. Stewart

4. What did each person do? Write notes near related words. Think of several things each person did and write them around that person's name. For example, around "Mr. Benton" you might write

interrupted my conversation

thesis

sent Gene, Sharmaine, and Brett outside

looked in both rest rooms several times

told James not to take another sandwich

stopped the band at midnight

watched the fire escape

5. What interesting ideas do my facts suggest? Think about your notes and fill another sheet of paper with the ideas they suggest. Ask yourself what's good and what's bad about the situation you're thinking about. The following diagram shows how part of the notes on the topic of high school might look.

Stopped the band at midnight → interrupted my conversation →

watched the fire escape → *Mr. Benton* ← Sent Gene, Sharmaine, and Brett outside

told James not to take another sandwich →

looked in both rest rooms several times →

Mrs. Seeley   Coach Watson

(Chaperones)   Mr. Drew

Dr. Stewart

Margaret Hansen

The facts about Mr. Benton suggest several interesting ideas.

Mr. Benton was very busy.

Mr. Benton worked hard at the prom.

Mr. Benton interfered with many people.

Mr. Benton is suspicious.

Mr. Benton worries about what other people are doing.

If you reached similar conclusions about other chaperones, you could make statements about the group. The whole page of notes about proms would produce many interesting ideas.

Perhaps now you're wondering about the difference between facts and ideas. A fact is determined by direct observation or measurement. People would hear Mr. Benton tell James not to take another sandwich and see him watching the fire escape and looking in the rest rooms. People would observe these facts. Your notes answering questions 3 and 4 above, telling who did what, should be facts. Ideas, on the other hand, are judgments or conclusions based on facts. After observing the facts and thinking about them, someone might decide that Mr. Benton worked very hard or interfered with many people. Ideas are not observed; they are created in people's minds. To convince people that your ideas are true, you must state them clearly and show people how you reached them by providing the facts on which they were based.

An essay is a device for communicating ideas in writing. To write an essay you must first decide what idea you want to communicate and state it clearly in a single sentence. That sentence is called the thesis statement. Now that you have some interesting ideas, you should decide which one you can prove most effectively and write a thesis that states it. You need a thesis that will focus your essay on a single narrow, interesting idea. The writers of the following faulty theses did not limit the subject to a narrow topic.

FAULTY (too broad)	REVISED (narrow)
Our society encourages people to spend too much money.	The proms at my high school taught young people to spend extravagantly.
Many people are engaged in illegal activities.	The proms at my high school promoted illegal activities.
Adults are always ruining young people's fun.	The chaperones ruined our senior prom.
People learn many skills in high school.	Working on our senior prom developed my organizational skills.
Sometimes people change.	Our senior prom changed Paula from a shy wallflower to a popular leader.

The good theses are narrow and exact. They make one specific point so that the reader knows the writer has something to say and knows exactly what that is. They are also good because they state ideas, not facts.

FAULTY (fact)	REVISED (idea)
We pay seventeen dollars per term for student activities.	Our student activity fees are being wasted.
This essay will discuss smoking.	Cigarettes should not be sold on campus.

Many college instructors give essay exams.	Essay exams don't accurately measure student knowledge.
I was a cheerleader in high school.	High school cheerleading is very competitive.

A factual thesis does not adequately restrict an essay. If you tried to write an essay proving the thesis "I was a cheerleader in high school," you wouldn't know what details to select from your experience and would probably write a boring essay describing everything that happened to you as a cheerleader. On the other hand, the thesis "High school cheerleading is very competitive" could lead to a fascinating essay describing attempted bribes, power plays, and dirty tricks.

A question would also be too broad for a thesis.

FAULTY (question)	REVISED (thesis)
How can our university help women improve their status?	Our university should provide free child care.
What can be done about trash pollution?	Trash problems could easily be solved at the neighborhood level.
Just how good are the Greenville elementary schools?	Students in the Greenville elementary schools are being denied the opportunity to develop their creativity.
What is it like to be poor?	Poverty taught our family to enjoy each other.

An essay with the thesis "What is it like to be poor?" would have no focus. You could describe anything in a poor person's life, and the reader wouldn't know what you wanted him to think. However, an essay proving the thesis "Poverty taught our family to enjoy each other" could describe such things as the days of the flood when your family had to live harmoniously in one small room, or the time you and your brother made a sled out of an old bureau. The reader would finish your essay convinced that poverty had indeed taught your family to enjoy each other. When you're tempted to use a question as a thesis, instead try writing an answer to that question. The good theses above are all answers to the questions asked in the faulty theses.

A thesis must also be a complete statement, not just a topic or title.

FAULTY (incomplete)	REVISED (complete)
The college cafeteria	The college cafeteria takes advantage of students.
Why I want to be a salesperson	Selling can be a lucrative profession.
Learning to ride a unicycle	Learning to ride a unicycle is very difficult.

Like questions, incomplete theses don't adequately restrict the essay. The thesis "The college cafeteria" doesn't take a stand. The writer could ramble around on the topic, making too many different and even contradictory points.

Some theses are too broad because they contain more than one idea.

FAULTY (too many ideas)	REVISED (one idea)
Property taxes are too high, and the local governments should lower them, or retired people will be forced to sell their homes.	Retired people should be exempt from property taxes.
Flowers brighten a yard, and vegetables, though some require a lot of work, are always welcome on the dinner table.	Every home should have a vegetable garden.
At our college scholars must struggle for their grades, but athletes aren't expected to perform well in class, and they get free tutoring.	Our college gives more support to athletes than to scholars.
Working in the summer has advantages and disadvantages.	Working in the summer solves many of a student's problems.

This last faulty thesis suggests that its writer is reluctant to take a strong stand.

The best theses are provocative and original.

FAULTY	REVISED
Jogging is good exercise.	Jogging can damage the body.
Television commercials portray women as sex objects.	Television commercials portray men as sex objects.
Every child should have a dog.	Every child should have a boa constrictor.
I enjoyed being class president.	Being class president taught me to manipulate people.

An original thesis lures readers into an essay, challenging and inspiring them to read on for more details. On the other hand, a thesis that says nothing new only reminds them that the ball game is on television and the dishes are in the sink.

thesis

Good writing commands attention. Writing cannot be effective if no one really wants to read it. An exciting essay, then, begins with an exciting thesis.

CORRECTION COMMENT: **Your thesis should state a single narrow, interesting idea.**

EXERCISES: From Subject to Thesis

I. Use the following terms to correctly label the thesis below.

Faulty (too broad)   Faulty (fact)   Faulty (too many ideas)

Faulty (incomplete)   Faulty (question)   Good

A.
1. My job at Hink's department store greatly strengthened my social skills.
2. What was my biggest mistake?
3. Performing in a play made me feel very powerful.
4. My aunt visited us last weekend.
5. Our economy is in bad shape.
6. Playing the piano keeps my morale high.
7. I'm aware of what I eat and exercise to stay in good health.
8. My friend Sojin is a pillar of strength.
9. What makes people happy?
10. A woman can never escape the burden of housework.

B.
1. Owning a 1978 Camaro changed me from a child to an adult.
2. I went camping with my friends at Yellowstone National Park.
3. Are parents too protective?
4. Dentists often use nitrous oxide for immoral purposes.
5. I go to school to meet people and to prepare myself for a career.
6. Competition for Soldier of the Year is tough.
7. I was a service station attendant.
8. What is the typical American?
9. From an abundant number of choices I have chosen to write about the personality of my son Tom, the only blond in our family, a tall sportsman unusually sensitive to people and the possessor of a certain charisma.
10. Shi-tou, a real paradise

C.
1. What did I learn in first grade?
2. I own a nice and comfortable car built in the United States.
3. Excessive consumption of sugar can cause mental illness.
4. Establishing a new record in plowing made me feel proud.
5. I will try to talk about Mexican music.
6. Playing soccer invigorates me.

7. The perfect country would have to be flawless.

8. What can be done about noise pollution?

9. Studying gymnastics taught me self-control.

10. Power has many forms, but the power that is the most mysterious and intrigues me the most is the hidden power at work within man: the power of love, the power of the mind, and the power of faith.

II. *Write sample theses on the following subjects. Be sure to narrow them down to one part, but you don't need to go through the whole question-asking process because you won't write essays on them all.*

A.   1. college

2. your neighborhood

3. cheerleading

4. grandparents

5. a good car

6. going back to school

7. getting along with a difficult person

8. a place you love

9. culture shock

10. the dangers of the street

B.   1. leaving home

2. your major

3. television and you

4. a talent you have

5. an amusement park

6. libraries

7. secondhand books

8. a way you had fun as a child

9. learning to write

10. a trip

III. A. *Working with other students in your class, choose one of the following topics and explore it by asking yourselves the five questions in this chapter. Follow the instructions for jotting down answers, thinking about those answers, and writing interesting ideas on another sheet of paper. Then write and refine some sample theses.*

college buildings	studying writing
college courses	college food
college catalogues	college students

B. *Choose one of the topics in II A or B for your first essay and explore it by asking yourself the five questions in this chapter. Follow the instructions for jotting down answers, thinking about those answers, and writing interesting ideas on another sheet of paper. Then write and refine some possible theses.*

IV. *Compare the following informal essay to the diagram of Figure 1 and the essay of Figure 3. Label the introduction, the conclusion, the body paragraphs, the thesis, the supports, and the evidence to prove them.*

How do you remember your high school days? Some people remember them as a joyful succession of football games, proms, and parties. Others, however, think of acne, fear, and awkwardness. Most people's high school memories focus on their success or failure with the opposite sex. Everyone wanted to be going steady, but before that a person had to get past the hurdle known as the first date. My first date was a disaster.

Our problems began as soon as we left my house. On the way to dinner, we got a flat tire, and guess who changed it. Being mechanically adept is one of the many advantages of being the youngest daughter in a family with no sons. The scene is indelibly printed in my memory: an embarrassed seventeen-year-old girl wrestling with the tire on a car belonging to an even more embarrassed nineteen-year-old boy. Though no one bothered to stop and help, most passing motorists slowed down for a good close look. If I'd known the fate in store for me, I'd have taken a taxi home to mother!

Dinner wasn't much better. I ended up wearing veal à la Oscar on my new crêpe dress. I was trying to cut my meat with the itty bitty knife they'd provided, and it slid off my plate into my lap! I mopped up what I could with my napkin, which had been neatly tucked under my chin. I opted for no dessert, feeling it was safer to leave well enough alone. There were twelve steps down to the exit, and I made it to seven before the heel of my shoe fell off. Rather than stoop to retrieve it, I limped down the remaining steps, hoping it was dark enough for me to go unnoticed.

My final humiliation occurred on the way home. Safely back in the car, we headed for the notorious Kissing Point. I had no idea where it was located and stupidly thought we were taking a scenic route home. When we pulled off the road and he turned off the ignition, it finally dawned on me that something was up. He slid closer to me on the seat and leaned over to kiss me. I chose this very moment to sneeze violently. Without a word, he wiped off his glasses and started the car. We were on the road home once again.

It goes without saying that I never heard from him again. Now I can look back on the whole experience and laugh and appreciate how much I learned on that first date. Perhaps the motto "If at first you don't succeed, try, try again" is not so outdated after all. Even if the dating game starts badly, it can only get better, and one day it may even be fun.

INDEPENDENT STUDY: From Subject to Thesis *(answers in the back)*

V. *Use the following terms to correctly label the theses below.*

Faulty (too broad)   Faulty (fact)   Faulty (too many ideas)

Faulty (incomplete)   Faulty (question)   Good

A.   1. Everyone should take vacations.

2. Did I enjoy my trip to San Diego?

3. Rain can sometimes destroy life.

4. I took my last dance class in high school.

5. What do I need from my English class?

6. Young women should have higher goals.

7. I started kindergarten when I was four years old.

8. Basketball is a great game and an entertaining sport that gives one good exercise.

9. Many consumers hurt themselves by buying on credit.

10. What are my career goals?

B.   1. A lawn is more trouble than it's worth.

2. My car is fun to drive and has attractive features.

3. Going to a party in disguise allowed me to enjoy myself in new ways.

4. My parents have found me many part-time jobs.

5. What I like about Michigan State

6. The food in the cafeteria is a gourmet's delight.

7. Chicago

8. That morning our family got a new dog.

9. What does it mean to be educated?

10. A camping vacation may be feasible when all other types are impossible.

thesis

BUILDING AN OUTLINE

You can't write a good essay if you don't know where you're going any more than you can get to a party if you don't know where it will be held. An exact thesis is like an address. Knowing the address, however, is not enough. You must also know what streets to follow to get to that address. Like a map, an outline shows you exactly how to get to your destination, exactly how to prove your thesis.

After perfecting your thesis, you must decide how you will prove it, determining the best logical route along which to lead your reader to your thesis. You can determine that route by following these four steps:

1. Study the notes you made when answering the five questions in the unit on thesis. Find the batches of facts that led you to the idea that finally became your thesis, copy them onto a fresh sheet of paper, and write your thesis across the top.

2. Then expand those facts by giving more answers to these questions.

> Who was involved?

> What did each person do?

3. Then add your answers to these questions.

> Where?   Why?   When?   How?

4. After filling your sheet with notes, draw lines around at least three groups of related facts. Look at each group one by one and ask yourself:

> Why is my thesis true?

> What do these facts show that proves my thesis?

Express your answers in statements that prove the thesis.

For example, the person who wrote the thesis "Television commercials portray men as sex objects" had a page full of notes about men in television commercials. They covered mainly the way those men looked, the way they dressed, and the way they were treated. Looking at each group and asking "Why is my thesis true? What do these facts show that proves my thesis?" led the writer to these three statements:

> The men on commercials are handsome.

> The men on commercials wear tight clothes.

> Television commercials show women ogling the men.

These statements became the supports in the outline.

> *Thesis:* Television commercials portray men as sex objects.

> 1. The men on commercials are handsome.

> 2. The men on commercials wear tight clothes.

3. Television commercials show women ogling the men.

Your outline should have at least three clearly different supports for its thesis. Here are some good outlines supporting theses from the previous unit.

Thesis: Jogging can damage the body.

1. Breathing polluted air damages the lungs.

2. Jogging can cause leg problems.

3. Jogging can cause foot problems.

Thesis: Every child should have a boa constrictor.

1. Boa constrictors are clean.

2. Boa constrictors require little attention.

3. Boa constrictors are educational.

Thesis: Being class president taught me to manipulate people.

1. I learned to direct the student vote.

2. I learned to control the student council.

3. I learned how to make administrators change their policy.

Be sure your supporting arguments are complete sentences so that you won't get off the subject.

FAULTY

Thesis: Gardening is a good way to exercise.

1. Tilling the soil

2. Planting the seeds

3. Cultivating the plants

Following this outline, you might slip into discussing the best tools to use or the best depth to plant seeds and forget about describing exercise. With the following outline, you would be much less likely to get off the subject.

REVISED

Thesis: Gardening is a good way to exercise.

1. Tilling the soil is good exercise.

2. Planting the seeds is good exercise.

3. Cultivating the plants is good exercise.

support

The argument of this outline and the sentences that state it are clear and simple. Such an outline holds both writer and reader on course. The writer knows exactly what he is committed to prove and can choose the best possible evidence to prove it, and the reader knows exactly what the writer wants to say.

Also be sure that all the arguments are worded so that they do indeed prove the thesis.

FAULTY

Thesis: Cats are a nuisance to anyone trying to travel down my street.

1. They annoy people by yowling for attention.

2. Once someone stepped on my cat.

3. Sometimes they even attack people.

The second support above doesn't prove the thesis. As it's now worded, it proves that people are a nuisance to cats, not that cats are a nuisance to people. The support can be rephrased so that it does prove the thesis.

REVISED 2. They make walking difficult by getting underfoot.

Also be sure that your three supports present completely different arguments. The first two supports below are almost the same.

FAULTY

Thesis: My older sister has been very helpful to me.

1. She is generous.

2. She buys me clothes.

3. She helps me solve problems.

The first two supports both state that the sister is generous. The second one should be replaced by a completely different point.

REVISED 2. She introduces me to her friends.

After the supports are finished, perfect the outline as a whole. Arrange the supports in the most logical order, with the strongest one last if possible. Check to see if the thesis could be improved now that the argument is written. Could the thesis be narrower? Could it be more clearly or precisely expressed? Take time to perfect the outline; it's almost impossible to write a good essay with a bad outline.

CORRECTION COMMENT: Your outline should have at least three clearly different supports for its thesis.

EXERCISES: Building an Outline

I. Study the following outlines. Circle each faulty part, note the weakness in the margin, and rewrite that part.

A. 1. *Thesis:* Laughter lightens the burden of school work.

    1. Laughter relieves nervous tension.

    2. Laughter relieves boredom.

    3. Some people laugh at the wrong time.

2. *Thesis:* Keeping healthy is difficult for a student.

   1. Students often have no time for exercise.

   2. Nutritious food is not readily available.

   3. Studying often interferes with sleeping.

3. *Thesis:* I am intuitive, persistent, and honest.

   1. Intuition guides many of my actions and decisions.

   2. My persistence drives me to complete my goals and seek solutions to my problems.

   3. A sometimes annoying trait of mine is honesty.

4. *Thesis:* An ocean cruise can be a learning experience.

   1. A person can try many new activities.

   2. A person can meet people from all over the world.

   3. A person can try a variety of new foods.

5. *Thesis:* I plan to visit my sister in Atlanta this weekend.

   1. Preparation for the weekend

   2. Cleaning the whole house

   3. Visiting my sister

   4. Making time to study

6. *Thesis:* It is hard for me to get back money I lend my friends.

   1. When I was younger, my friends always asked me to lend them money.

   2. When I was in sixth grade, I decided to watch out for people who asked me to lend them money.

   3. In high school, people asked to borrow clothes, books, and records.

7. *Thesis:* Taking care of a small child can be very difficult.

   1. A child creates a lot of work.

   2. A child creates a lot of laundry.

   3. A child needs a lot of attention.

support

8. *Thesis:* Budgeting their income is a way of life for many people.

   1. A person with a set income should have some kind of budget.

   2. The good things about a budget

   3. Budgeting one's income helps one to know what to buy.

9. *Thesis:* An ideal job should have certain qualities about it.

   1. The job should have a good health plan.

   2. The job should have good working hours.

   3. The job should pay well.

10. *Thesis:* Seafood is my favorite meal.

   1. Shrimp is delicious.

   2. Crab is inexpensive.

   3. Lobster is expensive.

B. 1. *Thesis:* These days an American teenager has a lot of freedom.

   1. Schools are relaxing their rules.

   2. Parents aren't as strict as they used to be.

   3. Teenagers themselves have become more liberal.

2. *Thesis:* I took badminton classes for two quarters.

   1. History of badminton

   2. Badminton is harder than one thinks.

   3. Badminton has played an important role in my life.

3. *Thesis:* I have had many disagreements with my parents, and I'm quite sure I'll have many more, but as a family we have learned to resolve our disagreements through mutual understanding.

   1. It isn't easy having to tell my parents in advance my plans for the weekend.

   2. According to law I am capable of assuming responsibility for myself and not having to depend on my parents.

   3. I have had a license for over six months, and I do believe it's time for my parents to let me drive at night.

4. *Thesis:* An active person has many opportunities to meet people.

   1. I've made good friends at my church.

   2. I've made good friends at my baseball games.

   3. I've made good friends in my classes.

5. *Thesis:* Car travel gives a vacation flexibility.

   1. A person can travel at his own pace.

   2. Things about traveling by car that are fun

   3. Traveling by car will give a person more than one vacation.

6. *Thesis:* High school is one of the best times in a person's life.

   1. High school is a time for fun.

   2. Going to high school is a lot of fun.

   3. High school leaves a person with good memories.

7. *Thesis:* Moving away from home improved my relationship with my family.

   1. I no longer have to fight for my privacy.

   2. They don't have to nag me about my responsibilities.

   3. Now I appreciate all the work my mother was doing for me.

8. *Thesis:* Death can be painful, peaceful, or chosen.

   1. Terminal disease is the most painful way to die.

   2. My grandfather died in his sleep two years ago.

   3. Suicide is another kind of death.

9. *Thesis:* The foods of my country really seem to be a good remedy for me when I'm homesick.

   1. First I would like to introduce *sushi,* which is a traditional Japanese food.

   2. Second, I would like to introduce *sunomono,* which is a sort of salad.

   3. The third food I like is *udon,* thin buckwheat noodles, which look like macaroni.

10. *Thesis:* Kim was always there when I needed her.

   1. She helped me when I was in fights.

   2. When I got caught stealing, she lied for me.

   3. One day on the way home from school, she saved my life.

II. A. *Write possible supports to prove the following theses. You won't need to go through the whole question-asking process because you won't be writing essays on them.*

   1. *Thesis:* My older brother makes my life miserable.

      1. _____

      2. _____

      3. _____

   2. *Thesis:* A library assistant acquires valuable research skills.

      1. _____

      2. _____

      3. _____

support

3. *Thesis:* At my elementary school we had little opportunity for academic subjects.

   1. _____

   2. _____

   3. _____

4. *Thesis:* A determined person can have fun even doing housework.

   1. _____

   2. _____

   3. _____

5. *Thesis:* Without my own car, I could never finish college.

   1. _____

   2. _____

   3. _____

6. *Thesis:* I enjoyed selling television sets at Montgomery Ward.

   1. _____

   2. _____

   3. _____

7. *Thesis:* My video tape recorder changed my life.

   1. _____

   2. _____

   3. _____

8. *Thesis:* My weekend was exhausting.

   1. _____

   2. _____

   3. _____

9. *Thesis:* This year's fashions make most women look ugly.

   1. _____

   2. _____

   3. _____

10. *Thesis:* My grandparents treat me like a princess.

   1. _____

   2. _____

   3. _____

B. Write supports for ten of the theses you composed for exercises II A and B (page 11).

C. For your first essay (essay 1), choose one of the theses you wrote for exercise III B (page 12) and follow the instructions in this unit for writing supports to prove it. Check your outline carefully and perfect it.

III. *Compare the following essay to the diagram of Figure 1 and the essay of Figure 3. Find the introduction, the conclusion, the body paragraphs the topic sentences, and the evidence to prove them. Write the thesis and supports on a sheet of paper.*

People acquire pets for many reasons. I know a woman who has a mastiff to guard her house and a man who has a Persian cat to impress his guests. I even know someone who breeds and fights pitbulls for sport. I'm not sure if my father intended to expand our family when he bought our dog, but Shep did become an important member of our family.

Shep and I grew up together. As far back as I can remember, we were always together having fun. One time when I was about eight or nine we really tore up the back yard. I came out and saw him pulling the stuffing out of an old chair my father had put back there because it was falling apart. Well, Dad didn't need it, and Shep looked as if he were having fun, so I decided to give him a hand. We ripped off strips of cloth, pulled out bunches of stuffing, and threw everything up in the air. We staggered and fell and dragged the rapidly disintegrating chair around the yard. Within ten minutes, the yard looked as if it had been hit by a tornado followed by a light snowstorm. We both got punished, and I had to clean up the mess, but I'd love a chance to repeat that experience.

Shep even went on trips with the family. Every summer when we went to Oregon to visit our grandparents, Shep would come right along with us. We always drove in a station wagon, so there was plenty of room for Shep. We made stops along the way to sight-see, eat, and use the rest rooms, and Shep used the rest stops just like everyone else. When we reached the mountains, he loved to stick his head out the window and bark at cows and horses. Sometimes I would get tired from the long trip, so I would crawl into the back of the station wagon with Shep and take a nap, or at least try to. He would never let me sleep. He kept licking my ears and jumping on me.

The family was always concerned about his health. He had a meal of fresh meat every day, and we always made sure that he had clean water and a bone to chew on. Whenever it rained, we would bring him into the garage to keep him from catching a cold. He had a fine doghouse, but we didn't want to take any chances on his health when it rained really hard. I made sure he had enough exercise. We used to go out in the field in back of the house, and he would chase me. I guess we did that just about every Sunday afternoon. My parents made sure when they bought him that he had had all his shots, and we took him to the vet twice a year for a checkup. My father always complained about the bill, but we all knew he really would not have cared even if it had been expensive.

support

I think growing up with Shep was one of the brightest parts of my childhood. The family gave him a lot of love, and he gave a lot in return. Many parents today are so busy keeping their families fed and clothed that they don't have as much time to spend with their children as they would like. Such parents should consider adding a dog to the family. A dog always has time to play and love to share.

INDEPENDENT STUDY: *Building an Outline* (answers in the back)

IV. Study the following outlines. Circle each faulty part, name the weakness in the margin, and rewrite that part.

A. 1. *Thesis:* My dancing experience prepared me for cheerleading.

1. Dancing gave me the stamina that a cheerleader needs.

2. Dancing made my body flexible.

3. My experience dancing in public gave me the confidence to perform in front of crowds.

2. *Thesis:* Gardens can be enjoyable and creative.

1. There are many kinds of gardens.

2. Planting a garden is hard work.

3. People who plant gardens are creative.

3. *Thesis:* I enjoy celebrating Christmas.

1. I enjoy seeing my relatives.

2. I enjoy eating Christmas food.

3. I enjoy receiving gifts.

4. *Thesis:* The Japanese news on television keeps me in touch with my home.

1. I can hear updated news from Japan.

2. I can see Japanese scenery.

3. I can hear Japanese ideas about world affairs.

5. *Thesis:* I learned teamwork during my senior year of high school.

1. I learned teamwork on the basketball team.

2. I learned teamwork in the glee club.

3. I studied home economics.

6. *Thesis:* Dressing well on a low budget is hard.

1. Nice clothes are expensive.

2. I like to have a lot of clothes.

3. I like expensive clothes.

7. *Thesis:* High-heeled shoes are uncomfortable.

    1. They are dangerous.

    2. They are bad for one's health.

    3. They are expensive.

8. *Thesis:* The personality of my sister Yolanda

    1. She is friendly.

    2. She doesn't like to be criticized.

    3. She is very moody at times.

9. *Thesis:* Mrs. Stevenson is the ideal next-door neighbor.

    1. She never criticizes us.

    2. She enjoys talking to us.

    3. She puts other people's wishes before her own.

10. *Thesis:* Freedom is very important to me.

    1. I like to live alone.

    2. I like to be financially independent.

    3. I want to go many places.

support

WRITING BODY PARAGRAPHS

Ideas, statements, and words can be general or specific. General words refer to groups of things; specific words refer to one thing in the group. A word referring to a large group is more general than a word referring to a smaller group within the first one. The following words are arranged from general to specific.

General			Specific
pet	dog	border collie	my dog Frodo
teacher	music teacher	guitar teacher	Ms. Stevens
residence	apartment	studio apartment	apartment 321

Action words and descriptive words can also be general or specific.

General	Specific
take	grab
speak	snap
laugh	cackle
careful	thrifty
old	dilapidated
nice	friendly

Statements also can be general or specific. A specific statement describes one thing or one event, and a general statement groups together more than one thing or event. A statement referring to a large number of things or events is more general than a statement referring to a smaller number of those things or events. Theses must be somewhat general, supports must be less general than theses, and body paragraphs must present many specific statements to prove that the generalizations of the outline are true. The statements below are arranged from general to specific. All except the last one describe something that happened more than once.

Very general statement—a good thesis for a book
Many people escape their responsibilities through television.

Somewhat general statement—a good thesis for an essay
Many students watch television when they should be studying.

Less general statement—a good support
I often watch television instead of reading my philosophy assignments.

Specific statement—good evidence for a body paragraph
Last Thursday I watched *The Two Ronnies, Monty Python's Flying Circus,* and *Benny Hill* even though I had ninety-six pages of *Art and Philosophy* to read for a midterm at ten o'clock the next morning.

In contrast to the general statements, the specific statement describes just one event, something that happened only once.

Now that you have perfected your outline, you need to write body paragraphs full of specific evidence to back it up. You have lots of good evidence on the page of notes with the thesis at the top. First figure out the best order in which to present each of the three groups of facts by asking yourself these questions:

Do some facts come before others logically?

Do some facts come before others in time?

Can the facts be arranged from least to most important?

evidence needed

If you answered yes to one of these questions, organize your facts in that order. If you answered no to the above questions, simply group related details together and save the strongest evidence for last.

Begin each body paragraph by writing the support from your outline followed by a sentence or two of explanation if necessary. Then go to the notes from which you got that support, start with the part you decided to cover first, and write those facts out for your reader. Write sentence after sentence adding more details and explanation and answering these questions:

Who did what?   Why?

Where?   How?

When?

The following paragraph starts with the support and proves it with good vivid details. These details are arranged in time order, from the beginning of the hayride to the end.

support

The graduating seniors also enjoyed the class hayride. The senior class rented a large wagon filled with hay and pulled by two old horses. We boarded the wagon at Mr. Smith's stable and rode off over the rough dirt road. The country air was sweet and warm, the big yellow moon hung low, and the stars twinkled across the warm country sky. As the wagon jolted us up and down, we screamed and laughed as loudly as we could and listened to the echo of our voices. When Mr. Smith brought the horses to a stop, we climbed out of the wagon. The boys gathered wood, and the girls built a large campfire with it. Then we sat around the fire telling spooky tales, singing songs, and roasting marshmallows, peanuts, and a small pig. The moon had traveled far across the heavens, and the roosters were crowing when we gathered around the fire and sang a farewell song. We hated to leave, but we climbed aboard the wagon, tired and sleepy, and headed home.

these details prove the support

Although the mind *understands* generalizations, it *experiences* specifics. This paragraph's details, from the echo and the jolting wagon to the farewell song, are so vivid that they enter the reader's mind and stay there like a memory. The reader doesn't just *understand* that they enjoyed the night, he *knows* it.

When you write a paragraph out of groups of related details, begin each part with a summary point. As you write, be sure to follow every generalization with the facts that prove it.

Point 1 Restoring a lizard's health took *Support* careful thought and hard work. First, I had to feed her. I presented her with flies, moths, and hamburger laced with bone meal, but she refused to eat. In desperation, I pinched her mouth open and shoved some food in. The food disappeared, so I continued this method of feeding her. *Point 2* After a few weeks I decided to try to improve her color. I thought that perhaps she needed some sun, so I put her under a light. In less than an hour she changed from a drab gray to a brilliant turquoise with yellow and white dots and a collar of two black and two yellow rings. I could hardly believe my eyes. *Point 3* Healing her broken leg took more patience. Every day I gave her thirteen hours of light and force-fed her twice with bone meal. After a month she could move her leg with ease and would catch the insects that I threw into her cage. I was thrilled to have saved the life of this beautiful creature.

(marginal annotations: details to prove Point #1; details to prove Point #2; details to prove Point #3)

This writer states three things that had to be done to revitalize the lizard and follows each statement with specifics about the activity. The reader sees the difficulty of feeding the lizard, the spectacular success of the light treatment, and the prolonged attention necessary for the final cure. One by one the supports must be stated, explained, and proven with lots of specific details and concrete facts.

The more specifics you include, the more convincing your writing will be. The following paragraph includes only generalizations.

FAULTY

Many people enjoy seeing the defensive men hit the *Support* running back with a good hard hit. These men are important because they are responsible for keeping the other team's score down. When I go to a football game, I always watch the defense. I enjoy seeing a good block. When somebody gets hit hard, the fans applaud and cheer.

Instead of stating specific facts, all the sentences in the preceding paragraph describe something that happens more than once. It's frequently true that the defense must keep the other team's score down, the writer watches the defense, and the fans enjoy seeing a good block. Notice how much better the following revision is.

REVISED

Many people enjoy seeing the defensive *Support* men hit the running back with a good hard hit. When somebody gets hit really hard, the fans applaud and cheer. Once in a high school football game I had the opportunity to get a good hit on an opposing player. The other team was kicking off to us, and I was one of the five men up front to block. As the other team came running down the field, our front line drifted back to set up to block. We ran the ball to the left side near the stand. As I was running forward, a man from the other team came at me. I could have avoided him because our man with the ball had almost been tackled, but I hit him anyway and knocked him down. My teammates started yelling, the people in the stands too. When I saw what I had done, I got fired up and said to the man at my feet, "Stay down, Punk."

The writer has replaced the generalizations with an example, a description of one situation in which many people enjoyed seeing a good hit. Fill your body paragraphs with those specific details that happen only once and stay in the reader's mind like a memory.

Be sure to choose the best possible evidence. The writer of the following paragraph provided vivid details, but they don't prove the support.

FAULTY

support↲

    Public parks are inexpensive places to have fun. At the park there are lots of activities to get into. Roller skating at Lake Merritt can be fun if a person knows how to avoid falling in the water. I went skating with my boy friend two weeks ago. While he was whispering sweet nothings in my ear, I was trying to concentrate on my skating. Unfortunately, I shifted my attention to him instead of watching the pathway, and in a split second I was up to my neck in the dirty smelly water. I was so embarrassed that I did not even want to come out. After that experience, I decided to try jogging because I would have more control over my feet.

evidence needed

The picture of the writer falling into the lake is memorable, but it does not show someone having fun, so it does not prove the support.

CORRECTION COMMENT: Each body paragraph should be built by stating the support, explaining it if necessary, and then proving it with lots of specific details and concrete facts.

EXERCISES: *Writing Body Paragraphs*

I. Circle the most specific word in each of the lists below.

1. athlete   male   baseball player   Johnny Bench   catcher

2. book   *Tom Sawyer*   paperback   novel

3. Meg Walker   writer   person   woman   reporter

4. listen   hear   eavesdrop

5. lox   salmon   fish   seafood

6. sneak   move   walk

7. musician   Sonny Terry   blues harpist   harmonica player

8. greedy   terrible   self-centered   bad

9. drink   alcohol   beer   Genesee

10. run   hurry   dash   go

II. *Write a specific word next to each of the general words below.*

A.
1. child
2. bird
3. big
4. car
5. exciting

6. walk
7. eat
8. interesting
9. read
10. dance

B.
1. city
2. young
3. give
4. music
5. loud

6. put
7. movie
8. unusual
9. get
10. boxer

III. **A.** *Suggest specific details that might be used as evidence for the following sentences.*

1. When I first saw our new house, I was sure it must be haunted.
2. It was fun to see our classmates and teachers in their Halloween costumes.
3. When my son was two years old, he took his clothes off at very inconvenient times.
4. My brother borrows my things without asking.
5. I especially enjoy their pizza.
6. The secondhand stores are becoming the fashion consumer's best bet for stylish clothing.
7. The working conditions were very poor.
8. We live in a large building.
9. There are several statues in the park.
10. I got some clothes for Christmas.

B. *Write a paragraph proving one of the sentences in exercise A.*

IV. *Study the body paragraphs below. Decide which ones start with a support and have good specific details to prove all their generalizations, and label them "good." Label the others "evidence needed—too general" or "evidence needed—wrong details." Be prepared to suggest specific evidence that would be effective in the paragraph, and rewrite any that your teacher assigns.*

A.   1.   I like greasy foods. I enjoy eating pizza, French fries, and chicken. Greasy foods are nice when they are hot, but there is nothing more horrible than cold greasy foods. When I go to a fast-food restaurant, the French fries are cold and greasy. In high school I met a guy who ate French fries for breakfast and pizza and hamburgers for lunch. Recently, I went out to dinner with him at Pizza Hut. I thought after a couple of years his eating habits would have changed, but I was wrong. When he eats pizza, it looks disgusting. The pizza sauce was dripping down his face onto his clothes, and he looked like a greasy pig. Even the pizza began to look disgusting to me. For a while after, the sight of pizza turned me away because I associated it with his greasy face. However, I have gotten over the shock. I am a true pizza lover.

evidence needed

2.   The Omega Club's initiations were exciting. Every year the club initiated new members. When I was initiated, the old members came to my house at about seven-thirty in the morning. They woke me up and dragged me outside in just my pajamas, robe, and slippers. They pushed me into a car and took off after eight other cars filled with Omega members and girls in their night clothes. The cars were all decorated with balloons and black and gold streamers, and everyone was honking the horns and screaming out the windows. After they picked up the rest of the initiates, they took us all to Biff's for breakfast. When we finished eating, they made us go outside the restaurant to sing and dance. We all had fun acting silly while everyone watched us through the windows. Then they took us back to our homes.

3.   Ever since I can remember, Ray has put himself before others. He put his family into debt by borrowing money for himself. He would always try to make himself look good even if it made someone look bad. He went out with other women, leaving his wife home with five children. He just didn't care.

4.   I enjoyed getting out of my school work when I skipped school. Because I wasn't doing my homework, my grades in math class dropped. Mrs. Kirkhorn would assign homework every night for us, and I would miss the assignments when I wasn't there. Also my American Government class suffered because we were graded on our class discussions. Missing one counted against my grade.

5.   I enjoyed the class also because I liked programming the computer. One day I wrote a really good program using the quadratic formula. I was so enthused about the program I went early to second period and spent all period working on it. I just couldn't stop working on that program, so I came in during lunch and worked through fifth and sixth periods. I struggled and sweated and finally the mistake came to me. With a few minor corrections, it worked and ran as smooth as ice.

6.   Moving into a school dorm will give me independence. Moving away from my family and others that I often depend on will give me real independence. I like to make my own decisions and do what I want to do. Being on my own will allow me freedom, freedom to come and go as I wish and to choose what I think is best in my life.

7.   I have strong ties to my family because of the many hours we spent together. The projects we worked on used to keep the whole family together. When we repapered the living room of our house, we were all in one room for several days. We had to learn to get along with each other. When a freak thunderstorm hit our village, the water streamed down the hill and into our house. There was mud and water everywhere. The water wrecked most of the work we had done on the house. The entire family had to live together in the two upstairs rooms for several weeks, and once again we had to learn to get along. Now my family can sit down and talk for hours. We have a lot of fun. We really cherish these moments. Very few families can even begin to communicate amongst themselves today. We face family problems as a unit rather than as individual people. None of us makes an important decision without at least informing the rest of the family. I think as a family we are far better off than most because of the time we had together.

8.   My man must also be intelligent. There is nothing more frustrating than being with someone who cannot make heads or tails of a given situation. In high school I dated a guy who could not follow simple directions. He would often get confused if he left his neighborhood, and it took him quite a while to memorize the route to my house. Education isn't always enough; one must also have common sense. A friend of mine asks some of the silliest questions. One day when we were driving toward a dead-end road, he asked me whether or not to turn. We had often traveled down this road, and the arrow on the sign was very visible. When I laughed at him, he got angry. He received very high grades in school, but he doesn't apply his intelligence to his daily life. Education is part of being intelligent; however, common sense is also.

9.   I also enjoy talking to Lisa. We always tell each other our secrets. Many times when I have problems at school I talk to her. She helps me solve them or gives me the confidence to manage them myself. She is always there when I need her. I also try to help her whenever she needs me.

10.   Wanting to be an actress also helps me conquer fear. When I was fifteen years old, I decided to audition for a summer musical. I was petrified. There were about two hundred kids looking at the scripts, practicing dance steps, and warming up their voices. While all this was going on, I sat straight up in my seat with eyes as wide as saucers. I didn't want to audition; I just wanted to be somewhere else. Then I began to get angry and asked myself, "How am I ever going to be an actress if I can't even audition for this stupid musical?" After that I found the strength to get up on the stage and do my best.

V. *Leaving about half a page empty at the beginning for the introduction, write the three body paragraphs for your essay 1. Start each one with the support from the outline assigned on page 31. Then look back at your notes, choose the best evidence, and decide what order to put it in. Finally, write these facts out in sentence after sentence, adding more details and explanation and answering these questions:*

Who did what?   Why?

Where?   How?

When?

Be sure to back up every generalization with details, and be sure that the details really prove the support.

VI. *Read the following essay and list its strengths and weaknesses in the margin. Write comments like "good thesis," "poor supports," and "evidence needed" as they apply.*

evidence needed

There are times when we need cash quick, fast, and in a hurry. Sometimes we are not able to make it to the bank on time. Especially on weekends, everyone seems to be a "cashoholic," searching in the cookie jars, under the bed, anywhere that money could possibly be hidden. People often ask to borrow money from me, so I decided to go into business. Unfortunately, as in any business, there are certain advantages and disadvantages to lending money.

I charge interest on my loans. Five percent interest is not bad, considering that the banks have higher rates. I find that charging interest is good for business because people pay me back sooner. I remember lending my sister twenty-five dollars with interest. "But I'm your sister," she said. "How can you charge interest?" I said, very eloquently, "Because we are sisters, I should charge interest; furthermore, I'm taking advantage of you before you take advantage of me." She looked at me, puzzled; then she said, "I don't want your money." I stood there in shock. Apparently she misunderstood me. Well, it wasn't a loss at all. I think it is not good for business to lend money to relatives, because they want special treatment. Besides, how can a girl get ahead if she's easy?

Sometimes people forget that they owe me money. This is really a disadvantage. Most of the time I need the money back on time because I have made future arrangements for it. I have customers eagerly waiting to take out a loan. If I can produce the money on the spot, so should everyone else. There is nothing more frustrating than people not paying their debts. I remember fighting someone because he refused to pay me back. Unfortunately nothing was gained for me but a black eye, so I decided to pay my brothers to collect bad debts. I keep a little black ledger in my purse at all times. This is how I keep track of who owes me money. I take the people's addresses, telephone numbers (work and home), and the expected dates of delivery. I also ask them to sign their names next to the amount loaned. Some people believe that I am a bank because I always have cash on me. I remember a man named Ray who tried to rob me. I had often loaned money to him, and he was aware that I always have cash. One day he walked up to me and said, "I would like to make a withdrawal." I told him that I only make loans. He said, "I am aware of that, but one has to pay back loans." He stood there with a sneaky look in his eyes; however, I knew what he wanted to do. I smiled at him and reached in my pocket slowly. Then I pulled out my whistle. Guess what! Around the corner in a flash appeared my older brother. Ray ran as though he had wings.

It is nice to help people when they really need money. I have been lending money ever since I was able to count. Charging interest is important, because I use the money toward school. I believe everyone should learn how to save and earn money, because we never know what may happen next.

INDEPENDENT STUDY: *Writing Body Paragraphs* (answers in the back)

VII. *Study the body paragraphs below. Decide which ones start with a support and have good details to prove all their generalizations, and label them "good." Label the others "evidence needed—too general" or "evidence needed—wrong details." Rewrite any that your teacher assigns.*

1. One nice result of cooking my own food is that I get to eat as much as I want. If I want to eat a lot, I am free to do it. Since I cook at home most of the time, I don't waste any food. If I am not hungry, I can save the food for the next day.

2. Grandmother was cruel to my mother. I never will forget the time we were out of food. Grandmother brought a bag of home-cured ham, canned vegetables, and fruit over to our house. She also brought a large pail of milk. She told my daddy, "I don't want your wife eating any food and drinking my milk." There was another incident between my mother and grandmother. Daddy was at church, and Mother was down the road visiting Aunt Rose. She left a large pot filled with stew cooking over the fireplace, and I turned the hot pot over on my legs. Grandmother was the one who ran over and pulled my long cotton stockings off. Because Mother was out of the house at the time, Grandmother told everyone she was no good.

3. I also really enjoyed the senior ball. We rented a boat and hired a band to play on it. I was a little seasick at first, but I finally recovered. Our band was not very good because the musicians did not dress up or play any good songs. I had fun with my date. Before we went on the boat, he took me out to dinner. I was not used to my long dress because I had never worn one before. When I got up to go to the rest room, I stepped on my dress and tripped. There were lots of people there, and I was so embarrassed I nearly fainted. That was the last time I will ever wear a long dress. At least my whole night was not destroyed. I had a really nice night.

4. Parents have fun enjoying the antics of the young children on Halloween. The parents are just as excited as the children as they help them get ready to go out. Parents get a kick out of watching the neighbors' children come to the door and ask for candy. They say that each child is just as cute and adorable as the next. Parents also like helping the children sort out their candy to make sure that the candy is safe.

5.   I am looking forward to staying in a luxury condominium in the Aspen area. This condominium is really beautiful. It is a two-story structure with four rooms and two baths. The rooms are spacious, comfortable, and suitable for a large family like mine. The big kitchen has a full range, refrigerator, and dishwasher. The living room is the really special part of the house. It has two very cozy couches on either side of the huge fireplace, which is center stage. On the sides of the fireplace are two large sliding glass doors, which open onto a balcony overlooking a frozen lake with a backdrop of snow-covered mountains. Sitting on the couch, drinking hot cocoa before a roaring fire, looking at the scenery with a friend, I lose track of my worldly cares.

6.   My sister, Valencia, is a very friendly person. Her warmth of heart and personal magnetism attract many friends, who find her gentle, helpful, and kind. People tend to confide in her and cry on her shoulder because she is a good listener and understands their problems. Valencia appreciates her friends' troubles because she has a deep perception of human feelings and failings. She worries when her friends worry and laughs when they laugh. Altogether, Valencia may be too peaceful.

evidence needed

7.   Playing soccer taught my brother teamwork. Teamwork is the only way to be successful at anything. Let's take basketball for an example. There are five men on a team, and each man has an assignment. If one man misses his assignment, the whole team suffers. In this type of situation, you learn to use teamwork. You help your teammates out in every way you can. When someone makes a mistake, you don't get mad. Instead you pat him on the back and encourage him. Even in an individual sport, teamwork is very important. Boxers use trainers and sparring partners. Even though all the work is done before the main event, it's just as important as the teamwork that goes on during a football or basketball game.

8.   Many people are exercising to improve their health. Early one morning I was heading out the door to work when all of a sudden the air became still, the birds stopped chirping, and a couple of cats preparing to fight shot away with terror in their large eyes. Then, simultaneously on both side of the street, over a dozen residents emerged from their respective houses. I was terrified, for I knew what was to happen next. Each of them did what looked like a short dance; then all at once they started jogging. The ground trembled as they stampeded in my direction. Knowing I would be trampled like a spectator at a Who concert, I made a dive for the door of my car. Split seconds later I was in my car with the door shut tightly, and not a moment too soon, since directly behind me was the multi-colored band of enthusiastic joggers. As the last one bounced past my car, I breathed a sigh of relief and hoped getting to my car in the morning wouldn't always be like this.

9.   Art fills me with a feeling of accomplishment. There is a great feeling that comes to me when I finish a project that I have been working on for a long time. This feeling of accomplishment helps me strengthen my

personality and self-worth. While most people are faced with troubles and the frustration that goes with the routine of our daily lives, I find comfort and reassurance in my art.

10.   In my family the preparation for this holiday is a big part of the tradition. Approximately three weeks before Christmas, my family and I begin to decorate our house. My older brother, Al, is usually in charge of picking out the tree. While my parents and Al are out shopping for the Christmas tree, my other brother, my sister, and I stay home and get the decorations down from the attic. When the tree finally arrives, we all do our share of the work, decorating it with bells, stars, tinsel, and many ornaments that we have collected through the years. We also make sure that our stockings are neatly hanging on the fireplace mantel. When the decorating is done, my mother, sister, and I start to bake. We make our traditional cut-out cookies and thumbprint cookies along with Portuguese pastries. These pastries include *sonhos,* which are similar to doughnut holes, and *aletria,* which is a pudding made of very thin pasta. We also make a Portuguese-style custard pudding and rice pudding. We spend many hours preparing for Christmas.

WRITING INTRODUCTIONS

Now that you have proven your thesis, you must convince someone to read that proof. Much imagination goes into inventing ways to get an audience. A kitchenware salesperson attracts potential customers with food: a taste of juice from a blender, a fried banana from a non-stick frying pan. A hustler develops a clever line, an encyclopedia salesman puts his foot in the door, and an essayist writes a gripping introduction. They all have a product to sell. The essayist wants to sell an idea—a thesis.

It is difficult to generalize about introductions. Because they must be interesting, creativity and unusual techniques work well in them. The best ones grow out of the unique combination of a particular writer and a particular subject. Now that your body paragraphs are finished, scrutinize your experience of the subject for any good material you haven't used. Is there a great story that you couldn't fit into the body paragraphs? Is there an interesting point that you couldn't use in your outline? Such elements often make good introductions.

Introduction

Think about the ways in which people attract attention. Advertisers are obvious masters of the art, but you'll see others everywhere: in class, on the bus, at work, in the supermarket. Notice the beginnings of books, magazine articles, editorials, and other professional writing, and try adapting some of these techniques to your own introductions. Many people like to begin an introduction with an attention-getter:

a question	a vivid detail
a quotation	a newspaper headline
a definition	a shocking statement

These devices, however, take only a sentence or two and must lead into a coherent paragraph.

Like any other paragraph, an introduction develops one idea with good vivid detail. If you still haven't thought of a topic for your introduction, look at your thesis and ask yourself:

What comes before this?

Then build your answer into an introduction by explaining and describing in specific detail who did what, how, where, when, and why.

End your introduction with your thesis. Since supporting argument always seems to logically follow a statement of the thesis, and since the body paragraphs are designed to present and prove that argument as effectively as possible, the thesis should be the last sentence of the introduction.

Your introduction may follow one of a few common patterns. If you had trouble narrowing your thesis to one side of the argument, you might present the other side in an introduction like the following.

GOOD

I want to move away from home because I am tired of fighting with my parents. My mother is always yelling at me to do the ironing, but I think that anybody who knows how the iron works can iron his/her own clothes. My father always tells me to clean the bathroom, but I think whoever messes it up should clean it. Whenever I try to explain my point of view, my father and I get into an argument. Sometimes I think our fights won't end until I get a place of my own, but when I sit down and think about moving, I always reach the same conclusion. I can't afford to live by myself.

←thesis↵

This introduction describes the difficulty of living at home while the thesis and the rest of the essay discuss the difficulty of moving away.

Just as the introduction comes before the thesis and body paragraphs on the page, the material in the introduction often comes before the material of the thesis and body paragraphs in time. The history of the topic fits well here. You might introduce an essay on the pleasure of playing tennis with a brief history of the sport. You could begin an essay on the dangers of Halloween today by showing how safe it used to be. The following introduction takes that approach.

GOOD

What compels a person to go back to college after five years? Perhaps it is a thirst for knowledge or for something more in life. It was a combination of both for me. After five years as an LVN at Children's Hospital, I was performing my job effectively without thinking. I wanted to use my brain and master new subjects. I had also reached the highest possible position and salary for an LVN, and I wanted the opportunity to move into even more responsible positions. I wanted a new challenge. Iowa State has certainly given me that! Take it from one who knows; going back to school is no easy feat.

←thesis

This introduction discusses the reasons for going back to school. Then the thesis and the rest of the essay show how hard it was. Notice that this introduction begins with a question.

Sometimes an introduction makes and develops a point that comes before the rest of the essay logically. The argument of an essay moves from the generalization of the thesis through the narrower generalizations of the topic sentences down to the specific facts of the body paragraphs. The introduction may start with a point even more general than the thesis and develop that, as does the following introduction.

GOOD

People live out their fantasies in many ways. A child may turn into Superman or Cinderella with the simple addition of a bath towel. An older child may become Huck Finn or an Indian scout just by climbing a tree. Some women dress up in exotic attire and play at being Raquel Welch while many men swagger around imagining themselves to be Burt Reynolds. Doing this is not as silly as it may seem; psychiatrists have had patients acting out their wildest dreams for years. This expensive and time-consuming national pastime is known as "therapy." My therapy occurs in a Datsun 280Z; once behind the wheel I become "Cheri Slick."

←thesis

This introduction discusses many ways that people act out their fantasies, but the thesis and the rest of the essay focus on the writer's way.

Whatever approach you choose, be sure to develop the introduction fully. The most interesting writing is very specific. The introduction above sparkles with details. Notice how uninteresting that introduction was before the detail was added:

FAULTY

People live out their fantasies in many ways. I act mine out in a Datsun 280Z; once behind the wheel I become "Cheri Slick."
↳ thesis

Specific details are needed in every paragraph.

There are other common weaknesses to avoid in introductions. Never try to prove the thesis in the introduction. Evidence and argument belong in the body. Though a ten-page paper or a speech may need the arguments in the introduction, such repetition in short essays like these bores the reader. The following introduction has that problem.

FAULTY

My younger brother Jason is sixteen and a sophomore in high school. He doesn't help with any of the housework inside the house or outside. All he ever does is make a lot of noise, pick fights, and borrow things he never returns. My little brother Jason makes my life miserable.
↳ thesis

The arguments of the body paragraphs that follow are that Jason makes a lot of noise, picks fights, and borrows things he never returns. Reading the body seems like a waste of time. The first sentence of the introduction is good, and the writer should have gone on to give more details about Jason, details that would not be used later in the essay. She could have described anything else: his charm, his hobbies, his athletic ability, his good grades—anything but material from the body paragraphs.

Like any paragraph, the introduction should hang together as a unit, so plan your introduction before you begin writing. Don't limp along sentence by sentence as the writer of this one did.

FAULTY

Once a year I visit my grandparents. My grandparents live in Delaware. All year long I find myself looking at the calendar wishing it were summer. My grandparents don't look a day over fifty, but they are well into their seventies. When I visit my grandparents, I learn about life in the old days.   thesis ↗

The writer of this introduction did not plan ahead. Instead he stopped after each sentence to think of something else to say. He should have developed in detail just one idea—for example, the trip to Delaware, his grandparents' young appearance, or his eager anticipation of the trip. He should not have included several different ideas.

The introduction should lead up to and include the thesis gracefully. The following introduction breaks awkwardly before the thesis.

FAULTY

Soccer is a tough, fast, exciting game that requires its players to be in excellent physical condition. They need strong legs to outrun their opponents and kick the ball accurately. They also need great physical endurance because once the game begins, the players constantly move up and down the field. Play is stopped only when a goal is scored, when a foul occurs, or if a player is seriously injured. A soccer player must have good ball-handling skills.
↳ thesis

The addition of just a few words makes the thesis fit in much more smoothly.

GOOD

Soccer is a tough, fast, exciting game that requires its players to be in excellent physical condition. They need strong legs to outrun their opponents and kick the ball accurately. They also need great physical endurance because once the game begins, the players constantly move up and down the field. Play is stopped only when a goal is scored, when a foul occurs, or if a player is seriously injured. In addition to being in excellent physical condition, a soccer player must have good ball-handling skills. ← thesis

Often a thesis is built into a long sentence. In that case, the reader will assume that the last part of that sentence is the thesis, so the writer should be sure that it is.

CORRECTION COMMENT: **A good introduction develops one interesting idea with good specific details, does not repeat the content of the essay, and ends gracefully with the thesis.**

EXERCISES: *Writing Introductions*

I. *Study the introductions below. By each one write "good" or "faulty" and add a few words indicating the weaknesses of the faulty ones.*

1. The Pizza Place is located in Queens. It just opened up about two weeks ago. There is always a line of people waiting for service. There is wheelchair access, and they also have a free delivery service. I've already been there four times. The Pizza Place is an excellent restaurant.

2. Most people who have just moved into a new house or apartment immediately start decorating. Plants, mirrors, and pictures are just a few of the usual items people put in apartments and houses. Keeping an elephant in a city apartment is very inconvenient.

3. When I was a child, I was very eager to enter high school. I would gather the neighborhood children together, and we would play high school. The boys would line up behind the girls with their homemade drums, horns, and tambourines and pretend to be the high school band. In front the girls pranced to the music—twirling, turning, and kicking. High school turned out to be even better than I had imagined. When I finally got into high school, I had many good times.

4. Traveling across the United States by train can be fun. It allows one to view the scenes man and nature have created, and it allows people to mingle with others from morning to night.

5. Life starts out slowly. Then it soon progresses. We have to learn the ways of life and how to fit into the system of society. I feel that the only real way to get ready for the outside world is to stand on our own two feet. Soccer prepared my brother for life.

6. My father was in the United States Air Force for twenty years. Consequently my family traveled the world over: England, Germany, and virtually

every state in the union. However, for the majority of our lives we lived in small towns of less than ten thousand people. There we were cut off from the social pressures of the world. When we moved to the city of Baltimore, I was shocked by the social pollution in my neighborhood.

7.   Selfishness is a horrible trait. Everyone is naturally a little selfish; we have to be or we would go insane. However, selfishness can be carried to extremes of cruelty. Ray is an excessively selfish person.

8.   When I was in junior high I had many friends, and we were in many activities together. We were involved in an art class, a physical education class, and a yearbook class. My friends and I really enjoyed having the entire gang together because it made our boring times pass more quickly. We did other things besides our class work: we went out after school, on the weekends, and to football games. No other person but Dave was my best friend during junior high.

Introduction

9.   My brother Louis has just started working part-time at a very nice restaurant. He receives many tips and compliments from his employer and customers because he is a very good worker. When he is at work he is always on the go, trying to do his best. This is one side of my brother that I do not see very often. When he is at home, Louis can be somewhat lazy.

10.   I don't know how my mother does it. She seems to have more energy in one little finger than most people have in their whole bodies. No matter how much she does in one day, she never tires. I guess that's why she is my mother and I will always love her. She is truly an energetic person.

II. **A.** *Rewrite three of the introductions in exercise I above.*

B. *Discuss with your classmates possible introductions for the theses given in exercise II A on pages 19–20.*

C. *Write three of those introductions.*

D. *Following the instructions in this unit, write an introduction for essay 1 (exercise V, page 30).*

III. *Read the following essay and write appropriate correction comments in the margin. Label the thesis, the outline, the evidence, and the introduction "good" or "faulty."*

Each country has its own way to say "I love you" and to express its feelings of love. In Venezuela, we give pleasure to those we love with the serenade.
   A woman has her first serenade on her fifteenth birthday. If she does not have a boy friend, then her parents and friends prepare a serenade for her. The serenade begins at midnight and is played and sung by a group of friends. Each serenade begins with a song called "Despierta," and in the case of a fifteenth birthday serenade, it is followed by a special song calld "Feliz Quinzavos Compleanos" so that the girl begins her spring days with love and happiness. When my fifteenth birthday came, I didn't have a boy friend, but my older sister

did, so she, together with her boy friend and my parents, gave a serenade. I didn't expect that serenade because none of them knew how to play the guitar, but my father hired a trio called "The Chirolies" for the serenade. I can say that a serenade the night of the fifteenth birthday is one of the most beautiful presents that a girl can receive.

Boy friends express their love at other times with serenades. This kind of serenade might have two purposes. Sometimes serenades celebrate the beginning of a relationship—each month or every two months. Other times, the serenade expresses apology if there is a quarrel between a boy and his girl friend. I had a friend who had a big quarrel with his girl friend, and he had done everything possible to win her back but nothing worked. Finally he called and asked me to serenade her. The next night we went to his girl friend's house with a rose, a present, and a serenade. After that night his girl friend forgot what had happened, and they were together again.

Special occasions are also celebrated with a serenade. The most beautiful serenade I remember was the one my brother-in-law gave to my sister the day my niece was born. It was a special and beautiful occasion because my niece was the first one in both families. Each family was very excited but especially my brother-in-law. He spoke with the director of the hospital, and we were allowed to go to the hospital's garden and serenade my sister and the new niece. My sister has not forgotten that serenade, and I suppose my niece is the only woman who had a serenade just hours after being born.

The serenade is a beautiful way to express love. The silence of the night, the stars in the sky, and the love one puts in it make a serenade special. It is not just music, it is love and happiness. When a lady receives a serenade, she feels that everybody loves her and that nothing is more important at that moment than to hear the music and to feel the love from the others.

INDEPENDENT STUDY: *Writing Introductions* (answers in the back)

IV. Study the introductions below. By each one write "good" or "faulty," and add a few words indicating the weaknesses of the faulty ones.

1. Ever since I was a junior in high school, I have been trying to decide what my profession should be. I thought about going to business college, but I really didn't want to become a secretary. I also considered going into nursing, but ruled it out because I can't stand the sight of blood. Well, now I'm a freshman in college and still have no idea what I want to do. There is one profession, though, that I wish I had thought of a year ago. If I could have any profession, I would choose to be an airline steward.

2. As long as I have known Kim, she has been a very energetic person. She has been involved in many school activities. She is extremely active in student government, and she has devoted many years to track. Just recently she began modeling school, and she has already done a number of jobs.

3. Almost every day I hear people moaning and groaning about their jobs. Last week a friend said to me: "I am so sick of working that I could just die. Every day it's the same old one-two-three. I am so bored. I just watch the

clock all day at work." Many people see their jobs as one of the worst things in their lives, but I had a job that I really enjoyed. My job at Jordan Marsh was a great learning experience for me.

4.   There are many expensive recreational activities. Tennis equipment can cost anywhere from forty dollars to two hundred dollars. In order to safely play football, one must purchase equipment which costs approximately two hundred dollars. Skiing is a very expensive sport.

5.   I remember when I was standing in line to receive my first high school yearbook. I was so excited that it seemed as if I was in line for hours. When I finally received the book, I sat down on the lawn and began to go through it page by page. As I did, I imagined myself as a member of the yearbook staff. I thought it would be lots of fun to help put a yearbook together. I found out later that it was harder than it seemed. Being a member of the yearbook staff was hard work.

6.   If you like the subway, please read this. The subway is one of the best forms of transportation I have. Whenever I go somewhere, I go by subway. Well, before the system wasn't well organized, but the system has improved and I can depend on it now. The subway gets me anywhere I want to go within its boundaries. Traveling by subway is fun.

introduction

7.   Some people say that it is very nice being the only child in the family, but having an older brother or sister can be very nice too. My older brother was very helpful to me.

8.   Ever since I was in third grade, I have loved to write stories and give them to my parents as presents. I wrote mainly about things that confused me, such as Santa's eight reindeer and how they flew or the tooth fairy and how she got in through my locked window at night. All these stories took time and patience. They were also fairly good because I wasn't rushed to finish them. Each story took me about a day to write—definitely longer than an hour. My only objection to this course is that we have to write essays in class.

9.   Joe Morgan will be a real asset to the Giants. He is an expert at moving round the bases. Whether by walking or hitting, he gets to first base more frequently than most good baseball players. Once on first, he's hard to stop because he's an expert base stealer. He will also improve the team's morale because his determination and dedication inspire all who work with him. Joe Morgan will greatly strengthen the San Francisco Giants.

10.   Throughout life, people in America are forced to play the credit game. Creditors make major purchases like cars or houses virtually impossible without previous credit. Personal checks are next to impossible to cash unless a person has at least two major credit cards. This game can be dangerous because it can lead to very serious debt. Purchasing by credit can be hazardous to one's financial health.

WRITING CONCLUSIONS

As the introduction comes before the thesis and its proof in both time and logic, the conclusion comes after it. Although the introduction may move back a step in argument or in history from the thesis and its proof, the conclusion moves forward in logic, carrying the argument one step beyond the thesis, and in time, relating the thesis to the future.

Look back at your introduction and thesis. Then write a conclusion by doing the following two things.

First, explain why the thesis is important in today's world. Look back at your thesis and then ask yourself these questions:

So what?

Why is this topic important to people besides me?

To build the first part of your conclusion, write out your answer, telling who does what, where, when, why, and how. If your thesis is about the difficulties of going back to school, your conclusion could begin by talking about the large numbers of people who are doing that today. If your thesis recommends a television show, your conclusion could mention the widespread use of television for relaxation or the poor quality of most television shows. If your thesis comments on an economical car, your conclusion could talk about the increasing costs of gas or people's dependence on automobiles in our society.

Second, relate the thesis to the future with predictions and recommendations. Now that you've shown that the topic is important, ask yourself these questions:

What if nothing changes?

What should be done about this situation?

To build the last part of your conclusion, write out your answers telling who will do what, where, when, why, and how and who *should* do what, where, when, why, and how. If you wrote about the difficulties of returning to school, you might predict drop-outs and recommend programs to solve the problems: for example, child care, transportation, or tutoring programs. If you described an outstanding television show, you might predict that it will become popular or be copied, and recommend that people watch it or that networks create more shows of similar quality. If you wrote about an economical car, you could predict that it will become popular or be copied, and recommend that people buy one or that other companies make similar ones.

The conclusion, like the introduction, should not contain body material, neither thesis, arguments, nor evidence. The conclusion should assume that the thesis has been proven. If it hasn't, the body should be changed, not the conclusion. Instead of telling why the thesis is important, the following conclusion repeats the writer's arguments.

FAULTY

Thesis: Traveling by car can be very satisfying.

From all of my traveling experience, I can say that I enjoyed traveling by car the most because it allowed me to see beautiful scenery, become closer to my family, and sit back and enjoy the rest I needed. I recommend that people planning to travel do it by car because they can be sure that they will have fun and get the rest they deserve.

Instead, the writer could have talked about the increase in leisure time, the decline in popularity of automobile trips, or the need for relaxation in today's tense and busy world. A ten-page essay or a speech may need the supports repeated in the conclusion, but a five-paragraph essay does not.

conclusion

A good conclusion explains why the thesis is important today and relates it to the future with predictions and recommendations. The following conclusion does that.

GOOD

Thesis: A blind person must overcome many obstacles.

In these challenging and troubled times our society needs the help of all its citizens. Handicapped people are a vast, untapped resource that this country is only beginning to explore. To maximize its use of this resource, society must consider the needs of these people and adjust its plans to include them. A small investment of time and money will produce immeasurable returns as a whole new segment of the population becomes productive.

(margin note: explains why the thesis is important in today's world *)*
(margin note: relates the thesis to the future *)*

CORRECTION COMMENT: A good conclusion explains why the thesis is important today and relates it to the future with predictions and recommendations.

EXERCISES: *Writing Conclusions*

I. *In the following conclusions, circle the sentences that answer "so what?" and those which answer "what next?" and label them in the margin. Then label each conclusion "good" or "faulty."*

1. *Thesis:* Credit spending can lead to serious debt.

   What can be done to prevent such viciousness in this crazy game? If credit were used more wisely and less often, people wouldn't run into financial difficulties or even, in some cases, bankruptcy. If the public refused to be abused by the creditors and stood up for their rights, then all these problems might be prevented.

2. *Thesis:* My older sister has been a big help to me.

   I hope that in the future my younger sister can feel the same way about me as I do about my older sister. I also hope I can be just as helpful to her as my older sister has been to me.

3. *Thesis:* The free world and its civilized manner of conducting business are to blame for the energy crisis.

   We have a lot to learn from countries with non-democratic governments. Even in democratic countries, decisions are made and problems are solved quickly in times of war. We are fighting a war for oil, a war against time. With our present strategy we are losing the battles, and we will soon lose the war. Some decisions are going to have to be made. We must get together and show the world we can still solve the problems we face.

4. *Thesis:* The subway is a good transportation system.

    I have filled a lot of my needs by riding the subway, and I depend on it every day for school. If we didn't have the subway, I would have trouble getting around. A lot of business people ride the subway. It's cheaper than driving, and I have saved a lot of money. The system is also well organized. The subway is very helpful to me, and I'm sure a lot of other people feel the same way.

5. *Thesis:* The pollution in my neighborhood is very bad.

    How can people live in a neighborhood that looks like the city dump? If I could move out of my neighborhood, I would, because I am ashamed of it. I am surprised my parents still live in our house, but I think they are considering moving.

6. *Thesis:* My honeymoon trip to Acapulco was a real vacation.

    Our honeymoon in Acapulco was a real vacation. The people at the hotels and restaurants treated us like a king and queen. Everything was done for us, so we had no responsibilities. I hated to come home again.

7. *Thesis:* My family took on extra responsibilities when I went back to school.

    As students make commitments to school, the people around them are making commitments too. Our friends and families deserve a lot of credit, and we should express our gratitude in both words and actions. When I graduate, I will really mean it when I say, "I couldn't have done it without you."

8. *Thesis:* My high school English classes did not prepare me for college writing.

    All over the United States, high schools are producing semi-literate people who aren't prepared for life. We must give high school English teachers the training and support they need before it's too late. Rebuilding our writing programs may be expensive, but isn't it worth it?

9. *Thesis:* A day at my grandmother's house is not always fun.

    It may not always be fun staying at my grandmother's house, but it's always interesting. My grandmother may bug me sometimes, but she's the best grandmother in the whole world, and I love her.

10. *Thesis:* Having an elephant for a roommate has several disadvantages.

    Most people enjoy having roommates. It's nice to find a roommate that you have a lot in common with. I recommend that you avoid living with any animal that is larger than you.

II. **A.** *Rewrite three of the conclusions in exercise I above.*

B. *Discuss with your classmates possible conclusions for the theses given in exercise II A on pages 19–20.*

C. *Write three of those conclusions.*

D. Following the instructions in this unit, write a conclusion for essay 1 (exercise II D, page 39).

III. *Read the following essay and write appropriate comments in the margin. Label the thesis, outline, body paragraphs, introduction, and conclusion "good" or "faulty."*

My family lived in a small fishing village in Saudi Arabia called Jubail. It was a beautiful and a peaceful town. There was a very small number of families, but they were all wonderful people. Memories are difficult to trace; they tend to float to the surface in the wrong order. Several vivid memories come to mind when I think about those years in Jubail.

conclusion

I remember vividly, for example, that Saturday in our family was cleaning day and that each Saturday the washerwoman arrived early in the morning, lit the kitchen fireplace, placed a huge cauldron over the fire, and filled it with water that she pumped from the well in the garden. Then she sorted out the laundry. While the water was being heated, she gave the white linen materials preliminary washing with soap and water. Then she rinsed these and put them in the boiling cauldron. She let the laundry boil for some fifteen minutes, gave it a soaping and a couple of rinsings, and hung it in the sun. I remember the joy of sleeping in those clean sheets and pajamas Saturday night after a hot bath.

I remember too the glorious summers in Jubail when the nights were cool and clear. The stars were close by, and we and our neighbors would go out onto the flat roofs to sleep. On such nights we stayed awake late, fascinated by the spectacle of the sky. My father would point out one constellation after the other, and by the time I was five, the firmament was friendly because I could call many of its stars by their proper names. Occasionally some clouds would sail by, and we would play the game of suggesting what each of them looked like.

There were other nights when we felt social and neighborly. On such occasions we would climb to the higher roof level, which was adjacent to our neighbors' roof, and we would call them to come up. Before long all the neighborhood, crossing from one roof to another, would congregate, and as there was always someone with a beautiful voice, we would often stay there until midnight, singing, gossiping, cracking roasted watermelon and pumpkin seeds, or sometimes just sitting for long periods of silence; in those days we could sit, unembarrassed, with nothing to say.

All that, of course, was a long time ago, but it is a family tradition and, like certain incidents of childhood, it lingers in memory. I always like to go to the past and think about the good and pure relationships between my family and those who used to be our neighbors.

INDEPENDENT STUDY: *Writing Conclusions* (answers in the back)

IV. *In the following conclusions, circle the sentences that answer "so what?" and those which answer "what next?" and label them in the margin. Then label each conclusion "good" or "faulty."*

1. *Thesis:* I hope my summer will be exciting.

   My summer will be a full and fast-paced one, but I can't wait until it happens. I don't know if everyone's summer will be like mine, but I know my summer will be full of adventure.

2. *Thesis:* My job at the bank just wasn't worth the money.
   That job took a lot out of me. Although I didn't want to stay there, I had to because I needed the money. I advise everyone to look around carefully before accepting a job. It's best to have several choices.

3. *Thesis:* Playing soccer prepared my brother for life.
   Young people entering society are faced with many pressures. They must compete for grades in school and then for jobs in a tight economy.

4. *Thesis:* This show is a perfect example of the mindless garbage on television today.
   This show and the others like it should be taken off the air at once. When I think of it, there is only one good show on television today, and that is "Little House on the Prairie." There should be more shows like this one, for it has real-life action and real-life drama.

5. *Thesis:* Buying on credit can cause a lot of problems.
   I don't mean to discourage all credit. I am just saying that people should be careful with their credit and not bite off more than they can chew. If used right, credit can make life much easier, but misused credit can make people's lives miserable.

6. *Thesis:* The United States needs the draft.
   The United States needs the draft because our mineral and political interests abroad are being threatened. Also, the increase in military power that would ensue should the draft be reimposed would create such an effective deterrent that a war might never have to be fought.

7. *Thesis:* The best toy for a child is a toy gun.
   Children learn a lot about life by playing with toys. It would not be a bad idea to suggest a toy gun for a child because we need good soldiers and police for the future.

8. *Thesis:* Good food is important to me.
   With the business of fast foods and junk food growing all the time, fewer and fewer people are taking the opportunity to appreciate how good food can be. People should choose at least one night a week to either prepare a fine meal at home or go out to a nice restaurant. A little planning can produce a lot of pleasure.

9. *Thesis:* I am not ready to have children.
   I am not ready to have children because I am not mature enough to have children, and I am not ready to make the sacrifices a parent must make. In fact, I don't have enough money to raise a child even if I wanted to.

10. *Thesis:* Overeating is very harmful.
    It may take years before you realize that those spare tires around your midsection can be difficult to live with, so before you get to that point, do yourself a favor and watch your weight. Just remember, "Once on the lips, forever on the hips."

2. Identifying Subjects and Verbs

• To write effectively you must be familiar with the parts of a sentence and know how to combine them into the complex sentences required to express complicated ideas. Furthermore, most college and business people strongly prefer standard English, and for success in those worlds you should master all the little details of that language. This chapter examines the sentence elements you must know to write effectively in standard English.

THE ELEMENTS

An English sentence is a structure built around a core of subject and verb. Sometimes the subject is a person or force that is doing something, and the verb states that action, as in the following sentences. (The subject is underlined once and the verb twice.)

The children cheered.

Finally her secretary arrived.

Karen plays the trumpet.

Other times verbs aren't really action words; the verbs of the following sentences link the subject to something that describes it.

My sister is a doctor.

I always become hungry early.

His umbrella looked wet.

Any of the following verbs can be used as **linking verbs.**

be (am, is, are, was, were, being, been)		taste
become	feel	look
seem	smell	sound

To these basic sentences writers add details to create vivid pictures.

The <u>boys</u> <u>played</u>.

becomes

The two sleepy <u>boys</u> <u>played</u> quietly.

Prepositional phrases may also be added. Parentheses have been used to identify prepositional phrases.

(After dinner) the two sleepy <u>boys</u> <u>played</u> quietly (on the floor) (with the flickering light) (from the fireplace) (on their foreheads).

A prepositional phrase is a group of words that begins with a preposition and ends with a noun (a word for a thing) or pronoun (a substitute for a noun). Between those words there may be one or several words. The list below contains, in alphabetical order, the most common English prepositions in phrases. The prepositions are in bold type. This list and the list of linking verbs have been reprinted inside the back cover of this book for easy reference.

about the lesson	**beyond** repair	**on** the table
above his head	**by** the pound	**outside** the house
across the table	**concerning** your letter	**over** the top
after the ball game	**down** the street	**past** the gate
against the wall	**during** the summer	**since** Sunday
along the edge	**except** me	**through** the window
among the victims	**for** my birthday	**to** the store
around the corner	**from** Italy	**toward** the stands
at the counter	**in** a plastic box	**under** the table
before the game	**inside** the locked drawer	**until** tomorrow
behind the door	**into** the wastebasket	**up** the stairs
below the belt	**like** a fox	**upon** request
beneath him	**near** the end	**with** regrets
beside the car	**of** the list	**within** ten days
between his feet	**off** the wall	**without** further notice

Of course any other nouns or pronouns could be used in prepositional phrases, and more or different details could be inserted. Sometimes a prepositional phrase contains more than one noun or pronoun, as in the following sentence.

(Of course) he told her (about the history exam and the argument) (in the bookstore).

If you aren't sure whether or not a word is a preposition, check the above list or a dictionary. The following entry for "beside" begins with *prep*, indicating that "beside" is a preposition.

> **be·side** /bɪˈsaɪd/ *prep* **1** at the side of; close to:
> *Come and sit ~ me. She would like to live ~ the
> sea.* at the sea-side. **2** compared with: *You're
> quite tall ~ your sister.* **set ~,** put against; com-
> pare with: *There's no one to set ~ him as a
> general.* **3** ~ **the point/mark/question,** wide
> of, having nothing to do with (what is being
> discussed, etc). **4** ~ **oneself,** at the end of one's
> self-control: *He was ~ himself with joy/
> excitement.*

To write well, you will need to identify the subjects and verbs of your sentences. The process is easy if you follow these steps in the order given.

1. Put parentheses around the prepositional phrases. Subjects and verbs are never in prepositional phrases.

2. Put two lines under the verb. When looking for verbs, watch for the -*s* and -*ed* endings that are often used on verbs. If an action verb or a linking verb is not obvious, add the words "tomorrow" and "will" to rephrase the sentence into future time. The verb of the original sentence can be spotted because it will change to a new form with the word "will" before it.

3. Put one line under the subject. The subject usually comes before the verb. It is the doer of an action verb or the topic of a linking verb. To find the subject, put the verb you found in the blank of the following question and then answer it.

Who or what _____ ?

The answer is the sentence subject.

The sentence below looks very difficult, but its elements are easily identified by the process outlined above.

The father of the two children with the dark shadows in their eyes stood silently at the side of the road.

1. Put parentheses around the prepositional phrases.

The father (of the two children) (with the dark shadows) (in their eyes) stood silently (at the side) (of the road).

2. Put two lines under the verbs. Now that the prepositional phrases have been identified, the verb "stood" can easily be picked from the few remaining words. If you still weren't sure, you could add "tomorrow" and "will" and rephrase the sentence into future time.

Tomorrow the father (of the two children) (with the dark shadows) (in their eyes) will stand silently (at the side) (of the road).

The word "stood" in the original changed to "will stand," so "stood" is the verb of the original sentence.

The father (of the two children) (with the dark shadows) (in their eyes) <u>stood</u>

silently (at the side) (of the road).

3. Put one line under the subject. Putting the verb "stood" into the question suggested under 3 above produces the following.

Who or what stood?

"Father" is the answer to that question and therefore the subject of the sentence.

The <u>father</u> (of the two children) (with the dark shadows) (in their eyes) <u>stood</u> silently (at the side) (of the road).

EXERCISES: The Elements

I. **A.** *Compose new prepositional phrases for all the prepositions in the list on page 48.*

B. *Put two lines under the verbs and one line under the subjects of these sentences:*

1. The train glided.
2. The lady raised her hand.
3. The boys climb.
4. The hobo huddled.
5. The bulldog snarls.
6. The band marched.
7. The chimpanzee leapt.
8. The dress hung.
9. The Jaguar slid.
10. The man stands.

C. *Rewrite the sentences in Exercise B, adding details but no additional subjects and verbs, to create vivid pictures.*

D. *Put a subject and a linking verb before the following words.*

1. _____ stubborn.
2. _____ enthusiastic.
3. _____ sour.
4. _____ delicious.
5. _____ smooth.
6. _____ slender.
7. _____ difficult.
8. _____ strange.
9. _____ shrewd.
10. _____ quiet.

E. *Insert details into the following prepositional phrases to create a mood or tone.*

1. to the house

2. up the steps

3. across the porch

4. through the door

5. into the hall

6. in a box

7. on the table

8. under the chandelier

9. by the window

10. with the curtain

F. Now repeat exercise E with different details to create an entirely different mood.

II. *For the sentences below, do the following in the order given.*

    1. Put parentheses around the prepositional phrases.

    2. Put two lines under the verb.

    3. Put one line under the subject.

A.   1. Karen looked through the hole in the fence.

    2. The orange trees grew beneath the palms.

    3. He carefully adjusted the brim of his hat.

    4. At the last minute she climbed behind the wheel of the old Ford.

    5. The rain made dark spots on the concrete.

    6. People today are lazy.

    7. You seem angry about something.

    8. We painted the whole house in four days.

    9. Visitors from Mars always laugh at our shoes.

    10. I need a new bookcase by the head of my bed.

B.   1. The man in the plaid jacket took the jack from the trunk.

    2. Women with crew cuts and leather jackets ran down the aisles of the theater.

    3. At the same time, lilac is the theme color of the year.

    4. In the cool of the evening, my grandfather relaxed with his pipe in the old rocking chair on the front porch of our first house in Rochester.

    5. In the fall the leaves on the trees, plants, and bushes turn all different colors.

6. My brother watches everything from soap operas to "Sixty Minutes," from "All in the Family" to "Wall Street Journal."

7. The Hawaiian shirt is a popular item, especially during the summer.

8. With a look of disgust he nodded his head curtly toward the pail of soap and water on the worn linoleum by the iron sink.

9. During most of those years I lived very close to school.

10. The small black and tan dog with long silky hair is a Yorkshire terrier.

C. 1. The owner of the skating rink shoved Mork backward onto the ice.

2. Thomas always looks silly in a suit.

3. Some of the older children slipped under the heavy canvas into the big top without tickets.

4. One of my friends helped me down the stairs.

5. He really is a terrific father.

6. His shirt felt rough against her arm.

7. *Dallas* has something in it for everyone.

8. Most of the students in my drama class have no acting experience.

9. This terrible creature controls the members of my family.

10. After my last final, he bought me a large bucket of fried chicken.

D. 1. One of the last people at the ticket window reserved seven seats.

2. Many large ponds add to the country atmosphere.

3. Both of my brothers work at General Motors.

4. President Reagan now plans a large tax cut for the people with high incomes.

5. The nurses on the helicopter pulled the man from the icy water of the lake.

6. Some of the best answers come from the littlest children.

7. Many poor and ailing citizens became the city's responsibility.

8. Thefts of crude oil and gas are common.

9. Several of the best seats are still empty.

10. One golfer resented the additional charge of ten cents for each golf ball.

E. I am even afraid of examinations. Before finals I have nightmares about all sorts of crazy things. One time I even dreamt about the characters in my history book. The wives of Henry VIII told me about the dirty pots and pans in the palace kitchen. Then Henry himself quizzed me about their names and dates. On exam day the papers seem smooth and cold like the blades of the guillotine. They reflect the light of the classroom into my eyes. After examinations, I always thank God for my survival.

INDEPENDENT STUDY: The Elements *(answers in the back)*

III. *For the sentences below, do the following in the order given.*

1. *Put parentheses around the prepositional phrases.*

2. *Put two lines under the verb.*

3. *Put one line under the subject.*

A.
1. In the winter my father took me to school by bus.

2. I really loved that delicious cabbage.

3. A tiny girl with stiff pigtails and a freckled face softly asked the ice cream seller for a rocky road ice cream cone with sprinkles on it.

4. Two of my sister's friends went to Reed College.

5. Larry has a bad attitude toward personal property.

6. After fifteen minutes, the bored campers banged their knives and forks on the bottoms of their tin plates.

7. Some of the tastiest fruit looks very ugly.

8. A young goatherd lived near this wild girl in the same snowy country with the same mountains over his head.

9. Most of the citizens of Washington, D.C., ignored George Washington on his 250th birthday.

10. Without a word she ran up the stairs and into her room.

B.
1. The press distorted the meaning of the supervisor's letter to the accused congressman.

2. The short cooking process retains the nutrition of the seafood and vegetables in most Japanese dishes.

3. One of the ladies from the convention left her hat on the front steps of the hotel.

4. The play opens Friday at 8:00 P.M. at the community theater.

5. Stoves with porcelain tops are not very popular on the West Coast.

6. Several of my favorite teachers left the school last year.

7. Chicago's etiquette adviser resigned from her $35,000-a-year post only twelve days after her appointment.

8. I mailed the bill and my check to the main office in Topeka.

9. After a brief delay, the countdown for the test firing of the space shuttle's engines began.

10. In three seconds, she finished a hamburger and a milk shake.

COMBINATIONS

Sometimes the verb has more than one word in it, as in the following sentences.

The director must not have understood their problem.

My sister has only been living (near Austin) (since 1979).

One or a combination of the following **helping verbs** can be used before the main verb of a sentence.

am	were	will	may	being	do
is	has	would	might	been	does
are	have	shall	must	can	did
was	had	should	be	could	

This list has also been printed inside the back cover for quick reference.

Sometimes, as in the sentences above, the verb is interrupted by a word that is not a verb. Words like "also," "not," "never," "always," "just," "only," and other words that end in -ly are never part of the verb. If the word isn't on the list above, it's not a helping verb.

The two sentences above had only one verb each, though each verb had several words in it. A sentence may also have more than one verb. The subject may do more than one thing.

Slowly she opened her eyes and pushed the hair away (from her face).

(After Easter), he will fly (to Rochester) and visit his mother.

Sometimes a sentence has more than one subject, more than one doer of the action.

Her coach and her teammates had confidence (in her).

(Before noon) Charlie and Louisa had bought a piano.

Some sentences even have more than one verb *and* more than one subject.

A rooster and a small boy jumped out (of the window) and ran (into the barn).

Yvette and her father painted the walls and replaced the broken windows.

In other words, a sentence can name one, two, or more doers of one, two, or more actions.

EXERCISES: *Combinations*

I.   *A. Put one line under the subjects and two lines under the verbs in these sentences.*

1. The girl reads the newspaper.

2. The man looked tired.

3. The child watched the fish.

4. The movers pushed the sofa.

5. The baker kneaded the bread.

6. The shopper examined the skirts.

7. The teacher writes the exam.

8. The visitor parks his car.

9. The woman rang the bell.

10. The goat leaps.

B. Change the sentences in exercise A so that the verbs have more than one word in them.

C. Add details including prepositional phrases to the sentences created in exercise B.

D. Put parentheses around the prepositional phrases in those sentences.

II. *Put one line under all the subjects and two lines under all the verbs in the following sentences.*

A. 1. The boy and the girl flew the kite.

2. The dog finished his dinner and walked calmly away.

3. The man and the woman sat and talked.

4. My sister and I ate dinner.

5. She went downtown and bought a hat.

6. His father and mother make rules and enforce them.

7. The man entered the library and returned the book.

8. He shook his head, blinked his eyes, and rubbed his neck.

9. The aunts, uncles, cousins, grandmothers, and grandfathers worried and asked questions.

10. He ran and jumped.

B. Add details including prepositional phrases to the sentences above.

C. Put parentheses around the prepositional phrases in the sentences created in exercise B.

D. Change these sentences so that they have two verbs instead of just one.

1. The lion roared.

2. The leaves cluttered the street.

3. The woman ran.

4. Her husband had wet feet.

5. The child went outside.

6. The cook cleared the tables.

7. The teacher arrived late.

8. The old man sat in the front row.

9. The librarian sorted the books.

10. The bus stopped.

E. Now change the sentences in exercise D so that they also have two subjects.

III. A. *Write five subject-verb combinations with more than one word in the verb. Underline the subjects once and all parts of the verbs twice.*

B. *Write five subject-verb combinations with more than one subject. Underline the subjects once and all parts of the verbs twice.*

C. *Write five subject-verb combinations with more than one verb. Underline the subjects once and all parts of the verbs twice.*

D. *Write five subject-verb combinations with more than one subject and more than one verb. Underline all subjects once and all parts of all verbs twice.*

E. *Go back through exercises A, B, C, and D and add more details such as prepositional phrases. Put parentheses around the prepositional phrases.*

IV. *In the sentences below, do the following in the order given.*

   1. Put parentheses around the prepositional phrases.

   2. Put two lines under all parts of the verb or verbs.

   3. Put one line under the subject or subjects.

A. 1. The manager liked my suggestions and acted on each one.

   2. My friend and I played two girls from the tennis team.

   3. Mexican presidents have also studied here in the United States.

   4. The schools, for example, are not replacing frames on windows and other parts of buildings.

   5. He did not find an answer to that question.

6. We were in the open air with peace, quiet, and our own thoughts.

7. Every bite of food was washed down my throat by a mouthful of ice water.

8. He should have listened more closely to the commercial.

9. Andrew and his mother visited Joe at the jail.

10. I buy my Christmas decorations on the day after Christmas.

B. 1. James and Lawrence have known each other for only three months.

2. Mr. Briggs and his son tore out the old counter and built a new one around the stainless steel sink.

3. At least you could have stayed for the first act.

4. The origin of this recipe is lost in the mists of time.

5. I am not staying in this accursed village for another night.

6. During the week after the accident, Charlotte did not speak to me, spoke only in a distracted way to Lewis, and placed two phone calls to Mr. Turner.

7. A stage had been constructed over the swimming pool of the house in Beverly Hills.

8. Coffee and pound cake and pear brandy were served in the dining room.

9. At the sound of the siren, Rhonda got up from the table and walked in the direction of the ladies' room.

10. His lack of excitement, of curiosity, of surprise, of any sort of pronounced interest increased her distrust.

C. 1. None of the card players suspected Gregory or watched his hands.

2. The rhythmic thump and splash of the oars could be heard from the bridge.

3. Elena and her sister have always visited me on my birthday.

4. The boys dragged the heavy trunk onto the porch and quietly shut the door behind them.

5. He sat carelessly, rested both his emaciated arms on the oak table, drew his papers near his chest, and whispered to his colleague.

6. Once I stopped and stood on the almost white sand and felt the cool misty wind on my face.

7. During his visit, he stayed at his sister's house in the middle of eighty acres of forest.

8. Behind the falling water, the rock was covered with a glistening green moss.

9. The hotels, motels, and restaurants of the Catskills are also dependent on the tourist trade.

10. I have been living in the United States for four years.

D.
1. The ground was covered with brown pine cones and needles and felt soft under my feet.

2. He referred reporters to his pledge of swift and sure punishment but would not describe his plans in detail.

3. Men and women must live together, work together, and play together.

4. She thrust one of her hands nervously over the counter and shook hands with the owner.

5. The two of us were suffering from an attack of stage fright and could not remember our lines.

6. Gerald and Ronald did not waste much energy on smiles or polite words.

7. From the beginning she must have been puzzled by my brother's actions.

8. After a half hour's effort, Tess looked up and saw no one.

9. Alfred closed his hand around the pin with the broken clasp and tried not to think about war and death.

10. She put her gum in an empty nut dish and helped herself to a handful of potato chips.

E.
My first encounter with an electric magic box occurred on a cold morning with a light snow in 1960. An electric appliance store owner came to our house with a huge cardboard carton. He took the magic box from the carton, put it in the living room, and placed the antenna on the top of the roof. Soon fantastic pictures with voices came out of the magic box. In those days very few households had television sets. Our friends and neighbors soon heard about our television set and came to visit. In fact at first our house was often full of guests.

INDEPENDENT STUDY: *Combinations* (answers in the back)

V. *In the sentences below, do the following in the order given.*

1. *Put parentheses around the prepositional phrases.*

2. *Put two lines under all parts of the verb or verbs.*

3. *Put one line under the subject or subjects.*

A.
1. Some of the best hunting and fresh water fishing areas are in New Mexico.

2. A person can drive through my neighborhood and identify the rented houses.

3. By night these cats sit on fences and whine and yowl.

4. The prices for food, clothing, services, transportation, and housing have been steadily moving upward with no sign of stopping.

5. Bad reading habits and low grades on exams are related.

6. Guns can be used for hunting, target practice, or self-protection.

7. I will never forget my senior year at Thomas Jefferson High School.

8. This country is faced with both foreign and domestic problems.

9. The cats travel in small groups and chase the little dogs all around the block.

10. Since the rise in popularity of tennis, better equipment and facilities have been developed.

B.   This year, natural fabrics and blends are being shown. The sheerness and softness of silk attract a lot of attention. Its high cost, however, and the necessity of dry cleaning keep it out of reach for a lot of people. Cotton and terry are also nice natural fabrics and should be very popular this year. For busy women, natural fabrics are blended with synthetic ones for easy care. Pure artificial fabrics will never replace the natural ones, however.

SOME IMPORTANT DISTINCTIONS

A few unusual sentence structures are responsible for many subject-verb errors. Therefore you should be sure you can identify subjects and verbs in these situations.

1. Learn about subjects in advice, requests, and commands. When someone says to you, "Notice the little specks in the background of the picture" or "Please pass the salt," you know that *you* are expected to do the noticing or the passing. In other words, you understand that "you" is the subject of "notice" and "pass" even though the word "you" is not stated. A grammarian would say that the subject is "you" understood. Such sentences can be analyzed as follows.

(You) <u>Notice</u> the little specks (in the background) (of the picture).

(You) Please <u>pass</u> the salt.

2. Learn to find subjects and verbs in questions. In most statements the verb comes after the subject, but in questions, all or part of the verb comes before the subject. Be careful not to confuse question words with subjects, and be sure to find all the verb parts.

Where <u>are</u> my <u>gloves</u>?

What <u>would</u> <u>you</u> <u>like</u> (on your bagel)?

Why <u>is</u> <u>she</u> <u>wearing</u> kneepads?

<u>Does</u> the <u>subway</u> <u>stop</u> (near the Cloisters)?

<u>Has</u> the <u>janitor</u> <u>shoveled</u> the steps?

3. Learn to find subjects that come after verbs in statements. The words "here" and "there" are never subjects. They are just place holders. When one of these words comes right before the verb, the subject comes after the verb. Don't mistake place holders for subjects.

There <u>were</u> four <u>mice</u> (in the attic).

Here <u>are</u> the <u>books</u> (from your locker).

After prepositional phrases, subjects sometimes come after verbs.

(Beside the shop) <u>was</u> a tiny <u>house</u>.

(Down the street) <u>rattled</u> my grandfather's delivery <u>van</u>.

Remember that a subject can never be one of the words in a prepositional phrase.

4. Learn to find verbs in contractions. Sometimes writers replace some of the letters in a verb with an apostrophe to suggest speech. Don't overlook a contracted verb.

> Here's your change.

> They're already late.

> I'd prefer a high grade.

5. Learn to distinguish verbs from words that look like them. Verbs that have "to" in front of them and verbs that end in *-ing* but have no helping verb cannot work as verbs. They may even be subjects. In this sentence, "singing" has the helping verb "was," and so it is working as a verb.

> (In those days), he was singing (for a living).

However, in the next sentence "singing" has no helping verb and is working as a subject.

> Singing relaxes me.

Sometimes *-ing* words without helping verbs are used to describe other words.

> Singing canaries make nice companions.

> We heard Mike singing (in the shower).

If you are unsure which word is acting as a verb, add "tomorrow" and "will" to change it to future time. The verb will change form to include the word "will."

> Tomorrow we will hear Mike singing in the shower.

"Will" goes before "hear" but not before "sing," and so we know "hear" is working as a verb and "sing" is not.

In the following sentence, "worry" is a verb:

> He worried (about his daughter).

But here it has "to" in front of it, so that it is not working as a verb:

> He was inclined to worry (about everything).

Here, "to worry" is the subject:

> To worry is a waste (of time).

In fact, sometimes the "to" is no longer used, as in the following sentence.

> We helped him clean the kitchen.

Adding "tomorrow" and "will" to this sentence confirms that "help" is working as a verb and "clean" is not because "will" goes before "help" but not before "clean."

Tomorrow we will help him clean the kitchen.

Don't underline as a verb a word that's not working as a verb.

EXERCISES: *Some Important Distinctions*

I. *In the following sentences put parentheses around the prepositional phrases, two lines under all parts of all verbs, and one line under all subjects.*

A. 1. Jogging keeps me awake.

2. Here is his answer.

3. He wants to go into business for himself.

4. There are hot-dog and hamburger stands on every other block in Mexico City.

5. To err is human.

6. Put the green chair in front of the television set.

7. Would you prefer to stay at a motel with a swimming pool?

8. Around the corner strolled three young ladies in top hats.

9. The washing machine rescued women from their washboards.

10. Going to the dentist is a most terrifying experience for me.

B. 1. Where's the key to the back door?

2. Please leave my shoes at the cobbler's.

3. On the hill across the river stood an old castle.

4. I watched the children run down the hall of the empty apartment.

5. Please return these books to the library for me.

6. Roger scraped his thigh sliding into second base.

7. Any time during the day one can find a small terrier hiding under a bush or behind a house.

8. There are good fishing and hunting areas throughout the state.

9. During the last three years, there has been much political uproar about the quality of our schools.

10. Why did you ask about season tickets?

C. 1. Where's the man from the department store?

2. I watched the man go into the bank.

3. Hoping to arrive early, we left home at five in the morning.

4. Crying about it won't change anything.

5. Reply at once to avoid losing your place on the waiting list.

6. There is absolutely no communication between us.

7. Going to the barber was a big treat for my brother.

8. For years I have been wanting to learn to play backgammon.

9. Has John's swimming improved?

10. On the other side stood a thin old man wearing a white lambskin cap.

D. 1. Expecting to pass easily, he didn't work hard at learning to write.

2. Sitting on the grass under the willow, they watched the sun disappear behind the dark hill.

3. We are expecting to entertain visiting relatives this weekend.

4. Be sure to check your writing for spelling errors.

5. In front of the restaurant was parked a long, shining, black Lincoln.

6. Watch that man standing by the door.

7. There's no possibility for advancement in this job.

8. She watched him pick up his napkin and wipe his forehead.

9. Waiting for someone always upsets me.

10. Please knock on the door and give her my message.

II. A. *Read the following essay and then answer these questions.*

1. *What is the thesis of this essay?*

2. *How many supports does it have?*

3. *What are they?*

4. *Do they all prove the thesis?*

5. *How could this essay have been improved?*

6. *What do you like best about this essay?*

At Last, a Cheap French Restaurant

At the corner of University Avenue and Milvia Street, there stands a nicely decorated restaurant. At 6 A.M. the line starts to form at the counter. Customers are waiting for their croissants and coffee. Very soon, the customers fill the dining room too. Au Coquelicot is an excellent inexpensive French restaurant.

Au Coquelicot has a pleasant atmosphere. Looking through the tall glass windows from the front, one will see a large dining room with high ceiling, tile floor, and an exposed brick wall. This dining room seats forty to fifty people. The espresso machine at one end of the bar operates sixteen hours a day. At the other end there are delicious cakes and tarts. Through the small hallway at the right corner of the front dining room is a larger back room with a capacity of more than sixty people. Both dining areas are very pleasant.

Au Coquelicot offers many inexpensive high-quality beverages. They have a large variety of French and Italian coffees, including espresso, cappuccino, café au lait, café mocha, and some Italian sodas. All the beverages are reasonably priced with almost everything under a dollar. Wine and beer are also available at very competitive prices. Au Coquelicot is one of the fastidious coffee drinker's favorite cafés.

The dinner menu is written on a small blackboard at the doorway to the inner dining room. There are always at least two choices. Weekend specials include leg of lamb, seafood Coquelicot, and veal in a mustard sauce. Porc à l'orange, boeuf bourguignon, and poulet basquaise are offered during the week. A complete dinner includes hors d'oeuvre, soup, salad, entrée, vegetable, bread, dessert, wine, and coffee for only $8.99. This is the cheapest French country-style dinner in the city.

They also have excellent desserts. Being a picky dessert lover, I never tire of this restaurant's strawberry tart. The juicy strawberries cover a layer of luscious almond-flavored filling inside the flaky tart shell. Just thinking about it makes my mouth water. The chocolate cake is always moist and lavishly covered with almond slices. The quality of the croissant is also very high.

French cooking is never low priced. All the dishes call for good meat and expensive wine. Au Coquelicot tries to serve a high-volume business with good quality and pleasant atmosphere at a reasonable price. I heartily recommend Au Coquelicot for an excellent French meal at a low price.

B. *Go back to the essay in exercise A, and put parentheses around the prepositional phrases, two lines under all parts of all verbs, and one line under all subjects.*

III. A. *Write an essay about a restaurant. Find your topic, your thesis, and your supports by following the instructions in the units called "From Subject to Thesis" and "Building an Outline." Check your outline with your instructor. Review the instructions in the unit called "Writing Body Paragraphs" and keep the model essay on page 4 in front of you as you write. Review the units on introductions and conclusions before beginning those paragraphs.*

B. *Write an essay on one of these subjects, following the instructions in exercise A above.*

shopping malls	a course you are taking
a job you have had	high-heeled shoes
a trip you have taken	a sport you play

INDEPENDENT STUDY: *Some Important Distinctions* *(answers in the back)*

IV. *In the following sentences put parentheses around the prepositional phrases, two lines under all parts of all verbs, and one line under all subjects.*

A.
1. There was no traffic on the road except for me and the nine other bike riders.

2. Has anyone been hired to replace Mrs. Brown?

3. For example, he did not hear me start the car.

4. There's a lot of vandalism in my neighborhood.

5. On the bottom of the leaf was a tiny snail.

6. My sister and I watched my father shoveling the heavy snow.

7. Frowning slightly, she folded her arms and began to speak.

8. There is no spicy sauce to cover up the freshness of the meat and vegetables.

9. Cleaning the yard took up most of my day off.

10. From the kitchen came the welcome odor of stew.

B.   Japanese food is simple to cook. Once I broke my cooking record by preparing a dish for twelve people in thirty minutes. After a hard day of skiing, everyone was tired and reluctant to go out for dinner. I decided to prepare a sukiyaki. I got everything out of the refrigerator and asked everyone to help. Soon everyone was chopping vegetables and slicing meat. Within half an hour, there were an electric skillet, plates of meat, and bowls of vegetables on the table. Everyone enjoyed cooking his own way at the table.

3. Understanding Sentences

• The sentences discussed so far have had only one subject-verb combination each and so can express only the most elementary ideas. Intricately interrelated subject-verb combinations are needed to communicate the subtleties of more complex ideas. In this chapter we examine such structures so that you can learn to use and punctuate them effectively.

CONNECTING CLAUSES

A clause is a group of words with a subject and a verb. Clauses may be dependent or independent. Independent clauses can stand alone as complete sentences, but dependent ones cannot. Here are some independent clauses.

INDEPENDENT CLAUSES

we arrived (at the house)

Japan's economy has grown phenomenally (since the war)

she lives eighty miles (from Goodyear)

he did not have any female relatives

An independent clause can be punctuated as a sentence, with a capital letter at the beginning and a period at the end. It makes sense by itself.

A dependent clause is formed by putting one of the following words at the beginning of an independent clause. This list has also been printed inside the back cover for easy reference.

after	before	unless	when	how	who
although	if	until	where	which	whom
as	since	whether	what	that	whose
because	though	while	why		

The following dependent clauses were formed from the independent clauses above.

DEPENDENT CLAUSES

when we arrived (at the house)

because Japan's economy has grown phenomenally (since the war)

although she lives eighty miles (from Goodyear)

that he did not have any female relatives

A dependent clause cannot be punctuated as a sentence, with a capital letter at the beginning and a period at the end. Dependent clauses do not make sense by themselves, and so they must be attached to independent clauses.

Thoughts are complex, and since sentences must communicate ideas, they too must be complex. A complicated idea is obscured by the simple sentences of this passage.

FAULTY

She lived eighty miles from Goodyear. She drove down and delivered her application in person. She was afraid. The postal service might fail her again.

The following sentence is much clearer.

REVISED

Although she lived eighty miles from Goodyear, she drove down and delivered her application in person because she was afraid that the postal service might fail her again.

The simple sentences of the faulty passage have been combined into one intricate sentence that expresses and reflects her reservation about the trip, her reason for going, and the nature of her fear. Clauses must be carefully combined, and the words that make clauses dependent must be carefully chosen to reveal rather than conceal each idea. The following faulty combination is harder to understand than the original simple sentences were.

FAULTY

She lived eighty miles from Goodyear because she drove down and delivered her application that she was afraid unless the postal service might fail her again.

The best writers carefully combine independent and dependent clauses to express subtle and complicated ideas.

Before you can combine clauses effectively and punctuate them clearly, you must be able to identify the independent and dependent clauses in a sentence. Dependent clauses can be easily distinguished from independent clauses because they begin with one of the words from the list at the beginning of this section. In the following sentences, the dependent clauses are underlined with a broken line and the independent ones with a solid line.

Although she lives eighty miles (from Goodyear), she drove down and delivered

her application (in person) because she was afraid that the postal service might

fail her again.

When <u>we</u> <u>returned</u> (to the house), <u>light</u> (from the kitchen windows) <u>filled</u> the

garden and <u>lit</u> the stone steps that <u>we</u> had <u>stumbled</u> down.

When a sentence has two or more independent clauses, they must be connected by a comma (,) and one of these words:

for

and

nor

but

or

yet

so

These words are easy to remember because their first letters spell the word "fanboys." Be careful not to confuse these words with the ones that make clauses dependent.

The following sentence has one dependent clause and two independent clauses.

Because Japan's <u>economy</u> <u>has</u> <u>grown</u> phenomenally (since the war), people's

<u>lives</u> <u>are</u> <u>changing</u> very rapidly, and <u>many</u> (of their traditions) <u>are</u> <u>being</u> <u>lost</u>.

The "economy has grown" clause has the word "because" at the beginning, and since "because" is on the list of words that make clauses dependent, that clause is dependent. In contrast, the "lives are changing" clause has none of these words at the beginning, so it is independent. Finally, the "many are being lost" clause does not have a word that makes clauses dependent at the beginning. Instead it is linked to the material before it by a comma and the word "and," one of the "fanboys" words that link independent clauses, so it is independent.

The sentence below has two dependent and two independent clauses.

If <u>any</u> (of his friends) <u>had</u> <u>seen</u> Mr. Snelling (in the boutique), <u>they</u> <u>would</u> <u>have</u>

<u>been</u> <u>astonished</u>, for <u>they</u> all <u>knew</u> that <u>he</u> <u>did</u> not <u>have</u> any female relatives.

The "any had seen" clause is dependent because it begins with the word "if," and the "he did have" clause is dependent because it begins with the word "that." On the other hand, neither of the other two clauses begins with a word that makes clauses dependent and the clauses are linked by a comma and the word "for," one of the "fanboys" words that link independent clauses, so they are both independent.

EXERCISES: Connecting Clauses

I. **A.** *Change the following independent clauses to dependent clauses.*

1. the cats were always in our yard

2. I have four older sisters

3. my family and I planned to have a big picnic and go to the fair

4. I like to run on the beach

5. my brother and I built a fort

6. our car was very old and always breaking down

7. I redecorated my apartment in Middle Eastern pillows and carpets

8. she wore a white blouse stained with beer and tomato paste

9. I received a summons for disturbing the peace

10. my job required me to pack groceries and keep the shelves stocked

B. *Change one of the sentences in the pairs below to a dependent clause by adding a word from the following list. Then combine it with the other sentence to make a two-clause sentence.*

after	before	unless	when
although	if	until	where
as	since	whether	
because	though	while	

1. They drove to Revere Beach. She loves the ocean.

2. I'm getting older all the time. I don't feel any different.

3. His car got wrecked. He has to take the bus.

4. Her children are out of town. She gets very lonesome.

5. My sister visited Japan. She stayed with me.

6. The telephone was ringing. She looked for a pencil.

7. The man walked down the street. He twirled his cane.

8. I worked hard. The fishermen became more friendly.

9. He was surprised. She was very angry.

10. She wanted to go out. She went to a movie.

C. *Put dotted lines under the dependent clauses and solid lines under the independent clauses of the sentences you created in exercise B.*

D. *Expand the following single-clause sentences by adding details and prepositional phrases as well as dependent clauses.*

1. The music began.

2. The boy watched the ball game.

3. The girl played.

4. The cheerleaders leapt.

5. The man swaggered.

6. The woman sat.

7. The dog rested.

8. The baby laughed.

9. The car stopped.

10. The man read.

E. *Go back to exercise D and do the following five things.*

1. Put parentheses around the prepositional phrases.

2. Underline all parts of all verbs twice.

3. Underline all of their subjects once.

4. Put dotted lines under the dependent clauses.

5. Put solid lines under the independent clauses.

II. *Do the five things listed in exercise I E to the following sentences.*

A. 1. When we reached the theater, the doors were already open.

2. He was always excited as he waited for the train.

3. Before she could finish, the boy began to cry.

4. We stopped at the ditch because we were afraid of Raymond.

5. When the police came, she was holding the box tightly between her hands.

6. As he spoke, she rose to her knees and put her hands on his cheeks.

7. After he had entered the room, there was a loud crash.

8. Mr. Wilson and the cow were out of sight when she got to the gate.

9. While Miss Golly waited for an answer, she studied the house.

10. We wondered if they would bring some food.

B. 1. She had not seen the kitchen before, but Mr. Stewart had described it to her in detail.

2. As he was going through the door, he had a second thought and went back to his desk.

3. When the snow is melted, the sun takes over again and burns the gray fields.

4. Brian held back his horse, so the group moved slowly.

5. If one of the big brothers came, he could supply them with grain.

6. It all came back to me when I was looking at that picture.

7. Sharon watched him as he squinted at the scale.

8. He worked with the chisel and the wooden mallet as a jeweler might work on a watch.

9. Mr. Reed paid me with apples when I worked for him.

10. As he passed the broken window, he cleared his throat and wet his thumb.

C. 1. If the children don't sit down, they'll be exhausted before we ever get started.

2. When I think of Warren as he was in those days, I always see him sitting there in that big hat as we rode the bus through Nevada on the way to Utah.

3. She doesn't bother me a bit, and if I don't know the answers to her questions, I tell her so.

4. When I go to the shopping center and see all those boys and girls, I wonder if any of them have ambitions as we did.

5. We both went in and sat down on those high stools before the counter and ordered ham and potatoes and coffee.

6. There were labels on the bags from all the hotels where they had spent nights.

7. When he came back, he walked through the restaurant, where people were eating breakfast and talking quietly.

8. She held the paper firmly by one corner as she turned and went back to her seat.

9. When Gloria tired of watching the stars, her glance dropped to Market Street, where colorful signs announced the names of the stores.

10. When Lori returned to Keene from Boston, where she had studied economics, a great future was predicted for her.

D. 1. Although he had always been considered an old bachelor, the matchmaker proposed several rich girls for him, but Mr. Miller declined to take advantage of these opportunities.

2. Sometimes after she left the library, she would stop at the bookstores on Granville where all sorts of old books and magazines could be purchased cheaply.

3. When Ms. Mead arrived at the restaurant, she was surprised to find a group of friends and admirers who forced her to sit at the head of the table while they made speeches about her.

4. She expected her quarterly allotment at the beginning of July, but as day after day passed, she began to worry.

5. Although the war had just started, sunburnt soldiers were marching through the dust in full battle dress.

6. I must have dozed off because I imagined that I was in my home town.

7. Over the bed hung a picture of a man who was wearing a broad ruff around his neck.

8. Remembering his attitude toward bookkeeping, she put every receipt into the file as soon as she returned to the office.

9. He must have been gone three days before anyone visited him or called his house.

10. She realized that the stairs, the hallway, and the sliding doors were all the same as they had been on that day.

III. *Read the following essay and then answer these questions.*

1. *What is the thesis of this essay?*

2. *What are the supports?*

3. *Does all the material in the body paragraphs prove the thesis?*

4. *What do you like best about this essay?*

5. *What do you like least?*

My Neighborhood

I was born in Hong Kong, and I have been in the United States for six years. Currently, I am living in my tenth apartment. I have lived in neighborhoods where judges, lawyers, doctors, and other rich people lived and in slums where I could hear shooting almost every night. Although I have lived in many different neighborhoods in this country, none was as interesting as my very first one in Hong Kong.

The street itself was interesting. My family lived in Wan Chai (The Small Bay) until I was thirteen. Our street was so small that people called it a lane, Wong Lok Lane (The Lane of Happiness). Four three-story houses were located on this lane. We lived on the second floor of the first house, overlooking the traffic of the whole lane as well as the backyard of a bakery. The lane was so small that no cars could drive through it. There was only foot traffic. A food booth was located at one end while the other end was blocked by a wall about thirty feet tall with steps on the side leading to another street.

I loved to sit on the balcony and watch the activities downstairs. I watched the short man make the noodle roll in the morning. I still remember his magic fingers dancing on a big piece of hot noodle. Within a few seconds, a noodle roll turned out. On the other side of the booth, his partner fried Chinese donuts while his assistant cut the dough. The long chopsticks kept the donuts turning over without a break. Since the food booth was open seventeen hours a day, there was always something to watch.

Our neighborhood supported many interesting occupations. The family on the ground floor of the last building made their living in pickles. The father made all kinds of pickles by himself and sold them in a portable food booth. There were carrot, radish, garlic, cabbage, and pepper pickles. I always watched him trimming the leaves of the cabbages and peppers. He seemed to enjoy his work so much that I always dreamt of being a cabbage trimmer one day. When mid-autumn festival was approaching, there would be a lot of workers in the backyard of the bakery preparing the moon cakes for the festival. Some ground tons of lotus seeds to make the filling of the cakes while others separated the salty eggs.

This year, I am going back to Hong Kong and will visit my old neighborhood. I know that the buildings were torn down, the food booth was moved, and things will not be the same. However, my sweet memories will never be destroyed.

INDEPENDENT STUDY: *Connecting Clauses* (answers in the back)

IV. In the sentences below, do the following five things.

1. *Put parentheses around all the prepositional phrases.*

2. *Underline all parts of all verbs twice.*

3. *Underline all of their subjects once.*

4. *Put dotted lines under the dependent clauses.*

5. *Put solid lines under the independent clauses.*

A. 1. I started kindergarten when I was four years old.

2. Since I had to be at school at eight o'clock in the morning, I had to get up at seven.

3. As I stepped out of the house, I heard my father snoring.

4. Locking the door behind me, I could smell the fresh air and the delicious odor from the ribs stand at the corner of the street.

5. When I reached the end of the street, I had to climb forty steps.

6. Those steps were so high that I almost had to claw my way up.

7. I didn't dare look back because I was afraid that I might fall down.

8. After I reached the top, I had to walk for another two blocks through dirty, smelly streets.

9. I was always afraid that I would see a rat.

10. When I did, I would feel sick all day.

B.   In those days when Japan was still poor and oppressed by the memory of the lost war, many heroes came from television. Rikidahzan was a professional wrestler who defeated rascal white wrestlers with his karate chop as if he were driving out the war-beaten Japanese people's inferiority complex. Tetsuwan was a boy robot cartoon character who always defeated villains. All the heroes fought against those who teased the weak. These heroes helped Japan recover from her war-beaten condition.

INSERTING CLAUSES

Good writers work comfortably with clauses of all types and know how to combine them effectively to express different ideas and create passages with an interesting variety of sentence types. Sometimes clauses are most effectively combined by putting a dependent one inside an independent one. The following sentences could be combined by making either one into a dependent clause and inserting it inside the other.

FAULTY

McMichael tackled Mrs. Winston.

McMichael had played a little football (in high school).

REVISED

McMichael, who had played a little football (in high school), tackled Mrs. Winston.

REVISED

McMichael, who tackled Mrs. Winston, had played a little football (in high school).

The independent clause hasn't changed, but now it has a dependent clause between its subject and its verb. Usually the idea that is most important to the argument should be in the independent clause. If you were writing about violence at cocktail parties, you would probably use the first sentence, and if you were writing about the virtues of playing sports, you would use the second.

When you are analyzing sentences, watch out for dependent clauses within independent ones. Here are more such sentences.

Leaning back (against the defense table), the judge, who is now officially dying, sings (in a soft, rough voice).

The boys who had dropped out (of football) watched eagerly (for the slightest mistake).

(In the heavy armchair), Mrs. Finley, who had studied ballet (in sixth grade), concentrated (on sitting straight and pointing her toes).

Sometimes the word "that" is working as the subject of the clause, and at other times it comes before the subject. Compare the following examples.

The city workers removed the maple tree that grew (in front) (of our house).

The city workers removed the maple tree that I had planted (in front) (of our house).

Often a dependent clause is hard to identify because the word "that" has been dropped from the sentence. If the word "that" can be inserted into the sentence before a clause without changing the meaning of the sentence, that clause is really a dependent one. The sentence

I knew she wanted me to answer

could be

I knew that she wanted me to answer

so the first sentence would be analyzed

I knew she wanted me to answer.

Here are some more such sentences.

As she picked up her pen, the man she had seen (on the sidewalk) swept (into her office).

(After peering) (at the mailboxes) (for a long time), she finally found the name she wanted.

He gently touched the face (of the man) he had shot.

EXERCISES: Inserting Clauses

I. Using words from the following list, change one of the sentences in the pairs below to a dependent clause and insert it next to the word it describes in the independent clause.

that   who   whose   which

A. 1. The woman just arrived in the country. She brought me the book.

2. The man owns a restaurant. He rented our house.

3. The lady sits in the back row. She got an A on her essay.

4. My mother rarely goes out of the house. She has nine children.

5. Robert Thompson spent three years in a concentration camp. He was working as an exporter when the war began.

6. The car was destroyed in the fire. We had bought it only three weeks earlier.

7. Charlie Smith is 134 years old. He has many fascinating tales to tell.

8. Mr. Brown refused to sell them the house. His intuition is usually sound.

9. Mrs. Stacy had been a member for three years. She will take the responsibility for the election.

10. Richard Edgar will play Polonius. He got rave reviews for his perform-ance as Bottom.

B. 1. Mary Saunders was elected to the city council. She studied with my daughter.

   2. I reheated the soup and finished it all. My father had left the soup for me.

   3. Mr. Brown was offered a contract with RCA. He had trained with Ms. Stevens.

   4. Alice Town wrote her first book when she was sixty-four. She has just written her third best-seller.

   5. Traditional student dueling fraternities have once more become popular in Germany. Their members wear colorful capes, pill-box hats, and brightly colored sashes.

   6. The glasses have large pink plastic frames. She chose them.

   7. Chen Chu designed her suit. He makes all her clothes.

   8. John Smith stood motionless with his lips tightly compressed. He had heard only my last sentence.

   9. Jerry Feldman stayed out of the conversation and leafed through the magazine. He wanted to see if he was really needed.

   10. Manning was sitting by a campfire on the bank of the river. His nickname was Jerusalem Slim.

C. *Could the word "that" be gracefully left out of any of the sentences you created for exercise B?*

D. *Add details, including dependent clauses, to make sentences out of the following subject-verb combinations.*

   1. _____ woman   _____ should wait _____

   2. _____ man   _____ swims   _____

   3. _____ child   _____ went to bed _____

   4. _____ dog   _____ sat   _____

   5. _____ girl   _____ laughs   _____

   6. _____ cat   _____ moaned   _____

   7. _____ my friend _____ must leave _____

   8. _____ the crowd _____ cheered   _____

   9. _____ the dentist _____ whistled _____

   10. _____ the boy _____ will hope   _____

E. Add dependent clauses beginning with the words "who," "which," "that," or "whose" to the following sentences.

1. The lady parked the car.

2. The girl went to the circus.

3. The child entered the school.

4. The man wore a long cape.

5. The woman touched the man.

6. The car struck the tree.

7. The boy fell off the bike.

8. The writer autographed the book.

9. The people congratulated him.

10. The bus stopped.

F. To the sentences created in exercise E add dependent clauses beginning with words from the following list.

after	before	unless	when
although	if	until	where
as	since	whether	why
because	though	while	

G. Now put solid lines under the independent clauses and dotted lines under the dependent clauses in the sentences created in exercises E and F. Could the word "that" be gracefully omitted from the beginning of any of the dependent clauses?

II. *In the sentences below, do the following five things.*

1. *Put parentheses around all the prepositional phrases.*

2. *Underline all parts of all verbs twice.*

3. *Underline all of their subjects once.*

4. *Put dotted lines under the dependent clauses.*

5. *Put solid lines under the independent clauses.*

A. 1. Thomas, who was seated in the front of the boat, looked over his shoulder toward the lonely, gray shore.

2. The path that had brought them to the hill reappeared on the north side.

3. Suddenly she realized she was moving backward.

4. The others looked toward the tree that he described, but they could see only branches and a few dead leaves.

5. The money he left his wife was gone within a year.

6. I know you must be exhausted after your long trip.

7. He thought he must have dropped it when he changed his shirt.

8. Coming to an opening between the trees, she found that she had climbed far beyond the farmhouse.

9. I am sure that they will hear about this problem before the night is over.

10. The people we visited in Mexico had a maid who washed their sheets by hand.

B. 1. When the innkeeper asked for volunteers, the man I had seen in the market stood up.

2. The book you need has been missing for three weeks.

3. The girls that had come up from Tokyo stared at them curiously.

4. He said he was thinking of writing a book and needed the names of subscribers.

5. It seemed that the men who understood had decided to keep quiet.

6. Joe and Robert, who were now feeling quite at home, chatted eagerly and drank deeply.

7. After we finished eating, one of the waiters, who had lived in Westmoreland years ago, questioned us about local gossip.

8. Each time they climbed out, the sky seemed darker.

9. The suit I wanted had been sold only a few minutes before I arrived.

10. He suspected he had met a mugger and was glad he had only a little money with him.

C. 1. I had learned that he was carrying with him a secret that concerned me and my friends.

2. When she finished talking, I realized I wanted to hear much more about that school.

3. He decided she was trying to avoid talking about the friends she had left in Montreal.

4. When he told me that much of the advertised merchandise was not available, I began to be suspicious.

5. I would give everything I have to get my father back and go camping in the country with him.

6. We are willing to listen, but they must demonstrate that introducing coyotes to the island will control the deer population with the minimum of animal suffering.

7. Sharon Jackson, who never did anything more athletic than balancing a bag of groceries on her hip while she opened her front door, has become an avid motorcyclist.

8. The leader of the group from Concord became a news-media personality, and people soon recognized her voice.

9. The woman who acted as translator attended Highland Park Elementary School from kindergarten through third grade.

10. Visitors had to pass through a wooden hut-like structure that was decorated with tribal feathers, leopard cloth, and mosquito netting.

III. A. *Read the following essay and then answer these questions.*

1. *What is the thesis of this essay?*

2. *What are the supports?*

3. *Is the outline good?*

4. *Is the evidence specific?*

5. *Does the evidence prove the thesis?*

6. *Is the introduction good?*

7. *Is the conclusion good?*

I live in the back of your closet. It is a lonely spot, dank and musty from the smell of old shoes and old clothes. I spend my time thinking of better days when I was more useful and carried shiny new shoes. Now I'm growing old and time has not been a friend to me. Life sure is tough for a shoe box.

Most of my friends don't like me because I'm too square. I sit in the corner of my closet all by myself waiting to make new friends. Occasionally a pair of shoes will stop in and see me, but usually they don't stay for long. The shoes that do stop have rounded heels and smooth rounded tips. They're usually full of life and view me as too structured and too square on all points. I would enjoy having a shirt or a blouse as a friend. Once in a while a blouse or a shirt will come down to see me, but only because they fell off their hangers. I watch them above me, so loose and free flowing, so soft and bright. It's easy to see how they see me as rigid and dull.

I age quickly from mistreatment. When I first came to this closet, I carried bright new shoes from a shoe store; my colors were bright and my tissue was firm. Look at me now. My colors have been worn off by rubbing against other objects in the closet. My tissue is smashed and ripped by careless shoes that have dropped in unexpectedly. The shoes that I hold are scuffed and smell of perspiration from working all day. My nice rigid corners have been smashed and beaten as careless shoes stumbled over them.

I'm in love with the shoe box at the other end of the closet, but I will never get a chance to meet her. I sit through long days making corners at that cute little shoe box. She is a slight little box that once carried some very elegant high heels. She is a little worn with age, but I don't mind because I am too. The vast distance between us is filled with old shoes and boots. I'd like to shout, "I love you" to her, but I wouldn't want the other clothes and shoes in the closet to laugh at me. I can only sit here and dream.

I know I'm not getting any younger and life is certainly tough, but I still have tomorrow. I have tomorrow to hope and dream about. I may still just sit here and do nothing all day long, but my dreams are big and as long as I have big dreams, I will survive.

B. *Correct any errors you find in the essay above.*

IV. A. *Write an essay about some common object you have in your home. Start by jotting down notes. Then write a thesis and supports that prove it, and check this outline with your teacher. As you write the essay, be sure to include lots of good details that prove your thesis and nothing that doesn't. Also be sure not to slip into telling a story* instead of *proving your thesis.*

B. *Write an essay on one of the topics below, following the instructions in exercise A.*

your career plans	a prom you went to
getting to school	bicycles
the real you	a car you like

INDEPENDENT STUDY: Inserting Clauses *(answers in the back)*

V. *In the sentences below, do the following five things.*

1. *Put parentheses around all the prepositional phrases.*

2. *Underline all parts of all verbs twice.*

3. *Underline all of their subjects once.*

4. *Put dotted lines under the dependent clauses.*

5. *Put solid lines under the independent clauses.*

A. 1. The forms that were on the table have disappeared.

2. The answer I expected was much simpler.

3. The woman who found the body saw no other person in the room.

4. They rushed me through the line so fast I don't even know what I bought.

5. The U.S. Secretary of Education said the federal role in enforcing laws against discrimination in education should be trimmed.

6. It seems we go from month to month anticipating the holiday that each month brings.

7. The house I remember was huge and had a round stained-glass window in the front.

8. Whenever she opened that door, she expected to see her uncle sitting in the heavy chair by the window.

9. He sat there wondering why he had come, what he would say, and how he would get away.

10. The lady who brought the eggs always wore a low flat-brimmed hat.

B. 1. Because he was originally a priest, Vivaldi's long-term friendship with the French prima donna Anna Girand, who accompanied him on his travels, eventually generated awkward questions, and Vivaldi lived out his last days in rejection and poverty.

2. The topics Brown addressed then are still very much in the news, so we decided to publish his remarks in fuller form.

3. Gordon Jackson, who played Mr. Hudson, was recently stopped in Piccadilly by an American woman who wanted him to become her butler.

4. Over at Bloom's, customers who entered through the main door found themselves in the middle of a Southeast Asian jungle, where camouflage-print clothing was displayed amid large cloth palms.

5. The town was founded at the turn of the century and settled by workers for the Santa Fe Railroad who filled the marshes separating the island from the mainland.

The Conventions

4. Separating the Sentences

fragment

• In speech, people use pauses, intonation, facial expressions, gestures, and other devices to punctuate their words and underline their ideas, but writers use only little marks on paper. Because the options are so limited, each mark on the written page has its own special meaning and function. You should master the language of punctuation so that you can write what you mean. This chapter shows how to use punctuation to separate words into sentences.

SENTENCE FRAGMENTS

A sentence is a group of words that contains at least one independent clause (subject-verb combination that makes sense by itself). A sentence is punctuated with a capital letter at the beginning and a period at the end. A group of words without an independent clause and wrongly punctuated with a capital letter and a period is called a sentence fragment. A complete sentence makes sense by itself, but a fragment does not.

FAULTY

When I visit Memphis. I always stay at the Palomino Motel.

"When I visit Memphis" does not make sense by itself. It is a *dependent* clause and should not be punctuated with a capital letter and a period as if it were an *independent* clause. This error is corrected by eliminating the extra period and capital letter and attaching the dependent clause to the independent clause either before or after it in the essay.

REVISED

When I visit Memphis, I always stay at the Palomino Motel.

The following passage also contains a fragment.

FAULTY

The owners are trying to control the industry. By dictating minimum and maximum salaries for all players. If the owners succeed, the players will lose a lot of power.

"By dictating maximum and minimum salaries for all players" is a fragment. This time it's an *-ing* phrase, not a dependent clause, but still this group of words is not an independent clause and should not be punctuated like one. This fragment too is corrected by removing the extra period and capital letter.

REVISED
The owners are trying to control the industry by dictating minimum and maximum salaries for all players. If the owners succeed, the players will lose a lot of power.

When eliminating a fragment, be sure to connect it to the material that logically goes with it. The following revision doesn't make sense.

FAULTY
The owners are trying to control the industry. By dictating minimum and maximum salaries for all players if the owners succeed, the players will lose a lot of power.

Here is another passage with a fragment.

FAULTY
Everything in her office reminded me of my own. For example, the typewriters, copy machines, telephones, desks, and people. People also discussed the same boring subjects.

"For example, the typewriters, copy machines, telephones, desks, and people" is a fragment, and it must be corrected by eliminating the extra period and capital letter and connecting it to the independent clause that makes sense with it.

REVISED
Everything in her office reminded me of my own, for example, the typewriters, copy machines, telephones, desks, and people. People also discussed the same boring subjects.

Usually a fragment is a punctuation error. The writer has used the correct words but has included an extra period and capital letter. Sometimes, however, the wording is not quite right.

FAULTY
Some people enjoy lending money. Like my cousin Gladys. I don't understand them.

This fragment doesn't really go with the material either before or after it. In a case like this, a sentence must be rewritten and the fragment built in properly.

REVISED
Some people, like my cousin Gladys, enjoy lending money. I don't understand them.

Here's a similar example.

FAULTY
I don't like riding the bus when the people are rowdy. People who carry large radios and play them loudly interfere with my thoughts and make me feel like finding other transportation. Also when the bus is especially crowded. Sometimes my trip to school ruins my whole day.

"Also when the bus is especially crowded" is a fragment, a dependent clause punctuated like an independent one. This fragment doesn't make sense with the independent clauses on either side, so a new independent clause can be added to solve this problem.

I don't like riding the bus when the people are rowdy. People who carry large radios and play them loudly interfere with my thoughts and make me feel like finding other transportation. I also feel uncomfortable when the bus is especially crowded. Sometimes my trip to school ruins my whole day.

The independent clause "I feel uncomfortable" has been added to the fragment to make a complete sentence.

Sometimes beginning writers mistake a complete sentence for a fragment because the sentence has a pronoun in it as this example does.

He carried all the furniture to the garage.

This is a complete sentence because it contains an independent clause whose subject is "he" and whose verb is "carried." Even though we do not know who "he" is when we read this sentence by itself, we still know that some male person carried the furniture to the garage, so the sentence makes sense by itself and is not a fragment.

fragment

CORRECTION COMMENT: **To eliminate fragments from your writing, use a capital letter and a period only around a group of words containing at least one independent clause (subject-verb combination that makes sense by itself).**

EXERCISES: Sentence Fragments

I. *Write sentences that begin with the words below. Remember that a sentence must have at least one independent clause.*

A. 1. Because _____

    2. If _____

    3. When _____

    4. Although _____

    5. For example _____

    6. Trying _____

    7. Before _____

    8. Avoiding _____

    9. Since _____

    10. While _____

B. 1. Tapering _____

    2. Unless _____

    3. For instance _____

    4. Worrying _____

5. As _____

6. Until _____

7. Knowing _____

8. Whether _____

9. Though _____

10. After _____

II. *Write sentences with the following words somewhere in the middle of them.*

A. 1. _____ especially _____

2. _____ trying _____

3. _____ maybe _____

4. _____ such as _____

5. _____ like _____

6. _____ because _____

7. _____ so that _____

8. _____ which _____

9. _____ that _____

10. _____ if _____

B. 1. _____ perhaps _____

2. _____ for example _____

3. _____ since _____

4. _____ wondering _____

5. _____ when _____

6. _____ although _____

7. _____ wishing _____

8. _____ then _____

9. _____ accusing _____

10. _____ except _____

III. *Write the letter* F *above each fragment in the exercises below. Then correct it. The first one has been done for you. If you are not sure about a group of words, do the following analysis.*

1. Put parentheses around the prepositional phrases.

2. Put two lines under all parts of all verbs.

3. Put one line under their subjects.

4. Put dotted lines under the dependent clauses.

5. Put solid lines under the independent clauses.

Then if there is no solid line under a group of words starting with a capital letter and ending with a period, you know those words are a fragment.

A. 1. **EXAMPLE** Before I was able to work with the doctors, I had to observe the procedures of the other clinical assistants.

2. I went to bed early. Because I had an eight o'clock class in the morning.

fragment

3. Grown men shouldn't argue about trivial things. Like a wrong call by an umpire.

4. We went to every class. We didn't want to miss anything.

5. Now that I have gotten used to college work. I can be depended on to do my homework and attend class.

6. Gradually I would create local banks. Then textile industries.

7. In 1977, I was the number one varsity player on the badminton team. I led my team to victory against five other schools.

8. The cruise liner. Although somewhat expensive, it is worth the money.

9. I can remember my brother was sitting in his room doing his homework. When I came in.

10. Whenever he has problems with notes, I like to help him. We have a lot of fun playing the piano.

B. 1. Instead of riding home, we walked. Because she had given the money for our fare to the beggar.

2. The music begins, and I pray that my voice will hold together. Knowing that the previous week I had been ill with strep throat.

3. Some people read about three hundred words per minute. Some about two hundred.

4. Everybody seemed to get quiet and sad. Because I didn't want to think, I tried to laugh and joke.

5. It's exciting to ride the bus. Things are always happening.

6. The conductor drives the train, the chef cooks the food, and the waitresses serve the meals. Because all of these services are part of the traveling arrangement.

7. It seemed as though every Friday every girl in high school had a date. Every girl except me.

8. When I got there, another of our friends was with her. All of us went to pick up Amelio, Jesse, and Pedro.

9. Since I cannot find a presidential candidate that I like. I decided not to vote this time.

10. The fancy styles and new fabrics of today's clothing are not really very practical. Like plastic tops and bottoms.

C. 1. I always thought my watching television when I was supposed to be practicing my guitar or doing my homework wouldn't matter. Until my brother told me what happened to him.

2. She carefully read the labels on each different brand of wheat bread. Finally settling on one brand whose label read, "All natural stone-ground whole wheat bread."

3. The Vietnamese government was taken over by the communists on April 29, 1975. Everyone was terrified.

4. One day while I was sitting there struggling and begging for help. Suddenly my brother came to the rescue.

5. My whole way of life is different now. Living in a dorm is more distracting than I thought it would be. Also more expensive.

6. Other English classes have taught me how to organize a paper before starting to write. Organization such as getting a good outline.

7. Sometimes I think that Americans are spoiled people. Look at the way they waste energy. Leaving the television or the stereo on all night.

8. Since this is my first year in college and this summer our family is planning to go to Poland. I am glad that the end of the school year is here.

9. Her sister always has something funny to say. She makes a lot of jokes, especially about husbands.

10. Only a grandmother takes the time to do the extra special things like taking a small girl to shop for materials for an embroidery project. Then selecting just the right colors for the flowers.

IV. A. *Write the letter* F *above the fragments in the following passages, and correct them in the best possible way.*

1. We faced two hearings. One on a Thursday and the other on a Friday. The first judges chose the representatives for the final hearing on Friday.

2. It is always good to read something. Even if it is just for fun. Many people enjoy reading newspapers.

3. It is fun to go for a walk in the park when the flowers are in bloom. To

see the butterflies and the hummingbirds enjoying the beautiful blooms. I especially enjoy going on picnics with my church groups.

4. Parks, movies, and discos are places to meet people. Although they may not be the right places. The place I go depends on the mood I am in.

5. My brother Sam is always teasing me. For example, last week when I was washing the dishes. Sam came into the kitchen, pulled out a glass, and took a drink of water. To irritate me even more, he got a bowl from the cupboard and ate some Jell-O.

6. A pack of gum a week costs about a dollar a month. Plus the dentist bills. Fifty dollars a visit plus a dollar a month is a lot of money going down the drain.

7. I had my own share of accidents last year. Two which stand out very clearly. The first one came during a donkey basketball game.

fragment

8. Stores begin to fill up hours before the kickoff of the first game. People getting everything from ice-cold beer to dip and chips. Once out of the store, they rush home to get organized.

9. Some people read slowly because they have fallen into the habit. Therefore causing problems for themselves. When they have important pieces of material that have to be read in a limited amount of time.

10. A few years ago, money meant nothing to me. I ran in and out of the house asking for money. Spending it as fast as my parents gave it to me. Never having to worry about getting more. When my father put me on a budget. Everything went wrong.

B.   This year's fashions are suitable only for very slim people. One afternoon when I was strolling through a department store. Glancing towards the latest in women's apparel, I caught sight of a comical but pathetic character. A woman of considerable girth had attempted to squeeze into an evening dress that only a fashion model could wear. After much squirming, tugging, and pulling in front of the mirror, she finally gave up and went back into the changing room only to face a new problem. Getting out of the dress. Which I might add must have been quite a task. Women are not the only ones afflicted with this problem. Because jeans are cramping the style of men everywhere. Even a tiny derriere can change the slogan "Cut to fit" to "Fit to cut" in the minds of the poor souls trying on a pair of pants. Though it is written that the Lord created man in his image. Those undernourished, underweight designers from France don't have to style clothing in their own image. As it stands now, the overweight person must manage to fit into these clothes. Or go through life out of style.

V.   A. Label and correct all the fragments in the following essay.

People living in middle-class neighborhoods have few worries. They may worry about the house burning down. Thieves breaking in and stealing the valuables. The television set or the dishwasher breaking down. These people don't have to worry about traffic, noise, or pollution, but my neighborhood has a pollution problem.

A trucking company in my neighborhood causes a lot of noise and air pollution. Every day the trucks come roaring down the street. Their loud noise irritating people's ears. People new to the neighborhood are kept awake by the sound of the engines and freezers. Which stay on all night. They also must get used to the bad air in the neighborhood. They can get irritated eyes and an upset stomach. From breathing all the fumes.

Right beside the neighborhood, a freeway causes more pollution. People who work in the neighborhood's factories create smog as they drive into the streets. During the rush hour, the traffic gets heavier and slows down. Making motorists stand still and give off even more exhaust. Looking down on the neighborhood from the hills during rush hour, a person cannot see through the smog created by the motorists and factories.

On the other side of the neighborhood, there's a railroad crossing with regular trains. Making thundering noise, keeping people awake, or preventing them from hearing someone talking. At the rush hour, the train distributing materials to the factories stops motorists in the neighborhood. Making some of them go through the back streets creating more air pollution and making them unsafe for children.

As living conditions get worse, landlords sell their land to factories. Making houses lose even more value. The city gave the people in the neighborhood five years to clear out because they plan to make it into an industrial area. The city should improve its neighborhoods. Not destroy them.

B. Reread the essay in exercise A now that its fragments are corrected. Label its thesis, supports, evidence, introduction, and conclusion, and add notes telling which parts are good and how others could be improved.

INDEPENDENT STUDY: Sentence Fragments (answers in the back)

VI. A. Write the letter F above all fragments in the following sentences and then correct them.

1. We are all proud of my mother. She's the electrician, the plumber, the painter, the cook, the housecleaner, the shopper, and the washerwoman.

2. I try to alert my friends to the instructions on all medicine. Especially those new higher-strength aspirins.

3. A child learns at an early age. That gravity is a powerful force.

4. I spent many hours learning to drive a stick shift through those narrow and winding streets. Stalling on every hill I came to and grinding gears along the way.

5. Women today receive far less pay than men for the same amount of work. Many of these women support families too.

6. When I was a senior high school student in Korea. I had three friends whom I still remember well.

7. Many corporations find some way to take advantage of the situation and make a profit. Like our famous oil companies.

8. In ninth grade I joined the band. Every evening at seven I had to be at school to practice.

9. You probably have eaten fried shrimp but not marinated overnight in a special sauce. So that the shrimp absorbs the sauce and becomes tender.

10. After that, I will work in my father's company. Of course, as an employee.

fragment

B.   Democracy is slow because of the basic principles upon which it is founded. Most democratic governments elect representatives to legislative bodies that consider the policies of the country. Also the laws. Afraid of losing future elections, representatives are reluctant to pass legislation that might hurt their constituents. For example, there have been many bills in the United States Congress designed to solve the energy problem. Bills appropriating money for research and development of breeder reactors, fusion reactors, solar energy, and coal exploitation. All have been killed or severely reduced. Even the president's comprehensive energy package was scrapped. The measures were killed in large part due to the influence of special interest groups. Groups whose members were voting constituents of the representatives.

RUN-TOGETHER SENTENCES

Independent clauses (subject-verb combinations that make sense by themselves) can be separated into different sentences by a period and a capital letter. However, good writing has many sentences that contain more than one independent clause. When independent clauses are combined into a single sentence, they must be separated by a comma (,) and one of these words:

for

and

nor

but

or

yet

so

As mentioned earlier, these words are easy to remember because their first letters spell the word "fanboys." They are called coordinating conjunctions.

The error of eliminating the "fanboys" word and incorrectly punctuating two independent clauses as though they were just one is called a run-together sentence.

FAULTY My mother has a job, I do all the housework.

This group of words is set up like a sentence, beginning with a capital letter and ending with a period. It contains two clauses. "Mother" is the subject and "has" is the verb of the first one; "I" is the subject and "do" is the verb of the second. Since neither clause begins with one of the words that make clauses dependent, both are independent. These two independent clauses in the same sentence are not separated by a "fanboys" word, and so they constitute a run-together sentence.

There are three easy ways to correct run-together sentences:

1. The two independent clauses can be separated into two sentences.

REVISED My mother has a job. I do all the housework.

2. A comma and a "fanboys" word may be added.

REVISED My mother has a job, and I do all the housework.

REVISED My mother has a job, so I do all the housework.

3. A word may be added to make one clause dependent.

REVISED Since my mother has a job, I do all the housework.

REVISED Because my mother has a job, I do all the housework.

REVISED When my mother has a job, I do all the housework.

REVISED While my mother has a job, I do all the housework.

REVISED If my mother has a job, I do all the housework.

REVISED As my mother has a job, I do all the housework.

REVISED My mother has a job since I do all the housework.

REVISED My mother has a job because I do all the housework.

REVISED My mother has a job when I do all the housework.

REVISED My mother has a job while I do all the housework.

REVISED My mother has a job if I do all the housework.

REVISED My mother has a job as I do all the housework.

All the revisions above correct the run-together sentence, but they all have slightly different meanings. You should choose the one that best fits your meaning, your sentence, and its context. The first solution is good when you have a very long sentence, but beginning writers usually write too many single clause sentences. The second solution will be appropriate when you haven't written a lot of similar sentences, but linking independent clauses together with "and" frequently reflects lack of careful attention to meaning. The third solution is often best because it offers many opportunities to express subtly different ideas.

A fourth way to correct run-together sentences is possible in some situations. Sometimes a writer can correct a run-together sentence *and* eliminate wordiness by condensing the two clauses into one, as in the following example.

FAULTY I had a very special friend her name was Sharon Arnold.

REVISED I had a very special friend named Sharon Arnold.

People combine independent clauses incorrectly for a number of reasons. There may be a lot of dependent material between the two independent clauses so that the writer forgets about the first one, as in the following example.

FAULTY He borrowed my sweat jacket without asking before I missed it, the jacket was faded and torn.

This sentence would be analyzed as follows.

FAULTY He borrowed my sweat jacket (without asking) before I missed it, the jacket was faded and torn.

The first and last clauses of this sentence are independent, and there is no "fanboys" word between them, and so this is a run-together sentence and must be corrected.

REVISED He borrowed my sweat jacket without asking, and before I missed it, the jacket was faded and torn.

run-together

When a sentence contains two independent clauses, no matter how much other material separates them, a "fanboys" word must also be used. Of course if the clauses are separated into two separate sentences, the "fanboys" word is unnecessary.

REVISED He borrowed my sweat jacket without asking. Before I missed it, the jacket was faded and torn.

Here's a similar example.

FAULTY I didn't want Mary's part because it was the biggest part of all I thought that my part was enough.

REVISED I didn't want Mary's part because it was the biggest part of all, and I thought that my part was enough.

REVISED I didn't want Mary's part because it was the biggest part of all. I thought that my part was enough.

Sometimes people write run-together sentences because they confuse introductory words at the beginning of an independent clause with the words that make clauses dependent and mistake an independent clause for a dependent one. The chart in Figure 4 lists both types of words. Clauses beginning with words from the first list do not make sense by themselves, but clauses beginning with words from the second list do. For example, "When we went home" leaves the reader waiting for something else, but "Then we went home" makes sense by itself. The reader knows that after something, the people went home. The following run-together sentences might have been caused by confusing these types of words.

FAULTY She played well, then she acknowledged her audience with a bow.

The word "then" does not make a clause dependent, so both clauses are independent. Since there is no "fanboys" word, this is a run-together sentence and must be corrected.

REVISED She played well, and then she acknowledged her audience with a bow.

Similarly, the word "besides" does not make a clause dependent.

FAULTY I wanted the best possible education, besides I've always enjoyed a challenge.

REVISED I wanted the best possible education. Besides, I've always enjoyed a challenge.

If you're ever unsure about a word, check the list in Figure 4. It is also printed inside the back cover for easy reference.

There is another way to distinguish between words which make a clause dependent and those which do not. The words that make a clause dependent must go at the beginning of a clause. We would say "When we went home" but not "We when went home." The words that don't make a clause dependent can be moved to other places in the sentence. We can say both "Then we went home" and "We then went home." We can say "Therefore the professor

Figure 4. Connecting words and clause punctuation

Connecting Words   *Correct Punctuation*

Words that make clauses
dependent:

after	whether
although	while
as	when
because	where
before	why
if	that
how	what
since	which
though	who
unless	whom
until	whose

        dependent   independent
Because my folks are away, I am staying alone.

        independent   dependent
I am staying alone since my folks are away.

Some of the words that *don't*
make clauses dependent:

also	moreover
besides	nevertheless
consequently	now
finally	otherwise
first	sometimes
furthermore	then
however	therefore
likewise	

        independent   independent
My folks are away. Consequently I am staying
alone.

        independent   independent
My folks are away, and now I am staying alone.

Words that connect inde-
pendent clauses:

for	or
and	yet
nor	so
but	

        independent   independent
My folks are away, so I am staying alone.

        independent   independent
My folks are away, and I am staying alone.

run-together

was late to class" and "The professor, therefore, was late to class." If you are wondering if a certain word makes a clause dependent, try moving it to a new place in the sentence. If such a move makes no sense, the word probably makes the clause dependent.

> CORRECTION COMMENT: **When a sentence has more than one independent clause, separate those clauses with a comma and a "fanboys" word (for, and, nor, but, or, yet, so).**

EXERCISES: Run-Together Sentences

I. **A.** *Write two independent clauses that fit around each of the following.*

1. _____ , for _____

2. _____ , and _____

3. _____ , nor _____

4. _____ , but _____

5. _____ , or _____

6. _____ , yet _____

7. _____ , so _____

8. _____ . Sometimes _____

9. _____ . Then _____

10. _____ . Besides _____

B. *Write five sentences with two independent clauses correctly connected.*

C. *Write five sentences with at least two independent clauses and some dependent clauses. Put solid lines under the independent clauses, and be sure they are correctly connected.*

II. *In the sentences below, write the letters RTS (for run-together sentence) after all the sentences in which two independent clauses are incorrectly punctuated as one. Then correct them. The first one has been done for you. If you are unsure about any, do the following things.*

1. Put parentheses around the prepositional phrases.

2. Underline all parts of all verbs twice.

3. Underline their subjects once.

4. Put dotted lines under the dependent clauses.

5. Put solid lines under the independent clauses.

6. Check sentences with two independent clauses to see if they are connected with a comma and a "fanboys" word. Any that aren't are run-together sentences.

A.
1. **EXAMPLE** A person should avoid junk foods they're not good for the teeth or the body.

2. Tennis isn't really hard it takes a little practice.

3. This will be a long weekend for me, I have several homework assignments.

4. He buys the groceries when she cooks the dinner.

5. He buys the groceries then she cooks the dinner.

6. The tomatoes have to be perfectly ripe for pepper steak otherwise they will turn into a mess.

7. This saved them money they didn't have to worry about hiring a sitter.

8. Production of coal has increased therefore our need for other fuels has decreased.

9. When the dusty stranger reached the horizon, Mrs. Stevens returned to her porch.

10. The clerk takes the credit information then the manager approves the sale.

B.
1. Early one morning, we took the boat to Angel Island for a picnic, in the evening we had a dance on the boat.

2. More families should take up roller skating it is excellent exercise.

3. After our first scrimmage, we had watermelon at our next scrimmage we had a barbecue.

4. She said, "I don't want to walk, I'm tired."

5. When my mother asked me to stop seeing Steven so much, I had to speak up.

6. Then a loud yell came from behind the plate "Play ball!" said the umpire.

run-together

7. I do my best to ignore the pain, and when I'm done stretching, it all seems worthwhile.

8. I'm not coming to the sale, I have to go somewhere with my boy friend.

9. Living in the city, many people don't get the chance to observe and admire the beauty of nature.

10. I enjoy spending a few days at their house nobody gets upset and their lives are easy and relaxed.

C. 1. She was very happy that day, and my parents were just as excited, they let her have the car that Friday night.

2. It's tea time come out, girls.

3. Running is an excellent way to stay healthy, it's good for the arteries and the heart.

4. As I walked into the house, I spotted Pam sitting on the couch with a photograph album spread out in her lap.

5. I figured it would be easy to get twenty-eight points, boy, was I wrong.

6. We drove to three drive-ins until we found something decent to watch, *King of Hearts* after the movie we went home.

7. This toy prepares kids psychologically for life it gives them the experience of using self-control.

8. I've been to a couple of other concerts since then, and none of them seemed as bad because I knew what to expect.

9. We were always happy at Christmas, wondering what secrets were hidden in the colorful packages.

10. Baseball is a boring game because it has too many faults, some are inevitable but others could be eliminated by penalizing the offenders.

D. 1. My uncle, for example, is now a retired commissioned officer, and he's receiving good benefits, also he has another job to support his family.

2. One time when my mother had just come back from the hospital after a serious operation and I wanted to be with her, my father said, "What are you doing inside you should be outside burning the trash."

3. The rewards included some of the things a boy my age would appreciate such as using his car on the weekend, in addition to an allowance, he would pay my way to almost any event.

4. His behavior embarrassed me because all my friends knew he liked me, and they always teased me about him.

5. She adored my older sisters and brother one day they broke into the pantry and cut a cake she had made for Grandfather the oldest children gave me a piece of the cake, and I forgot to wipe my mouth clean.

III. A. *The following sentences have been incorrectly punctuated. Figure out what is wrong, and then correct them.*

1. We then packed up our camping gear after loading the vehicles. We had a farewell party, then went home.

2. Skating really helps me to stay in shape. Because I am constantly moving my arms, legs, and stomach muscles. I once skated so much my body started to get stiff.

3. I ordered a double-cut prime rib steak when the waitress brought the steak to my table. My mouth suddenly started to water like a faucet.

4. My life so far has been happy, and if I had been asked two years ago to write a prediction of my life at twenty. I probably would have guessed what I am doing now.

5. Usually I decide a couple of days beforehand, and bang, bang. I'm off like a shot four-wheeling up the side of a hill in the Appalachian Mountains.

B. *Use periods and capital letters to correctly separate the sentences in the following paragraph.*

Lance doesn't watch us only when we have friends over, he peeps and peers every day I can't even walk by the window without dodging his eyes, and it's my house when I take a shower downstairs, I sometimes forget the soap our linen closet is upstairs, and this is where the soap is kept when I go up to get it, instead of getting all dressed, I usually just wrap a towel around me when I come to the top of the stairs, I remember the beady eyes that, nine times out of ten, are looking at me I then get down on my hands and knees and crawl under the window to the linen closet for the soap going back to the shower I do the same thing all over again until we get shades, I guess I'll just have to continue to crawl like a baby under that window.

IV. A. *Correct the run-together sentences in the following essay.*

Raja, the Grasshopper Who Loved to Drink Tea

Our family loved pets very much. I cannot think of a time during the course of my life that we did not have a pet of some kind. Our pets ranged from dogs, cats, and rabbits to parrots and canaries, none of them was as unusual as my pet Raja Gulab Khan, the grasshopper who loved to drink tea.

This story about Raja goes back to the time when I was in the first grade. I found him one summer afternoon while we were having our afternoon tea. We used to drink our tea in the garden where it was nice and cool. There was a rosebush near the table, it was on one of its branches that I saw Raja for the first time. I asked my mother if I could give him some tea. She told me he would not like it, but since I insisted, she agreed to let me do so. I put a drop of tea on a matchstick and held it close to him. To everybody's surprise he liked it very much. From that day, he became my pet and my friend.

run-together

After much discussion between my sister, my brother, and me, we agreed to call him Raja Gulab Khan, which means king of the rosebush. He never understood his name, but we felt it was unfair not to give him a name. He was called Raja for short I used to see him every day at the same time on the same bush. He loved to drink tea, and this habit seemed very unusual to everybody. I never knew why he came to that tree every day. I thought it was because he loved to see me, but then it might have been that he loved tea.

As the days went by, I loved him more and more, and I hated the neighbor's kids because they thought he was ugly and dirty. One day my mother told me that he was not going to be with us a long time because a grasshopper does not live very long besides he might be eaten by birds or cats. Although I was worried about all the bad things that could happen to him, I did not want to keep him in a box. I wanted him to be free. He was faithful, he never left our garden. I tried to teach him tricks, but he was a slow learner. He learned to jump to my finger when I held it close to him. He loved to eat lettuce. I did not feed him very often except for afternoon tea.

At last the day which I dreaded came. Raja was killed by the neighbor's boy. He crushed him under his foot under the same bush. His death was very painful, and it was very hard to get over it. I buried him under the rosebush. After that day I never drank tea. This experience taught me that all creatures have feelings and intelligence. Having a pet adds joy to our lives.

B. *Answer the following questions about the essay in exercise A.*

1. *This essay does not have three arguments that prove its thesis. How is it organized?*

2. *What is the thesis of this essay?*

3. *Does the whole essay prove this thesis?*

4. *What do you like best about this essay?*

5. *What do you like least? How would you change it?*

V. A. *Write an essay about an unusual pet. Organize the essay either by supports or as one long story. If you choose the story form, be sure that your essay has a thesis and that everything in the essay proves that thesis.*

B. *Write an essay on one of the following topics. First, narrow the topic and jot down notes. Next, write a thesis and three supports that prove it. Check this outline with your instructor, and then write an essay that follows the outline.*

your neighborhood	gardening
your best friend in first grade	a challenge you've faced
a sporting event	the death of a close friend

INDEPENDENT STUDY: Run-Together Sentences (answers in the back)

VI. A. *Write the letters* RTS *(for run-together sentence) after all the sentences in which two independent clauses are incorrectly punctuated as one. Then correct them.*

1. At first, the rain was coming down lightly, then it began to come down hard.

2. The bright colors of the late seventies still remain, however, they appear in prints now.

3. They had many types of activities planned such as picnics, dances, and volleyball, once they rented a party boat.

4. Inflation is the biggest enemy of employment if we can slow down inflation we might be able to solve some of our employment problems.

5. Her ancestry is Korean, her radiant smile points to large, dark, expressive eyes.

6. I think it's really good for a girl to have an older brother because he can keep an eye on her at school.

7. We got our safety briefing from the safety officer, then we went to get our ammunition.

8. Cities began to emerge, with them came pollution.

9. My nephew would begin to walk, then all of a sudden I could hear a clump, he had fallen again.

10. I went upstairs for a few minutes, when I returned to the kitchen, I looked in the oven and saw that his chocolate chip cookies were burned.

B. Add periods and capital letters to correctly separate the sentences in the following paragraph.

In early summer I competed in the Southwest Regional High School Chess Championship two days after school was out, seven of my cohorts and I got out of bed at five in the morning and set out for Houston, Texas, the site of the tournament the tournament lasted six days as a team, we finished seventh out of thirty-two schools individually out of 340 players, our top player got third place, I was next with seventeenth place although the tournament took up most of the day, we still had time to see the sights around Houston we saw the Astro Dome, the zoo, and NASA we all had a great time.

run-together

5. Matching the Parts

• The parts of a written passage in English are tightly linked by a network of word forms that indicate such information as who is speaking, who is listening, when something happens, what is being described, how many things are involved, and who owns what. Casual writing and speech often communicate these ideas in other ways and ignore the subtle distinctions among word forms, but the distinctions are fundamental to the formal written English of the academic and business worlds. This chapter examines this intricate word form system.

NOUNS

A noun is a word that refers to a person, place, thing, or idea. Some nouns are names; others may combine with the word "the" into a unit like "the cat," "the houses," or "the answer." Nouns are often used as subjects of sentences and as the last word of prepositional phrases.

The dictionary gives much valuable information about words. The small *n* in the following entry shows that the word "thesis" is a noun.

> **the·sis** /ˈθisɪs/ *n* (*pl* theses /-siz/) statement or theory (to be) put forward and supported by arguments, esp a lengthy written essay submitted (as part of the requirements) for a university degree.

Nouns referring to things that can be counted have plural forms to refer to more than one thing. Words referring to things that can't be counted, that have to be measured, have no plural forms.

Can be counted (have plurals)		*Must be measured* (have no plurals)	
one cookie	many cookies	some milk	much milk
one bush	many bushes	some vegetation	much vegetation
one lake	many lakes	some water	much water

Cookies, bushes, and lakes can be counted, but milk, vegetation, and water cannot be counted. They must be measured by the cup, the acre, or the gallon and have no plural forms.

Most plurals are formed by adding the letter *s* to the singular form, but a few words require *es*.

	Singular Nouns	*Plural Nouns*	
	teenager	teenagers	**add** *s*
	bookstore	bookstores	
	umbrella	umbrellas	
	truth	truths	
	valley	valleys	
	toy	toys	
words ending in *s*, *sh*, *ch*, **and** *x*	boss	bosses	**add** *es*
	wish	wishes	
	match	matches	
	box	boxes	
words ending in *y* **preceded by a consonant**	fly	flies	**change** *y* *to i* **and add** *es*
	philosophy	philosophies	
	company	companies	

plural

A few plurals do not follow these rules.

child	children	(*ren* **added**)
man	men	(*a* **changed to** *e*)
woman	women	(*a* **changed to** *e*)
foot	feet	(*oo* **changed to** *ee*)
sheep	sheep	(**no spelling change**)
self	selves	(*f* **changed to** *v* **and** *es* **added**)

All such irregular plural forms are given in the dictionary. The above entry for "thesis" includes the letters *pl* for plural followed by the word "theses," the irregular plural form of thesis.

Plural forms are sometimes unpredictable, and beginning writers occasionally use wrong plural forms. More frequently, however, they neglect to use any plural form at all where standard English demands one. Plural forms should be used to refer to more than one thing that can be counted.

FAULTY Cigarette manufacturers spend millions on television commercial.

Television commercials can be counted, and the writer is referring to more than one, so a plural form is necessary.

REVISED Cigarette manufacturers spend millions on television commercials.

Sometimes logic is required to determine if more than one thing is being referred to.

FAULTY We both laughed until tears came streaming down our face.

Obviously the two people in the sentence don't share one face, so the plural form "faces" must be used.

REVISED We both laughed until tears came streaming down our faces.

Plural forms should be used to refer to more than one thing that can be counted.

FAULTY One of my friend went to San Antonio.

The plural form is needed because the sentence refers to one of several friends. If it didn't, the sentence would have read, "My friend went to San Antonio."

REVISED One of my friends went to San Antonio.

The words "this" and "that" refer to one while the words "these" and "those" refer to more than one.

FAULTY He can't answer these type of question.

REVISED He can't answer this type of question.

REVISED He can't answer these types of questions.

This sentence was revised in two ways, first to refer to one type and then to refer to more than one type.

CORRECTION COMMENT: Plural forms should be used to refer to more than one thing that can be counted.

EXERCISES: Nouns

I. Form the plurals of the following nouns.

A.   *Singular*   *Singular*

1. monkey _____   6. victory _____

2. wristwatch _____   7. Jones _____

3. hostess _____   8. church _____

4. freeway _____   9. textbook _____

5. mailman _____   10. typewriter _____

B. 1. ditch _____ 6. dish _____

2. tax _____ 7. reply _____

3. sailboat _____ 8. Brown _____

4. theory _____ 9. sparrow _____

5. pie _____ 10. comedy _____

C. *Write five sentences using plurals you formed for exercises A and B.*

D. *Use a dictionary to find the plural forms of the following nouns.*

Singular   *Singular*

1. medium _____ 6. fungus _____

2. analysis _____ 7. phenomenon _____

3. quiz _____ 6. antenna _____

4. deer _____ 9. brother-in-law _____

5. bus _____ 10. tomato _____

E. *Write five sentences using plurals you formed for exercise D.*

II. *Correct all errors in the use of plurals in the following sentences.*

A. 1. Two week ago I saw him hiding under the fountain in our garden.

2. We were all lined up, worried our cap would fall or we would cry.

3. Then you can learn about the different salary and position that are offered in the company.

4. Can you imagine one of my friend jumping and chasing a basketball with her glasses on?

5. I would recommend that you try some of their buttermilk pancake with butter on top, a scrambled egg with two breakfast sausage, and a glass of juice.

6. The class covered various popular dance steps and included a field trip to one of the popular night club.

7. With all the advertisement about saving gas, some car company have not sold their new cars.

8. I try to be very courteous even with those type of people.

9. Her jeans were covered with mud, paint, and grease.

10. All my best girl friend sat at the same table.

B. 1. Now we're getting close to that big earthquake, and we need to learn emergency procedures like standing in doorways and getting under a desk.

plural

2. I went down to the basement and pulled out one of my mother's old dress.

3. While nations talk about keeping peace, they are improving their army and their weapons.

4. These type of restaurant always kept us waiting.

5. My dad would pay me twenty-five dollar a week for working.

6. One day she wore a beige dress with all kind of fancy designs with stocking and high-heeled shoes.

7. After graduation, we went to different high school, but we still stayed the best of friend.

8. There are many thing to do in Bermuda.

9. I remember when some students got their mouth washed out with soap by Mrs. Clark.

10. These type of toys are not only safe but inexpensive as well.

C. 1. A loaf of bread cost about fifty-nine cent a year ago, and today it costs a dollar five cent.

2. Two quarter passed.

3. She can tell me which brand of toothpaste works best on bad breath and which one is best for preventing cavity.

4. He and I both have a car.

5. Often I have seen my friends disregard these directions and pop six aspirins into their mouth.

6. These sort of mistakes show me how careless people can be.

7. The park has many lake and animals.

8. Have you ever tried sharing a room with three sister?

9. Then I had to walk for another two block through those dirty streets.

10. I haven't seen any of Ronald Reagan's movie, but I imagine he must be one of those hero in the West.

III. A. *Correct any errors you find in the plurals below.*

1. There are all types of toys and games for childrens on the market today.

2. Last year we enjoyed having a snowball fights.

3. With all this good things about baseball, it's still boring.

4. Television provides people with a lot of job, people like actor, actress, cameraman, and make-up person.

5. Packages, letters, magazines, and newspapers had overflowed from the mailbox onto the porch.

6. Parents shouldn't take young people to live in countrys other than their own.

7. At the museum one can see the prehistoric animals and cavemans.

8. He knows how to please womens, for he buys them clothes, flowers, candys, and anything else they desire.

9. My eyes lit up whenever I passed the table, with the desserts spread out to the left and the soft drink to the right.

10. The dining room had one big table that could seat eight peoples.

B. *Add any missing plurals to the following paragraph.*

In every war innocent people get hurt. The families in little town in the battle areas, women and children, teenager and babies, lose their possessions, their home, and sometimes their life. The soldiers who are forced to fight for someone else's cause are also victim. Young men, some still in their teens, may be injured or even killed before they have really begun to live.

IV. A. *Write a paragraph about a different situation in which innocent people are hurt. Begin the paragraph with a sentence that tells what the paragraph will prove.*

B. *Write a paragraph about the things that we see and use on a specific holiday and at no other time of the year. Begin the paragraph with a sentence that tells what the paragraph will prove.*

`plural`

V. A. *Read the following essay and correct it so the numbers are consistent.*

I entered college in 1977, and for three straight year I didn't take a single quarter off. By the end of the third year, I was so tired that I decided to take a summer off and spend almost two month traveling across the country. By the end of that summer, I was even more exhausted than before. Now I have everything planned for this summer and am praying that it will work out right.

For the first time in my life, I had enough courage to see a dentist before I had a toothache, but he disappointed me by referring me to an orthodontist and an oral surgeon. After several consultation, they all agreed that I should have my teeth braced for a couple of month, then undergo oral surgery to correct my underbite. Just a month ago, I thought my teeth were well qualified for a toothpaste commercial, but after listening to the experts, I wonder whether they will last another day. When I look into the mirror, I wonder how I will look with each tooth decorated with metal wiring. Well, it won't be long before I'll know.

After I have the oral surgery in a few month, I won't be able to eat for a while. To make up for this loss, I decided to indulge myself with all kind of food. I hope this will help me to satisfy my appetite for a while as well as give me a few extra pound. I have already started checking out good restaurant including Angelo's on Chestnut Street, Mai's on Clement Street, and Little Joe's on Broadway. However, I will avoid milk shake and ice cream for I am sure that I'll have plenty of those after my operation.

I have never been to a hospital in my life, and the idea of surgery shakes me up a little. How far is life from death? How can anyone say that she is going to be alive tomorrow? I realize I should enjoy my life while I am healthy and happy. When I lie in my bed, feeling the pain in my mouth, I think I will be more comfortable in a full-sized bed than in a twin-sized one. I need a new bookshelf by the bedside so that I don't have to claw my way to the living room for a book. New curtain may brighten up my room and ease the pain. I also need a new carpet so that I won't have to step on the icy floor. How will I rearrange the furniture? Well, I'll plan it after finals.

Since I have so many activity planned for this summer, I don't think I will have time to sit on the beach and enjoy the warm breeze with an ice cream cone in my hand. However, by the end of summer, I will have experienced something new, exciting, and, I hope, not too painful.

B. Look back at the essay in exercise A and then answer these questions.

1. *What is the present thesis?*

2. *Do all the body paragraphs begin with a topic sentence?*

3. *If not, write topic sentences that would fit the paragraphs that lack them.*

4. *Do those topic sentences prove the thesis?*

5. *Improve the thesis if possible.*

6. *How could the evidence in the body paragraphs be improved?*

7. *What else might be done to improve this essay?*

8. *What does the conclusion lack?*

9. *Write a better conclusion for this essay.*

INDEPENDENT STUDY: *Nouns* (answers in the back)

VI. A. Correct all errors in the use of plurals in the following sentences. Some sentences may be correct.

1. When I visited Oklahoma City, I saw many high building and crowded freeways.

2. Most parent agree with him, and I don't blame them.

3. Designers are blending these color together to create the new fashion.

4. The shrimp cocktail is one of my favorite.

5. People hit their brake and slide into other cars or telephone poles.

6. I would rather not take one of these type of jobs.

7. Usually the mall is crowded with teenager hanging out.

8. In college he played thirty-one game a season.

9. Will we be able to afford these nuisance in the future?

10. Young people run their own life, but they still listen to the opinions of the elders.

B.   The space shuttle *Columbia* will cut the cost of space exploration. This shuttle was designed to be used over and over again, so the cost of transporting astronaut to outer space will be greatly reduced. Before the shuttle was built, Apollo rocket were used to send astronaut to outer space. Scientist and engineer took several year to build each rocket, and once its mission was completed, the rocket could not be used again. The space shuttle will eliminate this expensive waste and allow man to enter space as easily as he enters our own atmosphere.

plural

PRONOUNS: Number

Pronouns are words that are used to replace nouns to avoid repetition. For example, the following sentence is unnecessarily bulky.

I bought a pair of navy blue shoes, but when I tried the shoes on with my dress, I found that the shoes were the wrong shade for my dress.

Notice how much pronouns improve it.

I bought a pair of navy blue shoes, but when I tried them on with my dress, I found that they were the wrong shade for it.

Pronouns may be singular or plural.

Singular Pronouns				Plural Pronouns		
he	him	his	himself	they	them	their
she	her	hers	herself	theirs	themselves	
it	its	itself				

Other variants like "hisself," "themself," "theyselves," and "theirselves" are never correct.

Pronouns should agree in number with the word or words they refer to.

FAULTY My sister would rather make clothes than buy it.

Here the singular pronoun "it" has been used to refer to the plural word "clothes." Instead the plural pronoun "them" should have been used.

REVISED My sister would rather make clothes than buy them.

In addition to being the same in number, pronouns must be of the same sex as the word they refer to. When the sex of that word is clear, people use pronouns correctly without thinking as in the sentences below.

My mother always dries her hair in the sun.

Here the feminine pronoun "her" is correctly used to refer to the feminine word "mother."

John made himself a salami sandwich.

Here the masculine pronoun "himself" is correctly used to refer to the masculine name "John."

However, when the sex of the word being replaced is not clear, people frequently make errors like the following.

FAULTY My grandmother can't pass a little child on the street without touching them.

In this sentence, the plural pronoun "them" has been incorrectly used to refer to "a little child," which is singular.

When a word can refer to either sex, writers often feel reluctant to replace it with a masculine word like "him." In the past, English used the masculine pronouns to include either male or female when the sex was not clear, but today many people feel this practice unfairly excludes females, and so most people prefer phrases like "he or she" or "him or her."

REVISED My grandmother can't pass a little child on the street without touching him or her.

Such errors can also be eliminated by making both pronoun and antecedent plural. This technique often produces the most graceful revision, especially when a sentence contains more than one pronoun.

REVISED My grandmother can't pass little children on the street without touching them.

Obviously such phrases as "a little child" and "a person" are singular. Sometimes the number of the word being replaced is not so clear, however. Words like "everybody" and "everyone" seem plural, but they are really singular. They refer to *each person* as an individual, even though together these people form a group. In contrast, plural words consider the group as a whole.

	Singular		*Plural*
none	nobody	no one	both
anyone	anybody	one	many
someone	somebody	each	a few
everyone	everybody	every	several

FAULTY Everybody should have Thanksgiving dinner with their families.

pronoun number

Here the plural pronoun "their" has been used to refer to a singular word "everybody." One of these words should be changed.

REVISED Everybody should have Thanksgiving dinner with his or her family.

REVISED People should have Thanksgiving dinner with their families.

Since "everybody" is singular, it must be referred to by "his or her." However, "people" is plural, so it can be used with the plural pronoun "their."
Sometimes these number changes require that the verb too be changed.

FAULTY Everyone was happy and smiling as they climbed onto the bus.

REVISED People were happy and smiling as they climbed onto the bus.

CORRECTION COMMENT: Pronouns should agree in number with the word or words they refer to.

EXERCISES Pronouns: Number

I. *Write sentences using the following words with at least one pronoun referring to each one.*

1. young people
2. a senior
3. everyone
4. everybody
5. every child

6. nobody
7. sociology courses
8. a woman
9. somebody
10. one of my sisters

II. *In the following sentences, circle each pronoun, and draw a line to its antecedent. Then change either the pronoun or its antecedent to correct any errors in numbers. Change the verbs too when necessary. Some sentences are correct.*

A.

1. **EXAMPLE** A woman has to take care of (themselves.) *herself*

2. Everyone disagrees with their parents.

3. Wherever a person travels, they will find historical landmarks.

4. Athletes take showers because it relaxes them.

5. A good student reviews their notes regularly.

6. Everybody has times when they need help.

7. The robbery victim is rarely compensated for their loss.

8. Someone left their cap in the kitchen.

9. A teacher should care about their students.

10. As television commercials become more effective, consumers must practice self-discipline to protect himself.

B.

1. Students start worrying about their midterms weeks before they take it.

2. After a cat has had a satisfying meal, he or she will usually clean and groom themselves.

3. Each person who has a garden has some idea of the design they want before they plant it.

4. Managers may not like the call, but they don't have to show how well he can insult the umpire.

5. Senior proms come every year, but people who go to it will never forget it.

6. If he was sitting and a woman would walk by, Bud would always stand, tip his old gray wide-brimmed hat, and greet them with a warm "Good morning."

7. Bruce Lee's movies seem kind of phony, but they show how the martial arts should be done.

8. Physical education courses are good for young boys because they will make men out of them.

9. Today people are becoming very materialistic. He wants to possess a thing the moment he sees it.

10. In times of war every citizen should do their best to protect their country.

C. 1. People can tell a little bit about a person by the way they keep up their garden.

2. Most parents don't have the money to send their child through school and also give them money to spend.

3. As a person gets the hang of budgeting their income successfully, they can get on with the rest of their life and worry about other problems.

4. Every city in the United States has their own police force. Their job is to protect and to serve the people of the community.

5. The rocket launcher is loaded with sharp plastic rockets that can be fired with such velocity that it sticks into the object it hits.

6. In most cases, the student will be penalized by grades they receive from the professor and in some cases get kicked out of school because of their poor grades.

7. Everyone should try taking some kind of dance at least one time in their life. One never knows; he may become a professional dancer.

8. My counselor listens to my problems and tries to help me out with it.

9. If a customer comes in often, the waitresses must get familiar with their names so that they may address them by it when they come in.

pronoun number

10. Physical education classes are great because it enables students to take a rest from their academic courses, it keeps students physically fit, and it allows them to meet other students.

III. *A. Correct errors in the pronouns in the following sentences. Change the verbs too if necessary. Some sentences may be correct.*

1. Many people live at home until they become able to take care of their selves.

2. After leaving the contaminated area, the soldiers must decontaminate themselves with the kit.

3. I like to see women taking pride in herself.

4. People who are old enough to take care of theyself have bills.

5. People can choose any books that they like, but my favorite books are my books of poetry.

6. College gives young people a chance to express theirselves.

7. The movie industry plays an important part in society. Without them, thousands of people would be out of jobs.

8. Working makes students feel that they are supporting themself instead of their parents supporting them.

9. The ship would also save me the hassle of moving my baggage each time I arrived at a new spot. I would just leave them in my cabin while at dock throughout the trip.

10. This course helps people help themselves.

B.   At the age of twelve, a person can be very easily excited, especially when they find that over the summer they will be going to Canada to visit one of his favorite relatives that he hasn't seen in two years. My trip to Canada when I was twelve strengthened an old relationship.

C.   A good musician must be strong. This person must be willing to sacrifice a lot of things in order to achieve his goal. At times this person won't be sure if he or she has a place to stay or where his next meal is coming from, but once they have overcome these obstacles, the rewards that can be obtained are worth the trouble they have to go through. An entertainer that has overcome these obstacles and then some is Stevie Wonder.

IV. *Read the following essay. As you read, correct any errors you find and note weaknesses that would require rewriting. Share your findings with your classmates in whatever way your teacher recommends. Then rewrite any parts your teacher assigns.*

With the health fade of today, people are trying many different way to stay healthy. They join health clubs, take exercise classes, jog, and take vitiamins all to keep healthy. Most people wouldn't need these things if they would just eat right, especially at breakfast. Everyone should eat something for breakfast to start out their day.

Breakfast is the easiest meal to prepare. All one has to do is pour some fortified cereal into a bowl and put milk on it, while they pop a couple of pieces of bread in the toaster and butter it when it's done. And for those people who are to lazy to fix breakfast for themselves, there is alway a nearby restaurant, like Jack in the Box, McDonald's, or Carl's Jr., that serves a good breakfast.

Breakfast is the most important meal of the day. After going without food for more than eight hours the person starts to feel fatiged and has to rely on the stored energy in the body until lunch, which is sometimes as much fifteen to sixteen hours from the last time they ate.

Eating breakfast regularly will make one healthier. Studies have shown that most people who don't eat breakfast, as compared with those who eat breakfast regularly, dont think as quickly, and don't have as good of reaction either. In most cases the people who didn't eat breakfast had a less positive and sometimes even a negative attatude toward their life and their jobs.

I feel we should all eat a good breakfast on a regular bases instead of trying to replace it by taking vitamins.

INDEPENDENT STUDY Pronouns: Number (answers in the back)

V. A. *Correct the following sentences so that the pronouns agree with their antecedents in number. Change the verbs too if necessary. Some sentences are correct.*

1. How many times does a person carry an extra pair of shoes with them?

2. Some people disliked their high schools, saying it was a waste of time and nothing was achieved there.

3. Sometimes a person dreams he will be famous.

4. Many years will be remembered because of the joys or sadness it brings.

5. I'm sure every child is afraid of something in the first grade and remembers their fear.

6. The prison walls are telling the prisoner that what they did was wrong.

7. A working student doesn't have time to go out as they would like to.

8. All the people packed out of the bus and went their separate ways.

9. A person who wants to be independent should have their own apartment.

10. Every young person needs someone to tell them about life.

B.   The best athletes in the world compete in the Olympics. These people have devoted most of their twenty-four-hour days to working hard and striving to be the best in his or her respective events. Some of the great athletes who have participated in the Olympics are Jesse Owens, Mark Spitz, Jean Claude Killy, and Bob Beamon. These athletes worked hard enough to get to the very top. Each day of their scheduled workout, each person went over a series of different exercises to keep their muscles in tone.

pronoun number

PRONOUNS: Person

In addition to agreeing in number, a pronoun must also agree in person with the word or words it refers to.

First Person Pronouns

Singular (to refer to the writer)

I   me   my
mine myself

Plural (to refer to a group that the writer is part of)

we   us   our
ours   ourselves

Second Person Pronouns

Singular (to refer to the reader)

you   your
yours yourself

Plural (to refer to a group that the reader is part of)

you   your
yours yourselves

Third Person Pronouns

Singular (to refer to a person being written about)

he   him   his   himself
she   her   hers   herself

(to refer to a thing being written about)

it   its   itself

Plural (to refer to people or things being written about)

they   them   their
theirs   themselves

The third person pronouns are obviously perfect for essay writing because they are used for people or things being written about. Also, because most nouns fall in this group, the third person pronouns are usually correct. The first person pronouns are valuable too because personal experiences make excellent evidence in informal essays.

On the other hand, second person pronouns are usually incorrect in student essays. Although they are used loosely in speech to refer to people in general, strictly speaking they should be used to refer only to the reader or the reader's group. They are also used to give instructions and may offend a sensitive reader by appearing to give uninvited advice. Finally, second person pronouns are often incorrectly used instead of first or third person words, as in the following example.

FAULTY Anyone would be foolish to buy a car that you cannot afford.

Referring to a person being talked about, "anyone" is in the third person group, so it should be referred to by a third person pronoun like "he" instead of the second person pronoun "you."

REVISED Anyone would be foolish to buy a car that he or she cannot afford.

Most errors in pronoun person can be corrected by eliminating the second person pronouns, "you," "your," "yours," "yourself," and "yourselves." Here is another example.

FAULTY We got report cards, and your parents had to sign and return them.

This sentence uses the second person pronoun "your" in the first person situation. The reader's parents didn't have to sign the report cards, so the second person pronoun "your" should be replaced by the first person pronoun "our."

REVISED We got report cards, and our parents had to sign and return them.

When referring to people in general, use words like "people," "students," "everybody," and third person pronouns to refer to them.

FAULTY When you buy new clothes, you never know what you are getting.

The writer is talking about all people, not just the reader, so third person words should be substituted for second person pronouns.

REVISED When people buy new clothes, they never know what they are getting.

Sometimes reducing the number of clauses creates the best revision.

FAULTY Visiting a college gives a person a good idea of what it would be like if you went to that school.

This sentence has a second person pronoun "you," referring to a third person word, "person." The pronoun "he" could be substituted, or the clause "if he went" could be replaced by "to go" for a less wordy sentence.

REVISED Visiting a college gives a person a good idea of what it would be like to go to that school.

Unfortunately, second person pronouns are sometimes hard to find because they lurk behind instructions, requests, and commands as understood subjects.

FAULTY One should think carefully, and don't rush.

The subject of the verb "do" in the second clause is "you" understood, and it's incorrectly used to refer to the third person word "one." This sentence is best corrected by reducing the second clause to a second verb in the first clause.

pronoun person

REVISED One should think carefully and not rush.

CORRECTION COMMENT: Most errors in pronoun person can be corrected by eliminating the second person pronouns, "you," "your," "yours," "yourself," and "yourselves."

EXERCISES   Pronouns: Person

I. Write sentences as requested below.

    1. Write two sentences with three first person pronouns each.

    2. Write two sentences with three third person pronouns each.

3. *Write two sentences with two third person singular pronouns each.*

4. *Write two sentences with two third person plural pronouns each.*

5. *Write two sentences each of which correctly uses one first person pronoun and one third person pronoun.*

II. *Correct errors in person in the following sentences. Change the verbs too if necessary. Some sentences may be correct.*

A. 1. One should minimize your coffee consumption.

2. Voting gives a person a chance to affect your country.

3. Anyone would like to improve your chances of getting a job.

4. When we went out on dates, your parents always told you to be home by midnight.

5. I would like to read everything twice, but you don't have enough time.

6. Everyone who goes to the Museum of Modern Art will enjoy yourself.

7. One should seek professional help, and don't try to cure yourself.

8. Take my advice. One should never work on a holiday weekend.

9. College teaches a person to be independent, to do things for himself and not let other people do everything for you.

10. Most of our lives are spent working and studying. It is refreshing to get a vacation and do the things you like to do.

B. 1. One can learn to communicate with the lower forms of life if you will take the time.

2. Reaching back into one's past for your earliest memory can be an enlightening experience.

3. The wife must obey her father-in-law and mother-in-law totally because if you don't you are considered bad.

4. Four years ago I moved into a house with two guys named Mike and David. They're both pretty nice guys, but sometimes they get on your nerves.

5. I usually don't go anywhere when I have a cold because I feel terrible. You have a fever, sore throat, and other uncomfortable symptoms.

6. Everyone who hasn't tried disco dancing should try it. You will probably get a great thrill.

7. One day I happened to be in her area so I decided to drop in on her. As she opened the door, you could see the entry way sparkling freshly.

8. A person would never touch the stereo because someone who did would find a 250-pound monster yelling and jumping on you.

9. I detested changing the oil of cars, especially for those customers that stood over you and watched your every move.

10. My roommate had hardly any fingernails at all. If he ever had to peel something off, he would ask you to help him.

C. 1. Many people on their jobs have check pools into which you pay a certain amount of money.

2. A person can get to know someone by offering him help with his problems.

3. In the winter months I need extra clothing to protect me and keep me warm. I don't like wearing extra clothing because I feel tied down. Some coats are very heavy with thick linings, and you have to wear heavy sweaters and pants.

4. I dislike driving in the heavy rain. The roads are very slippery and cause accidents. You have to be very careful and especially watch out for other drivers.

5. People who plant gardens are creative. You have to know what you want to plant and how much and what you want to put where.

6. I know I will enjoy the food at McDonald's no matter what you order.

7. The waiters and waitresses serve fresh soup and salad and then the meal of one's choice. They take time with a person and make you feel special.

8. If a person wants to enjoy life more, watch your eating habits. When you see five extra pounds, diet for a week to get them off.

9. When I ask questions about something, they never get answered because the teacher always tells you, "I answered that question in class."

pronoun person

10. Friendship can be important in college, but I have done without it. I learned that you have to keep myself company and study by myself.

D. My job as a cashier is very exhausting. You have to concentrate on pleasing the customer and also being very careful that you take the correct amount of cash on every transaction. Also, you are standing on your feet all day and get really tired. It is difficult to study after you have worked all day and are exhausted. It is also difficult to use your brain if it has been working all day and concentrating on other things.

III. A. *Beginning with a summary sentence, write a paragraph telling what happens to a person who gets hungry while on campus. Use only third person pronouns.*

B. Write a paragraph telling what happens to someone who must register late for a class. Begin with a summary sentence and use only third person pronouns.

IV. A. *Examine the following essay and mark its strengths and weaknesses. Some weaknesses may be of a type that has not been covered in class. Compare your findings in class and discuss with your teacher ways the weaknesses might be corrected.*

My elementary school, Luther Burbank, has really changed since I attended there. There has been some major changes to make the quality of the school take a big drop.

When I was there the school grounds were always sparkling clean. There was a beautiful garden of roses in the front of the school that the gardener cherished dearly. No student dared to walk near the bed of roses or even on the narrow strip of grass that surrounded the roses. Now the roses are very shabby looking. The rose bushes need pruning and when the roses bloom they look sick and brittle. I have passed by the school when the children are playing between the rose bushes and they're even throwing potato chip and candy wrappers down and on the rose vine. Not just in the front garden is there trash but on the playground trash is found. You never saw any trash on the playground when I was there. It was just something you never thought about doing. Even if some careless person did throw something down, someone else would soon pick it up. And you got punished for littering on the school grounds. One other thing that has changed the atmosphere is the building. The building is looking drab. The paint is wearing thin and a lot of the foundation is cracking. The window shades are fading and also tearing. It sure wasn't like that when I was there. The building was always kept painted and if the cement was cracking it was fixed immediately. I never saw a faded shade (I was shade monitor) because every time you turned around they were replacing them with new ones.

The students that went to Burbank were very well behaved children. Very seldom would you see a kid talk back to a teacher, let alone cuss at a teacher. Now you might hear anything come out of a student's mouth. They now tell the teacher what to do instead of the teacher telling them what to do. We never had a lot of fights at Burbank. The students were mostly very friendly. Not long ago someone told me that a fourth grader brought a gun to school in order to shoot an enemy. Also when I was going there the majority of the students were neat and clean. Now you see a lot of children who come to school filthy because the parents don't care enough to wash their clothes.

When I attended Burbank I had the best teachers in Little Rock. They really cared about the students. There was no fooling around in the classroom because the teachers didn't put up with it. The parents really worked hard with the teachers to keep their child on the right track. And in the classroom learning went on. We had a good time when we were learning because the teacher kept our interest and spent her time teaching. A good deal of that has changed now. Most of the teachers I had are gone. The teachers that have replaced them aren't as dedicated. The students run the class instead of the teacher and the teacher is too scared to discipline the students for fear of a parent coming down to school and cussing at her or threatening her. Few parents come to school to talk to the teacher to find out how their child is doing, instead they wait until the child is going to flunk before they talk to the teacher to see what they can do. It's too late then.

I'm sad to say that my elementary school has gone to the dogs. Everything that I loved it for has taken a drastic step downward. The students don't cherish Burbank. The parents don't cherish Burbank. And seemingly the faculty don't cherish Burbank. The school where I learned to read and write is deteriorating.

B. *Write an essay on one of the following topics. Narrow your topic; then write a good thesis and outline. Finally, flesh it out with specific evidence and examples. As you write, be conscious of the strengths and weaknesses of the essay above, and by your example show your teacher how it should have been written.*

a place that has changed	joining a new group
elderly people	car repairs
a special occasion	income tax

INDEPENDENT STUDY Pronouns: Person *(answers in the back)*

V. ***A.*** *Eliminate any errors in person from the following sentences. Cross out the incorrect words and write the correct ones above them. Change the verbs too when necessary.*

1. Our evening was full of laughter. It was a perfect time spent with your best friends, great food, and a beautiful sunset.

2. When her children become ill, a mother will sacrifice any and everything to improve their condition. A mother will stand behind you when no one else will.

3. When I worked at Sears, the other employees were always trying to help you with your work.

4. Since living on my own, I've learned the hard way that there's more to being on your own than staying up late, going to parties, and being your own boss.

5. I discovered that you enjoy the drive to Denver when you do it on a motorcycle.

6. I learned you have to work for what you want.

7. We walked into the reception room and announced to the hostess that we had reservations. From that room, you could see the whole dining area.

8. Every time one of these parts came up in the movie, I suddenly felt as if I were right up on the screen with the actors.

pronoun person

9. If my parents had sat down and talked with me about all the problems of moving away, I would have understood more about the responsibility of having your own place.

10. Having a small child also creates a lot of extra laundry for a mother, especially when you have a daughter who enjoys washing her hands with a clean cloth every time she eats.

B.   I had trouble studying for that history class. All those dates you had to memorize made you sick to your stomach. What bothered me most was all the reading you had to do. I could only remember so much after reading eight chapters. That class was so boring that you didn't read the book until the very last minute after you'd studied those notes that you were half asleep on in class.

PRONOUNS: Form

With More than One Person

Besides agreeing with the words they refer to, pronouns change with their function in the sentence. A writer who has settled on the third person plural pronoun, for example, still must choose between "them," "they," "their," "theirs," and "themselves." This is usually easy. Most people wouldn't be tempted to write "Them want to come with we." However, sometimes beginning writers confuse subject and nonsubject pronoun forms when words for two people are used together.

Subject Pronouns	Nonsubject Pronouns
I	me
we	us
he	him
she	her
they	them

The subject pronouns should be used for subjects of clauses, and the nonsubject forms should be used in all other places. Here's a typical error:

FAULTY Me and my mother went to the supermarket.

The nonsubject pronoun "me" has been incorrectly used as a subject. Instead the subject form "I" should have been used.

There's another way to find the correct pronoun form. Since native speakers of English automatically use the correct form when there's only one word for a person, the sentence can be checked with one person at a time. "Me went to the supermarket" is obviously incorrect, so "Me and my mother went to the supermarket" is also wrong. "I went to the supermarket" is correct, and adding another person doesn't change the form of the pronoun. Usually a writer puts himself last, so that "I and my mother" should be turned around to "My mother and I."

pronoun form

REVISED My mother and I went to the supermarket.

Here's another example.

FAULTY He asked my sister and I to play with him.

Here the subject form "I" has been incorrectly used since "he," not "I," is the subject of the verb "asked." The nonsubject form "me" should have been used here. To check this the other way, "He asked I to play with him" is incorrect, and "He asked me to play with him" is correct, so "He asked my sister and me to play with him" is also correct.

REVISED He asked my sister and me to play with him.

Sometimes a sentence combines two pronoun forms.

FAULTY They agreed to double date with he and I.

Since the pronouns "he and I" are not working as subjects, they are incorrectly used here. The nonsubject forms should be used. To check this the other way, "They agreed to double date with he" is wrong, and "They agreed to double date with him" is right. Similarly "They agreed to double date with I" is incorrect, and "they agreed to double date with me" is correct.

REVISED They agreed to double date with him and me.

CORRECTION COMMENT: The subject pronouns should be used for subjects of clauses, and the nonsubject forms should be used in all other places.

EXERCISES Pronouns: Form

I.   Write sentences using the following word groups correctly.

A. 1. Marsha and me   6. them and their children

     2. my cousin and I   7. Mr. Stevens and he

     3. my boy friend and me   8. they and the cheerleaders

     4. grandmother and she   9. my uncle and her

     5. the teachers and us   10. my cousins and them

B. 1. his brother and we   6. she and Donald

     2. he and his daughter   7. her and me

     3. Gerald and me   8. he and she

     4. Molly and him   9. she and I

     5. him and his cousin   10. her and him

II. Check the forms of the pronouns in the following sentences and correct the errors. Some sentences are correct.

A. 1. Me and the saleslady removed the price tags.

     2. The instructor asked Diana and I to collect the papers.

     3. Him and his brother lived behind the store.

     4. Me and my family enjoy eating out.

     5. Aunt Louise visited my sister and I in Hawaii.

     6. My grandfather gave quarters to my brother and me.

     7. Her and the supervisor often eat lunch together.

     8. He and a friend attended a lecture on Chinese Art.

9. Me and my cousins would sit in the house and drink soda all day because it was too hot to go outside.

10. Her and I used to dance together most of the time in our dancing session.

B.
1. The policeman saw me and him run behind the car.

2. I remember when me and some friends of mine took a ride on our motorcycles to Highland Lake.

3. My aunt used to like to play with me and my sister.

4. Me and my father are beginning to have too many conflicts.

5. He and his friends like to ride around and listen to the radio.

6. Susie, my best friend, asked my sisters and I to go to the lake with her on Saturday.

7. One couple wanted to take a picture of April and I falling.

8. At the end of the summer, me and my family went to King's Island.

9. All week she told my husband and I that she really loved that special desk.

10. One day me and two of my friends went over to Monique's house for lunch.

C.
1. My mom spends a lot of time with my brother and I.

2. I've discovered that me and him have similar personalities.

3. They and their friends have much more freedom than we did when we were young.

4. She and her husband are trying to find a bigger home.

5. One day me and about five of my friends went up to Jefferson High.

6. She kept me and my husband awake for the first six nights she was home.

7. Me and him have many things in common.

8. Every time a new student came to school, we would always introduce ourselves and ask he or she to play with us.

9. One Halloween when me and my brother went trick-or-treating, we received apples.

10. I recall one time when my father let my sister and I gather firewood.

D.   I remember another time my grandmother convinced me of her kindness. A few years ago my brother and I suffered a bad bike accident. Both my parents work and could not stay home with us while we were recovering. My grandmother came down from Athens to stay with my brother and I as long

pronoun form

as necessary. It was a lot of hard work for her. She made sure we got our medication and felt comfortable. In the long afternoons we would talk and play cards. Just having her with my brother and I made me feel better.

III. *Correct the errors in pronoun form in the following sentences. Some sentences are correct (answers in the back).*

1. Her and my dad went to sleep.

2. My sister and I have three children each.

3. One day when me and my friend were coming home from a movie we stopped at a traffic light.

4. In my childhood my brother and me had many great times.

5. Once me and a couple of my friends went up to Memphis for a day.

6. When there is something happening on the weekend, me and my sister may go.

7. He and I like to be the best dressed couple there.

8. The professor gave he and I the highest grades in the class.

9. Me and some friends were in the weight room, and there were some girls lifting weights also.

10. We could talk about some of the good times me and him have had.

"Who" and "Whom"

So many people are confused by "who" and "whom" that these words are often avoided, but the distinction between them is really not difficult to master. "Who" is a subject form and "whom" is a nonsubject form, so "who" should be used as a subject of a clause and "whom" in all other places.

FAULTY Whom broke that lock?

The nonsubject form "whom" has been incorrectly used here as a subject instead of the subject form "who."

There's another way to determine whether "who" or "whom" is correct. "Whom" should be used where "him" would fit and "who" where "he" would fit. In the sentence above "He broke that lock" is correct and "Him broke that lock" is not, so "who" should be used instead of "whom."

REVISED Who broke that lock?

Unfortunately, the words of clauses that begin with "who" and "whom" are often in unusual order, so that the subject may be hard to determine. When in doubt about the subject of such a clause, change the words to a more familiar order to find the subject.

FAULTY Who should the director have hired?

This question could be changed to read "The director should have hired "who." Now "who" is clearly not a subject, so obviously the nonsubject form "whom" should have been used. To use the other approach, "The director should have hired him" is correct and "The director should have hired he" is incorrect, so that "whom" is correct and "who" is incorrect. Now the words can be returned to their original order with the correct pronoun form.

REVISED Whom should the director have hired?

"Who" and "whom" often begin dependent clauses, so that when there is more than one clause, be sure to analyze the dependent clause, not the independent one.

FAULTY The director hired Harold, who he can trust.

Here "who" is in a dependent clause which can be changed to "He can trust who." In this sentence, "who" is obviously incorrect because it's not working as a subject. Also "He can trust him" is correct, and "He can trust he" is incorrect, and so "whom" is the correct form for this sentence.

REVISED The director hired Harold, whom he can trust.

Here's a similar example.

FAULTY The director hired Harold, whom is honest.

Here "whom" has been incorrectly used as the subject of the dependent clause. Using the other approach, "He is honest" is correct and "Him is honest" is not, and so "who" would be correct in this sentence.

REVISED The director hired Harold, who is honest.

Remember that sometimes a dependent clause may be inserted into the middle of an independent one.

FAULTY Marion Stewart, who he evicted, will testify.

"He evicted him" is correct, so "whom" should be used.

REVISED Marion Stewart, whom he evicted, will testify.

"Whoever" can be used in the same places as "who," and "whomever" can be used in the same places as "whom."

EXERCISES *Pronouns: Form*

I. *Change the following sentences to questions by substituting either "who" or "whom" for one of the words and adding a question mark at the end.*

1. Sam is always late.

2. Mr. Marcos brought the secretary some flowers.

3. They left their daughter with my husband.

4. Debra showed Ms. Sand the letter from the registrar.

5. The dungeon master refused to give us any information about the wizard.

6. The union members chose Jerusalem Slim to visit Joe in jail.

7. Oberon ordered Titania to give him the changeling.

8. The Western Airlines passenger representative called my mother about the ticket for Vanessa.

9. Joyce named her son after Pete Seeger.

10. Ashley asked Scarlett to take care of Melanie.

II. *Using "who" or "whom," rewrite the following pairs of sentences into single sentences.*

1. We looked everywhere for the hobbit. He found the invisibility ring.

2. She went to Charleston to visit a friend. She had met him at Oberlin.

3. Please give me the telephone number of the woman. She runs the Wildlife Rescue Operation.

4. The policeman accused Thomas. He had been out of town on the night of the robbery.

5. The delivery man drives a white van. He brought us our newspaper.

6. Calvin Jones wants to talk to them. He rents their house in Ohio.

7. The public relations manager called me on the telephone. I had written him a letter about my vacuum cleaner.

8. The lady became very sick. She ate some mushrooms from her lawn.

9. Two girls from Japan are staying in my camper. They want to see Nebraska.

10. The salespeople can buy the product at wholesale prices. We call them distributors.

III. *Write the sentences assigned below.*

1. *three sentences with "who"*

2. *three sentences with "whom"*

3. *three sentences with "who" in a dependent clause*

4. *three sentences with "whom" in a dependent clause*

5. *three sentences with "who" in a dependent clause inserted into the middle of an independent clause*

6. *three sentences with "whom" in a dependent clause inserted into the middle of an independent clause*

IV. *Correct errors in the use of "who" and "whom" in the following sentences. Some sentences are correct.*

A.
1. Whom is the boss here?
2. You gave the money to who?
3. Who won the last game?
4. She married who?
5. Whom wants to come with me?
6. They suspect whom?
7. Whom left these papers on the floor?
8. Whom did you visit?
9. Who did you recommend?
10. Who should we avoid?

B.
1. Who do they prefer?
2. Who should have handled this case?
3. They take orders from Brown, who runs the repair shop.
4. They take orders from Brown, who they despise.
5. Max knows the woman who wrote this article.
6. I need a secretary whom can type.
7. My father, whom left home years ago, came back for Christmas.
8. The man who operates the copy machine owns a sailboat.
9. Mrs. Tope, who took care of my children, has moved to Palm Springs.
10. Mr. Tope, who they feared, had a large, white beard.

pronoun form

V. *Correct errors in the use of "who" and "whom" in the following sentences. Some sentences are correct (answers in the back).*

1. Give the ribbon to the man who crosses the finish line first.
2. Mary Stone, who invented this process, has the patent on it.
3. Who is that letter from?
4. They usually select people who can think for themselves.
5. The people whom they visited have an estate on the mountain.
6. The witnesses who disappeared know the real story.
7. With whom would you prefer to travel?
8. They gave a gardenia to whoever they wanted kidnapped.

9. They gave a rose to whoever looked lonely.

10. They can never predict who the winner will choose.

With "than" and "as"

Problems with pronoun form also occur after the words "than" and "as." These words usually introduce clauses, though sometimes the verb is understood rather than stated. When using one of these words, mentally supply the missing words to determine the correct pronoun form.

FAULTY My sister is older than me (am).

Mentally supplying the missing word "am" shows that "me" is the incorrect pronoun form, because "I am" is correct, not "me am." Since the pronoun is the subject of the verb "am," the subject form "I" must be used, not "me," even though the verb is not stated.

REVISED My sister is older than I (am).

Here's another example.

FAULTY No one else is as fast as him (is).

Supplying the missing word tells us that the subject form "he" is needed.

REVISED No one else is as fast as he (is).

However, subject forms are not always used after these words, and incorrect pronoun form can sometimes completely change the meaning of a sentence.

He visits her more than me.

He visits her more than I.

He visits her as much as me.

He visits her as much as I.

Supplying the missing words in the sentences above shows that they mean very different things.

He visits her more than (he visits) me.

He visits her more than I (do).

He visits her as much as (he visits) me.

He visits her as much as I (do).

EXERCISES Pronouns: Form

I. Write the sentences described below.

1. three sentences with subject pronouns after "than"

2. three sentences with nonsubject pronouns after "than"

3. *three sentences with subject pronouns after "as"*

4. *three sentences with nonsubject pronouns after "as"*

II. *Correct errors in the pronouns in the following sentences. Think of the missing words to determine which form is correct.*

A. 1. Wendell is shorter than me.

2. Sharon is not as fast as him.

3. No one can believe she is heavier than he.

4. It's odd because he's four years older than me.

5. Today we have become much richer than them.

6. People in Asia are really the same as us.

7. I can boss her around because she is shorter than I.

8. I haven't met a finer or more enjoyable person than he.

9. I used to think they thought they were better than me.

10. The oldest person in the show was a year younger than me.

B. *(answers in the back)*

1. They don't realize that these women have the same purpose as them.

2. Her other students are moving faster than we.

3. He gets mad because someone smaller than him can beat him.

4. I was never very familiar with what they were saying because they were all older than me.

5. He said that he had known me for a long time and that I could handle the car even better than him.

6. I learned that he was ten years older than me and was a student at the University of the Philippines.

7. He may learn faster than I, but he's not as intelligent as I.

8. He is seven years older than me, and when I was still a boy, I remember him listening to the baseball and basketball games on the radio.

9. Even though he is short, he's just as old as me.

10. Her husband is much stronger than her.

pronoun form

III. *This paragraph contains pronoun form errors of mixed types. Cross out the errors and write the correct form in the margin.*

The first time I remember being treated like a child occurred when I was about four years old. I had big plans for a tea party and wanted to invite my friend whom lived down the street. When I arrived at her house, I found that she was not there, and in desperation I invited her sister, whom was two years older than us. This move was very bold. Her and my friend hated each other, so I hardly knew and greatly feared this girl. A short while later, me and her and our dolls were seated around a cardboard box set with jar lids and real food—raisins. I was fiddling nervously, afraid my set-up would be found wanting, when I glanced at my guest and saw her smiling at me, her eyes twinkling. I was shocked. I was prepared to be considered incompetent but not to be considered "cute."

IV. *A. Write a paragraph about an experience you shared with someone when you were very young. Use pronouns in situations like the ones we studied in this section. Begin the paragraph with a summary sentence.*

B. Write a paragraph about what you and your best friend have in common. Use pronouns in situations like the ones we studied in this section. Begin the paragraph with a summary sentence.

NOUN AND PRONOUN REVIEW *(answers in the back)*

I. *The following sentences contain errors in number, person, and form. Change the nouns, pronouns, and verbs if necessary to correct them.*

A.
1. When I am writing an essay and you hear your mother yelling at your brother, studying is impossible.

2. His answers never seem to be the answers an adult would give, but it is usually logical.

3. Everyone who watches the cheerleaders try out thinks cheerleading is really fun.

4. When an overweight person steps on a crowded bus, they roll their eyes at the thought of having to stand and hold themselves up for the duration of the ride.

5. Why, it's unheard of for a grandmother to spank a grandchild. They're supposed to spoil you.

6. Me and my sister together weighed less than him.

7. The way she smiled, all thirty-two teeth together and white as they could be, made you wonder if me and her were meant to be.

8. Sometimes my best friends get on the bus, and you talk to them so you don't get bored.

9. I had been looking for my clothes and found out when I calmed down that it was right in front of me.

10. I proved that smaller people can do whatever his mind wants him to do. If you just concentrate and don't let anything stand in the way of you and your goals, you can become whatever you want.

B.
1. The smoker whom is always looking for a cigarette or a match may seem happy, but are they really?

2. All the seniors agreed on the steak dinner because the other choices would dirty your clothes because it would have been too greasy.

3. I don't mind riding the bus, but when you're in a hurry things seem to go wrong on them.

4. This person at times is not sure whether he or she has a place to stay or where their next meal is coming from, but once they have overcome these obstacles the rewards are worth the trouble you have to go through.

5. Everyone has crazy things happen to them, but the funniest things happen when you are a child.

6. Every young adult should get a summer job because they can save up more money to buy a car. You can also buy yourself some school clothes so that your parents won't have to buy them for you.

7. Physical education classes take my mind off the pressures of school. It provides the perfect time and place to let yourself loose.

8. A person may think they have passed the exam with at least a C but finds out that the scale is so high you end up with an F. Teachers don't care how hard a person studies. If their grade matches the scale in such a way, the teacher does not care if you end up with a D or an F. A grade to a teacher is just a letter, but to a student they are their future.

9. Around the corner came a devil, a goblin, and a witch. I stood there and stared. I had never seen such things walking around before, but I wasn't scared because they were smaller than me.

10. There are a lot of thing in the outdoors that can hurt or even kill a person, for example, snake, poison oak, wild animals, hunters, and forest fires.

VERBS: Present Tense

In standard English the correct form of a verb depends on its subject and its tense. Tense indicates time. The present tense is used to express things that happen or are true when the words are spoken or written. Most present tense verbs in English are always the same, always without ending, except that a third person singular subject must have a verb that ends in s.

Present Tense "to help"

	Singular	*Plural*
first person	I help	we help
second person	you help	you help
third person	he helps	they help
	she helps	
	it helps	

FAULTY She respect nature.

Third person singular subjects must have verbs that end in s. "She" is a third person singular subject, so its verb must end in s.

REVISED She respects nature.

The spelling rules for adding s to nouns (pages 102–103) also apply to verbs.

A few common English verbs are siightly irregular in the third person singular form.

present verb

Present Tense "to do"

	Singular	*Plural*
first person	I do	we do
second person	you do	you do
third person	he does	they do
	she does	
	it does	

Present Tense "to go"

	Singular	*Plural*
first person	I go	we go
second person	you go	you go

third person	he goes	they go
	she goes	
	it goes	

Present Tense "to have"

	Singular	*Plural*
first person	I have	we have
second person	you have	you have
third person	he has	they have
	she has	
	it has	

If these verbs were strictly regular, the third person singular forms would be "dos," "gos," and "haves" instead of "does," "goes," and "has," but outside of these variations, these verbs too fit the pattern. They are always the same, always without ending, except in the third person singular where they always end in *s*.

Here are some typical errors.

FAULTY He don't really listen to anyone.

The third person singular subject "he" must have a verb that ends in *s*, so "does," not "do," is correct.

REVISED He doesn't really listen to anyone.

FAULTY They has three children at home.

"They" is not a third person singular subject. It is third person *plural,* and so its verb must not end in *s*. Therefore, "have," not "has," is correct.

REVISED They have three children at home.

Unfortunately, the most irregular verb is a very common one.

Present Tense "to be"

	Singular	*Plural*
first person	I am	we are
second person	you are	you are
third person	he is	they are
	she is	
	it is	

Once more, the third person singular verb ends in *s* and the others don't, but this time the first person singular verb "am" is also irregular.

This verb causes frequent errors. People frequently substitute "be" for the correct forms given above.

FAULTY He be the best catcher in the league.

The chart of the verb "to be" forms shows that "is," not "be," should be used with "he."

REVISED He is the best catcher in the league.

FAULTY They be too late to get tickets.

The chart shows that "are," not "be," is the correct verb form for "they."

REVISED They are too late to get tickets.

All singular subjects (except "I" and "you") take the third person singular verb form, the form that ends in *s*.

she	Kathy	
it	he or she	
a person	John or Mary	
audience	honesty	helps, does, goes, has,
my mother	exercising	is, needs, gets, etc.
school	to read	
everybody	music	
man		

All plural subjects take the third person plural verb form, the form that does not end in *s*.

present verb

they	he and she	
people	John and Mary	
audiences	honesty and sincerity	help, do, go, have,
mothers	dieting and exercising	are, need, get, etc.
schools	to read and to write	
both	music and art	
men		

The charts above give sample subjects of many kinds. If you are in doubt about the correct verb form for a particular kind of subject, look on these charts for a similar one and use the verb form associated with it.

FAULTY Listening to recordings of the big bands are always fun.

The chart shows that the *ing* subject "exercising" must have a verb ending in *s,* so the *ing* subject "listening" must also have a verb ending in *s.*

REVISED Listening to recordings of the big bands is always fun.

FAULTY High school and college is very different.

The chart shows that two subjects joined by "and" must have a verb that does not end in *s*.

REVISED High school and college are very different.

The information above can be summed up in the following rule: In the present tense, singular subjects (except "I" and "you") must have verbs that end in *s*. No other subjects should.

he is	they are
cat is	cats are
school does	schools do
it does	they do
box has	boxes have
mother has	mothers have
visitor stays	visitors stay
boy friend wishes	boy friends wish
child watches	children watch
plumber fixes	plumbers fix
student worries	students worry

Another look at this rule reveals that either a subject or a verb may end in *s*, but not both.

FAULTY Summer jobs gives young people valuable experience.

Verbs with plural subjects should not end in *s*. If the subject ends in *s*, the verb should not. The plural subject "jobs" ends in *s*, so the verb should not.

REVISED Summer jobs give young people valuable experience.

The rule above cannot be applied to words that already end in *s*. Subjects like "waitress," "loss," "Charles," "United States" and verbs like "miss," "caress," "fuss," "embarrass" don't follow the rule because they always have an *s* at the end.

Pronouns like "who," "which," and "that" may be singular or plural, depending on the words they refer to.

I like the lady who teaches French.

I like the people who teach there.

In the first sentence, the subject of the dependent clause "who" refers to "lady" and therefore is singular, and so the singular verb form "teaches" is required. In the second sentence, "who" refers to "people" and therefore is plural, and so the plural verb form "teach" is required.

FAULTY People who goes to work have to shovel ashes from their cars.

The subject "who" refers to "people," so it is plural, and its verb should not end in "s."

REVISED People who go to work have to shovel ashes from their cars.

CORRECTION COMMENT: In the present tense, singular subjects (except "I" and "you") must have verbs that end in *s*. No other subjects should.

EXERCISES *Verbs: Present Tense*

I. A. *Correctly complete the second sentence of the following pairs by rewriting the first one to agree with the changed subject.*

   1. The teams take the field.

       The team _____ .

   2. The dictionary gives plural forms.

       Dictionaries _____ .

   3. The zoo protects the snow leopards.

       Zoos _____ .

   4. The professors expect too much.

       The professor _____ .

   5. This restaurant has reasonable prices.

       These restaurants _____ .

   6. The planes are always late.

       The plane _____ .

   7. A couple sits down.

       Couples _____ .

   8. The audiences always cheer.

       The audience _____ .

   9. Birch trees grow outside my window.

       A birch tree _____ .

   10. My brother has courage.

       My brothers _____ .

present verb

B. *Circle the verb forms that go with the subjects on the left. Cross out the verb forms that don't.*

1. she	raises	insists	is	do
2. he	visit	has	wants	be
3. they	risk	ask	do	are
4. studying	offer	begins	have	works
5. my sister	resent	step	puzzles	have
6. to visit	becomes	exhaust	makes	does
7. Raymond and he	catches	shift	anticipate	races
8. hope	surge	lift	keep	has
9. waiter	bring	recommend	are	snaps
10. pity or envy	destroys	provoke	do	disturb

C. *Write the sentences described below.*

1. Write five present tense sentences that have singular subjects.

2. Write five present tense sentences that have plural subjects.

3. Write five present tense sentences with subjects connected by "or."

4. Write five present tense sentences with subjects ending in ing.

D. *Return to the sentences you wrote for exercise C. Put two lines under the verbs and one line under the subjects. Check that those subjects and verb forms are correct.*

E. *Correct the verb forms when necessary so that they agree with the subjects on the left.*

1. cheating	helps	weaken	destroy	prevents
2. everybody	know	have	offers	avoids
3. I	respect	wishes	tries	see
4. it	do	slip	vary	cuts
5. neighbors	invade	rebuilds	washes	has
6. she and my sister	break	celebrates	laugh	joins
7. hesitation	limit	provides	lead	does
8. they	attempts	prevent	climbs	rows
9. you	hopes	works	visit	dance
10. both	enters	choose	prefer	resents

II. *Put parentheses around the prepositional phrases, two lines under the verbs, and one line under the subjects in the following sentences. Then cross out incorrect verb forms and write the correct ones above them.*

A.
1. She help me with my homework.
2. They go to church every Sunday.
3. Our cat have a large fluffy tail.
4. The fireplace is clean.
5. She close the door quietly.
6. James and Monica has a new apartment.
7. James or Monica has a new apartment.
8. Suitcases does not fit behind the back seat.
9. Dogs always digs up my vegetable garden.
10. Welfare and charity is humiliating.

B.
1. A person need help sometimes.
2. People need help sometimes.
3. Everybody need help sometimes.
4. Swimming build his back muscles.
5. Swimming and rowing build his back muscles.
6. Home gardens adds beauty to one's yard.
7. I wonder if the fountain of youth really do exist.
8. A person have to win many small competitions to go to the Olympics.
9. Valencia and our father get into it all the time.
10. When our teeth starts to turn yellow, we use baking soda.

present verb

C.
1. At night games, we be so busy yelling that we are not cold.
2. There's many flowers beside the lake, and a bridge of bamboo goes over it.
3. The volcano grumble, and smoke, fire, ash, and lava growl in her belly like indigestion.
4. House prices ranges from $40,000 to $500,000.
5. I enjoy a newspaper that cover a variety of subjects.
6. As the number of computers grow, the need for programmers, systems analysts, and key-punchers grows also.
7. There is seven chair lifts and a lot of mountain.

8. Every year in May, my neighbors takes me out for my birthday.

9. Every athlete who get the opportunity to compete in the Olympics train very hard.

10. People gets stuck in the elevators between classes because there is too many people in them.

D.

1. Most of the boys my mom wants me to date looks like dogs anyway.

2. The food in both places are exceptionally good.

3. The United States have a little of every nationality in it.

4. Activities in school allows the students to have fun and meet people.

5. It really please me when resort owners take pride in keeping their places clean and neat.

6. Although college and high school has their differences, they are both very helpful.

7. The cars is not new, but they are in good condition.

8. Her warmth of heart and personal magnetism attracts many friends.

9. Many people on welfare doesn't really need it.

10. There's vegetables, used clothing, and lots of used household items that people want to get rid of.

III. *Change nouns, pronouns, or verbs to eliminate errors in number from the following sentences.*

A.

1. There's many things that we have to do since we are in the wedding.

2. The senior year activities are important. It's something every student looks forward to.

3. No matter how many times I dip the prawn in the sauce, it never come out too salty or spicy.

4. The bus driver can't see in the mirror because people's head are in the way.

5. Kids who has no love from their parents commits many crimes in society.

6. Pizza Chalet rewards the talented people who works for them.

7. Regular checkups with a dentist is also important.

8. The main issue of the strike between players and owners are power.

9. Riding the bus isn't bad at all if one ignores the other people that be on the bus.

10. These is just a few of my brother's honest and sincere thoughts and beliefs.

B.   1. Many poor people's homes are like a volatile volcano, ready to erupt at any moment.

     2. The best job are office or school job. These type of jobs last only five days a week.

     3. Some people think a boy is better than a girl, but my parents don't agree.

     4. The social events lets students inquire about various firms from people who work there.

     5. The diorama almost seem real when one is looking at it, but everyone know it is unreal.

     6. The professors who teaches at these colleges are here to see that we get our education.

     7. In addition, the necessity of parking lots have made the department store and the shopping center move from the downtown area to the suburban area.

     8. There is usually small lines, and one can get away from the crowds in several areas.

     9. Concerts is an occasion to get dressed up.

   10. Some people resorts to stealing.

IV. *Correct the verb forms in the following paragraphs.*

    A.   High school teachers are different from college instructors. Teachers are more conservative in their teaching habits than instructors are. Teachers always says, "You have to do your homework," and instructors says, "It is up to you if you want to do your homework." It is more relaxing knowing that I really do not have to do it, but if I decide to, it will help me. Teachers help the students more themselves while instructors sends them to a tutor.

present verb

    B.   Ronald is a very neat and clean young man. Last year when his mother died, I thought he might start letting things go. I was afraid that he just would not care any longer, but I was wrong. He wake up every morning, take a shower, and get dressed. Since he be alone now and live in his mother's house, he have to keep everything up to par. He do his own laundry since he have a washer and dryer. He dust the house, do the dishes, and vacuum the carpets by himself.

V. ***A.*** *Read the following essay and label its thesis and supports ʺgoodʺ or ʺfaulty.ʺ*

     Karate is a unique sport that test one's physical ability, patience, and determination. Karate does not come easily to me, and therefore I must spend two to five hours a day, four to five days a week, training. The workouts are strenuous and include painful stretches, hundreds of kicks, and a few rounds of sparring that usually leaves you with a new set of bruises each day. After a workout, I be drenched with sweat, and my muscles and joints ache as I hobble out of class. Many people think that I am unfeminine, foolish, or insane for taking up this sport, but I really enjoy the challenge of karate.

Karate requires all of my muscles to be flexible. The stretching is the most difficult and most important part of karate. It is painful because there is usually someone working with you that stretches you farther than you can stretch yourself. For example, in one stretch I try to do the splits as far as I can go, and then someone pull my legs out farther. There are also stretches in which a person puts all his weight on my back while I'm sitting on the floor to stretch out my hamstrings. It is best to stay in these positions as long as you can stand it, usually about three to five minutes. This may seem masochistic, but it's the only way to get height in your kicks. I do my best to ignore the pain, and when I'm through stretching, it all seem worthwhile.

Kicks, blocks, and punches also requires a lot of work. There are about fifteen different kicks that I work on, standing, spinning, jumping, or both spinning and jumping. They all require a lot of strength and balance that I am developing through repetition. I try to do each kick about twenty or thirty times with each leg. Sometimes it's boring and frustrating, but I usually manage to push myself because I am not satisfied. Practicing my punches and blocks gives me a chance to catch up on my breath and relax for a bit. The punches and blocks aren't too difficult but does require accuracy and speed. Once you develop good form in kicking, punching, and blocking, you are ready to start sparring.

Sparring is the last part of my workout and the real test of my ability. Applying my techniques in sparring take a lot of endurance, planning, and quick thinking and reacting. We wears shinguards and boxing gloves for protection and has no heavy contact with each other. Even with all these precautions you usually end up with a few bruises. I learn a lot about karate during our sparring matches, and everything seem to come together.

The real sense of accomplishment come when I am promoted to a higher level. The judges have high expectations and do not allow many mistakes. When I do live up to their standards, all of my workouts seems worthwhile. I have become hooked on karate over the last year and have developed a lot of control over my mind and body because of it.

B. *Answer the following questions about the essay above.*

1. *Are there any verb form errors? Where? Correct them.*

2. *Find the shifts in pronoun person in this essay and correct them.*

3. *What is the best thing about this essay?*

4. *What is the weakest part of this essay? Why? How could it be better?*

VI. A. *Write an essay about something unusual that you like to do. Be sure that your outline is correct before you start to write.*

B. *Write an essay on one of the following subjects. Be sure that your outline is correct before you start to write.*

a magazine you read	football
a good way to exercise	someone you live with
contact lenses	leaving home

INDEPENDENT STUDY   Verbs: Present Tense *(answers in the back)*

VII. *Put parentheses around the prepositional phrases, two lines under the verbs, and one line under the subjects in the following sentences. Then cross out incorrect verb forms and write the correct ones above them.*

A.
1. Although ballet and African dance are different, the spirit required for these dances are the same.

2. The top and the bottom of this fruit is not smooth like the rim of a glass cup.

3. This game consist of nine innings, and when there is a tie, the innings continue until the game is untied.

4. The refrigerator allows people to have a large variety of food at any time of the day.

5. Learning to write essays are very important to a student.

6. My family's teeth is always in good shape.

7. There is also the fights between the pitchers and players that has just been hit with the ball.

8. Although our bodies are not alive after death, our spirits remain.

9. If I ever has to go again now, I don't think it will be as bad because of the new cross-harbor tunnel.

10. When the pitcher is not doing well, the manager come into the field and talk to him for a couple of minutes.

B.   James and Lewis hates each other. I stop to talk to them to tell them we is only friends, but they seems to misunderstand our relationship. Now it has come to the point that my mother tells me to stop seeing both of them because they comes over and gets upset if the other one be there. My problem is that I tell one to stop coming over. Then I miss him and end up inviting him right back over. I guess it has gotten to the point that I have let James and Lewis grow closer to me than I had intended.

present verb

VERBS: Past Tenses

Verb forms also change with tense. English verbs have two past forms, the past participle form, which is used with a helping verb, and the simple past form, which is used alone. The simple past tense is used to refer to something that happened or was true in the past.

I lived in Leakey in 1973.

She had a Ford in high school.

The present tense of "have" and the past participle of a main verb are used to refer to something that started in the past and continues to the present.

I have lived in Keene for three years.

She has driven this Honda since January.

The past tense of "have," which is "had," and the past participle of a main verb are used to refer to something that occurred before another past event.

I had lived in Leakey for three years when I joined the army.

She had driven the Honda for only a few weeks when it blew a head gasket.

In the above sentences, "had" is used with "lived" and "driven" to show even earlier past times than those expressed in the simple past tense by "joined" and "blew."

Most verbs use the *ed* form for both simple past and past participle.

FAULTY Barry has always want to control his wife.

"Want" is a regular verb, so its past participle form is "wanted."

REVISED Barry has always wanted to control his wife.

Some common verbs, however, have irregular past and past participle forms. The following list includes the irregular verbs that cause errors most often. You should master these so that you can use correct verb forms when you write.

Present Tense	Past Tense (used alone)	Past Participle (used with "has," "have," "had")
become	became	become
begin	began	begun
break	broke	broken
bring	brought	brought
build	built	built
catch	caught	caught
choose	chose	chosen
come	came	come
cost	cost	cost

Present Tense	Past Tense (used alone)	Past Participle (used with "has," "have," "had")
do	did	done
draw	drew	drawn
drink	drank	drunk
drive	drove	driven
eat	ate	eaten
fall	fell	fallen
feel	felt	felt
find	found	found
fit	fit	fit
give	gave	given
go	went	gone
grow	grew	grown
have	had	had
hear	heard	heard
hurt	hurt	hurt
keep	kept	kept
know	knew	known
lay (place)	laid	laid
lead	led	led
leave	left	left
lie (rest)	lay	lain
light	lit	lit
lose	lost	lost
pay	paid	paid
quit	quit	quit
ride	rode	ridden
ring	rang	rung
rise	rose	risen
run	ran	run
say	said	said
see	saw	seen
shake	shook	shaken
sing	sang	sung
sink	sank	sunk
speak	spoke	spoken
spend	spent	spent
spread	spread	spread
steal	stole	stolen
strike	struck	struck
swim	swam	swum
swing	swung	swung
take	took	taken
teach	taught	taught
tear	tore	torn
tell	told	told

past verb

Present Tense	Past Tense (used alone)	Past Participle (used with "has," "have," "had")
think	thought	thought
throw	threw	thrown
wear	wore	worn
win	won	won
write	wrote	written

Irregular verb forms are also listed in good dictionaries. The entry below for "spring" includes the letters "pt" followed by the past tense, "sprang," and "pp" followed by the past participle, "sprung."

spring³ /sprɪŋ/ *vi,vt* (*pt* sprang /spræŋ/, *pp* sprung /sprʌŋ/) **1** [VP2C] jump suddenly from the ground; move suddenly (*up, down, out,* etc) from rest, concealment, etc: *He sprang to his feet/sprang out of bed/sprang forward to help me/sprang up from his seat. The branch sprang back and hit me in the face.* **2** [VP2C] ∼ *(up),* appear; grow up quickly from the ground or from a stem: *A breeze has sprung up. Weeds were* ∼*ing up everywhere. The wheat is beginning to* ∼ *up.* (fig) *A suspicion/doubt sprang up in her mind.* **3** [VP3A] ∼ *from,* arise or come from: *He is sprung from royal blood, is of royal ancestry. Where have you sprung from,* suddenly and unexpectedly appeared from? **4** [VP14] ∼ *sth on sb,* bring forward suddenly: ∼ *a surprise on sb;* ∼ *a new theory/proposal on sb.* **5** [VP6A] cause to operate by means of a mechanism: ∼ *a mine,* cause it to explode; ∼ *a trap,* cause it to go off. **6** [VP6A,2A] (of wood) (cause to) warp, split, crack: *My cricket bat has sprung. I have sprung my tennis racket.* ∼ *a leak,* (of a ship) crack or burst so that water enters.

Past tense and past participle verb forms must follow standard English usage. If you are not sure about a verb, check a good dictionary or refer to the list above. Here are some typical errors:

FAULTY My slacks costed twenty-five dollars.

The list of verb forms above shows "cost," not "costed," as the past tense of the verb "cost."

REVISED My slacks cost twenty-five dollars.

FAULTY Before that day, I had keeped my word to myself.

The chart shows that "kept," not "keeped," is the past participle of "keep."

REVISED Before that day, I had kept my word to myself.

All verbs except the verb "to be" use those same past and past participle forms for all people, singular and plural. The past participle of the verb "to be," "been," is the same for all people, but the past tense is different.

Past Tense "to be"

	Singular	Plural
first person	I was	we were
second person	you were	you were
third person	he was	they were
	she was	
	it was	

Once more the third person singular verb form ends in *s,* but this time the first person form does too.

Memorize the correct forms of the verb "to be" so that you can use them without thinking. Correct use of this verb is absolutely necessary in the written English of the business and academic worlds.

FAULTY We was lonely without Susan.

The table of past forms of the verb "to be" shows that "were," not "was," should be used with "we."

REVISED We were lonely without Susan.

FAULTY She were too old to join the army.

The table shows that "was," not "were," should be used with "she."

REVISED She was too old to join the army.

past verb

In the past tense, the verb "to be" follows the same rule as in the present tense. Singular subjects (except "you") must have verbs that end in *s,* and plural subjects must have verbs that don't end in *s.*

I was	we were
she was	they were
he was	they were
it was	they were
school was	schools were
cat was	cats were
box was	boxes were
mother was	mothers were
visitor was	visitors were

Either a subject or a verb may end in *s,* but not both. Once more, this rule does not apply to words that always end in *s.*

FAULTY The teacher were late.

The singular subject "teacher" needs a verb that ends in s, that is, "was," not "were."

REVISED The teacher was late.

FAULTY The exercises was too difficult.

Either verb or subject may end in s, but not both. Plural subjects take "were," not "was."

REVISED The exercises were too difficult.

CORRECTION COMMENT: Past tense and past participle verb forms should follow standard English usage.

EXERCISES Verbs: Past Tense

I. A. *This first exercise is designed to help you find out which correct past and past participle forms are already stored in your memory. Without referring to the list on pages 146–148, complete the following sentences using the listed verbs. One set has been done with the regular verb "visit" as an example.*

	Now I _____	Yesterday I ___	I have _____
1. **EXAMPLE** visit	*visit*	*visited*	*visited*
2. become			
3. begin			
4. break			
5. bring			
6. build			
7. catch			
8. choose			
9. come			
10. cost			
11. do			
12. draw			
13. drink			
14. drive			
15. eat			
16. fall			
17. feel			

	Now I _____	Yesterday I ___	I have _____
18. find			
19. fit			
20. give			
21. go			
22. grow			
23. have			
24. hear			
25. hurt			
26. keep			
27. know			
28. lay (place)			
29. lead			
30. leave			
31. lie (rest)			
32. light			
33. lose			
34. pay			
35. quit			
36. ride			
37. ring			
38. rise			
39. run			
40. say			
41. see			
42. shake			
43. sing			
44. sink			
45. speak			
46. spend			
47. spread			
48. steal			

past verb

	Now I _____	Yesterday I ___	I have _____
49. strike	_____	_____	_____
50. swim	_____	_____	_____
51. swing	_____	_____	_____
52. take	_____	_____	_____
53. teach	_____	_____	_____
54. tear	_____	_____	_____
55. tell	_____	_____	_____
56. think	_____	_____	_____
57. throw	_____	_____	_____
58. wear	_____	_____	_____
59. win	_____	_____	_____
60. write	_____	_____	_____

B. Check your completed exercise A against the list on pages 146–148. Circle the incorrect forms and write the correct forms above them in another color (for example, switch to pen if you used pencil to complete A).

C. Memorize the forms that you got wrong in the exercise above.

II. *A. Use a dictionary to find the past and past participle forms of the following verbs.*

	Past Tense	Past Participle
1. lend	_____	_____
2. prove	_____	_____
3. sell	_____	_____
4. send	_____	_____
5. shoot	_____	_____
6. shrink	_____	_____
7. shut	_____	_____
8. sleep	_____	_____
9. speed	_____	_____
10. swear	_____	_____

B. *Write ten sentences using the following subjects and verbs in the past tense form.*

Subject	Verb
1. he	to be

EXAMPLE *He was lonesome when his brother left for school.*

2. you	to have

_____

3. I	to go

_____

4. my mother	to have

_____

5. my friend and I	to be

_____

6. audience	to enjoy

_____

7. Lambert or Kathy	to be

_____

past verb

8. students	to earn

_____

9. Roger	to leave

_____

10. clothes	to cost

_____

C. *Write ten sentences using the following subjects and verbs with the present tense of "to have" and the past participle.*

Subject	Verb
1. relatives	to visit

EXAMPLE *Our relatives have visited all the museums in the city*

2. we	to slide

_____

3. teacher	to speak

_____

4. Emmy Lou Harris   to sing

_____

5. I   to do

_____

6. girls   to swim

_____

7. you   to wear

_____

8. team   to win

_____

9. catcher   to throw

_____

10. Lenny and his wife   to quit

_____

D. *Write ten sentences including clauses using the following subjects with the past tense of "to have" and the past participle of the given verb. In each sentence add a past tense clause or a phrase to show the contrast in time.*

Subject	*Verb*
1. my sister	to see

EXAMPLE *I didn't want to mention the man my sister had seen.*

2. grandfather	to write

_____

3. girl	to tell

_____

4. lady	to swim

_____

5. dancing	to give

_____

6. lawyer	to leave

_____

7. hitchhikers	to save

_____

8. dogs   to tear

_____

9. orchestra   to play

_____

10. Wanda and her friend   to finish

_____

III. *In the following sentences, cross out the incorrect verb forms and write the correct ones above them.*

A.   1. Their passports costed them five hundred dollars each.

2. It was the first time we had did anything like this.

3. One day Gerald lefted his wallet at my house.

4. The salesman even showed us how to set the margins.

5. You haven't answer my question.

6. The teachers in high school was so nice.

7. I solded it because I needed the money.

8. We had ate many kinds of food.

9. When I was alone he kept the phone in working order in case I called.

10. Before I was even nominated, I had already wrote a thank you speech.

B.   1. I builded a fire and fried fish.

2. Because she had drove to Dodge City, she had a car to use there.

3. The social conditions of the job was rotten.

4. It has been hard, but I have manage so far.

5. His tuxedo costed him two weeks' pay.

6. I accepted them as if we had known each other for years.

7. House prices in Houston has rose drastically.

8. We planned it so that I rung up the sales items and collected the money while she took off the tags and put the items in a bag.

9. There was many problems with my first love.

10. Since ancient times, men have generally been stronger than women.

1. A selling wave hit the stock market last week.

2. The cost of housing has soared, gasoline prices has increased, and employment has declined greatly.

3. Mount Saint Helens have awaken!

past verb

4. The economy of the United States is not going to weaken to the point of a depression because the country has already pass through that experience.

5. There was only three people to give me trouble over loans.

6. Mr. Straight emphasized that he had flatly rejected the attempt to recruit him as a spy.

7. I became frustrated when I founded out that the vegetables were not fresh.

8. Getting married at fifteen was the greatest mistake I have ever made. I have lost my good relationship with my family.

9. I found out that two of us was in the lead.

10. That actually keeped me busy for my college years.

D.
1. Living away from my parents has help me to become more responsible.

2. Last year I had a car accident, and I was feeling terrible, but getting a letter from her light up a couple of days.

3. We had walked three miles before my father picked us up.

4. When I was a senior, my mother start letting me travel by myself.

5. When our next door neighbor moved, the cats disappeared.

6. There has been times when I have felt the presence of my mother's spirit.

7. Conrad told reporters that he planned to become an art teacher.

8. The full skirt fit much better than the straight one.

9. He left Baton Rouge three years ago and opened a night club in New Orleans.

10. Finally she spread mustard over everything.

IV. A. *Read the following essay and discuss its strengths, weaknesses, and possible corrections with the other members of your class. Then divide into five groups, each group taking the responsibility for one paragraph of the essay. Discuss in detail the weaknesses of your group's paragraph. Then rewrite it together, producing one good rewritten paragraph. Read the rewritten essay to the rest of the class, each group reading its paragraph in turn. As you hear the other paragraphs, note their strengths and weaknesses and share your findings with your classmates.*

Washington, D.C.

When I was in the twelfth grade, I took a trip to Washington, D.C. The purpose of my trip was to see how the government operates. The trip was an educational experience, as well as a social experience. When I arrived in

Washington, D.C. it was very cold and snowing. I had never been in falling snow before, therefore I didn't like it. It took me almost three days to get used to the change of time which was three hours different from California time. I had problems going to bed at night and waking up in the morning. The transportation in D.C. was very slow. When I wanted to go downtown I had to wait almost thirty minuets for a bus. Although there were many disadvantages, everyone should visit D.C. for an educational experience.

You can attend many important lectures, seminars, and workshops. This was the most exciting experience to me. When I attended my first seminar, I had no idea that Alan Cranston was the speaker. Since I was from California, this seminar was important. Alan Cranston spoke about the main issues in California such as: welfare, jobs, and taxes. I was able to ask him important questions, which was an advantage to me. Most of the questions I asked him had to do with jobs for teenagers. After the seminar, I spoke with Alan Cranston personally. He told me some of his new ideas for the coming years. I was very pleased with Alan Cranston's ideas. I attended seminars and workshops that discussed public transportation and other economic situations I learned that the cost for public transportation would increase in the coming years. Simply because the price of gasoline is increasing and people can't afford to drive. Therefore, many are using public transportation.

You can see things you have never seen before. I was never taught the significance of historical events. I visited all the monuments, such as: The Jefferson Monument, and The Lincoln Memorial. I bought books to guide me as I visited the monuments. I learned that The Lincoln Memorial signifies not only a historial point, but as a remembering point. Many people go to most of the monuments for silent prayer on the birthday's of the leaders. I seen museums, libraries, and institutes. The Smithsonian Institute was very exciting. There were things there that I had never seen in my life. I learned about my culture when I visited the African Art Museum. I took pictures and wrote down important facts.

You can visit Capital Hill and see how the government works. When I asked about Capital Hill, I thought it was just a big hill. Well, I amazed and embarrassed when I seen Capital Hill. I sat in on the House and Senate meetings. The House of Representatives is located on the far right side of Capital Hill, and the Senate on the far left. The whole Capital is made of marble stone. When you walk in the main entrance, there are many pictures. When you enter Capital Hill, you have to give the guards most of your personal belongings, such as: cameras, purses and keys. You only can take pictures of certain things on Capital Hill. I sat in on one of the meetings in the House of Representatives. I was very bored because I couldn't hear anything they were saying. The whole room is like a big coliseum. When I got lost on Capital Hill, because its so hugh, I seen Ron Dellums. I spoke with him in his office for two hours. When I finally found my way out, I went to the Supreme Court, which is also located on the hill. There was a hearing in session. I fell asleep in there. I couldn't see all of Capital Hill in a few days, but what I seen was very educational.

Everyone should make it a point to visit D.C. It's an educational experience as well as an enjoyable one. You can discuss many problems

past verb

that you have wondered about. You can meet people that you have never met before, and see things that you have never seen before. The enjoyable part is when you come home. You can share what you have learned with your family and friends. You can encourage them to visit the Nation's Capital and judge it from their point of view.

B. *Write a paragraph about a place you visited where you learned something. Begin that paragraph with a summary sentence, and fill it with good vivid details about the place and the things you learned.*

INDEPENDENT STUDY   Verbs: Past Tense *(answers in the back)*

V. *In the following sentences, cross out the incorrect verb forms and write the correct ones above them.*

A.
1. Badminton first appeared in India and then spreaded all over the world.

2. I had saw some pictures from books and from television before then.

3. Over the past fourteen years I've suffered an attack once or twice a week.

4. Grandpop and I packed a lunch and was off.

5. I have visited many small towns in Nebraska.

6. If they wanted to stay there was movies and games for all ages.

7. We sung, laughed out loud, and told jokes until I became hoarse.

8. We was always doing something fun in class.

9. I founded that eating at the Sizzler was a good idea.

10. You haven't traveled until you've drove down a highway feeling the wind across your face or smelling the wildflowers alongside the road.

B.   Both of the young men want me to stop talking to the other one. This past Saturday, Lewis took me out to lunch. While I was gone, James had came up to my office to take me out to lunch also. I hadn't known either were coming. After returning from lunch with Lewis, I kiss him and went back to work. Just a couple of seconds later, I seen James walking toward me with the angriest look on his face. It scared me so much I didn't even want to talk to him. He started yelling at me. I told him that we're all just friends.

VERBS: Combinations

Main verbs also combine with helping verbs other than "to have" to express other ideas. The chart in Figure 5 tells which verb forms or endings follow which helping verbs. Referring to this chart helps one correctly form such verbs as

can ask	am asked	is seeing
must be	was seen	was being
must fly	had visited	were wondering

In addition, if the added verb part is also a helping verb, even more parts may be added. In other words, the verb part from the second column on the chart may be one of the following five forms, which are also in the first column.

be	being	been
have		had

If it is, it may be followed by more verbs of the form indicated on the chart, creating such verbs as

must have asked

will be named

could be hoping

In fact, this process can be expanded to such less frequently used forms as

shall be being visited

might have been being shocked

Applying the following process to the chart in Figure 5 would generate the last verb form above. As a type 1 helping verb, "might" may be followed by "have." As a type 2 helping verb, "have" may be followed by "been." As a type 3 helping verb, "been" may be followed by "being."

As a type 2 helping verb, "being" may be followed by a past participle form like "shocked." The result is the verb "might have been being shocked." This chart could also be used to construct verbs that make no sense, so be sure to use it as a guide for determining the forms used in familiar verbs and not as an opportunity to generate structures that no one will understand!

Sometimes a helping verb can combine with more than one main verb as in the following sentences.

You should go to the usher and ask for help.

verb combination

Instead of saying "You should go to the usher, and you should ask for help," we omit the words that are repeated at the beginning of the second half of the sentence, in this case "you should," and let "ask" go with the first "you should" as in the above sentence. The following sentence is similar.

Figure 5

These helping verbs   can be followed by   *these verb forms.*

			No ending (the form used with "to," the dictionary form)
Type 1			
Present	*Past*		
can	could		ask
may	might		like
shall	should		name
will	would		shock
do	did		do
does			steal
must			write
ought to			be
	used to		have
			etc.

		Past participle (the form used with "have")
Type 2		
am		asked
are		liked
is		named
was		shocked
were		done
*_____ be		stolen
*_____ been		written
*_____ being		been
other linking verbs		had
has		*etc.*
had		
have		

		Present participle (the *ing* form)
Type 3		
am		asking
are		liking
is		naming
was		shocking
were		doing
*_____ be		stealing
*_____ been		writing
		being
		having
		etc.

*_____ before a verb indicates that the verb must have a preceding helping verb.

You should have gone to the usher and asked for help.

Instead of repeating "you should have" before "asked," we just let "asked" go with the "you should have" at the beginning of the sentence. The reader realizes that the sentence means "You should have gone to the usher, and you should have asked for help."

Verb combinations should be formed according to the chart in Figure 5. Here are some typical faulty sentences revised:

FAULTY I had to pay my fees before I could danced.

The chart shows that the form without an ending should follow "could."

REVISED I had to pay my fees before I could dance.

FAULTY He was suppose to unlock the door.

The chart shows that the form we use with "have" should follow "was."

REVISED He was supposed to unlock the door.

FAULTY The tomatoes would be spoil by then.

The chart shows that the form we use with "have" follows "be."

REVISED The tomatoes would be spoiled by then.

FAULTY She should have went to class more often.

The chart in the previous section (pages 146–148) shows that "gone" follows "have," not "went."

REVISED She should have gone to class more often.

Sometimes the helping verb is missing or faulty.

FAULTY We hasn't brought our books.

The chart on page 136 shows that "have," not "has," is the correct form with "we."

REVISED We haven't brought our books.

FAULTY We use to go to church every week.

"Use to," without the *d,* is *never* correct.

REVISED We used to go to church every week.

FAULTY They always going out drinking.

If it's working as a verb, an *ing* word must have a helping verb.

REVISED They are always going out drinking.

verb combination

Be careful not to add endings to words that are not working as verbs.

FAULTY I taught him to danced.

A verb used with "to" is not working as a verb, and so it should not have an ending.

REVISED I taught him to dance.

In questions, the helping verb goes before the subject.

FAULTY How do he do it?

Rearranged to sentence order, the core of this question is "he do do," but we already learned that "does" should be used with "he." From there the chart shows that "do" follows the helping verb "does." After checking the verb forms, we can return the words to the question order.

REVISED How does he do it?

Words like "not," "never," "always," "just," "only," and other *ly* words should be ignored because they're not verb parts.

CORRECTION COMMENT: Verb combinations should be formed according to the chart in Figure 5.

EXERCISES   *Verbs: Combinations*

I.   A. Write ten sentences using at least three helping verb–main verb combinations from each of the three groups in Figure 5.

B. Write ten sentences with verbs of more than two parts. Be sure the verb combinations make sense.

II. Using the chart in Figure 5, write the correct verb forms in the blanks in each of the following sentences. Look back at the preceding unit if necessary.

A.   1. I can _____ my mother tonight about this weekend. (to ask)

2. He has been _____ this book for seven years. (to write)

3. We were _____ to be here at 8:00 P.M. (to tell)

4. The librarian was _____ by our talking. (to disturb)

5. You might _____ _____ pneumonia out there. (to have) (to catch)

6. The typing was _____ in thirty-five minutes. (to finish)

7. _____ you believe in free enterprise? (to do)

8. They were _____ to get there first. (to suppose)

9. Many inexpensive meals can be _____ with cheese. (to make)

10. The teacher should have _____ those papers sooner. (to return)

B.   1. The clerk must _____ _____ a break. (to have) (to need)

2. Could you _____ what he wanted? (to guess)

3. Johnny is always _____ for trouble. (to look)

4. She would _____ asked permission if she _____ had time. (to have) (to have)

5. You should _____ the poet's club and _____ some new people. (to join) (to meet)

6. They _____ to keep their boat in our driveway. (to use)

7. That cake should _____ been _____ for dessert. (to have) (to serve)

8. He was _____ that you didn't _____ it. (to disappoint) (to buy)

9. She might have _____ right about this teacher. (to be)

10. They haven't _____ gas in two weeks. (to buy)

III. *Find the faulty verb forms in the following sentences. Cross them out and write the correct ones above them.*

A.
1. My friend Diane can talked for hours without stopping.

2. He was suppose to be in the board room by two.

3. I use to skip meals during the day.

4. How do the doctor want them to paid?

5. They always trying to increase their power.

6. The administrators hasn't made a decision.

7. The president should have went back to France.

8. The child would be finish school in 1990.

9. I had one more week in high school before I could graduated.

10. This automobile doesn't uses a lot of gas.

B.
1. This would have enable them to do well on the exam.

2. I discovered many interesting things that happening in the world.

3. We decided to go to the gym where we wouldn't be spot.

4. I went to the orientation that was offer for the freshmen.

5. I should had gotten a raise sooner because I did plenty of work accurately.

6. I have to find someone that really do love me.

7. I should have went to a counselor in advance and asked for help, but I tried to plan my own schedule.

8. One morning I overslept and would had been stranded without a car.

9. We were call the Manchester Marching 100, and 1979 was a very good year for us.

10. He was rich and so he could hired several employees in his store.

verb combination

C. 1. The schedule would always be change right before my day off.

2. How do it feel to be dead?

3. I could have gave him an answer right then, but I don't like blind dates.

4. When I am finish I feel like I have done ten sit-ups and four push-ups.

5. My friends would always told me to walk home and not ran.

6. In elementary school I use to be very frighten by my grandmother.

7. Everyone was feed so much food.

8. The class is suppose to start at 10:40 A.M. every day.

9. On the freeway, the traffic was back up.

10. My husband would sat on the bed and listen to the baby's heart beat.

D. 1. I did straightened up and flew right.

2. A good dish can be spoil if poor quality ingredients are use.

3. You can be the dummy in the class and not even know how to spell your name, and you'll still pass.

4. He don't want to waste time merely making money.

5. Now she has me twirling around and around, and at the same time I'm suppose to be concentrating on someone's hand. I can't do it.

6. Does success come as suddenly as winning a new car?

7. Months later I was shock because both schools accepted me.

8. She would always wanted to have conferences with me, and they made my record look bad.

9. They always together drinking wine and talking about how to manage their land and people.

10. The Tigers should be prepare because the Bulldogs plan to wins the next three games.

E. Superior beings from another planet could help the world in many ways. These superior beings could teach us ways to eliminate cancer, diabetes, blindness, and birth defects. Many other diseases could be minimize or totally wipe out. Maybe we could live longer or even forever if the aliens gave us a miracle drug. These aliens could also help us in agriculture. Barren wastelands could be turned into fruitful soil. Places like India and the Soviet Union could supply their own grain. Our energy in this world is running out, so we need to find alternate energy sources. The aliens could help us solve that problem. They must know plenty of energy sources because they couldn't traveled that many miles without knowing how to produce energy.

IV. A. *Write a paragraph about changes that should be made in university classrooms to make them better places to learn. Begin the paragraph with a summary sentence, and give lots of examples and details to show what you mean.*

B. *Read the following essay and write out the outline.*

"No, please don't hit me any more can't we just talk this over, Mom?" shouted Karen. "No, you children don't understand talk this is the only thing that will get across to you," answered Mrs. Jackson. Some of my friends has to go through such agony every time they makes one little mistake. I'm fortunate to have a mother who's not like this but instead tries to be very understanding. She lets me share things with her, as women do.

My mother didn't treated me like a child when I was in high school. When I was in the ninth grade, I hung out with the older people because the people my age couldn't do the things I could do. My mother would say yes when I ask to go to a party then I would see my friends could go along with me. They either couldn't go at all, or they had to be home so early that there wasn't any point in going at all. When I started being with the juniors and seniors every day, I began to do things that they did, like ditching. This caught up with me, and my mother found out. Instead of whipping me or putting me on restriction, she sat me down as a woman and lectured me about the responsibilities I had to myself in order to achieved the things I wanted out of life. By treating me like an adult, she made me realize that I wasn't a child any more. From that day on it was my decision to either make something out of my life or not.

In high school, I use to chat with my girl friends, but if I wanted to talk about them, I would talk with my mama instead. She can be a listener or a suggester whichever the case calls for. When I was in the eleventh grade, I had a neighbor who let her boy friend beat her up all of the time. I advised Mary in the best ways that I could, but nothing seemed to help. I seeked my mother's advice, and with her help I came through this okay.

My mother is usually in a loving and playful mood. I have always been a late sleeper, that is whenever I get the chance. One summer, about three years ago, I decided I wasn't going to work or go to summer school but just stay home and rest. My mama change that plan every morning when she woke up, she would came into my room, pull my covers up until she found my feet, and start tickling. If she didn't do that, she would opened my curtains as wide as they would go and say, "It's time to gets up." I would fuss, but it never did any good. At the end, we would both be smiling and laughing about it. Whenever I get mad at her, she always messes with me and won't leave until she makes me laugh.

My mother and I have a good relationship, and I hope that some day the whole world will be able to share such happiness with their families. The children have to be more open with their parents, and the parents have to be more understanding.

verb combination

C. *Answer the following questions about this essay.*

1. Is the outline good?

2. *Which of the body paragraphs could be improved? How?*

3. *Could the introduction or conclusion be improved? If so, how?*

D. *Correct all the errors in the essay above.*

E. *Write a paragraph about your parents' rules about curfew when you were in high school. Start the paragraph with a summary sentence.*

F. *Write a paragraph about someone you can talk to. Start the paragraph with a summary sentence.*

INDEPENDENT STUDY   Verbs: Combinations *(answers in the back)*

V. *Correct the verb form errors in the following sentences.*

A.   1. If our poor people are not given the same opportunities as others we will still be face with a high crime rate.

2. She moving home soon.

3. He was hospitalize quite often because he got really sick.

4. Doesn't American teenagers have better things to do?

5. The stores are not very crowd.

6. I wasn't finish with school yet.

7. My older brother, Sam, was always bothering me while I was doing my housework.

8. These programs are need to improved our communities and the personal lives of the middle and lower class people.

9. I'll always know that my teeth is going to be taken care of properly.

10. By then, I was very relax.

B.   The aliens could tell us about our world. If the aliens could traveled billions of miles, they must know about this universe. They must know about atoms that make up matter and chemicals that produce life. The universe is constantly changing, and the aliens might know how the universe produced our solar system. The aliens must have acquire a lot of knowledge which they could passed on to us.

VERBS: Tense Shifts

Be sure to use the verb tense that fits the situation you are describing.

FAULTY After an hour had passed, I became worried and call his house.

The "had" form in the first clause suggests that a contrasting past tense will follow, and it does, but then the sentence shifts to the present tense for no reason. The present tense verb "call" should be replaced by the past tense form "called."

REVISED After an hour had passed, I became worried and called his house.

Check your work closely to be sure that the verb tenses are consistent. Here's another example of a tense shift revised:

FAULTY One summer I don't know what I was going to do.

"One summer" suggests a past time, but the first verb "do" is in the present tense. Then the last clause is in the past tense. The sentence should be corrected so that it is consistent. The present tense verb "do" can be changed to the past tense "did" to correct this error.

REVISED One summer I didn't know what I was going to do.

If the verb or verbs of an independent clause are in the past tense, the verbs in the dependent clauses of the same sentence should not be in the present tense. Many errors are caused because people don't realize that the following words have past tense forms.

For Present Tense Sentences	*For Past Tense Sentences*
can	could
may	might
shall	should
will	would

FAULTY We were told that there will be eighty targets.

"Will" is correct for a present tense sentence.

REVISED We are told that there will be eighty targets.

"Would" is correct for a past tense sentence.

REVISED We were told that there would be eighty targets.

Either of these revisions makes the sentence consistent. The correct form can only be chosen by checking the rest of the essay because the tenses throughout the whole essay must be consistent. Here's a similar sentence:

FAULTY I can go anywhere at any time if I wanted to.

"Can" in the first clause does not go with the past tense verb "wanted" in the second clause. One or the other should be changed.

tense shift

REVISED I can go anywhere at any time if I want to.

REVISED I could go anywhere at any time if I wanted to.

Tenses should be consistent, but they should not necessarily stay the same. The following sentence comes from a passage that was all in the past tense.

FAULTY I remembered going bicycling with my boy friend two weeks ago.

This sentence would have been correct if the remembering had gone on in the past, but the essay makes it clear that the writer is remembering while writing, and so the verb must be in the present tense.

REVISED I remember going bicycling with my boy friend two weeks ago.

As the writer moves through different situations—remembering the past and the remote past, generalizing about what's true today, looking ahead to the future—the verb tenses express those time changes. The line below represents time from past through the present to the future, and important moments and time periods in someone's career have been noted on this line.

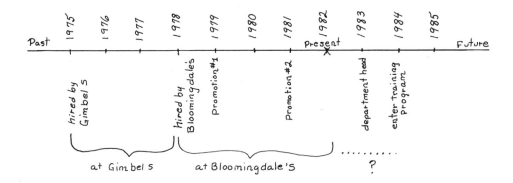

The sentences below describe this same job history. Note the use of verb tenses to indicate the time relationships.

I had worked at Gimbels for three years when I landed a job at Bloomingdale's.

I remember my excitement when my boss called me in to work. Since that day, I have received two promotions, and I am now a department head. Next year I will enter Bloomingdale's buyer training program.

The first sentence states that the writer worked at Gimbels before landing the job at Bloomingdale's and indicates this time contrast with the contrasting verb forms "had worked" and "landed." Then, while writing, she remembers the excitement of the call to work. Because that remembering is going on as she writes, the writer expresses it in the present tense, "remember," but the call itself occurred previously, so that verb, "called," is in the past tense. Next, the writer talks about two promotions that occurred during the period between beginning at Bloomingdale's and the present, and indicates the idea of a time period up to the present by using the "have received" verb form. Then the writer indicates her present position with the present tense verb "am." Finally, she looks ahead and indicates this fact by using the future tense, "will enter."

CORRECTION COMMENT: Check your work closely to be sure that the verb tenses are consistent.

EXERCISES Verbs: Tense Shifts

I. *Complete the second sentence of the following pairs, changing the tense as required for consistency.*

A. 1. As the day comes to an end, we go to her apartment for dinner.

   EXAMPLE As the day came *to an end, we went to her apartment for dinner* .

2. I spend about fifty dollars on clothes my daughter needs.

   I spent _____ .

3. I wonder where we will sleep.

   I wondered _____ .

4. If she doesn't cook, she won't get any supper,.

   If she didn't _____ .

5. After I weed the garden, I have to mow the lawn.

   After I weeded _____ .

6. I hope someday I can watch the whole show.

   I hoped _____ .

7. When he gets there, they have already started dancing.

   When he got _____ .

8. She was supposed to come home as soon as the dance ended.

   She is _____ .

9. He comes right up to me and says I can leave.

   He came _____ .

10. The old man explains, but they won't listen.

   The old man explained _____ .

tense shift

B.   1. Her mother is really sick and needs an operation.

   Her mother was _____ .

2. He is so nervous he can't sit still.

   He was _____ .

3. He sits outside her old house hoping she will return.

   He sat _____ .

4. When I try to study, my husband wants to talk.

   When I tried _____ .

5. Whenever we visit my cousin, he takes us to the beach.

   Whenever we visited _____ .

6. He is hoping the check has come.

   He was _____ .

7. She is looking for the belt she left there.

   She was _____ .

8. She staggers and leans on the car for support.

   She staggered _____ .

9. My watch falls on the floor three weeks after I bought it.

   My watch fell _____ .

10. His mother is relieved that he survived.

   His mother was _____ .

II. *Correct the tense inconsistencies in the following sentences. Cross out the incorrect ones and write the correct ones above them.*

A.   1. I never realize that bills took up most of the money.

2. My father and I always get there early so we could watch batting practice.

3. Now that I am in college, I fondly remembered my high school days.

4. The guy was really mad and ask the other man to say he was sorry.

5. I straighten up my face and began walking down the stairs.

6. When I open the door, I couldn't believe what I saw.

7. I spend another $175.00 on parts for work I did myself.

8. I suggest that we should play some tennis, and everyone in my family agreed.

9. When I was a kid, I could not understand why my parents will have to die.

10. Ancient men looked at the sky and tried to relate what happen in the universe to the world around them.

B.
1. My hair was so curly that it looks like millions of tiny ringlets.

2. We arrived as early as we dare with three small children.

3. A lady got on the bus and knock my friend's bags on the floor.

4. Since my parents left North Korea, we have not lived near any close relatives.

5. Thousands of people left their homes before the volcano erupt.

6. As I look back, I remembered working with a particular doctor who made me uncomfortable.

7. After I finished my homework, I played softball for three hours with some Japanese people.

8. He was famous for finding things about the cadets that he can use against them.

9. The dog sat by the hole wishing another rabbit would run in.

10. I would always wonder why they never ask me for help.

C.
1. I took lessons in school and remembered how my music teacher use to encourage me.

2. When they move from Maine to Norfolk, Virginia, the neighbors thought that they were transferring from a private school.

3. When I was still young, a couple of boys come to our house to see my brother.

4. I asked my mother who had come over, and she name thirteen or fourteen people.

5. I was wondering what's wrong with him.

6. I couldn't understand exactly what they sang about, but they might have sung about Christianity.

7. Babysitting makes me mad because I have to clean up the mess my brother used to make.

8. I remembered going to the senior ball with a guy I did not like.

tense shift

9. Knowing what time it was terrified me, for I know what is going to happen when I arrive home.

10. If I didn't watch "Private Benjamin," I won't know what my classmates were talking about on Monday morning.

D.
1. Whenever we are sitting down talking about some of our friends or reminiscing about old times, she or I would say, "You know I was thinking that same thing."

2. The school nurse told me that 90% of the asthma was mental and if I would challenge it by exhaustion from some sort of vigorous exercise, I may be cured.

3. I remembered that I used to tease her, saying, "Hey, if you want to exercise, why don't you walk? Walking is exercise too!"

4. My parents had told me several times that girls can interfere with my studies.

5. As she struggle to read, they forced her to listen.

6. I close my eyes and began to touch the outside of the apple.

7. It is important to know what I want to say and what comes first, second, and third.

8. Whenever I have a difficult problem I always think of her words and ask myself whether or not the problem can be solved if I worry about it. If the answer is no, then I said to myself, "Well, I will think about it tomorrow," and go to sleep like a small child.

9. One summer I decided to visit my cousins who were living in Hong Kong. I understand that traveling to other places is really expensive, and I needed a lot of money to spend for the tour.

10. As I made the police report, my brother Larry pull up in my car.

III. A. *The following paragraph has errors of many kinds. Find and correct as many as possible.*

Datsuns are very fast. One day me and one of my friends were riding around in his 240Z. He says, "Do you want to see how fast she'll go." I say, "Yes." Next thing I know I am pinned to the seat. I began looking at the speedometer it was reading 120 then it rose to 140. I said that he could slow down now, so we began to slow down. That ride proved to me that the car had power.

B. *Correct the verb errors and run-together sentences in this essay.*

Women and men are not physically equal, but that doesn't mean that they are not mentally equal. Many a woman surpasses men in her ideas. In this world although people are created the same, they have different values and cultures. People differ from one place to another in my culture, the woman is supposed to take care of the family and the house.

Men and women have different roles in my culture. Usually the man is the one who goes to work and get the money to support his family. The woman, on the other hand, stays at home to cook the meals, clean the house, and look after her children. When the husband gets off work and goes home, he found his wife waiting for him with a smile on her face which makes him forget his tedious day. Husbands are usually very helpful to their wives, They help them with the housework and try very hard to get what their wives want.

When a woman gets married, she is supposed to stay with her husband and not see anybody else. Because most of the people back in my country are Muslims, we use Islam as our law. Islam says that a woman must not see a man other than her father, brother, grandfather, and husband. If the woman is seen with a stranger, her husband may divorce her or forgive her. Islam tries to make sure that the children are from one mother and father. Brothers from the same mother and father are closer to each other than half brothers.

Women are highly respected for what they do. Back where I came from, women are treated very nicely. No one raises his voice to a woman. I know when my mother tells me to take her and my sisters to the shopping center, I have to go get the car, open the doors, and waits until my mother and sisters get into the car then I would close the door quietly and drive very carefully. When we get to the supermarket, I will push the cart, and they would tell me to get what they want as we walk through the aisles in the store. I was taught by my father to respect women.

All over the world there are different people. Women are very happy with their treatment back home. I don't think that we should try to be up to date by copying the western world I think that we should be proud of what we are and work hard to make our country a nice place to live. We should give the world an example of how people who are considered to be living in the past can get the highest standards of living and still keep their old customs.

IV. A. Write an essay about the role of women or men. Narrow the topic down to one particular situation or place. You might want to discuss the essay above. Be sure you have a good outline before you begin to write, and include lots of details and examples to prove your thesis.

B. Write an essay on one of the following topics. Be sure to narrow the topic and write a good outline before you begin. As you write, include many vivid details to show, not just tell, the reader the truth of your thesis.

a place you love	the police in your neighborhood
a pollution problem	living with a small child
culture shock	lending money

INDEPENDENT STUDY   *Verbs: Tense Shifts (answers in the back)*

V. A. Correct tense inconsistencies in these sentences.

tense shift

1. Also during my last year in high school, we traveled all over Alabama.

2. After the floor is mopped, I had to clean all the equipment before placing it back in the shop.

3. My grandmother's size was the first thing that frighten me.

4. I did not remember how many times I murmured, "Dummy," to myself while I was reading.

5. One time after my brother had returned from jail, I noticed some of my personal goods were missing.

6. Traveling to school could be a lot better if I don't have to drive and deal with all that freeway traffic.

7. Another time I was watching television and minding my own business. He comes right up to the television and changes the channel.

8. The minute I started enjoying myself it's time to go home.

9. The Egyptians had strong soldiers in the Middle Ages. They conquer many neighboring countries.

10. The rat would then be x-rayed to see if the scanning medicine is doing what it is suppose to do.

B.   The police are always harassing people in my neighborhood. Once I was coming home from a party at about three in the morning. The police pulls up and start asking me questions. I told them immediately that I was coming from a party. Before I knew it, there were about eight more cars. One of the officers grabs me and throws me against the car. I ask him what I'm being arrested for, and he tells me burglary. I told him that he has the wrong guy. I waited there in the car for twenty minutes until another police car pull up and the officer says that they have the wrong guy.

VI. *Some of the verbs in the following sentences are incorrect. Cross out the incorrect words and write the correct ones above them.*

A.
1. Whenever a man look down on another, he is asking for trouble.

2. Their trips costed them a year of suffering.

3. Before she could even finish the sundae, she wanted a pickle.

4. The dentists always does a good job on our teeth.

5. Most Japanese cooks like to broil, stir fry, and deep fry their food quickly, so fresh ingredients are required.

6. If there's any casts, I would do away with them.

7. If a person want to manage his own life, he must first learn how to manage his money.

8. He tolded Michael if he didn't start coming in on time, he would be terminated.

9. While cruising, I notice things I never notice before.

10. We has use up a lot of gas by the time we finally get home.

B.
1. They are nice to me, but I don't always like to lend them the money I had saved.

2. The manufacturer were subsequently sued for damages, but the kid is still minus one eye.

3. Summer came to an end, and I realized I learned many new skills.

4. The last game of the championship he score forty-two points and lead the Lakers to a big win.

5. I was allowed to participate in sports during my last year in high school, something I always wanted to to.

6. Since the early 1970s, the department stores has been suffering from the attack of the shopping center.

7. Have you ever went into your purse and found that you had only ten dollars left to last you for two more weeks?

8. In 1975 the television industry alone contribute over ninety million dollars in income to baseball.

9. My meal costed me ten dollars, and the food was not worth what I paided for it.

10. He was taken to the hospital and had to wait three hours with the pain because there were not enough space in the emergency room.

C. 1. Money comes fast and gone faster.

2. My brother used to pulls me out of my room and introduced me to his friends.

3. She know that if she keep on grumbling, her brothers and sisters will flee from her and seek a place of refuge.

4. The cheese be melted so well that it stretches from my plate to my mouth.

5. The housing authorities were force to make some people move out of their neighborhoods because the houses had become so rat infested.

6. Sometimes the problems can be solve with medicine.

7. The night of the prom was so exciting that I could not standed up.

8. My brother don't want to miss "Three's Company," my uncle wants to watch "Star Trek," and the others wants to see "Paper Chase."

9. I haven't receive my money yet, so to avoid future disagreements I just forget about the four hundred dollars.

10. There is one female and two males, so I am again waken in the night by the sound of cats fighting and moaning.

D. 1. High school is suppose to be a place to prepares for college.

2. My head, my looks, and my future is being controlled by my hairdresser.

3. I was so scare that I bribed my brother with everything from movie tickets to dates with my girl friends so that he would sit with me to watch the ghost story.

4. Every time I put on my coat, she automatically thinks she suppose to come with me.

5. She such a skinny small child. You would never guess she ate like a pig.

6. If the family was traveling by bus or airplane, they could not stop because the bus or airplane have a set schedule to follow.

7. There's so many men that one of them would have to be the one.

8. I may be prejudice because I don't believe that all men are equal.

9. Also this weekend the Datsun were racing at Seers Point, but I couldn't go because of my job.

10. She would always watch the house until mother gets back from the store. Sometimes we would stay with her until my mother comes back. She taught me to hid my valuables or sometimes even lock them up.

MODIFIERS: Past Participles as Modifiers

The section on verb combinations covered structures with the verb "to be" and a past participle.

The woman was exhausted.

The car was stolen.

She is named Susan.

Past participles may also be used as modifiers. They may be inserted into sentences to describe words they are next to. Used in this way, they add detail and make the sentences denser and more vivid. For example, the following sentences could be improved.

FAULTY The woman was exhausted. She collapsed on the sidewalk.

The past participle "exhausted" can be put before "woman," the word it describes. Then the weak words "she" and "was" can be eliminated and the two choppy sentences combined into one sentence that is more effective because it has a higher density of significant words than the original sentences.

modifier ending

REVISED The exhausted woman collapsed on the sidewalk.

The following sentences have been similarly strengthened.

FAULTY The car was stolen. It was found at the bottom of the cliff.

REVISED The stolen car was found at the bottom of the cliff.

FAULTY I have a friend. She is named Susan.

REVISED I have a friend named Susan.

FAULTY The business major turned in her marketing report. She was finished at last.

REVISED Finished at last, the business major turned in her marketing report.

REVISED The business major, finished at last, turned in her marketing report.

Words that describe other words are called modifiers. The only problem that arises from the use of past participle forms as modifiers occurs when people forget the past participle endings.

FAULTY My favorite drink is ice tea.

REVISED My favorite drink is iced tea.

FAULTY A student name John left a message for you.

REVISED A student named John left a message for you.

FAULTY High-heel shoes are dangerous.

REVISED High-heeled shoes are dangerous.

FAULTY I wish I had a king-size bed.

REVISED I wish I had a king-sized bed.

Once again the dictionary is helpful. The following entry for *size* ends with its use as a verb and gives an example of its use as a modifier in "medium-sized."

> **size¹** /saɪz/ *n* **1** [U] degree of largeness or small-
> ness: *a building of vast ~; about the ~ of* (=
> about as large as) *a duck's egg; of some ~,* fairly
> large. *They're both of a ~, are the same ~.*
> **That's about the ~ of it,** (colloq) That's a fair
> account of the affair, situation, etc. **2** [C] one of
> the standard and (usu) numbered classes in which
> articles of clothing, etc are made: *~ five shoes;*
> *three ~s too large; all ~s of gloves. I take ~ ten.*
> □ *vt* [VP6A] **1** arrange in ~s or according to ~.
> [VP15B] *~ sb/sth up,* (colloq) form a judgement
> or opinion of. **-sized** /-saɪzd/ *suff*(in compounds)
> having a certain ~: *medium-sized.* `**siz(e)·able**
> /-əbl/ *adj* fairly large.

Modifiers that come from past participles of verbs must be in the past participle form. Be especially careful to include all *ed* endings. They tend to disappear because they are often slurred over in speech.

> **CORRECTION COMMENT: Modifiers that come from past participles of verbs must be in the past participle form.**

EXERCISES *Modifiers: Past Participles as Modifiers*

I. *Write sentences using the following words as modifiers.*

1. short-sleeved
2. overstocked
3. undernourished
4. advertised
5. barbecued
6. promised
7. protected
8. warned
9. called
10. endangered

II. *Combine the following pairs of sentences or clauses by inserting a past participle form next to the thing it describes.*

A. 1. I wore my new shoes to the party. They were high-heeled.

2. The politician refused to compromise. He was hard-nosed.

3. His waterbed fills the room. It is king-sized.

4. A person should always eat a breakfast. It should be well balanced.

5. I went to Miami Beach with a friend. She was named Sandra.

6. She was married in a white satin dress. It was made by her mother.

7. My cousin called her long distance. He was puzzled by her letter.

8. The quarterback staggered to the bench. He was drenched with sweat.

9. We raced to the airport. We were afraid of missing our plane.

10. The candidate couldn't decide what to say. He was amazed by his success.

B. 1. Her mother insists that she be home by ten o'clock even on weekends. Her mother is old-fashioned.

2. People cannot use this entrance if they are handicapped.

3. A person with a refrigerator that is well stocked will never starve.

4. The snack bar has good food. It is also low-priced.

5. Milk that has been powdered is cheaper than fresh milk.

modifier ending

6. The people on the bus were very uncomfortable because it was overcrowded.

7. The lawyer slammed the door. He was disturbed by his client's self-pity.

8. The hummingbird darted away. He was frightened by the faces in the window.

9. The winner of the second round decided to continue playing. She was carried away by her good fortune.

10. My sister took a camping trip with her high school girl friends last summer. She was tired of seeing only her husband.

III. Cross out the incorrect modifier forms in the following sentences, and write the correct forms above them.

A. 1. One time she went into the hospital with fracture bones.

2. The personnel department is looking for an experience key-punch person.

3. We saw one show title *The Horrors of Gin*.

4. Every weekend we pitch pennies and win stuff animals.

5. The rear bedroom has a large walk-in closet, a regular-size bed, a nine-drawer dresser, and two night stands.

6. There is a ride call the Tidal Wave.

7. They serve many kinds of mix drinks.

8. "Roots" was the most watch television show in history.

9. They saw a strange metallic cigar-shape vehicle.

10. The last course will be ham cover with brown sugar.

B.   1. Every morning I eat a soft poach egg.

2. At ten I was a hard-head little girl.

3. The men wear baggy pants, low-heel shoes, and tight shirts.

4. The whole thing was funny, but my friend was a little scare because he doesn't like strange people.

5. We met a lady name Rena from Alaska.

6. My summer will be a full and fast pace one, and I can hardly wait.

7. Then I had to hose down the floor with water, add powder soap, and scrub it down with a broom.

8. We took a whip-cream pie to one birthday party.

9. The witness, disturb by the prosecuter's insinuations, refused to reply.

10. Employers prefer skill laborers because they do the jobs better.

C.   1. Contacts are very expensive compare with glasses.

2. *Star Wars* is one of the best movies ever develop.

3. Stoves are more common in today's industrialized societies than in the less developed ones where people still cook the old fashion way.

4. The most impressive sight is the stain glass partition showing little girls and boys playing in a meadow.

5. No girl has to wear a wrinkle dress if she has an iron.

6. Anyone wanting the stuff toys, fish bowls, or dishes might as well buy them from a store.

7. I also drive the handicap people of Dublin so they can conduct their business.

8. We the people know that the verdict was a bias one, not a just one.

9. Our primary function is keeping emotionally disturb people from going back to a mental institution.

10. I can also remember very vividly a guy name Terrance in eighth grade. He sent one of his friends to give me a long-stem rose and a box of candy shape like a heart.

IV. A. *Correct all errors in the following paragraph.*

Although our bodies are not alive after death, our spirits remain. All of us who have experienced the death of a love one doesn't really believe they are dead. I feel that the deceased will always live within my heart. There has been times when I felt the presence of my mother's spirit. I remembered feeling depress about not having her alive to talk to about my problems. I cursed her for not being there when I needed her. I was sitting in the dark crying, and I felt a warm, comforting sensation around me. I was convinced that my mother's spirit was reaching out and touching me. Whenever I'm feeling depress about something, I sit and talk to my mother as though she is there body and soul.

B. The paragraph above is about an idea that comforts someone. Write a paragraph about an idea that comforts you. Start the paragraph with a summary sentence, and give vivid details to show the comfort that it gives you.

V. A. Read the essay below, and answer these questions:

1. What do you like best about this essay?

2. Does this essay follow a good outline?

3. How could the essay be changed so that everything proves the thesis? Try to find an outline that will be supported by as many as possible of the present body paragraph details.

4. How could the introduction be improved?

5. How could the body paragraphs be improved?

6. How could the conclusion be improved?

modifier ending

Dallas is a beautiful city. There are many places and things to see in this city. I spent eight years growing up in Dallas, they were very fun years. The place that I grew up in was not very far from downtown, but it was very excluded from the everyday hussle and bussle of everything. In our area, during the day, there were only kids running about, especially during the summer. It was a very poor neighborhood and the kids ran about so wildly, because all of our parents had to work and could barely afford food, let alone babysitters. So there we were with nothing better to do but play. We'd play from morning until dark. We all knew that as soon as the darkness began to come that we had to go inside. Every night it was the same when dark came the streets were totally bare of children. That is when I would retreat to my favorite place in the house, our kitchen. While in our very small kitchen, I would sit at the window and look outside. The reason that I liked this spot the best was because it was warm, quiet, and gave me view of the parking lot.

Our kitchen was very small with only enough space to walk in and turn from one piece of furniture to another. The kitchen had no door and only one small window. The room was square and the ceiling rather low. The room had such bad areation and the walls were a yellowish brown from cooking. It always had a warmth about it and never really smelled. That was one of the reasons that I enjoyed staying in the kitchen, considering that the rest of the house was usually cold and drabby. Anyway, the floors that were once a light gray lineoleum had turned to a dark gray with dirt build up in the corners. My father (my only parent then) never really expected much from my sister and I, only that we clean our rooms and the dishes, so the floors usually stayed the same.

Since the kitchen was so small, only the necessary appliances were in there. There was a small four burner stove that was right next to the window. The flames from the burners usually caught onto the window shade, but never caused too much damage. Next to the stove, so close that the door barely opened, was the refrigerator. The refrigerator was quite big, much too big for the amount of food we had. It had a curve front that with the words "Cold Spot" print on it. The noise from this monster (refrigerator) was the only sounds that my mind had to compete with. The noise it made was never really distracting, only a "hum." The only other thing that could fit into our crowd kitchen was the sink. It was on the opposite side of the stove and refrigerator. Our sink was not very large, it had a single tub with hot and cold water valves (the cold didn't work) and a dish rinse which my sister and I used as a squirt gun. That was all that was in the kitchen beside a large picture of a meadow that hung over the sink.

The last and most important thing about our kitchen (to me) was the small window. By the window there was only one cramp corner that nicely fitted a stool. Which I sat on. This was my spot. With all of the warmth from the stove to my right and the support of the sink, I leaned on it, I would sit and stare out of my window. The reason that window was so important to me was because it gave me a view of all of the cars in the parking lot. I sat in this corner and waited for my father to return home from work. The window had always become fogged when I sit there so I had a towel to wipe it. When my father drove up, usually about 3 A.M., I'd pull down the shade and run into my room. My father had always know that I was there because there was always a peep hole through the fog window.

Although, in front of the window was my favorite spot to be in, all of the other things in our kitchen made it comfortable. There was the rhythmic hum of the refrigerator that kept me company, the warmth of the stove, and the support of the sink that kept me from falling when I dosed off. I have never found a spot or room quite like it. Maybe except in my Pinto, but then again it is usually cold and not quite as comfortable.

B. Reread the above essay and underline any errors you find. Share your findings with your classmates. Then rewrite one of the paragraphs, correcting these errors and the weaknesses identified in exercise A.

INDEPENDENT STUDY   Modifiers: Past Participles as Modifiers
(answers in the back)

VI. A. Cross out the incorrect modifier forms in the following sentences and write the correct ones above them.

1. A balance diet is unheard of in this society.

2. Overcook meat will turn hard and flavorless.

3. The J. O. Club conducted delightful activities to raise funds for sick and handicap people.

4. My paper has to be two or three pages long, single-space and type.

5. I met a lady name Connie about two years ago.

6. This movie keeps audiences amuse and in good spirits.

7. Marion also furnished safety glasses, protective shoes, and a long-sleeve blouse.

8. My mother doesn't want to give her more money because she spends most of it on junk like barbecue potato chips, strawberry soda, and Hershey candy bars.

9. Whatever fashion designer came out with the idea of high-heel shoes was very lucky.

10. Sometimes soldiers got wounded, and the doctors had to treat them, like on the show call "M*A*S*H."

B. *Correct the errors in the following paragraph. Some were covered in previous chapters.*

modifier ending

     Yvette help me when I was in fights. There was a girl name Velna who bullied us around. She was bigger than Yvette and me. Velna was fat and very powerful and seem to enjoy picking on me the most. I would sometimes talk back to her when I was a distance away from her, and she would catch me and pull my hair. One day I decided that I wasn't going to let her bully me anymore. The next time she tried to pull my hair, I grab her hand and bit it. Consequently she overpower me, and Yvette came to the rescue. I also remember a boy name Kevin who used to make us pay five cents to get on the monkey bars. One day I refused to pay, he then told me that I had to give him a kiss. I told him that I would give him a kiss with my fist. He dared me to hit him. As I swung to hit him, Yvette jump between us. She said, "Don't fight him, I'll give him a kiss."

MODIFIERS: ADJECTIVES AND ADVERBS

There are two types of modifiers: those which describe nouns or pronouns are called adjectives, and those which describe verbs are called adverbs. Adjectives tell how many or what kind, and adverbs tell when, where, how, and to what extent. People rarely make mistakes with adverbs that tell when or where, but they often use an adjective when they should use an adverb that tells how.

Here are some of the words that cause problems.

Words to tell what kind (adjectives)	*Words to tell how* (adverbs)
good	well
bad	badly
real	really
regular	regularly
serious	seriously
easy	easily
most	mostly

Notice that adverbs usually end in *ly*.

If you need to know whether a word is an adjective or an adverb or if you want to find an adverb form of an adjective, check the dictionary. The following entry for the adjective (*adj*) "serious" gives adverb (*adv*) and noun (*n*) forms and sentences for each.

> **seri·ous** /ˈsɪərɪəs/ *adj* **1** solemn; thoughtful; not given to pleasure-seeking: *a ∼ mind/ appearance/face; look ∼.* **2** important because of possible danger: *a ∼ illness/mistake. The international situation looks ∼.* **3** in earnest; sincere: *a ∼ worker. Please be ∼ about your work.* **∼·ly** *adv* in a ∼ manner: *speak ∼ly to sb; be ∼ly ill.* **∼·ness** *n* state of being ∼: *the ∼ness of the country's financial affairs.* **in all ∼ness,** very ∼ly; not at all in a light-hearted way: *I tell you this in all ∼ness.*

Do not use a word that tells what kind of thing when you need a word that tells how. Here is a typical error.

FAULTY She would have to know her job good.

"Good" is one of the words that tell what kind of thing. It answers the question "what kind?"

What kind of book?	a good book
What kind of baby?	a good baby
What kind of game?	a good game

In contrast, "well" is one of the words that tells how.

How did he play?   well

How did she cook?   well

How did they sleep?   well

In the faulty sentence above, the word "good" is used to tell *how* the person must know her job instead of the word "well."

REVISED She would have to know her job well.

Be sure to use the correct form for a word that tells how. Here are some more faulty sentences revised:

FAULTY My brother took school serious.

How did he take school? Seriously.

REVISED My brother took school seriously.

FAULTY It is important to write clear.

To write how? Clearly.

REVISED It is important to write clearly.

The word "real" should be used to describe a thing, to tell what kind.

Quitting school was a real mistake.

What kind of mistake? A real mistake.

Overpopulation is a real danger.

What kind of danger? A real danger.

However "really," not "real," should be used to tell how. Use "really," not "real," where "very" would fit.

FAULTY Her mother was real sick.

How sick was she? Really sick, very sick.

REVISED Her mother was really sick.

FAULTY The setting was real nice.

How nice was it? Really nice, very nice.

REVISED The setting was really nice.

FAULTY She talks real loud.

How does she talk? Loudly.
How loudly does she talk? Really loudly, very loudly.

REVISED She talks really loudly.

FAULTY They started out real slow.

How did they start out? Slowly.
How slowly? Really slowly, very slowly.

REVISED They started out really slowly.

Determining the correct form for a describing word after a linking verb may be tricky. After forms of "to be" and words like "seem," "feel," "smell," "taste," "look," and "sound," the describing word may seem to tell how, but it really describes the subject, as in these correct sentences.

She smells nice.

He felt comfortable at my house.

His hat looks elegant.

My sister should be careful.

CORRECTION COMMENT: **Do not use a word that tells what kind of thing when you need a word that tells how.**

EXERCISES *Modifiers: Adjectives and Adverbs*

I. A. *Write five sentences for each of the following words.*

1. really

2. real

3. well

4. good

B. *Write one sentence for each of the following words.*

1. slow

2. slowly

3. clear

4. clearly

5. emotional

6. emotionally

7. excessive

8. excessively

9. smooth

10. smoothly

II. *Figure out what questions the modifiers in the following sentences answer. Then cross out any incorrect modifier forms and write the correct ones above them.*

A. 1. I decided to try the shoes on, and they fit perfect.

2. When I first got the car, it ran smooth.

3. Things were going good.

4. I need a good car to drive to school.

5. I thought for sure I had done bad and been rejected.

6. Then I get on the inner tube and sit comfortable on it.

7. The interviewer knows that the applicant can dress good.

8. The dentist scared me really bad.

9. If you ever meet Chuck, please do not take him serious.

10. A person has to get a ticket real early.

B.   1. When I'm driving alone, I can think very clear.

2. Sometimes an insult can hurt a person real bad.

3. They were nice girls and real good friends.

4. The desserts are made just as good as the dinners.

5. Many young people dress real nice when they go to college.

6. I have many loud friends, but I'm real quiet in class.

7. Many people dance professionally while others may not take dance as serious.

8. Luck is accidentally.

9. Jeff always ate good and would get mad at me for not eating my vegetables.

10. Every morning I helped her make breakfast and then did the housework very enthusiastic.

modifier form

C.   1. When he didn't give me the money, I knew he was serious.

2. Some students feel it's real important to get to class on time, but if I'm late I don't care.

3. Sometimes I would be doing bad in one of my classes, and I would tell Mr. Mewsom.

4. A good pair of plates should fit perfect at the edges and leave a small space between.

5. Real discrimination is harder to see.

6. In heavy traffic, people become very frustrated and begin to drive erratic.

7. Too much money is needed to get the real good prizes.

8. Many young people do not believe in marriage as strong as they used to.

9. At the same time these corporations pay off the rich and influential people to keep things running smooth.

10. A person who gets nervous on big tests and flunks them may do good on many little tests.

D.   1. My cousins play very good and should be on a professional team.

2. I enjoyed this amusement park because it doesn't have any real scary rides.

3. I answered her back very calm.

4. In most clothing stores, nice clothes will go on sale at the end of each season.

5. He didn't get paid because he was official dead.

6. The real terrible tragedies have also happened on Halloween.

7. As soon as a young person starts doing good for himself, he gets fired.

8. He and I both love to smell nice, and we have dressers full of colognes and perfumes.

9. As we are dog owners, we should treat them nice.

10. My parents didn't have much money, but they always managed to keep me dressed nice.

E.   Fortunately, the next class went smooth too. It was in the same room as my previous one, so I didn't need to move. As the students began to file in, I started feeling nervous, but once the teacher arrived and began speaking Spanish real slow, I felt comfortable. I relaxed and listened to the teacher. I usually do good in Spanish, and as I sat there I began to feel confident that I would do good in this class and enjoy it.

III. *Read the following essay and discuss its weaknesses with your class-mates. Rewrite the introduction as a group. Then rewrite by yourself one of the other paragraphs in the essay.*

    I enjoy wearing high-heel shoes because they make me feel real casual and jazzy. Every time I put a pair on I feel better about my appearance. I remember once when I went out to a party, and I wore a dress and a nice pair of open-toe high-heel shoes. Let me tell you! I got lots of compliments about how pretty my feet were and how sexy my ankles looked. High-heel shoes seem to add to a womans sensuality. This makes her feel enchanted. And when you look good you feel good. You'll feel so refined, but take it from me, those high-heel shoes are hazardous and expensive.

    They are harmful to our health, and can cause us to have terrible backaches that can lead to a real serious problem. I can recall times when I'd wear high heels continuously, for about a month. Then I'd begin to get this aching feeling in the lower part of my back. That was my signal to cool off on the wearing of high heels. Wearing high-heel shoes can lead to the infliction of leg spasms and it will off-set your posture. The problem that I most frequently hear about regarding the high-heel shoes is the way they derange your instep. I have a girl friend who had been wearing high-heel shoes for eight years. Last year she had to have an operation on her feet. The heels on the majority of shoes she had been wearing were too high. The ligaments surrounding her instep had been pulled and torn apart.

    These high-heel shoes are likewise dangerous because more than half of them have skinny heels. This makes it easier for you to miss a step and fall, while walking down the stairs or step down on the stairs too hard and force the heels to bend under your feet and break. These heels even get caught in the cracks in the streets. Once when I was walking down the street with a friend of mine, and I was just talking and laughing calmly, real relaxed. Then suddenly my left foot got stuck in a hole in the street pavement. As a reflex reaction I pulled my left leg forward and with my heel being stuck in the hole I fell to the ground on my right knee. When I got up I notice the heel of my left shoe was broken in half.

High-heel shoes are pretty expensive. The only reason why I can see their being expensive is because there so feminine and they enhance a womans feet. I remember the last time I went shopping for some shoes. The prices were so high I couldn't believe it. For a pair of black leather ankle straps the price was $56 and for black leather pumps the price was $64. But if you're a woman who like to look and feel her best as much as possible, then you'll have to pay the price.

In these times there is always something unsafe or wrong with everything we use. The economy has gone haywire and inflation has increased so much I can barely afford to buy a pair of high-heel shoes. But there will always be that desire to "keep up with the Jones," as far as fashionable footwear goes especially among women. As long as the stores continue to market this expensive but hazardous footwear problems like these will stay problems.

modifier form

INDEPENDENT STUDY Modifiers: Adjectives and Adverbs (answers in the back)

IV. **A.** *Figure out what questions the modifiers in the following sentences answer. Then cross out any incorrect modifier forms and write the correct ones above them.*

1. In the fall quarter I didn't do very good in my earth science class.

2. I never took school serious.

3. He's a nice man, but he looks fierce.

4. Everyone could dress casual, and people would come for a quick dinner.

5. Blind marriages turned out good sometimes, and the couples were very happy.

6. It is real entertaining watching people do dances like the Freak, the Worm, and the Dog.

7. A teenager who feels free to talk about sex is less likely to get into trouble.

8. Judy jumped up and screamed real loud, and we saw the tack stuck in her good pants.

9. The motorcycle was fun but also dangerous because people didn't know how to ride it good enough.

10. Dogs can scare burglars away with their loud barking.

B.   I feel very unattractive when I go to parties. The gentlemen rarely ask me to dance. I may dance three or four times out of a four-hour party. After someone dances with me, he seems to get away as quick as he can. I sometimes wonder if I am dressed distasteful or bizarre, but I look around me and see others dressed similar, in neat clothes, maybe a nice skirt and blouse. My roommate tells me there is nothing wrong with my dress or me, but I still get this ugly feeling.

MODIFIERS: COMPARISONS

Comparisons add valuable detail to writing, but they must be accurate to be effective. Follow these six guidelines to powerful comparisons.

1. Use the correct comparison form. There are two kinds of comparisons: one thing may be compared to one similar thing, or it may be compared to two or more similar things. English expresses such comparisons with *er* and *est* or "more" and "most," depending on which combination is easier to say. Generally shorter words take *er* and *est,* and longer words take "more" and "most." Some common words have irregular comparison forms. Study the chart in Figure 6.

comparison

> **FAULTY** My teacher's advice was worst than my mother's.

The chart in Figure 6 shows that "worse," not "worst," should be used to compare one thing to one other thing.

> **REVISED** My teacher's advice was worse than my mother's.

If you aren't sure whether a word takes *er* and *est* or "more" and "most," consult a good dictionary. The following entry for the word "young" indicates that the endings *er* and *est* should be used.

> **young** /jʌŋ/ *adj* (-er, -est) **1** (contrasted with *old*) not far advanced in life, growth, development, etc; of recent birth or origin: *a ~ woman/tree/animal/nation, etc.* **2** still near its beginning: *The evening/century is still ~.* **3** ~er, (used before or after a person's name, to distinguish that person from another; contrasted with *elder*): *the ~er Pitt; Pliny the Y~er.* **4** (used before a person's name to distinguish esp a son from his father): *The Y~ Pretender* (grandson of James II). *Y~ Jones is always ready to help his old parents.* **5** as a familiar or condescending form of address: *Now listen to me, ~ man/my ~ lady!* **6** having little practice or experience (in sth): *~ in crime.* **7** ~ *and old,* everyone; *the ~, ~ people*; children: *books for the ~.* □ *n* offspring; ~ ones (of animals and birds): *The cat fought fiercely to defend its ~, its ~ offspring. Some animals quickly desert their ~.* **with ~,** (of an animal) pregnant. ~**·ish** /ˈjʌŋɪʃ/ *adj* fairly ~; somewhat ~. ~**·ster** /ˈjʌŋstə(r)/ *n* child, youth, esp a boy.

2. Never use an *er* or *est* form with "more," "most," "less," or "least."

> **FAULTY** She is more happier since her divorce.

"More" and "happier" should not be used together.

> **REVISED** She is happier since her divorce.

> **FAULTY** I write more better under pressure.

"More" should not be used with "better."

> **REVISED** I write better under pressure.

> **FAULTY** I was the most worst speller in my class.

"Most" should not be used with "worst."

Figure 6. Comparison Forms

	To compare one thing to one similar thing:	To compare one thing to two or more similar things:
short words	*add* er	*add* est
loud	louder	loudest
warm	warmer	warmest
easy	easier	easiest
simple	simpler	simplest
long words	*add "more"*	*add "most"*
serious	more serious	most serious
dramatic	more dramatic	most dramatic
intelligent	more intelligent	most intelligent
expensive	more expensive	most expensive
ly words	*add "more"*	*add "most"*
loudly	more loudly	most loudly
warmly	more warmly	most warmly
easily	more easily	most easily
simply	more simply	most simply
seriously	more seriously	most seriously
dramatically	more dramatically	most dramatically
intelligently	more intelligently	most intelligently
expensively	more expensively	most expensively
irregular		
good	better	best
well	better	best
bad	worse	worst
badly	worse	worst
little	less	least

REVISED I was the worst speller in my class.

FAULTY The blue notebook is less fuller than the other.

"Less" and "fuller" should not be used together.

REVISED The blue notebook is less full than the other.

3. Use *ly* forms to tell how.

The previous unit covered the difference between words that tell what kind, adjectives, and words that tell how, adverbs. The same distinction must be made in comparisons. Adverbs, words ending in *ly,* should be used to tell how. For comparison, simply add "more" or "most," following Figure 6.

CORRECT We enlarged the clearer of the two photographs.

"Clearer" comes from "clear." Both words tell what kind of photograph.

FAULTY Channel nine comes in clearer than channel seven.

Here "clearer" is incorrectly used to tell how the channels come in. "Clear" and "clearer" should be used to tell what kind; "clearly" and "more clearly" should be used to tell how.

REVISED Channel nine comes in more clearly than channel seven.

CORRECT The easiest puzzle comes first.

Here "easiest" is correctly used to tell what kind of puzzle.

FAULTY He studies easiest at home.

"Easiest" comes from "easy." These words should be used to tell what kind. "Easily," "more easily," and "most easily" should be used to tell how he studies.

REVISED He studies most easily at home.

4. When you compare two things, be sure to state both things clearly.

FAULTY Usually Jean tries harder.

The comparison is unclear. Does Jean usually try harder than she did at some particular time or in some particular situation, or does she try harder than someone else and if so who? Both elements of the comparison should be clearly stated.

REVISED Usually Jean tries harder than she did last Tuesday.

REVISED Usually Jean tries harder than Steven does.

FAULTY Jerry challenged Mark more frequently than his mother.

This comparison is unclear. Did Jerry challenge Mark more frequently than he challenged his mother, or did Jerry challenge Mark more frequently than his mother did? All comparisons should be clearly expressed.

REVISED Jerry challenged Mark more frequently than his mother did.

REVISED Jerry challenged Mark more frequently than he challenged his mother.

5. Be sure to compare similar things.

FAULTY The chimpanzee is much like the human brain.

The things compared are not similar. An animal is being compared to an organ. Either the whole beings should be compared,

REVISED The chimpanzee is much like the human.

or the brains should be compared.

REVISED The chimpanzee's brain is much like the human brain.

FAULTY My problems are probably similar to other freshmen.

Here "problems" are being compared to "freshmen." Problems should be compared to problems,

REVISED My problems are probably similar to those of other freshmen.

or people should be compared to people.

REVISED I am probably similar to other freshmen.

6. When comparing something to all similar things, specify precisely the things being compared to avoid comparing something to itself.

FAULTY Louisiana is different from any state in the union.

Because Louisiana is a state, this sentence says that Louisiana is different from Louisiana. Adding the word "other" corrects this problem.

REVISED Louisiana is different from any other state in the union.

Here's a similar sentence:

FAULTY More people get married in June than in any month.

Because June is a month, this sentence claims that more people get married in June than in June. This sentence should compare June to other months, not to all of them.

REVISED More people get married in June than in any other month.

CORRECTION COMMENT: Use standard forms and rigorous logic to express meaningful comparisons.

EXERCISES   Modifiers: Comparisons

I.   Fill in the blanks in the following comparisons. You may have to add more than one word.

1. **EXAMPLE** a. John has a clear voice.

    b. John has *a clearer* voice than Raymond does.

    c. John has *a clearer* voice than any other singer.

    d. John has *the clearest* voice in the choir.

2. a. My white pullover is a warm sweater.

    b. My white pullover is _____ than the navy one.

    c. My white pullover is _____ than any other sweater I own.

    d. My white pullover is _____ sweater I own.

3. a. Uncle Gaylord's milkshakes are smooth.

    b. Uncle Gaylord's milkshakes are _____ than the Stanford Creamery's.

    c. Uncle Gaylord's milkshakes are _____ than those of any other ice cream parlor in town.

    d. Uncle Gaylord's milkshakes are _____ ones in town.

4. a. Hank is serious about an acting career.

    b. Hank is _____ about acting than Susan is.

    c. Hank is _____ about acting than any other actor in the company.

    d. Hank is _____ actor in the company.

5. a. Mr. Thomas is an enthusiastic lecturer.

    b. Mr. Thomas is _____ lecturer than Mr. Bordan.

    c. Mr. Thomas is _____ lecturer than any other English instructor.

    d. Mr. Thomas is _____ lecturer in the English department.

6. a. Mr. Thomas lectures enthusiastically.

    b. Mr. Thomas lectures _____ than Mr. Bordan.

    c. Mr. Thomas lectures _____ than any other English instructor.

    d. Mr. Thomas lectures _____ of all the English instructors.

7. a. Dan is a good basketball player.

    b. Dan is _____ basketball player than Floyd.

    c. Dan is _____ basketball player than any other player on the team.

    d. Dan is _____ basketball player on the team.

8. a. Dan plays basketball well.

   b. Dan plays basketball _____ than Floyd.

   c. Dan plays basketball _____ than any other player on the team.

   d. Dan plays basketball _____ of all the players on the team.

9. a. My brother has a bad cold.

   b. Now my brother has _____ cold than he had last December.

   c. Now my brother has _____ cold than any other he's had this year.

   d. Now my brother has _____ cold he's ever had.

10. a. I have little time to study.

    b. This semester I have _____ time to study than I did last semester.

    c. This semester I have _____ time to study than in any previous semester.

    d. This semester I have _____ time to study I've ever had.

II. *Correct any comparison errors in the following sentences.*

A.   1. It was the most funniest movie I saw all year.

   2. Today she is drinking lesser than in the past.

   3. He was the one cadet that rose faster in power than all cadets.

   4. The material is more thicker and solid than most.

   5. I had to grow up faster.

   6. With my new glasses I could see much clearer than before.

   7. This exam is worst than the last one.

   8. My situation made me a more stronger person.

   9. He sang the silliest song I've ever heard.

   10. The quicker such problems are resolved, the better I feel.

B.   1. I found it more easier to hand in preplanned assignments and survive in college when I stuck to a strict schedule.

   2. A person will react more quicker under stress.

   3. Now I am able to get along better with Valencia because I have matured and learned how to deal with her personality.

4. Today I can read the textbooks or a newspaper much easily than yesterday.

5. Finally I realized that my most specialest friend was gone for good.

6. This crisis taught me to talk to others easier and more open than ever before.

7. Meeting new people made my job funner.

8. Attending Kenyon College has made me the most happiest person I could be.

9. Teenagers have more freedom to do their own things.

10. I can handle stress much more easier today than at sixteen.

III. Rewrite the following comparisons so that they are correct, graceful, and accurate.

A.
1. After I finished the last course, my belly was at least twice the size of my entire body.

2. My camping experience improved my outlook better than before.

3. Soon the fears held within as a baby are directed like a young fawn taking its first steps.

4. My relationship with my mother was completely opposite compared to my relationship with my father.

5. My best year was my sophomore year because I went to a lot of older parties.

6. He played ever weirder as the concert went further.

7. My Datsun performs more better than any car would do on the road.

8. I won two first place awards, became athlete of the week for wrestling, and placed first in the John F. Kennedy Physical Fitness contest out of twelve other high schools.

9. One of the hardest things to leave behind was my friends.

10. This made me realize how happy I was to be a teenager now than to have been one then.

B.
1. Buying houses today is more expansive than the last ten years because more and more people are buying houses more than before.

2. We cannot let ourselves be victims when we least expect the worse in our streets.

3. I was the most happiest girl that day.

4. Until that day comes, the lonliest and painfulest part of all is saying good-by.

5. My little brother makes the problem even worst.

6. Johnny Carson has the most shrewdest investment councelor.

7. Being Oriental, my family is more closer than most of the other nationalities.

8. A person might use some powder or rouge to bring her color out more better.

9. A long running show, "Starsky and Hutch," was one of the most violent shows on television. It was also one of the most highest rated shows.

10. Evelyn knows better to keep quiet around us because my family will criticize back.

IV. A. The following essay compares two sports, boxing and karate.

Boxing has long been a favorite spectator attraction for millions of people throughout the world. The worldwide recognition given to Muhammad Ali is evidence of this. In contrast, professional karate is a relatively unknown sport, because of prejudice and ignorance. The aim in both sports is to defeat an opponent in a one-on-one situation, but boxing is much more popular than karate.

First of all, boxing is more visible than karate. Nearly every man has boxed in some form at some time in his life. Often the most memorable incident in a young boy's life is the fight he had with the school bully. During the fight the two boys undoubtedly imitated boxing's heroes as they flailed away. Unlike boxing, karate is one of the least common forms of fighting outside of the Orient. Occasionally a karate exhibition will draw a mildly interested crowd, but a child is never challenged to a karate bout in the school yard. With little knowledge of the art, people associate killing blows and instant death with karate. In the face of such ignorance, karate has attracted few followers.

Boxing is also easier to learn than karate. Any young man with an average build and stamina can be taught to box in a relatively short period of time. Needless to say, every man can't be a champion, but any man can learn the basics and do so quickly. On the other hand, to learn karate takes quite a long time. To even get in proper shape takes weeks. First, the student must develop flexibility through weeks of painful stretching exercises accompanied by aches and pains in previously unused muscles. Once the flexibility is acquired, mastering the techniques is much more difficult than learning to bob and weave in boxing. Boxing is a sport of relatively simple moves: left hand punches and right hand punches. Karate involves offensive strikes with either hand, either elbow, both feet, and the knees.

The common conception of sportsmanship also makes boxing more popular than karate. In most children's fights, the one who kicks his opponent is considered a dirty fighter and a cheater. Since the Marquis of Queensbury developed the Queensbury rules of human combat, many people feel that kicking a person in a fight is unsportsmanlike and, in turn, have a dim view of karate. Since boxing involves no foot strikes, it is considered a clean sport, and a boxing match is viewed as a test of a boy's manhood.

Few people realize that boxing is really more brutal than karate. People associate violent, murderous, and bloody spectacles with karate matches. They think a karate match is a life or death struggle after which the only man left standing is the winner. Boxing is by far a more brutal sport. Many people go to boxing matches just to see someone get pummeled into unconsciousness. Some of the greatest moments in boxing occur when a nearly beaten fighter rallies and smashes the opponent's face and head, continuously rocking his brain until the referee stops the punishment. Such brutality does not occur in karate. Most matches are decided on a point system and take comparatively little time. An average karate match lasts for five one-and-one-half-minute rounds and may be decided by a single technique. The bloodbaths of boxing do not occur in karate.

comparison

Boxing is more popular than karate because few people have had sufficient contact with karate to recognize its superiority. If our society would turn its attention from boxing, which teaches brutality, to karate, which teaches discipline, the highly evolved karate masters would replace the brutal sluggers as our young people's heroes. Better role models would make better people, which in turn would make a better, and especially a safer, society.

B. *Answer the following questions about the above essay.*

1. *What is its thesis?*

2. *Does the thesis mention both boxing and karate?*

3. *What are its supports?*

4. *Do the supports mention both boxing and karate?*

5. *Does the writer believe that boxing should be more popular than karate?*

C. *Write a comparison essay on one of the topics below. Begin with a thesis and three supports that mention both items being compared. Then develop this outline into an essay giving details on both items in every paragraph.*

two athletes	two cars
two neighborhoods	two people
two sports	the lives of a poor person and a rich person

D. *Write an essay on one of the following topics. Begin with a good thesis and supports that prove it. Express some of your evidence in sharp, rigorous, logical comparisons.*

a challenge you faced	a difficult relationship
your career choice	a triumph
your decision to go to college	learning to write

INDEPENDENT STUDY Modifiers: Comparisons *(answers in the back)*

V. *A. Complete the following comparisons. You may have to add more than one word.*

1. a. Ohio is flat.

    b. Ohio is _____ than Pennsylvania.

    c. Ohio is _____ than any other eastern state.

    d. Ohio is _____ state east of the Mississippi River.

2. a. Mr. Stevens is wealthy.

    b. Mr. Stevens is _____ than Mr. Nelson.

    c. Mr. Stevens is _____ than any other businessman in El Paso.

    d. Mr. Stevens is _____ businessman in El Paso.

3. a. Ms. Sullivan is helpful.

    b. Ms. Sullivan is _____ than Ms. Johnson.

    c. Ms. Sullivan is _____ than any other economics instructor.

    d. Ms. Sullivan is _____ economics instructor at our school.

4. a. Delphina won the race easily.

    b. Delphina won the first race _____ than the second one.

    c. Delphina won the first race _____ than any other race she ran that day.

    d. Delphina won the first race _____ of all the races she ran that day.

5. a. They served good pastries.

    b. They served _____ pastries than Goodnow's.

    c. They served _____ pastries than any other bakery.

    d. They served _____ pastries in town.

B. Correct the comparisons in the following sentences if necessary.

1. The president has more experience with inflation problems.

2. We grew closer to each other than ever before and therefore closer to mankind.

3. I write much more better since I took his course.

200 MATCHING THE PARTS

4. After I got on it, I realized it was much bigger and powerful than I had thought.

5. Standing up to your mother isn't the easiest thing to do, but it is the most wisest thing to do.

6. After winning the discus throw, I was able to handle everyday problems easier.

comparison

7. Sojin's view of the world around her is about three feet lower than the average person.

8. When matched against a skateboard, the bike is a rabbit and the skateboard is a turtle.

9. Since my father's remarriage, I am much more happier than I was before.

10. This experience made me a much more fair person, a much happier person, and a much easier person to get along with.

WRONG WORD FORM

As a word changes function in a sentence, its ending also changes. In addition to the *s, ed, ing,* and *ly* endings already discussed, other endings are used to change words to nouns, verbs, or adjectives. For example, a new ending may change a word from

a verb	to *a noun*	to *an adjective*
He always **succeeds.**	His **success** upsets me.	**successful** attempts
She **permits** smoking.	Her **permission** is needed.	a **permissive** teacher

or from

a noun	to *a verb*	to *an adjective*
The **drama** began.	They **dramatize** it.	**dramatic** fights
under his **dominance**	I **dominate** him.	**dominant** genes

Figure 7 lists these word endings. Of course, endings can't be added arbitrarily—we say "helpful," not "helpsome," and "loyalty," not "loyalness"—but this list should suggest the correct word form. If it doesn't, consult a dictionary. The following dictionary entry for the noun (*n*) "tragedy" gives its adjective (*adj*) form, "tragic," and its adverb form (*adv*) "tragically."

> **tra·gedy** /ˈtrædʒədɪ/ *n* (*pl* -dies) **1** [C] play for the theatre, cinema, TV, of a serious or solemn kind, with a sad ending; [U] branch of the drama with this kind of play. **2** [C,U] very sad event, action, experience, etc, in real life. **tra·gedian** /trəˈdʒidɪən/ *n* writer of, actor in, ∼. **tra·gedienne** /trəˈdʒidɪˈen/ *n* actress in ∼.

Be sure to use the form of the word that fits its use in the sentence.

FAULTY Jerry is much more intelligence than his boss.

Instead of the noun "intelligence," this sentence needs an adjective to describe Jerry. One *has* "intelligence" but *is* "intelligent."

REVISED Jerry is much more intelligent than his boss.

FAULTY My adolescent was very painful.

Instead of the adjective "adolescent," this sentence needs the noun "adolescence" to be its subject.

REVISED My adolescence was very painful.

CORRECTION COMMENT: Be sure to use the form of the word that fits its use in the sentence.

Figure 7. Word endings

Nouns (words for things)	Verbs (action or linking words)
-acy, -age, -al	-ate
-an, -ant	-en
-ance, -ancy	-fy
-ence, -ency	-ize
-er, -ar, -or, -ery	
-ier, -eer, -ee, -ess	
-ian, -ism, -ity, -ist	
-ion, -tion, -sion, -ation	
-dom, -hood, -ice	
-mony, -ment, -ness	
-ship, -tude, -ty, -th, -y	
Adjectives (words to tell what kind)	**Adverbs** (words to tell how)
-al, -able, -ible	-ly
-an, -ant, -en, -ent	
-esque, -ic, -ish, -ive	
-ful, -less, -some, -like	
-ose, -ons, -ory, -y	

EXERCISES: Wrong Word Form

I. Fill in the blanks in the following sentences with the correct form of the underlined word. Consult a dictionary if necessary.

A.
1. The president speaks <u>clearly</u>. He is a _____ speaker.

2. My brother is <u>bold</u>. He acts _____ .

3. She participates <u>actively</u>. She is an _____ participant.

4. She has <u>intelligence</u>, so she is _____ .

5. He prefers <u>independence</u>. He is _____ .

6. The boss is <u>patient</u>. She has _____ .

word form

7. He is a <u>king</u>, and Great Britain is his _____ .

8. She is very <u>neat</u>. Her _____ makes up for my sloppiness.

9. My friend acts like a <u>child</u>. He is very _____ .

10. Dick is an <u>actor</u>, and his wife is an _____ .

B. 1. Kathy loves <u>books</u>. She is _____ .

2. She <u>betrayed</u> her husband. Her _____ hurt him deeply.

3. Her father will <u>permit</u> her to come. She has his _____ .

4. Their <u>theory</u> is well-known. They _____ about life on other planets.

5. He wants to go to <u>sleep</u>. He is _____ .

6. He loves to <u>flirt</u>. He has many _____ .

7. She <u>admires</u> her boss. Her _____ is understandable.

8. I want to <u>know</u> all about France. I want to be _____ about France.

9. He plans to become a <u>priest</u>. He will enter the _____ .

10. The car has many <u>miles</u> on it. Its _____ is high.

C. 1. She <u>waits</u> on tables. She is a _____ .

2. The child must be <u>punished</u>. He must have _____ .

3. The master is <u>wise</u>. He has _____ .

4. This room is <u>pleasant</u>. It _____ me.

5. She has no <u>pity</u>. She is _____ .

6. He must be <u>warmed</u>. He needs _____ .

7. She adds <u>accurately</u>. Her addition is _____ . I admire her _____ .

8. I met a man who writes <u>novels</u>. He is a _____ .

9. My father's <u>nerves</u> are on edge. He is _____ .

10. He wanted some <u>advice</u>, so he visited his _____ .

II. *Correct the wrong word forms in the following sentences. Some sentences may be correct.*

A. 1. She was a very beautiful, elegant, and intelligence young lady.

2. They knew the Rabbit would out-sale all their other models.

3. Don't you want to be health?

4. Luck is accidentally.

5. I sympathize with your fear.

6. She is a teaching assistance.

7. Her reassurance easied my mind.

8. I've always wanted a large family, not gigantic but comfortably.

9. I learned how to operation two kinds of cash registers.

10. If they don't know when they can return the money to the lendee, they should say so.

B. 1. My brother is a big-headed, conceited, brat person.

2. Even though the prawn is deep fried, the batter is always light, fluffy, and greaseness.

3. After a year, traveling becomes boring and expense.

4. Iranians believe in Islamism and listen to the chief.

5. I prefer to go out at someone else's expensive.

6. I got the experience of being with people from different backgrounds.

7. Fighting shouldn't take place in a game because it is unsportsmen.

8. A few decades ago this assumption could possible have been correct.

9. I know arguments could break up a married.

10. I am so exciting about going to the party.

C. 1. Nevertheless, she did not negligent her studies.

2. The choosing of a place to skate is also important.

3. Many dangers things happen on the way to school.

4. High school was the started of my dunking career.

5. I prefer junk food, which is not very health.

6. Americans are fame for baseball, hot dogs, apple pie, and Chevrolets.

7. I was mere a guy with a big vocabulary, good grammar, and common sense.

8. Its engine is a 430 with a four-track carburetor, automatic transmission, power steer, and power brakes.

9. Her husband was fired by his employee.

word form

10. Television not only dominants the time and space. It also destructs the communication among members of the family.

D. 1. Dishes like sukiyaki make up a health diet.

2. You must also have a lot of patients to deal with the customer.

3. When my children's adolescents comes, I will properly educate them about the facts of life.

4. Each athlete at the Olympics has a different patriot feeling.

5. Inside the stove one can find harding cheese, grease, meat sauce, and other foods or food juices that have spilled.

6. After eating Chinese food, I feel like jogging because I feel full but very lightly.

7. I couldn't believe they were communication until the female crab decided to leave her home.

8. After graduate, I will seek a manager position.

9. It is very relaxing and not too riskful to take a ride in the open fields or through the woods.

10. Suicide should not be categoried as a violent crime.

III. *The following paragraph contains several word form errors, some of which were covered in previous sections of the book. Cross out the errors and write the correct forms in the margin.*

When I'm speaking in front of a group of people, I want everything to go smooth. If I forget a line or stumble over a word, I turn bright red, and my butterflies wake up. For example, during my senior year in high school, I ran for a class officer. At the rally, in the middle of my speaking, I forgot a line. I was terrorized. I stood there, shock, looking back at all those faces. I was so mix up I couldn't remember what I had said or what I wanted to say. I just turned around and went back to my seat.

IV. *A. Read the following essay and decide which body paragraph has the best evidence and which one has the worst. Be prepared to support your opinion with evidence.*

Perhaps, the person that I love the best in this world is my mother. She is not only a good wife to my father but also a sweet and terrific mother to me. My life is influenced by her because she is the one who has made me a better person.

First of all, she teaches me to love persons. She usually said to me that "love is worthless—If you love people and treat well them, you will obtain everything nice from them." What does she mean by that? Well, this means I need to understand persons, forgive them whenever they make mistakes. She agrees some person really bother me but try to control my angry and forget them. My mother also said that If I can help people, go ahead and do that. Assistance is also a form revealing that I love them, I am a benevolent person.

In order to help me to keep up my classes, my mother checked my homework every night when I was in junior high school. I remember she usually spent four hours every night to sit close to me at my desk and to open all of my notebooks. She carefully read all of the comments that my teachers wrote on it. She found out that I was bad in Mathematic. One day she bought a Math book and told me she would teach me this. Then night after night, I had to do some applied problems. After a couple months I became one of the best students who got the score highest in Math. My mom, she was very delighted when she heard this.

In addition, my mother persuades and protects me whenever I do something wrong. One time (when I was 11 years old) I played with some friends in front of my house. We were throwing the ball back and forth to each other. Accidently when one of my friend throw it to me, I did not catch it well; the ball hit the window glass and then "pang" the window glass is broken. I was scared and cried loudly. My mother run up to me to ask what happened. She held me in her hands and patted her hands over my head. She said "It's all right—honey—I'm glad you're not hurt. Don't worry. I will fix it." Well, she really made me feel better. When my father came home, of course he was very furious about what I did. My mother begged my father not to punished me, she told him that it was only an accident.

So I love my mother a great deal. I usually tell myself that I will try to please her, I will try to do anything that will make she feel good. She has done everything to make me a better person, this I will never forget. I hope when I am older and have enough money I will take her in a trip around the world because this is one of her wishes.

B. Reread the essay above and draw lines under its errors. Discuss these errors with your classmates. Then rewrite the first body paragraph, correcting all its errors.

V. *A. Write an essay about someone who has made you a better person. Write a good outline and check it with your instructor. Then write an essay using details and examples to show this person in action.*

B. Write an essay on one of the following topics. Remember to check your outline with your instructor and use vivid details to support your argument.

a childish thing you enjoy doing

smoking   praying

prejudices   junk food

choosing classes   assassination

INDEPENDENT STUDY: *Wrong Word Form* (answers in the back)

VI. *A. Correct the word form errors in the following sentences. Consult a dictionary if necessary.*

1. There's a big different between Taiwan and America.

2. There were some tragedy and some comedy stories.

3. On the train ride, one can view one of the world's famous nature wonders, the Grand Canyon.

4. Overpopulating began to appear gradual around the Middle Ages.

5. He was grateful for her friendness during his difficulty.

6. The white blossom shows up in only one of every four plants because the red flower dominants it.

7. The professor was very upset by the interrupting.

8. I will always feel a lost when that special someone dies.

9. We have become so dependence on cars.

10. All the students participanted in the boycott.

B.   I understand my problem. I am scare, fear of failure, afraid of a losing a good tooth, getting a disaster hair style, or giving a wrong answer. I have not found a solution to my problem. I will either have to see a psychiatric or plan to live with my fear for the rest of my life.

6. Punctuating Correctly

• Punctuation reveals and clarifies the relationships among words. It separates similar items and exposes independent clauses so that sentences are as easy as possible to understand.

COMMA RULES 1, 2, AND 3

Commas should be used only where rules demand them.

1. Put a comma (,) before an independent clause to separate it from words or groups of words that come before it.

Nevertheless, she called home every half hour.

Finishing the last problem, he breathes a sigh of relief.

While we cooked, our husbands drank beer.

Without the comma, a reader might assume the last sentence started "While we cooked our husbands," and then the rest of the sentence wouldn't make sense. The comma makes the reading easier.

2. Use commas to separate items in a list or series.

I looked into the bathroom and saw a dark ring around the tub, toothpaste on the mirror, and wet towels on the floor.

San Blas, Puerto Vallarta, and Manzillo have beautiful scenery and interesting people.

She turned in her essay, picked up her books, and left the room.

When all the items in the list are separated by "fanboys" words (for, and, nor, but, or, yet, so), commas are not used.

She accepted neither compliments nor criticism.

Socks and shoes and books dropped from the window.

When an address or date is being used in a sentence, in addition to the commas between the items, a comma must also be placed after the last item.

> She moved to 13 Little Kate Road, Park City, Utah, to be near her parents.

> The lobster in Marblehead, Massachusetts, is the best in the world.

> July 21, 1980, was the first day of registration.

3. Use commas before the "fanboys" words (for, and, nor, but, or, yet, so) when they connect two independent clauses.

> A large straw hat covered his hair, and sunglasses hid his eyes.

> He is trying to be nice, but she has made her decision.

> The train was early, so we didn't have to stand in the rain.

> She came out on the stage, and she addressed the audience.

Rules 2 and 3 dictate that commas should be used before "fanboys" words like "and" at the end of a list separated by commas and between independent clauses. In other places, commas should not be used before these words.

> **FAULTY** She came out on the stage, and addressed the audience.

Here "and" connects the two verbs "came" and "addressed," not two independent clauses, so a comma is wrong.

> **REVISED** She came out on the stage and addressed the audience.

> **FAULTY** He wondered when they would come, and what they would say.

Here "and" connects the dependent clauses "when they would come" and "what they would say," not independent clauses, so a comma is wrong.

> **REVISED** He wondered when they would come and what they would say.

> Here are some sentences with the comma use improved.

> **FAULTY** Before I can prepare my lessons I must spend two hours feeding my family.

Rule 1 dictates a comma after words before an independent clause, so a comma is required after lessons.

> **REVISED** Before I can prepare my lessons, I must spend two hours feeding my family.

> **FAULTY** They invited him in, when he arrived.

No rule dictates a comma in the sentence above. The words "when he arrived" are not an independent clause, and so rule 1 doesn't apply; there's no list, and so rule 2 doesn't apply; there's no "fanboys" word, and so rule 3 doesn't apply. A comma should be used only where a rule demands one.

> **REVISED** They invited him in when he arrived.

FAULTY One might expect her to be very frail but she is one of the strongest people I know.

Rule 3 demands a comma before a "fanboys" word when it connects two independent clauses.

REVISED One might expect her to be very frail, but she is one of the strongest people I know.

FAULTY He plays only a few minutes at a time, and can wear his uniform for two games before it needs washing.

Commas should be used before "fanboys" words like "and" only at the end of a list or between two independent clauses. Here "and" is between the two verbs "plays" and "can wear," not between two independent clauses, so the comma is incorrect.

REVISED He plays only a few minutes at a time and can wear his uniform for two games before it needs washing.

Many good sentences contain commas dictated by several rules, as do the following sentences. The number of the rule that demands each comma is printed above it.

After traveling to class in her wheelchair,¹ she must unload a heavy carrying bag full of books,² transfer a six-inch cushion from her wheelchair to a seat in class,² and finally use her crutches to get to her seat.

My mother spent the whole day kissing,² hugging,² and listening to the children,³ and when everyone was hungry at six o'clock,¹ she miraculously produced a delicious meal.

CORRECTION COMMENT: Commas should be used only where rules demand them.

EXERCISES: *Comma Rules 1, 2, and 3*

I. *Write sentences using the following elements in the given order, and use commas where rules demand them.*

1. *two independent clauses*

2. *one independent clause with three subjects*

3. *one dependent clause and one independent clause with two verbs*

4. *one dependent clause and two independent clauses*

5. *three prepositional phrases and one independent clause with three verbs*

II. The following sentences are correctly punctuated. Above each comma, write the number of the rule that demands that comma.

A.

1. When my alarm clock goes off, the cat starts crying under my window.

2. I spent my afternoon mowing the lawn, trimming the edges, and pulling the weeds.

3. Mr. Burt has the day off today, so the mail will be late.

4. When the blueberry season is over, we will drive over to Hampton Falls for some peaches.

5. President Carter won the nomination, but Senator Kennedy won the convention.

6. We will go to the park and cook corn, potatoes, and hamburgers over the coals.

7. My uncle in Tucson, Arizona, lives in a trailer park.

8. While my hands are busy pulling weeds, planting seeds, or raking leaves, my mind appreciates the beauty and serenity of the outdoors.

9. This assignment asks me to write about my favorite leisure activity, and my favorite leisure activity is writing.

10. Nothing beats packing my gear, buying some steaks, and zooming away in my car.

B.

1. Last week I was struggling with a project for my broadcasting class, and I finally decided to take the easy way out and do it as simply and uncreatively as possible just to get it done.

2. I'm a very impatient person, and when the road isn't smooth, I get frustrated.

3. It took me and the clutch a while to understand each other, but we eventually did.

4. I ran off my own Christmas cards, business cards, and graduation announcements.

5. If she wants to go somewhere, she either has to carry the baby, diapers, and bottles with her, or she has to find someone responsible to watch her baby.

6. Fireworks make me nervous and uneasy, and when the Fourth of July explodes, I hide.

7. When the whole gang finally arrives, we'll sit down for a breakfast of coffee cake, fresh fruit, and eggs.

8. Ever since I can remember, I've given my family handmade presents instead of expensive ones, and they seem to cherish my gifts the most.

9. I was never interested in biology and geometry, but they were required courses, so I struggled through them.

10. Babies and puppies are cute and lovable, but both grow up and need constant attention and care.

III. *Add commas to the following sentences where rules demand them, and write the number of the rule above each one you add.*

comma 1, 2, &

A. 1. When we were doing math or writing the teachers had to help.

2. The teachers had to help when we were doing math or writing.

3. She may have been the oldest but she wasn't the smartest.

4. I go camping swimming picknicking jogging and everything else.

5. I got tired of looking for her because it was hopeless.

6. If care is taken roller skating can be fun.

7. Lane was a very nice man and fun to work with.

8. It must also be easy to work on and parts for it should be easily obtained.

9. Jose Lopez Mateos studied in Berkeley California and other Mexicans have studied in Texas.

10. The baking soda gets the yellow off our teeth and makes them white again.

B. 1. It took some time and she finally came to accept it.

2. There were three other finalists waiting for the board to start when I got there.

3. I can remember another time when my parents would go to dances and leave me with a babysitter.

4. When I return home more inside work awaits.

5. I was thrilled over the idea of preparing meals and mending clothes.

6. Mother also would go out in the woods and pick huckleberries and blackberries and share them with her.

7. The command finally came and we started to fire at the pop-up targets.

8. Brushing one's teeth also keeps him from getting bad breath.

9. For example I went to the Hungry Tiger and heard Ron Lewis.

10. After the first couple of solo runs on your new wheels I'm sure you've realized there's more to skating than just suiting up and hitting the floor.

C. 1. I often came home crying because I couldn't catch on.

2. At the same time rice lamb and tomatoes are the main ingredients in most Greek dishes.

3. When she was born God probably had many things on his mind.

4. Being on my own has taught me many things and I'm grateful for the experience.

5. The answer would be yes if you had a brother with an attitude regarding personal property like my brother's.

6. Don't be afraid to ask and don't let the dealers try to sell you something right away.

7. I once planned to go to a picnic but had to finish my housework first.

8. When I was living at home with my family I never had to make any decisions.

9. Eggs spinach carrots and mushrooms are often added to the noodles.

10. Snowshoes may be rented for five dollars a day or one dollar and thirty cents an hour.

D. 1. We know when to laugh it off and when to be serious.

2. When you are going to high school you don't have to worry about paying bills and having a job.

3. We then started to unload the tents and sleeping bags and braced for a cold night.

4. Even though I lost a friend I learned a lesson from all of this. Now I never lend a friend anything unless I do not want it back.

5. Why do that when you can take another couple along share the gas expense and enjoy yourselves?

6. The next to the last page of the book is blank.

7. After we had gone through the board we waited for the results.

8. After the soil has been prepared for planting one has to arrange his garden by forming rows or beds for the seeds.

9. He was hated by the other cadets but his superiors liked him and their approval was what he wanted.

10. She quickly left for home and when she pulled up in front he was just getting out of his car.

IV. A. *Put commas in the following essay where rules demand them. Put the number of the rule that demands each comma above that comma.*

I shift down to third gear stamp on the accelerator and barely squeeze in front of another car as the lane ends. I keep the throttle wide open through a series of "S" curves and detect the tires starting to slide. Traffic appears and I weave in and out and barely make it each time. I grin and admit to myself that I have fun driving.

I like the sensation of hard acceleration. My body sinks into the cushioned seat. The streetlamps stores and trees that were next to me once shrink and blend with the horizon in two or three seconds. The rest of the cars shrink also. They do so more slowly but quickly enough to put a safe distance between them and me.

Going around curves quickly gives me a good feeling too. The cockpit leans to one side and my body leans with it. The tires make a squealing sound as they grope for contact with the road. At the end of the curve my pulse lowers and I become very calm and tranquil.

I like to disobey the flow of traffic. If one lane of traffic is much shorter than another at a stoplight I take the shorter one. Sometimes I make my own lane and out-accelerate the traffic next to me. On the freeway I do not wait for someone going slower than I to get into the slow lane. I go around him. And I never let anyone cut in front of me.

My way of having fun suggests that I am not at peace in safe situations. I must take a chance that my tires may give way or that I might hit a car.

B. Look back at the essay above and answer the following questions. Be prepared to back up your answers with evidence.

1. *Is the evidence good?*

2. *Is there enough evidence?*

3. *How could the evidence be expanded?*

4. *Is the conclusion good?*

5. *How could the conclusion be improved?*

C. Write a new conclusion for the essay above.

INDEPENDENT STUDY: Comma Rules 1, 2, and 3 *(answers in the back)*

V. A. Add commas to these sentences where rules demand them. Write the number of the rule above each one you add.

1. This statement is true because the car body protects the driver but the motorcycle doesn't provide any protection.

2. We'd go downtown shopping together buy the same colored skirts and blouses and wear them to school on the same day.

3. If I had to send my children to school there I would make sure I taught them as much as I could at home.

4. Everytime I want a good meal and don't feel like cooking I go to the Sizzler.

5. I met a girl from Calgary Canada named Gretta Wilson.

6. Having good looking teeth is important when meeting a beautiful woman or making a business deal.

7. Finally we talked ourselves into going so we quickly had to find our friends.

8. Most of the time when I go out with other girls I have to pay my own way but when I go out with guys they pay my way.

9. Working may not seem as enjoyable to others as it does to me.

10. If I didn't look and listen I didn't learn because they didn't have the extra time to help me.

B.   Saigon prospered right up until the communist takeover. It had about twenty theaters. The Rex Eden and Casino were big ones and they always presented French or American movies. During weekends many people stood in line and waited to buy tickets. Even though these theaters were expensive people preferred them because they showed the best films. Famous films like *Romeo and Juliet Doctor Zhivago* and *Gone with the Wind* usually played on their screens.

C.   Saigon also had a very big shopping center. Along Tu Do and Nguyen Hue Avenues there were department stores flower stores and television stores. On weekends people came from faraway places and assembled in this area. Restaurants stores and theaters were full and people in fancy clothes walked on the streets and laughed happily.

COMMA RULE 4

4. Words that interrupt a sentence should be set off by commas. They may be words moved to an unusual place in the sentence. For example,

> However, her apple pie is well known.

could also be written

> Her apple pie, however, is well known.

> On the other hand, real estate has continued to appreciate.

could also be written

> Real estate, on the other hand, has continued to appreciate.

Interrupters may also be extra modifiers that come after the thing they describe.

> Michael, waiting for the mailman, wandered idly around the yard.

> Lambert, exhausted from his trip, didn't even want to eat.

> My oldest sister, Mary, is a public accountant.

> Jeremy, who knew better than to talk in front of strangers, was describing their adventure to everyone in the tavern.

> My car, which had been parked in the street, had a long scratch along the side.

Sometimes these modifiers may not seem like interrupters because they come at the end of the sentence instead of in the middle, but no matter where they are, extra modifiers after the thing they describe should be separated from the rest of the sentence by commas.

> He enjoys listening to music, especially organ music.

> She waited patiently for Mr. Hart, who had promised to be back by two o'clock.

A modifier is extra if it is not necessary to identify the person or thing being discussed. A modifier that is necessary to tell which person or thing is being discussed is an essential part of the sentence, so no commas should be used around it. Compare the following correctly punctuated sentences.

> My mother, who wanted to leave early, forgot all about the time.

> The woman who wanted to leave early forgot all about the time.

Both of these sentences have the dependent clause modifier "who wanted to leave early" after the words it describes, "my mother" and "the woman." This modifier is extra in the first sentence because the words "my mother" completely identify the person being discussed, so commas should be used around the modifier. However, in the second sentence, the modifier is necessary to tell which woman forgot about the time, so commas should not be used around it.

Here are two correctly punctuated sentences:

I am looking for *The Art of Italian Cooking,* which tells how to make lasagne.

I am looking for a book which tells how to make lasagne.

These sentences have the same dependent clause modifier, "which tells how to make lasagne," after the words it describes, *"The Art of Italian Cooking"* and "a book." This modifier is extra in the first sentence because we already know the name of the book, so a comma is required. Since the end of the modifier comes at the end of the sentence, the period takes the place of the second comma. In the second sentence, however, the modifier is necessary to tell what book the writer is looking for, and so no comma should be used.

Though these modifiers are extra in the sense that they aren't needed to identify the things they describe, they are not extra in any other sense. Such modifiers strengthen sentences by adding valuable detail. Notice how much less interesting the following sentences are than the sentences above with the extra modifiers.

Michael wandered idly around the yard.

Lambert didn't even want to eat.

He enjoys listening to music.

She waited patiently for Mr. Hart.

Clauses beginning with the word "that" are always necessary, so commas should never be used with them. Similarly, a modifier that could be expressed as a "that" clause should not have commas. The sentences above could be expressed as follows:

The woman that wanted to leave early forgot all about the time.

I am looking for a book that tells how to make pizza.

Since the modifiers in these sentences can be expressed as "that" clauses, they are necessary, and so no commas should be used. In contrast, the modifiers in the other sentences don't convert gracefully to "that" clauses, and so the modifiers are extra and need commas.

FAULTY My mother that wanted to leave early forgot all about the time.

FAULTY I am looking for *The Art of Italian Cooking* that tells how to make lasagne.

Here are some examples of typical student errors corrected:

FAULTY Lillie Langtry a beauty from Jersey became the darling of London society.

"A beauty from Jersey" is a modifier after the words it describes, "Lillie Langtry," and it is extra because the woman's name identifies her, so commas should be used around it.

REVISED Lillie Langtry, a beauty from Jersey, became the darling of London society.

FAULTY The boy, that helps out at the clinic, wants to be a dentist.

A "that" clause is always necessary, so commas should not be used.

REVISED The boy that helps out at the clinic wants to be a dentist.

FAULTY John who is five years older than I, introduces me to his friends.

Here the writer has put a comma after the modifier "who is five years older than I" but none before it. Commas should only be used between a subject and a verb when there is extra modifying material after the subject, and then two commas are required to set the modifier off and emphasize the independent clause. There should never be one comma between a subject and its verb. The modifier in this sentence is extra because John has already been named, so commas are required.

comma 4

REVISED John, who is five years older than I, introduces me to his friends.

FAULTY The first thing she requested, was a sharp pencil.

Again, modifiers in the middle of a sentence need two commas or none. The modifier "she requested" is a "that" clause and therefore necessary, so no commas should be used.

REVISED The first thing she requested was a sharp pencil.

FAULTY I believe, she really wants to quit.

The words "she really wants to quit" are a "that" clause and therefore necessary, so a comma should not be used. *Never* replace the word "that" by a comma.

REVISED I believe she really wants to quit.

REVISED I believe that she really wants to quit.

CORRECTION COMMENT: Words that interrupt a sentence should be set off by commas.

EXERCISES: Comma Rule 4

I. A. *Write sentences to go around the following interrupters.*

1. _____ in my opinion _____

2. _____ without a doubt _____

3. _____ I understand _____

4. _____ he reflected _____

5. _____ furthermore _____

6. _____ you know _____

7. _____ we understand _____

8. _____ nevertheless _____

9. _____ she puzzled quietly _____

10. _____ of course _____

B. *Write sentences as requested below, and punctuate them correctly.*

1. *three sentences with extra modifiers after the words they modify*

2. *three sentences with necessary modifiers after words they modify*

3. *three sentences with -ing modifiers after the words they modify*

4. *three sentences with -ed modifiers after the words they modify*

5. *three sentences with "who" clause modifiers after the words they modify*

6. *three sentences with "which" clause modifiers after the words they modify*

7. *three sentences with "that" clause modifiers after the words they modify*

8. *three sentences with names and modifiers after them*

9. *three sentences with names as modifiers after the words they modify*

10. *three sentences with words moved to an unusual place*

II. *Write sentences to go around the following modifiers so that they will be necessary and need no commas.*

A. 1. **EXAMPLE** *The man* who just returned from Bermuda *has a terrific tan.*

2. _____ which I prefer _____

3. _____ stalking from the office _____

4. _____ chattering on mindlessly _____

5. _____ rescued from a fate worse than death _____

6. _____ who was looking nervously over his left shoulder _____

7. _____ wearing checkered pants and a white belt _____

8. _____ who always carried an extra handkerchief _____

9. _____ which smelled like mold and old ashtrays _____

10. _____ holding a glass of milk _____

B. 1. _____ who knocked over the chair _____

2. _____ backing slowly into the kitchen _____

3. _____ presenting *The Last of the Red Hot Lovers* _____

4. _____ defeated in the last ten seconds of the game __

5. _____ Henry J. Woessner III _____

6. _____ who was driven to the ends of his patience_____

7. _____ who slipped the gun into his inside pocket _____

8. _____ seated quietly in a dark corner _____

9. _____ who had mistaken me for a well-known rock

singer_____

10. _____ endangered by acid water _____

*C. Go back to exercises A and B, and write sentences around the same
modifiers so they will be extra and need commas.*

III. *Put commas in the following sentences where rule 4 demands them.*

A. 1. Mrs. Steele who has been out of school for twenty-two years wants to take a degree in law.

2. The lady who has been out of school for twenty-two years wants to take a degree in law.

3. Shi-Tou a summer resort in South Taiwan is between Tai-Chung and Tai-Nan.

4. Ms. Martin my tennis instructor is very patient with her students.

5. I wish that my high school English teacher had taught me to punctuate.

6. Customers that are still in the shop after closing leave promptly after getting a whiff of the aroma.

7. Darrell Watley the last master undertaker has more business than he can handle.

8. Over this long weekend especially this Friday I'm going to spend time with my best friend Wendy.

9. Mr. Brown who checked in last had to take a double room.

10. The steak was so juicy my eyes began to water from pure delight.

B. 1. I enjoy ice blocking which is the sport of sliding down a hill on a block of ice.

2. A tomato which is fresh from the garden has a flavor that cannot be surpassed by a tomato which has been sitting in the grocery store for days.

3. I enjoy the family picnic because there are always lots of good things to eat that I normally don't fix at home.

4. I wanted to help my mother who was cleaning the house for my party.

5. I wanted to continue my education at the University of Tehran which was one of the best universities in the Middle East.

6. I really cherish our new strawberry patch which is growing big beautiful strawberries.

7. Iran had only four colleges and universities which weren't enough for all the people who wanted to go to college.

8. A block of ice costs eighty-five cents plus four cents tax which comes to a total of eighty-nine cents.

9. The ideal roommate is someone who can share one's interests and goals.

10. I have a friend who had an American roommate.

C. 1. I advise anyone who will spend a day with a small child to get plenty of rest the day before.

2. My best friend Brigette had assured me that he was a nice person.

3. All parents should have their children close together about a year or two apart.

4. Winston Bridge who is a good athlete shared my grief and decided to do something about it.

5. The building was kept spotless at all times because the medicines that were made had to be germ and bacteria free.

6. A clerk who sells a sale item should remind the customer that it cannot be returned.

7. My present religion which is Holiness requires many sacrifices from a Christian.

8. The man I met on the road to Bath wore knickers and a cap.

9. After some miles however the road stopped rolling up and down.

10. Her age which was eighty-six almost matched the number of pounds she weighed.

IV. A. The following introduction requires commas demanded by rule 4 and the rules covered in the preceding section. Add those commas, and write the number of the rule that demands it above each one.

Summer my favorite season has always been associated with freshness new growth and change. I personally have done my most profound soul-searching during the summer. I usually find the time for a back-packing trip my way of finding the necessary peace for an inward glance. This summer however I may not get off to the mountains yet I am confident it will be a summer to remember. This summer is going to bring many changes for me.

B. *The following essay requires commas demanded by all four rules. Add those commas and write the number of the rule that demands it above each one.*

Remember when you were a child? Little boys played cowboys and Indians while little girls played with dolls and dreamed of someday becoming mommies. Even then the messege was: nice girls grow up and become someone's dear old mother. Oh I admit I went along with the game stuffing a fake bottle in my dolly's mouth and changing her "pretend to be wet" diapers but inside my heart was with those lucky boys outside playing "shoot um up." As I grew up I heard all about how a woman isn't fulfilled until she's held her first-born that every woman has an inborn maternal instinct and all that other pro-baby hogwash. I don't dislike children but I believe it's a woman's choice not her "destiny" to become a parent. Don't feel you're a freak if you have decided as I have that motherhood is not for everyone.

The thought of diapers and pablum leaves me cold. I tested my "motherhood is not for me" theory by working in the newborn nursery for a period of six months. (It only seemed like six years) As an L.V.N. on the day shift I would be presented with 4 to 5 little bundles of joy to take care of from 7am to 3pm. I can remember thinking how easy it was going to be and how I'd get a chance to catch up on all my novels while the little darlings slept. I never cracked a book cover! Contrary to popular belief newborns do not sleep 20 to 23 hours a day. Imagine if you can six wet and messy babies all crying at the top of their lungs add one impatient doctor and one very harried nurse and you can see how my six month sentence went. One child I'll never forget cried all day messed his diaper eleven times peed on my new uniform and threw up in my hair twice before going home that afternoon with his unsuspecting mom and dad. When I threatened to throw all the little brats out of a 4th floor window they gave me my old job back.

Children do not necessarily improve with age as I've witnessed with my nieces aged 6 9 and 16½. In one of my moments of temporary insanity I decided to take them to a nice place for dinner. If I'd known what fate had in store for me I'd have taken them to Taco Bell! After I settled them into a booth I took a potty break to freshen my make-up. I had only been there for a minute when I heard a strangely familiar little voice singing "Yankee Doodle Dandy" amid a chorus of slightly older giggles. I dashed back to my seat and there was Mia the youngest standing up singing loud and clear. I got her to stop only by threatening to break her legs and steal her snoopy pin. Soon dinner arrived which I'd hoped would solve their boredom problem. Wrong again! Gina 9 who doesn't like starches threw her baked potato three tables across from us into some elegantly dressed woman's bowl of soup. I quickly offered to pay her cleaning bill. Before they could get into any more mischief I paid the bill and got out of there. Needless to say from now on it's TV dinners for them!

Raising kids is a responsibility that takes its toll in many ways. Ask any psychiatrist about his clientele. I'll bet 90% of them are parents pulling their hair out over the kid's latest prank. I suspect many alcoholics and serious drug abusers are also parents in search of an escape. Not everyone can cope with the day in and day out responsibility and reality of rearing a child. Are you one of them?

I'm not advocating zero population growth or anything like shipping all children to a remote island until they reach 21. I just want a chance to point out to the many with grave doubts that they do have a choice. Leave motherhood and parenthood to those who truly want it; they will surely make better parents than those who do it for all the wrong reasons. As a 25 year-old female who has made my choice I can assure you there's more to life than "mommiehood." I've got the freedom to be me!

C. Correct all errors in the essay above.

D. Go back to the last essay that you wrote, and put the rule number above each comma.

INDEPENDENT STUDY: Comma Rule 4 *(answers in the back)*

V. A. Put commas in the following sentences where rules demand them, and write the number of the rule above each comma.

1. My only sister who is ten years older than I helps me by sharing her experiences of the hard times of marriage.

2. Walt Disney the creator of Mickey Mouse is a true American.

3. I can also remember my brothers and me fighting over the television set each trying to watch a different program.

4. The lady who ran the boarding house in London lived alone except for a large black Labrador retriever.

5. I think I crave these foods because I have stayed in a foreign country for a long time.

6. Mr. Lee who is from China married an American Irish lady named Sally.

7. Mary Jackson my best friend rides to college on a motorcycle.

8. A book that I enjoyed very much was *The American Caesar.*

9. My Uncle Anthony who lived in Georgia died about a month ago.

10. The first department store amazingly similar to contemporary department stores was founded in France a hundred years ago.

B. The following paragraph needs commas demanded by all four comma rules. Put the commas where rules demand them and write the number of the rule above each comma.

The employees are all my friends because I used to work there. My positions included busgirl hostess and sometimes waitress. I wasn't eighteen yet so I couldn't serve liquor as the waitresses were supposed to do. Liz the head waitress would help me keep the customers happy and show me the proper things to do. I liked her the best of all the waitresses because she was always ahead of everything. When the work was done she allowed us to relax and have a few laughs. Barbara the cook lived across the highway from us and she dished out the delicious plates of food every night. I thought she was a better cook than the owner. When Evelyn the owner was around it seemed as if all the fun stopped. She was all business but I guess that was what kept the restaurant going. Most of the time work was pleasant and everyone looked forward to going to work every day.

comma 4

COMMA REVIEW *(answers in the back)*

The following sentences need commas demanded by all four rules. Add those commas and write the number of the rule above each comma.

A.   The food was also superb. Every dish was prepared carefully and individually. On the tables there were a basket of homemade tortilla chips and a dish of delicious hot sauce. The restaurant served beef cheese and chicken enchiladas smothered with melted cheese. There were also delicious burritos with a creamy white sauce on top. The dinners included beans rice lettuce and an entree. There was so much on the plate it was impossible to see a white spot. Steak picado enchiladas verdes and juevos rancheros were the most expensive choices but they were worth it. My favorite I must admit was the special because it had a variety of foods. On the plate sat a chile relleno two enchiladas a taco and a handful of crisp lettuce with a red tomato on top.

B.   New foods can also cause culture shock. When I first arrived in this country I didn't know what a hamburger was. I wasn't accustomed to fast food restaurants or TV dinners. Before we came here my mother would take two hours preparing all the meals which I ate. Here most of the food is already cooked and frozen and she only needs to warm it up. I miss the foods which I ate regularly: crab stew octopus stew fresh meat and homemade bread. My mother now prepares those dishes once in a while and when she does the whole family enjoys a feast because we haven't adjusted to hamburgers TV dinners and warm-and-serve breads.

C.   My whole attitude changed one sunny day when our team was playing one of the toughest teams in the league. The score was tied and there were only a few minutes left in the game. I had sat out the whole game. Then all of a sudden the coach yelled to me to get in there. I gulped and ran into my position. I stood there and hoped the ball would not come in my direction. Then the ball flew through the air and dropped right in front of me. I blocked the ball with my body and passed it to the center forward who quickly scored. I had assisted a goal. I couldn't believe it. I had actually assisted a goal! We won the game and I had helped. I got smiles and recognition from everyone around me. I felt great confidence at last that I could play soccer. From that day on the coach had me play more and more until eventually I played for a whole game. My confidence was up and I practiced every day. I wanted to be the best soccer player in the world.

D. *Put commas where rules demand them in the following sentences, and write the number of the rule above each comma.*

1. Before World War II a man especially a father was supposed to be the strongest and the most authoritative person in his family.

2. The problem that I have just described is occurring all over the United States and the high schools are producing a world of illiterate people who aren't prepared for life.

3. Now for the more hearty appetite the Piper's located in San Leandro offers all that one can eat for under five dollars.

4. People who live in cities seldom see the sunrise breathe the fresh air or see the plants and flowers.

5. While he was in college Magic was a disc jockey at Bonnie and Clyde's a disco in Lansing.

6. When I looked around trying to find someone to assist me with a machine that didn't return my money I couldn't find a soul who worked there.

7. My friends on the other hand never gave me any trouble and if one of my friends could not repay me on the date promised he would tell me in advance.

8. People who have bad reading habits probably pick up a book read a few pages and put it down.

9. President Reagan who has had four years of experience in dealing with American problems is honest and interested in the welfare of the country.

10. Cars money diamonds and gold are only a few of the things we wish we had.

SEMICOLONS AND COLONS

A semicolon (;) may be used between independent clauses instead of a period and a capital letter. A lowercase letter, not a capital, follows a semicolon.

A sharp crack shattered the silence. The rabbit disappeared.

A sharp crack shattered the silence; the rabbit disappeared.

A semicolon is used instead of a period to indicate an especially close relationship between two sentences.

He agreed to stay; the children were delighted.

We saw them lose; we saw them triumph.

Often this close relationship between clauses is indicated by the words that introduce independent clauses listed in Figure 4 (page 95), and so semicolons are often used before these words.

He usually eats very little; consequently, his clothes hang loosely on his body.

She hoped her car would start; otherwise, she would have to take a cab.

His cowboy hat would keep the sun off his face; besides, women always noticed that hat.

Of course, these words don't always introduce independent clauses. Sometimes they are used as interrupters in the middle of a clause, and so a semicolon would create a fragment.

FAULTY The people they evicted; however, were not impressed by their excuses.

Here "however" comes in the middle of a clause, not at the beginning, and the semicolon creates two fragments out of a good sentence. Comma rule 4 demands commas around such interrupters.

REVISED The people they evicted, however, were not impressed by their excuses.

Use semicolons only between independent clauses.

FAULTY As he passed through the living room; he threw his coat on the sofa.

Here a semicolon was wrongly used instead of a rule 1 comma between a dependent and an independent clause, making the dependent clause into a fragment.

REVISED As he passed through the living room, he threw his coat on the sofa.

FAULTY I hope to see my whole family; except Jack of course.

Here a semicolon was used instead of a rule 4 comma, creating the fragment "except Jack of course."

REVISED I hope to see my whole family, except Jack of course.

Also, a semicolon should not be used instead of the word "that."

FAULTY He thought; she wanted him to stay.

At first glance this sentence may look as if it has two independent clauses, but a closer look reveals that the second clause is dependent, a "that" clause, and the semicolon distorts the meaning of the sentence.

REVISED He thought that she wanted him to stay.

REVISED He thought she wanted him to stay.

A colon (:) is used to add a list to the end of a complete sentence.

Last quarter I took four courses: French, English, geology, and art.

A colon often attaches a list to a noun that it expands as the colon above attaches the list to the word "courses." However, a colon should *not* be used when the sentence is incomplete without the list.

Last quarter I took French, English, geology, and art.

The list in this sentence is necessary to complete the sentence. A colon should not come directly after a verb or a preposition. Compare the following correctly punctuated sentences.

We competed in the following countries: Mexico, Panama, and Brazil.

Colons are often used after the word "following."

We competed in Mexico, Panama, and Brazil.

Here the list completes the sentence, so a colon would be wrong.

Use a colon only to attach a list to the end of a complete sentence. Do not use a colon in the middle of a sentence.

FAULTY She asked him to bring: a bridle, a whip, and a hat.

Here the list is necessary to complete the sentence, so a colon is wrong.

REVISED She asked him to bring a bridle, a whip, and a hat.

The sentence could also be completed with the words "the following." Then the colon could be used to attach the list.

punctuation

REVISED She asked him to bring the following: a bridle, a whip, and a hat.

FAULTY The meal includes: soup, rice, entree, and tea.

Here a colon comes directly after the verb and separates off a list that is necessary to complete the sentence.

REVISED The meal includes soup, rice, entree, and tea.

REVISED The meal includes the following: soup, rice, entree, and tea.

CORRECTION COMMENT: Do not create fragments by sticking semicolons (;) and colons (:) into the middle of complete ideas instead of between them.

EXERCISES: Semicolons and Colons

I. Write sentences to go before and after the semicolons and connecting words below.

A. 1. _____ ; consequently, _____
    2. _____ ; furthermore, _____
    3. _____ ; however, _____
    4. _____ ; moreover, _____
    5. _____ ; nevertheless, _____
    6. _____ ; otherwise, _____
    7. _____ ; therefore, _____
    8. _____ ; also, _____
    9. _____ ; besides, _____
   10. _____ ; then, _____

B. 1. _____ ; as a result, _____
    2. _____ ; thus, _____
    3. _____ ; meanwhile, _____
    4. _____ ; still, _____
    5. _____ ; for example, _____
    6. _____ ; on the other hand, _____
    7. _____ ; indeed, _____
    8. _____ ; in fact, _____
    9. _____ ; for instance, _____
   10. _____ ; at the same time, _____

II. Write complete sentences to go before the following colon-list combinations.

A. 1. _____ : shoes, slippers, socks, and boots.

    2. _____ : two chairs, a sofa, and a bookcase.

    3. _____ : a mixer, an electric frying pan, and a toaster.

    4. _____ : *Emma, Pride and Prejudice,* and *Sense and Sensibility.*

5. _____ : a bikini, one sneaker, two socks, and several comic books.

6. _____ : car keys, some change, a pocket watch, and three bullets.

7. _____ : a worn mace, a battered shield, and two broken swords.

8. _____ : oats, almonds, sunflower seeds, coconut, and honey.

9. _____ : three orcs, two clay golems, a purple worm, and some green slime.

10. _____ : Hawkeye, B. J., and Charles Winchester III.

B. 1. _____ : El Paso, Laredo, and Brownsville.

2. _____ : Dorothy Sayers, Margery Allingham, and Josephine Tey.

3. _____ : tacos, enchiladas, tostadas, and burritos.

4. _____ : Morocco, Algeria, and Libya.

5. _____ : Mike Wallace, Harry Reasoner, Dan Rather, Morley Safer.

6. _____ : Maine, New Hampshire, Vermont, Massachusetts, Connecticut, and Rhode Island.

7. _____ : Charles Schultz, Virgil Partch, and Gahan Wilson.

8. _____ : eggflower soup, chili pepper beef chow fan, and pressed duck.

9. _____ : *Time, Newsweek,* and *U.S. News and World Report.*

10. _____ : rocky road, mocha chip, and fudge ripple.

III. *Eliminate incorrect colons and semicolons from the following sentences.*

A. 1. We will study: Keats, Shelley, Wordsworth, and Coleridge.

2. We will study the following romantic poets: Keats, Shelley, Wordsworth, and Coleridge.

3. She packed up her: sleeping bag, ground cloth, cooking kit, and dried food.

4. She packed up her camping gear: sleeping bag, ground cloth, cooking kit, and dried food.

5. She was certain; however, that he would remember Mary.

6. She was certain; however, her father was not.

7. For example; a two-bedroom unit costs eight hundred dollars a month.

8. I know; he'll arrive on time.

9. When we arrived in Nikko; mist softened the landscape.

10. They grow: raspberries, blueberries, and strawberries.

B. 1. I'm not always off to myself; I can be a very outgoing person.

2. For example; mortgage interest has increased approximately ten percent within the last year.

3. We came back and had: steak, eggs, bacon, sausage, and chile with beans for breakfast.

4. Sometimes Mother would leave us with my grandfather; when she had to go to the field to chop or pick cotton.

5. It's a small cafeteria featuring hot sandwiches and dinner plates including: vegetable, meat, and potato.

6. When someone notices that luck has come down to him; it slips away.

7. In my senior year almost everything happened at night: parties, football games, and studying.

8. Udo really makes a person warm; therefore, it is a good food for winter.

9. Children can meet: Mickey Mouse, Pluto, Goofy, and other Disney characters.

10. We rode in a small car; with my father as the driver.

C. 1. I understand them; I wish everyone did.

2. The *Queen Elizabeth II* is like a city on water. It offers recreation such as: swimming, skeet shooting, shuffleboard, dancing, exercise classes, Ping-Pong, and card games. For those who are interested in developing their arms; there is even a room filled with slot machines.

3. My mother hardly ever asks to borrow money; she always seems to have it.

4. At the first school, I learned my basics: reading, printing, writing, addition, subtraction, and multiplication.

5. I was planning to sleep until about 7 o'clock. Suddenly at 4 o'clock, Jason woke up and couldn't go back to sleep; he decided to turn on his radio full blast. I thought; I had been given an electric shock.

6. A mariachi dresses like a charro with: a big hat, decorated trousers, matching jacket, a colored shirt, a string tie, and boots.

7. When the game finally starts; he watches each player with binoculars.

8. It wasn't fair; I felt that the mechanics should clean their own tools.

9. I've always worked for my dad, which meant: days off when I wanted them, showing up late anytime I wanted, and working the days I preferred.

10. Nobody ever said running regularly was going to be easy; but I feel no sympathy for those silverbells and cockleshells who skip a day.

D. After eighteen years of pure torture; my dream will come true; I will have a white Christmas. My parents and two other families rented a cabin at Lake Tahoe for a week. My boy friend and I will leave here on Christmas Eve. It will be the first time that either of us has seen snow, and if we both don't go absolutely hysterical, we should reach the cabin by noon. It's located on the north shore; twenty-two minutes from Heavenly Valley. During this week; I plan to act out all my childhood fantasies of the snow: homemade snowcones, a snowman, a snowball fight, and Alpine skiing. This year will truly be the merriest of all Christmases; because my childhood dream of a white Christmas will have come true.

IV. A. *Correct the use of commas, semicolons, and colons in the following essay.*

My family has always been very close. All my aunts, uncles, cousins, and my immediate family are constantly writing letters, making telephone calls, and visiting each other in order to keep in touch. I have relatives in many parts of the United States, and enjoy visiting them all, but I especially enjoy visiting my grandparents in Iowa.

The time spent traveling is an important part of making the whole visit a success. My family and I have always driven to Iowa. During our trip, we have always taken extra time out to visit: other relatives, national monuments, historic sites, and other interesting places. Even when we have had car trouble we have had a good time. One summer on the way to Iowa the rear axle on our car broke and we were stuck in a small town in the middle of Wyoming. While waiting the two days it took to get our car fixed; we got the opportunity to enjoy and explore the town from top to bottom. My whole family enjoyed seeing the bright side of an event that could have spoiled the rest of our vacation.

While in Iowa, I always enjoy doing new and unusual things. A popular pastime in many farming communities is tractor-pulling. At a tractor-pull farmers get their largest and most powerful tractors together and compete to see which one can pull the most weight. Two years ago my cousin took me to my first tractor-pull. I hadn't been very thrilled about the idea of going but after we got there I found that it was really very interesting and exciting. I had never imagined that men would go to such time effort and expense to

punctuation

make tractors both powerful and good looking. Everyone including me enjoyed the tractor-pull and I'm looking forward to going to another one.

Working on my grandparents' farm is always fun and exciting. When we go to Iowa; my grandparents don't expect us "city folks" to do much serious farm work. Since we don't have any standards to meet, my brother, sister, and I always turn our work into play. An easy job like: collecting eggs, feeding chickens, or milking a cow can take twice as long as it should. On more than one occasion when we were sent out to pick strawberries, raspberries, or cherries, my brother, sister, and I came home with half the berries either on our clothes or in our stomachs. My grandparents saw that we were wasting more berries than we were bringing home, and eventually they dictated the number of baskets of fruit we could eat, have wars with, and bring home. We always said that my grandparents were getting a great deal because of our free labor, but now I realize that we got the better end of the bargain.

Memories of the times I spent in Iowa are some of the best memories I have. There were some bad times, but there were so few that I find them hard to remember. I like knowing that I can still go back to Iowa and do the same things I did when I was younger.

B. *Write an essay about a place you enjoy visiting. Include lots of good detail to show the reader how much fun it is. Check the punctuation carefully.*

C. *Write an essay on one of the following topics. Use commas, semicolons, and colons only where rules demand them.*

the space shuttle   an unusual person

divorce   your first love

college writing requirements   vending machines

D. *Above each comma in your essay write the number of the rule that demands it.*

INDEPENDENT STUDY: *Semicolons and Colons* (answers in the back)

V. A. *Eliminate incorrect colons and semicolons from the following sentences.*

1. He plays four instruments: piano, harmonica, guitar, and fiddle.

2. Lunch consisted of: steak, beans, chicken, and potatoes.

3. When I first started going to Kansas State; I thought it would be easy.

4. We invited our best friends: Heidi, Mike, Lisa, Mary, Tom, and Fabia.

5. For example; the cost of gasoline per gallon has almost doubled within the last two years.

6. I've traveled by almost all the transportation available: airplane, train, car, bus, and cruise liner.

7. When the bullet hits one of these targets; it makes a loud plink, and the target goes down.

8. For the teenagers and young adults, there are games in the arcade such as: pinball, air hockey, computer games, shooting galleries, and many more.

9. When I picked up my diploma; I felt like a young lady.

10. She is raising four wonderful boys: Scott, Peter, Daniel, and Kevin.

B.   In addition to its primitive side, rock has a progressive side. Early hard rock groups include: Pink Floyd, Steppenwolf, The Doors, and Jimi Hendrix. Later groups include: Yes, Jethro Tull, Led Zeppelin, Queen, and Camel. This music is quite different from earlier rock styles. Hard or acid rock uses: more varied instrumentation, synthesizers, organs, and various electronic gadgetry. Yes; for example, uses an array of electronic keyboards plus the usual complement of: guitars, drums, and voices.

7. Polishing the Words

• People in the academic and business worlds are impressed by careful attention to the details of writing. This chapter covers those final touches you should add to any piece of writing before submitting it to a teacher or a business contact.

ARTICLES

The English articles are "a," "an," and "the." The following chart summarizes their use. Native speakers of English probably know these rules without thinking.

Before a noun that refers to one thing or group that can be counted	If the noun is general (refers to any one), use "a" or "an." He has decided to buy **a suit**. She ate **an apple**. If the noun is specific (refers to one particular thing), use "the." He has decided to buy **the brown suit**. She ate **the apple he gave her**.
Before all other nouns (plurals and nouns referring to things that can't be counted)	If the noun is general (refers to no particular ones), use no article. **Eggs** are nutritious. They always appreciate **honesty**. If the noun is specific (refers to particular ones), use "the." **The eggs we bought** are cracked. They admired **the honesty of her answers**.

Articles may be replaced by numbers, possessive nouns like John's or the teacher's, or any of the following words where they make sense.

my	no	this	both
your	any	that	some
his	each	these	many
her	every	those	much
its	either	most	few
our	neither	more	several
their		all	

Speakers of English as a second language sometimes forget the article when there is a modifier before the noun.

FAULTY They are looking for heavy oak table.

"Table" is a noun referring to one thing, and tables can be counted. The word refers not to a particular heavy oak table but to one of many, so the article "a" is required.

REVISED They are looking for a heavy oak table.

Here is another typical error:

FAULTY He finished his essay next day.

The word "essay" does not need an article because it has the word "his," but "day" refers to one thing, and days can be counted. Furthermore, the reference is to a particular day, and so the article "the" is required.

FAULTY He finished his essay the next day.

Although most names don't require articles, the article "the" should be used with descriptive names that include a modifier and a noun as in "the United States," "the Soviet Union," and "the Rocky Mountains."

FAULTY Television is very popular in United States.

REVISED Television is very popular in the United States.

Native speakers of English often have trouble with this next distinction. Because it is difficult to say two vowel sounds together, English uses "an" instead of "a" before words beginning with a vowel sound. Most words that begin with vowels (the letters *a, e, i, o,* and *u*) begin with vowel sounds.

an especially good play

an interesting question

an estimate

an optimistic approach

an ugly confrontation

Before words beginning with all other letters, *a* is used.

a worried man

a big decision

a demanding job

a hard time

a mistake

However, there are a few exceptions. Sometimes words that start with the letters *eu* or *u* start with a *y* sound, and so they don't need "an."

a university education

a union

a united front

a European car

Also sometimes the letter *h* is silent, and a word starting with the letter *h* really starts with a vowel sound, so "an" should be used.

an hour

an honorable woman

an honest person

CORRECTION COMMENT: **Be sure to use the correct article wherever one is required.**

EXERCISES: *Articles*

I. *Write sentences as described below.*

1. *five sentences correctly using "a"*

2. *five sentences correctly using "an"*

3. *five sentences correctly using "the" with singular nouns*

4. *five sentences correctly using "the" with plural nouns*

5. *five sentences including nouns without articles*

II. *Correct the use of articles in the following sentences. Cross out incorrect ones and add correct ones above them. Insert omitted articles.*

A. 1. I put most of my money in savings account.

2. I thought that the mother played a important part in the movie.

3. I read a book about two powerful men in small town.

4. Cooking isn't a easy task.

5. He took a long vacation.

6. I hope I can find better job later.

7. Also for children they have merry-go-round.

8. A well prepared omelet is like an work of art.

9. A ideal job should have certain benefits.

10. You can rent sailboat if you have license.

B. 1. Many girls are being hired just for a job of welcoming the customers.

2. The United States is sixth country I have visited.

3. He gave us an open book exam.

4. One was a old model, and the other was a new model.

5. My little green bug is a friend as well as a car.

6. Her husband came to United States five years ago.

7. My sister doesn't want an honest answer.

8. Having a older brother or sister can be very helpful.

9. When we are making an decision, the girls always win five to one.

10. I always wanted to go on a dates before I was old enough.

C. 1. I remember seeing a car identical to mine except it had a automatic transmission.

2. When I was younger, I was an accomplished flute player.

3. Working in a library was very helpful experience for me.

4. My brother played a important role in my success.

5. Park heard this rumor from his servants and did not sleep before wedding ceremony.

6. As I was walking out of the rest room, I had to stop to remove a ice cream wrapper that was stuck to my shoe.

7. It is more fun for them to go for a drive or to disco with their girl friends than to take part in festivals.

8. He never had a term "fatigue" in his dictionary.

9. I came to United States to enter the university and to study management even though I had succeeded in entering Japanese university.

10. Graduation gave me an unique feeling.

D. 1. Some people say that such music is for a unhappy person because it is usually about a unhappy time of the singer's life.

2. All groups played fusion, so I could enjoy them, especially Chick Corea and friends who lead jazz scene now.

3. After an hard day of work most people will head for the sofa to relax.

4. I was awakened in the morning by the singing of the birds.

5. On Saturday and Sunday, I went to Newport Jazz Festival.

6. When he came to United States, he couldn't find his parents.

7. When I eat, I feel like a angel floating in the air.

8. He plans to take a sociology class next semester.

9. Once in Japanese restaurant, we ordered six specials.

10. They paused for a minute and then plotted a important plan.

E. 1. A man can wear jeans and sport coat to social event and be as well dressed as if he wore a suit.

2. His mistakes and good choices helped me to a easy conclusion about the things that I wanted to explore.

3. We found the picture of nice-looking boy.

4. I had to be sent to a all-black school, and I was scared of this new atmosphere.

5. Having a older brother or sister can play a important role in growing up successfully.

6. I love the fun of licking on an frostie ice cream cone, trying to eat it all before it melts down my hand, and walking up and down the different rows looking for a bargain.

7. Park had sixteen-year-old daughter, and Kim had a fifteen-year-old son.

8. Music is a important part of our history. Jazz, blues, soul, and rock-and-roll all have a important meaning to us.

9. However, this book was so interesting that I could finish it next day without sleeping at all.

10. A ex-boyfriend of mine had to win a gold medal in boxing to get a crack at the pro heavyweight boxing title.

F. Sometimes during the warm summer nights, Grandma would sit out on the porch and tell me stories about when she was an little girl on their farm in the woods. She told me about a bear trying to get into their house and how frightened everyone was. She also told me about walking through the woods and being bitten couple of times by snakes. Her stories would always end on a unbelievable note. Many times my mother told Grandma to stop lying to me, but listening to the endings was half the fun.

III. A. *Correct the errors in the following essay.*

The Trip to Chen De

On the first summer vacation I had in the university, five of my best friends, my brother, and I took a trip to Chen De, small northern city in Hebei Province of China. It is only five-day trip, but it is also really interesting trip.

During this trip, we learned many things about the history of the Ching Dynasty. The emperors of the Ching Dynasty used to live in Chen De, so many important historical events happened there. When we were visiting emperor's palace, we saw a screen beside emperor's bed. We were told that the Empress CiXi hid behind this screen and listened to all dying Emperor DaoGuang said to his officials about preventing her from taking over power after he dies. Then the Empress CiXi took action in advance and stage a coup successfully. Under rule of the Empress CiXi, China experienced miserable time. Because of its geographic position, Chen De was also place where the emperors of the Ching Dynasty met with the leaders of northern minority nationalities. In those magnificent temples which the emperors built for those leaders, there are many stone tablets and the inscription on those stone tablets record in detail the circumstances of those meetings. Through visiting those temples we learned many things about relation between the Ching Dynasty and the northern minority nationalities.

Chen De is beautiful city. The emperors built big summer palace in Chen De. In summer palace there are many halls, pavilions, and big lake. The buildings there combine northern architectural style with the southern style to form new and distinctive style. We had very good time visiting those buildings, rowing boat on the lake, and seeing the sunset on a old tower. The palace is so big that there are some beautiful mountains in it. Hiking in those mountains, we admire the beauties of nature. We drank from a mountain streams, had our picnic in a ancient temple, and took a rest under a towering old trees. We forgot our fatigue and thought only about our glorious future.

I also enjoyed staying with my best friends and my brother in trip. Because all of us are students studying in different universities, even different cities, vacation is the only time for us to meet and to play together. During the trip we went out together in the daytime and at night we sat down and discussed interesting issues. Once a discussion became a debate which was so heated and interesting that some people living in same hotel came over and listened to us. At night we also played bridge, which is my favorite game. When we stayed together, we really had a great fun.

Although several years have passed, I often think of this trip, our happiness and my best friends. I hope that I will have chance to go to Chen De again with them, and I also hope that the trips which I will take in future will be as interesting as this trip to Chen De.

B. *Reread the preceding essay and write down three ways in which it could be strengthened. Share your findings with your classmates.*

INDEPENDENT STUDY: Articles *(answers in the back)*

IV. *A. Correct all errors in the use of articles in the following sentences. Cross out incorrect ones and add correct ones above them. Insert omitted articles.*

1. Then we have a hour and a half to eat.

2. Dallas was just wide and busy city.

3. Jogging is a escape from the stress.

4. They seem not to care about anything except maybe a unfriendly dog.

5. The health is necessary for happiness.

6. Music is a other way to tell about the things that are going on in the world.

7. We heard a extensive variety of songs.

8. They played for two hours and half.

9. It is Oriental custom that since he promised, he had to keep his word.

10. Valencia appreciates her friends' troubles because she has an deep perception of human feelings.

B.   Contact lenses must be handled carefully. They are made of plastic, and the soft ones are very pliable. During cleaning procedure, the edge of lens may be bent or torn by accident. This change may cause blurry sight. One of my friends lost soft contact lens temporarily, and when he found it next day, it had dried in folded position. The wrinkle has never really come out and still interferes with his vision.

242   POLISHING THE WORDS

CONTRACTIONS

In speech, some sounds are slurred over, and two words may be pronounced as one. This contraction is expressed in informal writing by joining the two words together and replacing the omitted letters with an apostrophe. Here are some common contractions:

there is	there's
it is	it's
here is	here's
that is	that's
what is	what's
I am	I'm
I have	I've
we are	we're
they had	they'd
they would	they'd
do not	don't
has not	hasn't
is not	isn't
let us	let's

Only one contraction behaves differently:

will not	won't

More confusing are the contractions that sound just like other words. Some contractions sound like the possessive pronouns.

you are	you're (sounds like "your")
it is	it's (sounds like "its")
it has	it's (sounds like "its")
who is	who's (sounds like "whose")
they are	they're (sounds like "their" and "there")
we are	we're (sounds like the verb "were")

Be sure to use the contraction form of the words above, the form with the apostrophe, only where the two words would fit into the sentence and nowhere else.

FAULTY Your never on time.

The two words "you are" fit into this sentence.

REVISED You are never on time.

Therefore the contraction form is correct, not the other form.

REVISED You're never on time.

FAULTY Bring me you're book.

Two words don't fit here. "Bring me you are book" doesn't make sense, so the contraction form "you're" should be replaced by the other form "your."

REVISED Bring me your book.

FAULTY Its too late now.

The two words "it is" fit into this sentence.

REVISED It is too late now.

Therefore the contraction form is correct, not the other form.

REVISED It's too late now.

FAULTY He lost it's handle.

Two words don't fit here. "He lost it is handle" doesn't make sense, so the contraction form "it's" should be replaced by the other form "its."

REVISED He lost its handle.

FAULTY Whose coming with me?

The two words "who is" make sense in this sentence.

REVISED Who is coming with me?

Therefore the form with the apostrophe should be used.

REVISED Who's coming with me?

FAULTY Who's book is this?

Two words don't fit here. "Who is book is this" doesn't make sense, so the contraction form "who's" should be replaced by the other form "whose."

REVISED Whose book is this?

FAULTY There going to be late.

The two words "they are" fit here.

REVISED They are going to be late.

Therefore the form with the apostrophe is required, not the other form.

REVISED They're going to be late.

FAULTY We brought they're essays.

Two words don't fit here. "We brought they are essays" doesn't make sense, so the contraction form is incorrect.

REVISED We brought their essays.

You cannot go wrong by spelling out both words, by the way, because many teachers do not like contractions in academic writing.

> **CORRECTION COMMENT:** Be sure to use an apostrophe to replace the letters that are left out when two words are contracted; however, do not use a contracted form where the two words it represents do not make sense.

EXERCISES: Contractions

contraction

I. Write the sentences described below.

    1. three sentences using "it's"

    2. three sentences using "its"

    3. three sentences using "you're"

    4. three sentences using "your"

    5. three sentences using "who's"

    6. three sentences using "whose"

    7. three sentences using "they're"

    8. three sentences using "their"

    9. three sentences using "we're"

    10. three sentences using "here's"

II. Correct the errors in the use of contractions in the following sentences.

    A. 1. Its best to run on a soft surface so that you wont hurt your feet.

        2. They are'nt responsible for the confusion.

        3. Were being evicted.

        4. Lets face the truth about this.

        5. Im not sure when Ill finish.

        6. Your going to be sorry its over.

        7. There sure theyll arrive early.

        8. Whose going to solve this problem?

        9. All in all their no help.

        10. Its typical of a car salesman.

    B. 1. The seeds make a tasty snack when theres nothing else around.

        2. Jeanette is unhappy because her mother doesnt care about her.

        3. Its my time of year again.

4. If your not so lucky, you may even be attacked by one.

5. I no longer wear tank tops, for Im not out to impress anyone anymore.

6. Their trying to get an education, so they can get out of the ghetto.

7. That's when I found out how messy and inconsiderate she really is.

8. With all of this taken care of, your ready to get rolling.

9. The dollar has practically lost its value.

10. She is mean and doesn't want to be bothered.

C.
1. You might say it's in Oakland and thats not convenient.

2. Politicians often are'nt as honest as they seem.

3. Were held responsible for so many things today, including how we talk, act, and dress.

4. These magazines help us to understand whats going on in our federal government.

5. The strike forced the manufacturer to lay off some of it's workers or take a loss in profits.

6. Roller skatings not an expensive sport.

7. Its almost impossible to get somewhere in a hurry without a car.

8. Your doctor is your best friend when your in the weight-watchers' game.

9. I wont tell you how many years I lived in Mexico.

10. There so rich they don't even work anymore.

D.
1. Im sure most people hate getting paid only once a month because they have to go through the trouble of budgeting their income to meet their expenses.

2. Erwin shouted, "Hey, Dad, lets not go to Texas this summer."

3. I asked Mrs. Jackson why most PE teachers have short hair. She told me that when their involved in physical activity, they don't want their hair getting in the way.

4. The child who is beginning to crawl reminds me of a turtle, moving slowly, just looking at whatevers in front of him.

5. It's up to the students to change their weekend habits so they can do all their assignments.

6. I had my heart set on Loyola Marymount University, but my family could'nt afford it.

7. "Lou Grant" shows whats happening in the world, and its a very entertaining program.

8. He told me he had a flat tire, but thats an old excuse.

9. After the students pay their registration fees, there entitled to privileges and benefits, but its up to them to find out whats due them.

10. Im sure they wont be late two times in a row.

E.　　The people in my family empathize with each other. When I had been searching for a job without success two months ago, I was in a really bad mood and wasnt talking to anyone. Then my parents said, "It's really discouraging to look for a job and time after time get turned down. It makes you feel like your worthless." My eyes opened wide, and I said, "Thats exactly it. You really helped me." Shortly after that I found a job. One night last week I came home from work feeling really down, and my brother said that I must really hate washing the floors. I said, "Your right," and he cringed and said, "Thats too bad."

III. A. *Read the following essay and underline its errors. Correct the errors in the use of contractions.*

contraction

The Things that Make Me Laugh

　　I have a good sense of humor and it usually doesnt take much to make me laugh. I laugh at things that most people laugh at like a good comedian, cute things (babies), and people's mistakes. I think this covers just about all of the things that make me laugh.

　　It takes a good comedian like Jerry Lewis for me to really have a good laugh. Most comedians cant get by without a good writer but Jerry Lewis is different. He doesnt have to say a word to make me laugh. He uses all these weird sounds like "WAA," and "Bop, bop um beemp." These sounds, along with his goofy facial expressions, make Jerry Lewis fun to watch. Other comedians like Steve Martin, Robert Klein, and George Carlin are also fun to watch. They're jokes come from personal experiences, and I can relate to them. When I see one of these comedians doing an imitation of their mother I can see my own mother. To me, theres nothing funnier.

　　Infants can be cute too. Last week, my godson Scott, who is six months old, went to a basketball game with us. He really enjoyed it. It was surprising how he watched the game. His little head moved as the teams went from one end of the court to the other. What was really funny was the look on Scott's face every time the scorekeeper's horn sounded. His eyes would get real wide and his little mouth would drop open. The little mouth would open again during a free throw, but then noise would be coming from it. Scott screamed the most when everything was quiet. Like when someone was trying for a free throw. I thought it was hilarious, but the guy shooting the ball didn't.

　　I also laugh at people's mistakes. I think its alright to laugh at mistakes as long as their not disastrous. Also, I dont limit myself to just laughing at other's mistakes; I laugh at my own mistakes too. Right now I cant think of any of my mistakes so Ill just have to use someone else's. The other night my mom, who crochets a lot, bought a pom-pom maker. The pom-pom maker could be used to make Christmas ornaments and mom was anxious to try it out. The kit consisted of two small plastic hoops about 2″ in diameter. The idea was to wrap some yarn around the hoops, cut the ends, and tie it off. So mom sat down and preceded to do just that. When she finished she held up the scraggilest looking pom-pom Id ever seen. She was so disappointed but she was laughing so hard she could barley stand up. The sight of that ugly pom-pom had the same effect on me; soon I was laughing right along with her. Sometimes people try very hard but end up with egg on their face.

One day, a couple of winters ago, it was so cold that a thin layer of ice covered the blacktop in front of our school. Along comes this guy on his bike whose going to show off in front of all the kids. He was going to get on his bike and skid all over the ice. Well, he did skid, but not on his bike. His bike slipped away from him. He ended up alone, sliding on his back past the group of laughing onlookers. The "daredevil" really blew it but it was a good comedy show.

So thats what makes me laugh; the funny people. There are the good comedians who are professionals at making people laugh. There are the babies who are so cute but arent trying to make people laugh. And lastly there are the everyday people who when they make mistakes, dont want people to laugh. But I laugh anyway, at all of them because there funny. One has to have a little humor in their life and now you know three ways of finding it.

B. Share with your classmates the other errors you found. Correct any your teacher assigns. Then evaluate the introduction and conclusion. How would they be better? Suggest material that could be used there.

C. Write a better introduction and conclusion for this essay.

INDEPENDENT STUDY: *Contractions* (answers in the back)

IV. A. Correct the errors in the contractions in the following sentences.

1. When I tell my daughter to take a bath, she comes running in to me, telling me she cant turn off the water faucet because its stuck.

2. I really feel good after Mondays over and Im through with writing for a week.

3. Dont be worried about the gas mileage; this Volkswagen gets a great twenty-five miles to the gallon.

4. In high school, I didnt have to walk nearly as far between classrooms as I do here in college.

5. Rich people have other problems; there always worrying about burglars and stock prices.

6. By the time you find your on your own, you will be able to handle your life with grace, dignity, and self-confidence.

7. A student does'nt have to be smart; he just has to put a little effort into his studies.

8. It's pretty obvious that he'll have higher heat bills in the winter than in the summer.

9. We try to get there by five in the morning. Thats the best time to fish for hornpout.

10. Ive always dreamed of visiting Japan; now that's my next vacation goal.

B. *Correct the errors in the use of contractions in this conclusion to an essay addressed to Alaskans who keep elephants in their hotels.*

contraction

The future for you all seems bleak. It looks like youll be thrown out of the hotels into the cold. Since your elephants will die, youll be sued by the humane society, the rest of the United States will hear of the scandal, and youll lose your jobs. Do you want all this to happen? Of course not! Now, Im willing to offer you sixty percent of the original price you paid for your elephants. Im starting a corporation called HELP, thats Hawaiian Elephant Location Plan. All of the interested people can come up to see me now to negotiate.

POSSESSIVES

Often in English we want to show that one element of an idea owns another element.

I saw his calculator on my desk.

Among other things, this sentence tells us that the writer has a desk and some male person has a calculator.

English has special pronouns to show ownership or possession.

my	mine	our	ours
your	yours		
her	hers	their	theirs
his	its		
whose			

People rarely have trouble with these possessive pronouns. However, sometimes they aren't exact enough, and so the writer must adjust a more specific word to show possession.

I saw Roger's calculator on my uncle's desk.

I saw my uncle's calculator on Roger's desk.

I saw Mr. Mason's calculator on my desk.

I saw the teacher's calculator on her desk.

I saw somebody's calculator on Mr. Mason's desk.

A name or noun (word referring to a thing) that doesn't end in *s* can be used to show possession if *'s* is added to it. If a noun already ends in *s*, only the apostrophe (') must be added.

the girl's jacket

both girls' jackets

the child's jacket

the children's jackets

Charles' jacket

If a word is both plural and possessive, the plural should be formed before the possessive.

Because English also uses the *s* ending on verbs and to make nouns plural, don't assume that an *s* ending always indicates possession and requires an apostrophe. Any of the following questions can be asked to determine if possession is involved.

1. Are there two nouns next to each other? If so, does the first one own the second?

my mother's boat

James' bicycle

both dogs' noses

the men's office

2. Can the words in question be turned around into an "of" phrase?

the boat of my mother

the bicycle of James

the noses of both dogs

the office of the men

3. Can one of the above possessive pronouns be used in place of the words that would end with the apostrophe?

her boat

his bicycle

their noses

their office

If the answer to any of these questions is yes, ownership is being expressed and an apostrophe is needed.

To use the apostrophe correctly, you have to know whether or not the owning word ends in *s*. To avoid confusing the possessive *s* with others, either turn the words into an "of" phrase or answer the question "who owns it?" Either of these processes will produce the true spelling of the owning word. If that word does not already end in *s*, add *'s*; if it already ends in *s*, just add an apostrophe. Then you can write that adjusted word in a sentence before the thing it owns.

possessive

FAULTY	"Of" phrase	Who owns it?	REVISED
my mothers boat	the boat of my mother	my mother	my mother's boat
James bicycle	the bicycle of James	James	James' bicycle
both dogs noses	the noses of both dogs	both dogs	both dogs' noses
the mens office	the office of the men	the men	the men's office

Here are some typical errors:

FAULTY A persons handwriting reveals many things about him.

"A persons handwriting" can be turned into an "of" phrase, "handwriting of a person," so we know that possession is involved and an apostrophe is needed. The last word of the "of" phrase, "person," does not end in *s*, so *'s* should be added to "person" when the words go back to the order they were in originally.

REVISED A person's handwriting reveals many things about him.

FAULTY Teacher's salaries should be higher.

"Teacher's salaries" can be turned into an "of" phrase, "salaries of teachers," so we know that possession is involved. The last word of the "of" phrase, "teachers," ends in s, so only an apostrophe should be added to it when the words are returned to their original order.

REVISED Teachers' salaries should be higher.

FAULTY Todays fashions are very unflattering.

"Todays fashions" can be turned into an "of" phrase, "fashions of today," so possession is involved and an apostrophe is needed. The last word, "today," does not end in s, so add 's to it and return the words to their original order.

REVISED Today's fashions are very unflattering.

FAULTY My parents' are still trying to give me orders.

"My parents' are" cannot be turned into an "of" phrase, so no possession is involved and the apostrophe is incorrect.

REVISED My parents are still trying to give me orders.

CORRECTION COMMENT: Possession should be indicated by adding 's to an owning word that doesn't end in s and by adding just an apostrophe to an owning word that does end in s. Apostrophes should be used only to show possession or contraction.

EXERCISES: Possessives

I. *Rewrite the phrases below as correct possessives after adding 's to the word at the end of the "of" phrase when it doesn't already end in s and an apostrophe when it does.*

A. 1. **EXAMPLE** the book of the boy *the boy's book*

2. the books of the boys

3. the mother of the boys

4. the books of the children

5. the slippers of the woman

6. the slippers of the women

7. the job of Lewis

8. the Pontiac of Mr. Smith

9. the Pontiac of the Smiths

10. the beard of the man

B.

1. the coats of the visitors

2. the advice of the counselor

3. the zipper of the jacket

4. the energy needs of the United States

5. the fashions of yesterday

6. the license of drivers

7. the office of the doctor

8. the office of the doctors

9. the gloves of Sugar Ray Leonard

10. the work of the day

II. *Change the following ownership words to "of" phrases, correct the use of plural if necessary, and insert 's or an ' in the original to correctly form possessives.*

A.

1. **EXAMPLE** my fathers hat   *the hat of my father*   *my father's hat*

2. one players goal

3. two players goals

4. the womans favorites

5. the womens favorites

6. my fathers rules

7. my parents rules

8. the mans guitar

9. the mens guitars

10. a lawyers case

B.

1. one familys car

2. two families cars

3. our customers needs

4. one mans opinions

5. both mens opinions

6. a lawyers case

7. the childs toys

8. the childrens toys

9. one months money

10. one days work

possessive

C. 1. one mans problem   _____   _____

     2. my mothers wishes   _____   _____

     3. my sisters hearts   _____   _____

     4. my fathers Ford   _____   _____

     5. the dentist drill   _____   _____

     6. three mens jackets   _____   _____

     7. a bulldog nose   _____   _____

     8. todays prices   _____   _____

     9. all shirts pockets   _____   _____

   10. some teenagers opinions _____   _____

D. 1. both childrens bicycles   _____   _____

     2. our principals decision   _____   _____

     3. Julies birthday   _____   _____

     4. the cups handle   _____   _____

     5. the jars lids   _____   _____

     6. the childs face   _____   _____

     7. the bookstores prices   _____   _____

     8. the womans face   _____   _____

     9. the babys bottles   _____   _____

   10. those womens hopes   _____   _____

III. *Find and underline the words showing ownership (an owning word and a word for something owned) by seeing if an "of" phrase can be formed. If one can, add 's to the last word of the "of" phrase if that word doesn't end in s or add ' to that word if it does end in s. Then correct the original sentence if it's incorrect.*

A. 1. A child imagination is very active.

     2. Most peoples marriages today don't work.

     3. Even in her late fifties my mother is still working.

     4. I found a penny on the way to the dentist office.

     5. My name is Katherine, but my mother name is Frances.

     6. This service is free because my familys insurance covers it.

     7. Grandmothers have their own special way of teaching children.

8. The health plan should cover all doctor bills.

9. One must make the essay interesting enough to catch and keep the readers attention.

10. High school is one of the best parts of a person life.

B. 1. My mother maiden name was Brown.

2. I would grin whenever I heard this certain players name mentioned.

3. I look at other people plates to see what they are eating.

4. My aunt kids are like parasites.

5. When I moved out of my parents home, I had a lot more privacy.

6. A person must be responsible in todays society.

7. We then increased our supply to meet consumers demands.

8. One can share her joys and sorrows.

9. We boarded the wagon at Mr. Smith stable and rode off over the rough dirt road.

10. The United States economy is not as bad as it seems to be.

C. 1. The entire process required the use of ones muscles.

2. Many such toys are on the market today.

3. Mount Saint Helens anger over her sudden awakening was too much for her to bear.

possessive

4. After a hard days work I go to my car and listen to some music.

5. When I was in high school my parents feelings toward me didn't change.

6. Genetics will govern the looks of animals offspring.

7. I would like to live in Caesar time with our modern knowledge.

8. My older brother friend introduced me to the district attorney.

9. They also had tacos which nearly made me faint whenever I looked at them.

10. The television at Monique house was blaring.

IV. *Insert 's or ' in the following sentences to make the possessives correct. If there is an error in the plural forms, correct that too.*

A. 1. There will be no hope in many of these peoples lives if these programs are eliminated.

2. Anytime we felt like it we'd go eat at somebodies house.

3. Her name is Angela Davis, and she was a member of and spokesperson for the Black Panthers.

4. The principals last words were, "No one could have ever predicted that Mr. Cooper wouldn't be back."

5. This smorgasbord offers all the regular standbys from salads to five different main courses.

6. The supervisor magnificent personality made Intel successful.

7. The neighbors who lived to the right of me, next door, were the Lees.

8. I became familiar with both doctors idiosyncrasies.

9. I want to move away from home because I'm tired of hassling with my parents.

10. The food is unsanitary and unhealthy for the customers body, and all of the hectic customer business is unhealthy for the employees nerves.

B.
1. It's best to take your childrens education into your own hands.

2. If the United States economy is failing, the government should cancel the financial aid to other nations.

3. Our senior class president parents went out of town, so we went over there for lunch.

4. Another toy which lets the imagination run wild is the new story book that has a tape recording of the story along with it.

5. My fathers criticism is only for Valencia own good, but she feels he is picking on her.

6. Earvin Magic Johnson big dream came true.

7. My sister kids always want to borrow money from me.

8. After we have taken the weeds from Jonny house to the dump, we will start fixing my sister Jacky house, so she can put it up for rent and make enough money to pay off her bills without losing the house.

9. Then the rest of my sisters agreed because they said that they didn't have much money.

10. If the United States goes into a deep recession or depression, Mexicos economy will suffer also.

C.
1. In an attempt to slow down my fathers work demands upon me, I have learned to beat him to the punch line by suggesting things for him to do before he suggests things for me to do.

2. Saving is no longer possible because the prices in todays market are increasing so quickly.

3. My fondest memory is of a Sunday afternoon at my parents house.

4. The best toy stimulates the childs imagination.

5. It comes in packages of two to four cans in four colors: red, yellow, blue, and white.

6. Kevins concern for me was obvious when I caught the chickenpox last year.

7. Yesterday discards are becoming today fashion.

8. Luck takes many forms: beginners luck, blind luck, lucky numbers, lucky streaks, lucky days, lucky horse shoes, lucky rabbits feet, lucky colors, ladies luck and Lucky supermarkets, which some people believe are not lucky at all.

9. She then began to take classes in a search for the attention she didn't get at home.

10. The four years an individual spends in high school are probably the most memorable years in a persons life.

V. A. *Read the essay below and correct the possessives.*

Mans best friend is the dog. For ages mans favorites have been the sporting breeds because they make great protectors, hunters, and companions. This group includes shepherds, Dobermans, and retrievers. The pit bull is a less common sport dog. This unusual breed includes some of the most ferocious dogs in the world.

The pit bull was bred in England for bull baiting. Its exact heritage is not known, but its ancestors include the British bulldog and the terrier. In bull baiting, two or three dogs were pitted against a mad bull in a duel to the death. The English wanted a dog that was solid as steel and had the strongest possible jaws. To show the jaw strength and determination of their dogs, the owners would chop one of them slowly in half while its powerful jaws still clung to a dead bulls neck. The dogs were also pitted against each other, wild boars, big cats, and anything else that would put up an exciting fight.

possessive

Pit bulls have to be carefully controlled. My uncle has a pit bull that he keeps in control. We wrestle with Buster a lot, and he has never turned on anyone. Busters jaws are very big and his neck is huge. Buster can jump up to a tree branch, lock his jaws on it, and hang there. One time when my uncles front door was open and nobody was watching, Buster spotted a Doberman and darted outside. The Doberman, not wanting to fight, ran off, and Buster chased after him. My uncle and I chased the dogs for two blocks. As we caught up to them, Buster snapped at the Doberman but missed. I grabbed him by the collar, and the Doberman took off. Buster could have killed that dog, and my uncle would have gotten in trouble. My uncles friends pit killed a neighbors dog, and the S.P.C.A. put it to sleep.

An uncontrolled pit is very dangerous. Bull baiting has been illegal for a long time, but the mad instinct is still in the blood of a pit. If anyone or anything gets a pit seriously angry, the dogs mad instinct takes over. Once a pit gets its deadly grip, it is most unlikely it will let go. Pit bulls have even been known to turn on their owners. Their fighting instinct is stronger than their loyalty. Recently I heard on the news about a jogger who was running with his shepherd. Suddenly a mad pit jumped out and attacked the shepherd for no reason. When the jogger tried to interfere, the pit attacked him. In Union City, a police cars tires were flattened by a pit. The dog just bit the tires.

Pit bulls may take a little watching, but they make nice pets. They are unique and have a tough reputation. When I was walking Buster on the beach one time, a couple, worrying about their own dog, asked me if Buster was a pit and if he was really mean. I said, "Yes, but he's a nice guy once you get to know him."

B. *Answer the following questions about the essay above.*

  1. Is the outline good?

  2. How could the thesis be improved?

  3. What do you remember most clearly about this essay?

  4. How could the conclusion be improved?

C. *Write an essay about something dangerous. Use lots of vivid detail to show how dangerous it is. In the conclusion suggest ways in which it could be prevented from hurting people.*

D. *Write an essay on one of the following topics.*

being a working student	owning a home
a movie that teaches something	the Sunday paper
a grandparent	midterm exams

INDEPENDENT STUDY: *Possessives* (answers in the back)

VI. A. *Insert 's or ' in the following sentences to make the possessives correct. If there is an error in the plural forms, correct that too.*

  1. I can still remember the horrid look on my fathers face when I missed second gear and almost ran into a bus.

  2. One of the hardest things for me to do in my teens was to challenge one of my mothers decision.

  3. My nephew enjoys these stories, especially when he is in bed.

  4. Borrowing will cause problems for ones next months budget because part of that money will have to be repaid to the person it was borrowed from.

  5. I also recommend parents spend as much time as possible with their children.

  6. From the very beginning he took wage surveys to inform himself about the workers wage conditions.

  7. Sharon and I would dress up in my mothers clothes and put on my older sisters make-up.

8. The poet may express his love for a place, a person, or a thing with words that bring images to the readers mind.

9. We told Carol that we were leaving, but I don't think she heard us because of her boy friends loud voice.

10. Due to the increase in prices, heads of households are forced to budget their incomes.

B.   "M*A*S*H" shows how hard it is to be away from home. In one episode, Radar shows home movies to the staff of 4077 "M*A*S*H" and then breaks into tears because he misses his family so much. In the same episode, Colonel Potter grandson is born, and the colonel cries because he can't see his grandson. In a later episode, Radar leaves Korea for home and is greeted by B. J. Honeycutt family. One of B. J. kids mistakes Radar for his father, and when he finds out, B. J. gets so upset he starts drinking heavily and finally expresses his anguish by hitting Hawkeye.

possessive

CAPITALS

Capital letters are used to indicate beginnings and names.

1. The first word of a sentence should be capitalized, and so capitals should follow periods but not colons (:) or semicolons (;).

He saw everything. She was cheating on him.

He didn't want to be an accountant; he wanted to be a clown.

He itemized the overhead: rent, utilities, and insurance.

2. The first word of a direct quotation should be capitalized.

She said, "Go get the tickets while I park the car."

Bartley says, "The best way to learn to write is by writing."

3. The first, last, and every important word in a title should be capitalized. Short prepositions, connecting words, and articles are not considered important words.

Gardening for Fun

The Rise and Fall of the Price of Gold

4. Names of races, ethnic groups, religions, languages, and nationalities should be capitalized.

Black	Catholic	Spanish	African
Indian	Methodist	Filipino	French
Chicano	Holiness	Chinese	Dutch

5. The official name of a particular person, place, thing, or group should be capitalized. Here are some detailed examples:

CAPITALIZE	DO NOT CAPITALIZE
Words used as names of people	*General words referring to people*
She consulted Dr. Drew.	She consulted a doctor.
We will visit Aunt Martha.	We will visit our aunt.
I asked Father for help.	I asked my father for help.
She wrote to Senator McGann.	She wrote to her senator.
Names of specific places	*General words referring to places*
They live on Pine Street.	They live down the street.
We vacationed at Highland Lake.	We vacationed at the lake.
She entered Tulane University.	She entered university.
I was born in England.	I was born abroad.

He teaches at Lincoln High School.

He got off at Victoria Station.

She grew up in the South.

He teaches at my high school.

He got off at the last station.

She grew up south of the river.

Names of months, days of the week, and holidays

We went camping in June.

School starts on Monday.

We returned on the Fourth of July.

He looks forward to Christmas.

General words referring to days, time periods, or seasons

We went camping last summer.

School starts next week.

We returned on the fifth of July.

He looks forward to winter.

Exact names of specific courses and historical events and periods

He is taking Chemistry 1001.

She teaches Business Machines.

They fought in World War II.

He wrote in the Romantic Period.

Words referring to general areas of study and types of events

He is taking chemistry.

She teaches a business course.

They fought in the war.

He wrote in an earlier period.

Exact names of companies and products

My Volkswagen needs repairs.

She works for Jordan Marsh.

Do dentists use Crest?

General words for industries or products

My van needs repairs.

She works in the fashion industry.

Do dentists use fluoride toothpastes?

CORRECTION COMMENT: **Learn to form all capital and small letters, and use capitals only where convention demands them.**

EXERCISES: *Capitals*

I. *Correctly capitalize the following titles.*

A.
1. my first mistake

2. child raising in greece

3. ridicule among friends

4. is cheapest best?

5. stop or I'll shoot

6. the importance of competition in education

7. your loss is my gain

8. oxidation prevention

9. nest-building rituals of the nuthatch

10. pueblo houses as homes

B.

1. cooking for twelve in Japan

2. is organic gardening really possible?

3. phonics for first grade

4. an upward-sloping demand curve?

5. body decoration among fiji women

6. alcohol and disease resistance

7. recycled rubber

8. solar powered calculators

9. peer tutoring in disadvantaged neighborhoods

10. save the sloughs

II. *Correct the capitalization in the following sentences by crossing out the incorrect letters and writing the correct ones above them.*

A.

1. Her Doctor recommends that she wear low heels for her safety and health.

2. Two years ago I lived in a quiet neighborhood in sarasota.

3. I had history and english exams that day.

4. On saturdays we have scrimmage, defense against offense.

5. When I was in High School, I wanted to live in my friend's family.

6. Last February, he toured a cheese factory in Oregon.

7. I'll be spending memorial day with my parents and sisters.

8. When I didn't have a car, gary had a cougar he would let me use to run my errands or go on dates.

9. We examined Pines, Cypresses, and Cedars.

10. I don't know what classes I will have until I talk to my counselor this friday.

B.

1. Whether my problem is in math, psychology, or english, she'll drop what she's doing and help me until it's solved.

2. I have lived all my life on the planet mars.

3. Dr. Martin Luther King, Jr., deserves a National holiday because he fought for the human rights of all people.

4. Switching from a catholic school to a Public school put me into many new situations.

5. They cooked my two favorite kinds of persian food for my birthday.

capital

6. Our first conversation was about the difference between College and High School.

7. My career counselor said, "computer specialists will remain in demand through the eighties."

8. It was fortunate that I got back to Brooklyn a few days before Registration because the college didn't have me in its files.

9. The rain, fog, and snow of Winter increase the chance of accidents.

10. Just last week I was presented with a mural of camp wa-wa drawn on my daughter's wall with some smucker's jelly and a bright orange crayon.

C. 1. He recommends applying at general telephone.

2. When we go to safeway and lucky stores, we don't pay for parking.

3. We never worked very hard in our english courses.

4. I have only been to eight Rock concerts in my life.

5. One friday night a friend of mine came home from College for christmas vacation and invited me out to dinner.

6. During the Winter months, the cost of electricity and heating goes up.

7. My Independence caused me to become self-supporting.

8. I know I will choose one of the business majors someday.

9. The american people must find alternate energy sources now.

10. My anthropology professor said, "the most important thing to learn in this course is cultural relativity."

D. 1. Last february I lent my brother Four Hundred Dollars.

2. The senior class President, two of my friends, and I went over to monique's house for lunch.

3. If one delegation has business with another and the Translator is not there, both parties usually speak french.

4. One weekend Jeff went to a party on friday night; then he got up saturday morning to go to a convention.

5. I have to start studying for final Exams in English, Costume Designing, and Senior Project.

6. After my boss assigned me this duty on thursday morning, he left town and didn't return to the ranch until saturday morning.

7. My first class on Wednesday is called Slavery of the Western World. Mr. Masare, an african professor from Tanzania, discusses the beginnings of slavery and its impact on america today.

8. I got off at the embarcadero station.

9. He said, "some women I can do without, but as long as I live I will be glad that God made us different."

10. When I finish my English requirement, I will take just sociology courses for a while.

E. Correct the errors in capitalization in the following introduction.

I haven't had many jobs that actually required a specific skill because I had no qualifications. My working experience included only baby-sitting and working as a Waitress at a Lake Resort. As I approached my junior year in High School, I began taking a lot of Business courses to help me get a part-time job as a secretary. I then applied for a job at Ellis Olsen Mortuary and to my surprise got it. That job was a big disappointment to me.

III. A. *Following the rules in this section, add capital letters to this essay.*

frank and babe were both professional baseball players. it's a shame they never had a chance to play against one another because there is a lot of doubt in the minds of many people as to which one of them was the best.

babe was a white man who played right field for the new york yankees. he lived in an era of bootlegged whiskey, 30-mile-an-hour speed laws, racketeers and elliott ness.

the rules of the game were pretty much the same as babe knocked 714 home runs out of the park. sometimes he'd hit two or three a day. he was loved by millions as he played the game from day to day. the voices of the fans would echoe like thunder as he would swing at the pitch, fastball, curve, knuckle or even a splitball.

old babe had a record surpassed by none, that is until frank came on the scene with 715 home runs.

frank is a black man, something new added to the major leagues long after babe played his last inning with new york.

now frank is an incredible man also. he's loved by millions and hated by quite a few too. he lives in a time of racism, discrimination, 747s and naypalm bombs.

the basic rules of baseball still hold true, but frank has to hit them a good 30 to 40 feet farther. he swings at change-ups, sliders, and some pitches babe never saw, and as frank got closer to that record mark of babe's, the pressure on frank was much greater than babe ever had to deal with.

who was the best. was it frank or babe. unfortunately, most people won't be able to see that game. when it's played on the field where all good players go when they've played their last game here at home.

B. *Reread the essay above for other errors and for weaknesses in organization. Share your findings with your classmates.*

INDEPENDENT STUDY: Capitals *(answers in the back)*

IV. *Correct the capitalization in the following sentences by crossing out the incorrect letters and writing the correct ones above them.*

A.
1. A totally Liberated woman should marry a liberated man or no one at all.

2. When president Carter announced his decision to recognize China, he surprised the whole world.

3. A Doctor should be consulted about weight problems.

4. Booksellers will be meeting in Denver this saturday and sunday.

5. The United States is one of the richest countries in the world, and our Government could contribute more assistance to poor nations.

6. Our economics professor said, "Fortunes have been made by following the simple rule of buying low and selling high."

7. This year I got together five of my friends to practice Christmas Carols every saturday in November.

8. I was hoping to spend my Holidays with my family, but I had to work on Memorial day.

9. My hands and legs were shaking as I stared at him. For a moment I thought it was halloween, but it was not.

10. A strong Bell Boy is more economical than a weak Bell Boy.

B.   My weekends are usually spent just hanging out. Last weekend we all drove up to fremont to watch the motorcycle races. After they were over, we drove to mcdonald's to get something to eat. There were three cars full of people from bellows falls, and everyone was looking at us as though we were from another world. After that we met at a park to decide what to do. We sat around all evening and talked about the parties that were going on in marlboro, winchester, dublin, and bellows falls.

SPELLING

Good spelling makes your ideas more believable. It is difficult to take ideas seriously that are expressed with misspelled words. The best way to learn to spell correctly is to develop good spelling habits.

1. Sound words out as you read or write them. Careful attention to the sounds will prevent confusion of words like these:

ever	every
except	expect
marital	martial
quiet	quite

When you're writing an essay, don't limit yourself to words you know how to spell. If you aren't sure about the spelling of a word, just spell it as it sounds and underline it lightly.

2. After everything else is done, check your spelling by looking up questionable words in a dictionary or word book. Figure out the first few letters of the word, turn to that page of the dictionary, and look for your word.

If you misspell more than two or three words per essay, check each word for spelling starting from the end of the essay. If you aren't positive that a word is spelled correctly, look it up. Misspelled words are often difficult to find because writers get caught up in the meaning of the sentences and lose sight of individual words. Reading backward allows you to see each individual word.

3. Keep a list of the correct spelling of words you misspell. This list can be consulted quickly and studied in those extra moments while you wait for the bus or walk across campus. The blank pages at the end of this book have been saved for this list.

4. Remember this jingle:

> *Put i before e except after c*
> *Or when sounded like ay as in "neighbor" and "weigh"*

Following this rule will allow you to correctly spell such words as

believe	ceiling	eighty
niece	deceive	sleigh
fierce	conceit	vein

The exceptions to this rule are contained in this odd advice:

Seize weird leisure.

5. Become familiar with the spelling changes required when adding endings to words. Usually word endings are simply added to the original word, but some words require spelling changes with some endings. In this list, the words requiring spelling changes are boxed and explained. Compare them to the similar ones near them that have no spelling changes.

content	contented	contentment
wish	wishful	wishing

Words ending in a consonant followed by a y	Change the y to i before endings beginning with all letters but i	
deny	denial	denying
study	studious	studying
vary	variation	varying
worry	worrisome	worrying

annoy	annoyance	annoying
convey	conveyor	conveying
play	played	playing

Words ending in a silent e	Drop the e before endings beginning with a vowel	
encourage	encouraging	encouragement
hope	hoped	hopeful
love	lovable	lovely
use	usage	useful

agree	agreeable	agreement
free	freeing	freedom

One-syllable words ending in a single vowel followed by a single consonant	Double the consonant before endings beginning with a vowel	
war	warring	warfare
red	redden	redness
sin	sinner	sinful
ship	shipping	shipment

warm	warmer	warmly

spelling

sink	sinking	sinkful
rest	rested	restless
treat	treating	treatment

Words with the accent on the last syllable ending in a single vowel followed by a single consonant	Double the consonant before endings beginning with a vowel	
allot	allotting	allotment
inter	interred	interment
commit	committee	commitment
regret	regretted	regretfully

humor	humorous	humorless
abandon	abandoned	abandonment
pocket	pocketed	pocketful

6. Become familiar with the distinctions between the following words that often cause errors. Whenever possible, spelling associations and strange sentences have been created to aid your memory.

accept/except

word	accept	except
meaning:	take	excluding
use:	verb	preposition

He accepted the praise.

They all left except Mr. Smith.

advice/advise

word:	advice	advise
use:	noun	verb

I advise you to follow my advice.

affect/effect

word:	affect	effect
meaning:	change	result
use:	verb	noun

The climate affected his health.

The climate had an effect on his health.

a lot/all right

	Always correct	*Always incorrect*
	a lot	~~alot~~
	all right	~~alright~~

already/all ready

The sentence that requires two words could be written without "all"; the sentence that requires one word could not.

We are all ready for dinner.

"We are ready for dinner" makes sense.

We are already far behind.

"We are ready far behind" doesn't make sense.

are/or/our

word:	are	or	our
use:	verb	connecting word	possessive

Our books are lost or stolen.

board/bored

word:	board	bored
meaning:	panel	tired
use:	noun	verb or modifier

They nailed a board across the window.

The school board must make a choice.

His lecture bored us.

The bored children squirmed in their seats.

choose/chose

word:	choose	chose
use:	present verb	past verb
pronunciation:	*oo* as in "booze"	*o* as in "rose"

She chose the rose; I'll choose the booze.

clothes/cloths

word:	clothes	cloths
meaning:	garments	pieces of fabric
pronunciation:	long *o* as in "note"	short *o* as in "not"

Most people note clothes but not cloths.

complement/compliment

word:	complement	compliment
meaning:	completer	praise

A 60° angle is the complement of a 30° angle.

I like compliments.

conscience/conscious

word:	conscience	conscious
meaning:	moral standards	aware

Conscience has an extra *n* because it usually says "no."

does/dose

word:	does	dose
meaning:	accomplishes	specified amount
use:	verb	noun

One dose does wonders.

idea/ideal

word:	idea	ideal
meaning:	thought	perfect
use:	noun	adjective

She has the ideal idea.

it's/its/its'

word:	it's	its	its'
meaning:	it is	something's	no meaning
use:	subject-verb combination	possessive pronoun	always incorrect

It's losing its impact.

knew/new

word:	knew	new
meaning:	understood	not old
use:	past verb	adjective

They knew all the new songs.

know/no/now

word:	know	no	now
meaning:	understand	not any	not later
use:	present verb	negative	adverb

I know no solution now.

led/lead

word:	led	lead
meaning:	guided	metal
use:	verb	noun

He led the parade.

The toys were made of lead.

loose/lose

word:	loose	lose
meaning:	free	miss
pronunciation:	rhymes with "moose"	rhymes with "news"

Loose the moose and lose the moos.

passed/past

word:	passed	past
meaning:	went by	earlier time, by
use:	past verb	noun, adverb, preposition, adjective

In the past, he passed past daily.

rise/raise

word:	rise	raise
meaning:	move upward	lift
pronunciation:	rhymes with "eyes"	rhymes with "days"

Things rise by themselves but raise other things.

The sun and I rise at the same time.

I have spent my life raising children, vegetables, and money.

than/then

word:	than	then
use:	to compare	like "when," to refer to time

Then she was heavier than I.

their/there/they're

word:	their	there	they're
use:	possessive	like "here," it points things out	substitute for "they are"

They're leaving their coats in there.

thorough/though/thought/through/threw/thru

"Thorough" is an adjective meaning "fully done."

Her revision was thorough.

"Though" makes clauses dependent and means almost the same as "although."

Though she had little money, she always fed her children well.

"Thought" is the past and past participle form of "to think."

I thought my essay was finished.

"Through" is a preposition meaning "in one side and out the other."

My son ran through the kitchen.

"Threw" is the past tense form of "to throw."

I threw the ball over the wall.

"Thru" is a colloquial spelling of "through" that should not be used in formal writing.

too/two/to

"Too" means "in addition" or "extra" (it has an additional or extra *o*).

She too is too late.

"Two" is the word for the number 2 (it has a "double *u*" in it).

We have two alternatives.

"To" is a preposition (it is a smaller word than the others and gets less emphasis in a sentence).

My friends plan to swim to the island.

wander/wonder

word:	wander	wonder
meaning:	travel	feel curiosity

We wander through the halls.

They wonder at his boldness.

Their eyes were full of wonder.

wear/we're/were/where

"Wear" is a verb meaning "to have on the body."

I always feel attractive when I wear new clothes.

"We're" is a contraction of the two words "we are."

"Were" is the past tense form of "are."

Today we're wiser than we were yesterday.

"Where" refers to location (it has the word "here" in it).

Where are my boots?

Good spelling is easy to master. Simply proofread carefully and look up any words that might be misspelled. As you develop the good spelling habits outlined above, your proofreading time will get shorter and shorter.

CORRECTION COMMENT: Correct your spelling by proofreading carefully and looking up any words that might be misspelled.

EXERCISES: Spelling

I. *Following the* ie, ei *spelling rule in point 4 of this section, correctly fill in the following blanks.*

spelling

A.
1. sh _____ ld
2. y _____ ld
3. rec _____ pt
4. th _____ f
5. v _____ n

6. perc _____ ve
7. rel _____ f
8. s _____ ze
9. w _____ ght
10. f _____ ld

B. 1. s ＿＿＿ ge   6. w ＿＿＿ rd

2. n ＿＿＿ ghbor   7. conc ＿＿＿ ve

3. gr ＿＿＿ f   8. r ＿＿＿ ns

4. pr ＿＿＿ st   9. p ＿＿＿ ce

5. sl ＿＿＿ gh   10. surv ＿＿＿ llance

II. *Add the prescribed word endings following the spelling patterns de-scribed in the list in point 5 of this section.*

A. 1. walk + ed =   6. carry + ed =

2. pay + ment =   7. carry + ing =

3. list + less =   8. destroy + ed =

4. nation + al =   9. play + ful =

5. rain + ed =   10. empty + er =

B. 1. like + able =   6. sincere + ly =

2. like + ness =   7. drop + ing =

3. arrive + al =   8. droop + ing =

4. write + ing =   9. pin + ing =

5. achieve + ment =   10. pine + ing =

C. 1. hop + ing =   6. admit + ed =

2. hope + ing =   7. control + ing =

3. cheap + ly =   8. refer + ed =

4. adjust + able =   9. begin + ing =

5. occur + ed =   10. differ + ing =

D. 1. unforget + able =   6. strip + ing =

2. submit + ing =   7. stripe + ing =

3. suffer + ed =   8. interfere + ed =

4. rob + ed =   9. beauty + ful =

5. robe + ed =   10. easy + er =

E. 1. imagine + ation =   6. lonely + ness =

2. compel + ing =   7. necessary + ly =

3. late + ly =   8. employ + able =

4. big + est =   9. amuse + ment =

5. condole + ence =   10. mighty + ly =

III. *In the following sentences, find the misspelled words, cross them out, and write the correct spelling above.*

A.
1. On the dance floor he had to left feet.

2. My nieghborhood supports more then a few cats.

3. If the owners get there way we will see more control over the baseball industry.

4. Everysince I was a little girl, I've wanted to visit Paris.

5. I went to my room, turned on my television, and studyed three times as long as in a quite place.

6. I usually go to Southland in Lansing to buy all my cloths and jewelry.

7. If these educated people where to be drafted, the country would be weaker in years to come.

8. We studied the rules and than answered the questions.

9. Many parents are to concerned about there children's education.

10. Teachers should give there students a chance to prove their responsible.

B.
1. For the passed too years, I have really enjoyed my car.

2. At school I get board more easyly than I do at home.

3. The full-time employees always had to worry whether are not they'd work enough hours to pay they're bills.

4. My professors lecture so fast that I loose the main ideals of there lectures.

5. He refused to go in a beat-up car, and I really didn't like the idea myself.

6. He's alright, but the motorcycle didn't quite survive the sudden stop with a tree.

7. Dr. King lead the civil rights movement nonviolently.

8. The decline in employment has had a deep psychological affect on many people, young and old.

9. I always new when the doctor was going to give me a shot because he got very quite and sneaky.

10. I think she's moving on to new material to fast.

C.
1. Today their are fewer people in the market for cars then they're were ten years ago.

2. She beleives her neighbors are getting evicted.

3. I see alot of people skating and enjoying it.

spelling

4. Our international policymakers have gone one step to far.

5. Finally my mother came too except my decision.

6. Men don't always approve of women earning more money than they do.

7. If parents would tell their children that libraries have fun activities to, then maybe there children would come to the library more often.

8. American teenagers mature to quickly.

9. At Christmas we have a houseful of poeple wondering around.

10. Their are always assistants helping the doctors, and they also make the patient feel better.

D. 1. Women where totally ignoring their responsibilities. Marriages where breaking up, and children where turning radical because there mothers were out fighting for high paying and masculine jobs instead of staying home.

2. Our neighborhood was alright except their was to much trouble for teenagers to get into.

3. My religion requires that an unmarried person not engage in martial situations.

4. We will rise our children carefully.

5. If our educational system prevents our youth from geting a good education, than our communities can only deteriorate.

6. When I recieved my draft notice, my friends started comming by and giveing me advise.

7. Parents never seem to understand their children. They're always trying to past on their own morals and expectations to them.

8. He kept telling me, "Never stop to close to the car in front of you."

9. His conscious told him it was wrong to chose death.

10. He new how to sew and made elegant cloths.

IV. A. *Go through all the essays you have written recently and write correctly in the pages at the end of this book all words that you have misspelled. Space them out in alphabetical order for easy reference.*

B. *Correct spelling and other errors in the following essay.*

It's three A.M. on Friday the 13th on a cold, stormy night. Herbert, a perfect example of the average American college bay, is sitting at his small desk covered with books and scattered papers. The house is dark and quiet except for a small desk lamp and the sound of Herbert chewing his nails. All at once, a lowed low pitched growl shatters the silence! Herbert quicly jumps up and runs for the kitchen where he keeps his weapons to fight of this terrible unseen threat. Herbert, with incredible speed, reaches the kitchen and quickly opens the cupboard where he keeps his small black cream filled weapon. Almost by reflex, he rippes off the safty storage foil and "munches out," defeating his enemy instantly! Americans don't know enough about the junk food they are eating.

Americans don't know what junk food does to their bodys. Junk food is the main cause of millions of deathes each year that could have been avoided, if it was not for junk food. A person may say "I have never heard of anyone dieing from eating junk food," this is because there deathes are listed as other diseases caused by eating junk food. Some prime exampls of theas killers are: Hart disease, Cancer, Arteral Sclarosses and Diabeaties. All of theas life-taking diseases were virtualy unheard of before the introduction of food additives into our diets. I beleive if theas additives were all tested conclusivly, and people were informd of the findings, the F.D.A. would be forced to pull the substances off the market.

Americans don't know what food is junk. Americans assume that if it is on the shelf it will not hurt them, and if it could harme them, it would have a warning on the lable. This is not the case, infact, it is the opposite. There are 3,834 food additives and perservitives used in prosesed food. Only three of theas additives have been tested conclusivly: Salt, Sugar, and sacrine. All three substances were found to be harmeful to our health, and one or more of theas three substances is found in all processed foods. In short, a good definition of junk food would be, anything in a box, bag, can, carton, package, or is not in its' natural form.

Americans don't know what food is good. A person might ask the question, "if I can't eat processed foods, what is left", thats right, natural foods. Natural foods sustained life for billions of years before the Ding Dong was ever thought of. Processed foods have only been around for the last century, and as we are now learning, and are not adequitly sustaining life. Natural foods are fruts, vegtables, grains, and cerials in thire natural state. If America was to go on the right natural food diet, we could all but wipeout hundreds of modenday diseases in one generation.

It is 25 yeas later, and Herbert is in bedd watching old reruns of Johny Carson. The roon is quiet, except for the faint sound of the T.V. in the background. When all of assudden that same fimilure monster within rolles, rumbles, and roars out lowed.

Reflex has Herbert out of bed and troting for the kitchen and his arsonal of weapons. Sunday Tribune, Page 25, obituary collem 2 reads as followes: Herbert W. Weston 45 years died of heart attack in home as he got up for a mid-night snack.

C. Reread the essay above and answer the following questions.

　1. What is the outline? Is it good?

　2. Does the evidence support the arguments?

　3. Is the introduction good? What is its weakest point?

*4. Is the conclusion good? Does it answer the questions "so what"
and "what next"?*

INDEPENDENT STUDY: Spelling *(answers in the back)*

V. **A.** *Following the* ie, ei *spelling rule in point 4 of this section, correctly
fill in the following blanks.*

1. ach _____ ve
2. bes _____ ge
3. I _____ sure
4. misch _____ vous
5. rec _____ ve

6. r _____ gn
7. retr _____ ve
8. fr _____ ght
9. f _____ nd
10. r _____ ndeer

B. *Add the prescribed word endings following the spelling patterns
described in the list in point 5 of this section.*

1. angry + ly =
2. marry + age =
3. destroy + er =
4. lose + ing =
5. receive + able =

6. god + ess =
7. transmit + ing =
8. interest + ing =
9. dignify + ed =
10. busy + ly =

C. *In the following sentences, find the misspelled words, cross them
out, and write the correct spelling above.*

1. Everyone nose that food is very important too us.

2. These children really enjoyed listening, and there enjoyment pleased me.

3. I new I would have to loose ten pounds to fit into those pants.

4. When visiting a good resturant, I except everything too be nice.

5. In the passed, society was more oppresive then it is today.

6. I worked durring my last to summers in high school, but after I
graduated I excepted unemployment gratefully.

7. I would advice him to accept that repreive.

8. Reaching an agreement with my advicer can be quiet a task.

9. In the junior department, we had to hang cloths, straighten racks,
unwrap and hang new items, do mark-ups and mark-downs, and still
have time to help are customers.

10. A dentist can catch cavities in there early stages, before to much
damage is done to the teeth.

Strong Writing

8. Good Materials

• A writer formulates impressions and ideas into words and builds those words into sentences and the sentences into larger structures. Since words are the basic units of all writing, they should be carefully chosen to fit the writer's idea and convince his audience. This chapter discusses the selection of solid words, especially subjects and verbs, that will most effectively support sentences, paragraphs, and essays.

EXACT WORDS

Standard English demands careful attention to word choice, so you should always be sure the word you use fits your idea and your sentence exactly. Many expressions that are common in casual speech should be avoided in writing.

1. Avoid the double negative. According to the rules of standard English, no two of the following words should be used together because they cancel each other out.

no	hardly	nobody	never
not	without	nothing	neither

FAULTY I get tired of talking without no answer.

The rules of standard English say that "without" and "no" cancel each other out, that "without *no* answer" means the same as "with an answer." Either "without" should be changed to "with," or "no" should be changed to "any."

REVISED I get tired of talking with no answer.

REVISED I get tired of talking without any answer.

FAULTY They didn't have no hope of winning.

In this sentence, the words "not," expressed as "n't," and "no" cancel each other out, and "didn't have *no* hope" means the same as "had some hope." Either "didn't have" should be changed to "had" or "no" should be changed to "any."

`wrong word`

REVISED They had no hope of winning.

REVISED They didn't have any hope of winning.

2. Use precise quantity words. English uses different words depending on the nature of the material being grouped.

With plurals, things that can be counted (people, wishes, bananas)		*With group words, things that can't be counted but can be measured (water, wealth, sugar)*	
many	number	much	amount
fewer	numerous	less	a lot of

FAULTY Mount Saint Helens caused much floods.

Since floods can be counted and "floods" is a plural, "many" should be used with it, not "much."

REVISED Mount Saint Helens caused many floods.

Alternatively, the word "flood" could be changed to a nonplural word that groups things, like "flooding."

REVISED Mount Saint Helens caused much flooding.

FAULTY The new process requires less machines.

Since machines can be counted and "machines" is plural, "fewer" should be used with it, not "less."

REVISED The new process requires fewer machines.

Also the word "machines" could be changed to a nonplural word that groups things, like "machinery." Then the word "less" would be correct.

REVISED The new process requires less machinery.

The dictionary tells which words refer to things that can be counted and which don't. The [C] in the following entry for "machine" indicates that this word stands for something that can be counted, and the [U] in the entry for "machinery" indicates it stands for something that can't be counted.

> **ma·chine** /məˈʃin/ *n* [C] **1** appliance or mechanical device with parts working together to apply power, often steam or electric power (*a ˋprinting-∼*), but also human power (*a ˋsewing-∼*). *We live in the ∼ age*, the age in which ∼s more and more replace hand labour. ˋ∼-**gun** *n* gun that fires continuously while the trigger is pressed. ʹ∼-ˋ**made** *adj* made by ∼ (contrasted with *hand-made*). ˋ∼ **tool**, tool, mechanically operated, for cutting or shaping materials. **2** persons organized to control a political group: (US) *the Democratic ∼*. □ *vt* [VP6A] operate on, make (sth) with, a ∼ (esp of sewing and printing). **ma·chin·ist** /məˈʃinist/ *n* one who makes, repairs or controls ∼ tools; one who works a ∼, esp a sewing-∼.
> **ma·chin·ery** /məˈʃinɹi/ *n* [U] **1** moving parts of a machine; machines collectively: *How much new ∼ has been installed? Cf How many new machines have...?* **2** (*pl* -ries) methods, organization (e g of government).

3. Use the word "where" only to refer to place. In speech it is frequently used instead of "until" or "when."

FAULTY There were many times where we could have said something.

Here "where" is incorrectly used to refer to time instead of "when."

REVISED There were many times when we could have said something.

4. Use "who" to refer to people and "which" to refer to things.

FAULTY I had a friend which worked at O'Neil's.

Here "which" incorrectly refers to a person, "a friend." "Who" would have been correct.

REVISED I had a friend who worked at O'Neil's.

5. Don't use "of" instead of "have." When "have" is used as a helping verb after words like "must," "could," "might," "should," "would," and "ought to," it is often pronounced like "of." However, "of" is always a preposition, never a verb.

FAULTY She could of done better.

Here "of" is incorrectly used as a verb part instead of "have."

REVISED She could have done better.

6. Don't use "and" instead of "to" after words like "try" and "be sure."

FAULTY When I try and study, he stops me.

This sentence doesn't have two verbs, "try" and "study," because the writer doesn't study; she only *tries* studying or *tries* to study.

REVISED When I try to study, he stops me.

CORRECTION COMMENT: Always be sure the word you use fits your idea and your sentence exactly.

EXERCISES: Exact Words

I. *Write three sentences using each of the following words.*

1. no	6. amount
2. less	7. without
3. of	8. numerous
4. many	9. where
5. hardly	10. much

wrong word

II. Find the wrong words in the following sentences, cross them out, and write the correct ones above them.

A.
1. My new school had less students then my old one.

2. Anyone could of won, but I had taken myself to the limit of my abilities.

3. Finally, we do reach the age, and that's where the problems start.

4. The second day I woke up early and decided to try and participate in all the activities.

5. There were hardly no people shopping in Penney's.

6. She could of done better.

7. The beach had less sand than my living room floor.

8. I hope when I finish my studies I will not have much difficulties in running our business smoothly.

9. Since that experience, I haven't never tried flying again.

10. When I try and do better, my grades improve.

B.
1. I've also noticed they are not selling much bows and arrows anymore.

2. If I hadn't waited, I never would of met my friends.

3. Married couples never have trouble renting a home.

4. We had a problem because the amount of hours was very short.

5. If I ever lost them, I don't think there is no one to replace them.

6. I now have less problems with my eyes.

7. It's impossible to try and take a nap once in a while.

8. Therefore, the Japanese haven't been reducing their employees as many as Americans.

9. There have been many incidents like this one where she or I would have the same thoughts in our heads, but neither of us would say them right out.

10. I had worked all day in an empty store, and they didn't save me nothing.

C.
1. I didn't want any help with my homework.

2. I couldn't believe the amount of people who were already there.

3. People which haven't seen *Star Wars* must of thought I was a genius to create such a catchy title.

4. His job demands a large amount of good will.

5. When I try and do sometimes nice for people, my parents think they're using me.

6. Who would of thought that I would get such an exciting graduation present?

7. I visited my cousin which had rented a condominium near the beach.

8. The only way my mother could manage to take care of us was to accept welfare for a few years until we reached grammar school age where we went to a public school.

9. Now they have less opportunities to talk to each other than before.

10. The boat which we rented had three beds.

D. 1. I guess I came home late too many times and didn't do my chores as well as I could of.

2. We didn't get no instruction from that teacher.

3. The man which wrote out the order entered the wrong date on the form.

4. After the soil has been raked where it is smooth, one can just plant his seeds.

5. He insists that people in Russia have less freedom than we do.

6. Only ten years ago it would not cost a student no more than forty dollars to take a trip from Istanbul to Bangkok.

7. I usually feel uncomfortable when I am at a party or disco with a large amount of people.

8. They never permit tourists to work.

9. During the time I was plowing, I did not have a good meal because it would of taken valuable time from work.

10. She didn't have much trouble answering the questions correctly.

E.   I won't never be able to buy a home with prices as bad as they are. When my parents and my husband's parents bought homes about ten years ago, they paid between $35,000 and $55,000. My parents' house didn't have no air conditioning, fence, or modern appliances. After they added those, they could of sold it for $79,000. The value has increased even more since then because they added a swimming pool and sun porch. I will have to pay twice that amount of money if I try and buy a house like that today.

III. A. In the following excerpt from Sherwood Anderson's "I'm a Fool," a young man describes the anguish he causes himself by pretending to be someone he isn't.

    And I was with that girl and she wasn't saying much, and I wasn't saying much either. One thing I know. She wasn't stuck on me because of the lie about my father being rich and all that. There's a way you know. . . . Craps amighty. There's a kind of girl you see just once in your life, and if you don't get busy and make hay, then you're gone for good and all, and

wrong word

you might as well go jump off a bridge. They give you a look from inside of them somewhere, and it ain't no vamping, and what it means is—you want that girl to be your wife, and you want nice things around her like flowers and swell clothes, and you want her to have the kids you're going to have, and you want good music played and no ragtime. Gee whizz.

There's a place over near Sandusky, across a kind of bay, and it's called Cedar Point. And after we had supper we went over to it in a launch, all by ourselves. Wilbur and Miss Lucy and that Miss Woodbury had to catch a ten o'clock train back to Tiffin, Ohio, because, when you're out with girls like that you can't get careless and miss any trains and stay out all night, like you can with some kinds of Janes.

And Wilbur blowed himself to the launch and it cost him fifteen cold plunks, but I wouldn't never have knew if I hadn't listened. He wasn't no tin horn kind of a sport.

Over at the Cedar Point place, we didn't stay around where there was a gang of common kind of cattle at all.

There was big dance halls and dining places for yaps, and there was a beach you could walk along and get where it was dark, and we went there.

She didn't talk hardly at all and neither did I, and I was thinking how glad I was my mother was all right, and always made us kids learn to eat with a fork at table, and not swill soup, and not be noisy and rough like a gang you see around a race track that way.

Then Wilbur and his girl went away up the beach and Lucy and I sat down in a dark place, where there was some roots of old trees the water had washed up, and after that the time, till we had to go back in the launch and they had to catch their trains, wasn't nothing at all. It went like winking your eye.

Here's how it was. The place we were setting in was dark, like I said, and there was the roots from that old stump sticking up like arms, and there was a watery smell, and the night was like—as if you could put your hand out and feel it—so warm and soft and dark and sweet like an orange.

I most cried and I most swore and I most jumped up and danced, I was so mad and happy and sad.

When Wilbur come back from being alone with his girl, and she saw him coming, Lucy she says, "We got to go to the train now," and she was most crying too, but she never knew nothing I knew, and she couldn't be so all busted up. And then, before Wilbur and Miss Woodbury got up to where we was, she put her face up and kissed me quick and put her head up against me and she was quivering and—Gee whizz.

Sometimes I hope I have cancer and die. I guess you know what I mean. We went in the launch across the bay to the train like that, and it was dark, too. She whispered and said it was like she and I could get out of the boat and walk on the water, and it sounded foolish, but I knew what she meant.

And then quick we were right at the depot, and there was a big gang of yaps, the kind that goes to the fairs, and crowded and milling around like cattle, and how could I tell her? "It won't be long because you'll write and I'll write to you." That's all she said.

I got a chance like a hay barn afire. A swell chance I got.

And maybe she would write me, down at Marietta that way, and the letter would come back, and stamped on the front of it by the U.S.A. "there ain't any such guy," or something like that, whatever they stamp on a letter that way.

And me trying to pass myself off for a big-bug and a swell—to her, as decent a little body as God ever made. Craps amighty—a swell chance I got!

And then the train come in, and she got on it, and Wilbur Wessen, he come and shook hands with me, and that Miss Woodbury was nice too and bowed to me, and I at her, and the train went and I busted out and cried like a kid.

Gee, I could have run after that train and made Dan Patch look like a freight train after a wreck but, socks amighty, what was the use? Did you ever see such a fool?

I'll bet you what—if I had an arm broke right now or a train had run over my foot—I wouldn't go to no doctor at all. I'd go set down and let her hurt—that's what I'd do.

I'll bet you what—if I hadn't a drunk that booze I'd a never been such a boob as to go tell such a lie—that couldn't never be made straight to a lady like her.

I wish I had that fellow right here that had on a Windsor tie and carried a cane. I'd smash him for fair. Gosh darn his eyes. He's a big fool—that's what he is.

And if I'm not another you just go find me one and I'll quit working and be a bum and give him my job. I don't care nothing for working, and earning money, and saving it for no such boob as myself.

B. *Return to the passage above, underline any variations you find from standard English, and answer the questions below. Support each answer by quoting words and sentences.*

1. *Do the verbs the narrator uses follow the rules of standard English?*

2. *Do his words follow the rules of standard English?*

3. *Does he use concrete words?*

4. *Are his sentences graceful and varied?*

5. *Why doesn't Sherwood Anderson use standard English in this story?*

6. *What does the narrator's language suggest about his education, social class, and occupation?*

7. *How does his language relate to the central idea that he is pretending to be someone he isn't?*

wrong word

8. *What do you like best about this passage?*

C. Write an essay about the language in this passage. Your thesis might answer one of the last questions above, and your supports might answer the earlier questions. Check your outline with your teacher. Then flesh it out into an essay by quoting words and sentences and explaining their effect.

D. Write an essay about the language that you use with your friends and your family or both. Talk about the ways in which it differs from standard English. Many people think standard English is boring or colorless, and so you might want to use the thesis that your informal language is richer or more colorful than standard English. On the other hand, you might choose the thesis that your informal language is less precise than standard English. Be sure to use lots of examples to prove your supports.

INDEPENDENT STUDY: **Exact Words** *(answers in the back)*

IV. **A.** *Correct any wrong words you find in the sentences below.*

1. I knew fifty dollars would not be enough for the amount of presents I had on my list.

2. We decided to try and usher.

3. The people who live in my neighborhood have hardly nothing in common with each other.

4. The United States sent a large amount of wheat to Russia.

5. Riding the bus is convenient, especially when one doesn't have a car or no other way of getting anywhere.

6. I'm sure you've had experiences where people who owe you money pay you back late.

7. She wants no part of this contract.

8. If we can get them trained, then there will be less people in the unemployment line and less demand on federal funds.

9. I never stayed at any jobs no more than three months.

10. Looking through a Webster's Dictionary, I was surprised to see a large amount of everyday words with three or more different meanings.

B. *Find and correct all the wrong words in the following paragraph.*

People which live in my neighborhood must of forgotten where the dump is. A few weeks ago when I took my brother's dog for a walk in the field across the street from my house, I saw numerous amounts of paper, car parts, aluminum cans, cardboard boxes, an abandoned refrigerator, a broken sofa, and even plastic bags full of garbage. I couldn't believe no one could be such pigs. They could of easily gone to the city dump, which is only five miles away.

CONCRETE SUBJECTS AND VERBS

The most powerful and memorable writing is built from concrete words: words that refer to objects and actions that can be perceived by the senses. Compare the following boring abstraction

> The form of literature was more interesting to Miss Groby than its meaning. Her reading of literature was a constant search for interesting phrases. One example was her examination of Shakespeare and Scott for their figures of speech.

with this concrete statement of the same idea.

> It is hard for me to believe that Miss Groby ever saw any famous work of literature from far enough away to know what it meant. She was forever climbing up the margins of books and crawling between their lines, hunting for the little gold of phrase, making marks with a pencil. As Palamides hunted the Questing Beast, she hunted the Figure of Speech. She hunted it through the clangorous halls of Shakespeare and through the green forests of Scott.
> —James Thurber

Thurber creates visual impressions in his readers' minds. They see Miss Groby climbing up the margins, crawling between the lines, and stalking through halls and forests. These active verbs, "saw," "climbing," "crawling," "hunting," add life and movement to the Thurber passage and contrast sharply with the dull repeated "was" of the first passage. Powerful writing requires active concrete verbs.

Concrete subjects also strengthen writing. The writer of the first passage uses vague, weak subjects, "form," "reading," "example," while Thurber uses particular people. The active force in the idea, Miss Groby, hides behind the dead abstractions in the first passage, but Thurber's sentences show her in action.

Writers of English build sentences around subject-verb cores, so concrete writing begins with concrete subjects and verbs. Generally, the subject of a sentence should be the strongest or most active force in the idea, and the verb should express whatever action that force is generating. A sentence should show "who does what."

Even the most abstract ideas can be expressed in concrete words. The following sentence conceals a powerful idea behind a boring abstraction.

> Obtaining the necessities for survival in nontraditional ways is illegal.

This sentence is built around the abstract subject-verb core "obtaining . . . is." In contrast, the concrete language of the following sentence *shows* the reader the truth of the statement.

> The law in its majestic equality forbids the rich as well as the poor to sleep under bridges, to beg in the streets, and to steal bread.
> —Anatole France

France builds his sentence around a concrete subject-verb core, "law . . . forbids." The law is the dominant force in the idea, so that it makes an excellent subject, and its action is expressed in the verb "forbids." This sentence shows "who does what." Around this core France constructs a sentence of concrete words, "sleep," "bridges," "beg," "streets," "steal," "bread," that show poor people barred from even the barest necessities for survival.

Choose the first words of each clause carefully because they will probably contain your subject.

FAULTY Those times with my father are something that I will cherish throughout my life.

The writer of this sentence seems to start with "those times with my father" because these words express an important element of the idea. Unfortunately, however, few good verbs can combine with the abstract subject "times," and the writer completes the clause with the empty words "are something," then goes on to the real actor-action combination of this idea, "I will cherish," which should have been the subject-verb core of the first clause.

REVISED I will cherish those times with my father throughout my life.

Here's a similar example:

FAULTY Another aspect of war is that it ruins the economy.

The writer starts poorly with "another aspect," and so "aspect" becomes the subject while the logical subject, the real operating force of this idea, "war," falls into a prepositional phrase. Then the writer is forced to pad the sentence with "is that it" to get to the real action word, "ruins," which should have been the original verb.

REVISED War also ruins the economy.

Transitions like "another reason" and "one example" improve the coherence of a written work, but they may become the subject, take a weak verb like "is" or "was," and throw the main idea of the sentence into a dependent clause. Words like "also," "in addition," "for example," and "because" express transition without interfering with the main clause.

Some form of the verb "to be" has undermined every abstract sentence examined here. Whenever possible, eliminate this overworked verb.

am	was	be
is	were	being
are		been

Especially avoid using forms of "to be" with "because," "if," "when," and "where." Combinations like

is because	was if
was because	is where
is when	will be when

waste words and weaken sentences.

FAULTY Another reason I preferred the first motel was because our room faced the ocean.

This "reason was because" structure destroys a perfectly good sentence. Removing the abstract subject-verb core "reason . . . was" allows the real actor-action combination "<u>I</u> <u>preferred</u>" to move from a "that" clause to an independent clause that works gracefully with the final "because" clause. The transition expressed in "another" can be expressed by "also" or "in addition."

REVISED I also preferred the first motel because our room faced the ocean.

The best sentences are built from concrete words, and most awkward sentences are caused by abstract subject-verb combinations.

> **CORRECTION COMMENT: Substitute concrete words for abstract ones whenever possible, paying particular attention to subjects and verbs.**

EXERCISES: Concrete Subjects and Verbs

I. **A.** *Look through the essays you've written and find sentences with good concrete words, especially forceful subjects and active verbs. Copy ten of those sentences onto a sheet of paper.*

B. *Proverbs are memorable because they express abstract ideas in concrete terms. Below each of the following proverbs write the abstract idea that it communicates.*

1. Don't change horses in midstream.

   _____

2. A new broom sweeps clean.

   _____

3. No man is a hero to his valet.

   _____

4. Still waters run deep.

   _____

5. Set a thief to catch a thief.

   _____

6. Look before you leap.

   _____

7. Birds of a feather flock together.

   _____

8. Don't cut off your nose to spite your face.

_____

9. Barking dogs never bite.

_____

10. A rolling stone gathers no moss.

_____

C. Write your own proverbs to express the following abstractions.

1. People can not survive if they destroy the world around them.

2. Lost things usually turn up in likely places.

3. Anyone can learn anything if he or she has a long enough time to work on it.

4. Basically people are the same even though they may look different.

5. People cannot be healthy without good food.

6. Individuals are what they want to be.

7. Only a person who is sure about something can convince someone else.

8. The human race can choose a wonderful future.

9. A person can do almost anything if he or she wants to do it badly enough.

10. People who waste a lot of time accomplish less than people who use time well.

D. Write your own proverbs to express some ideas that you value.

II. Rewrite the following sentences, replacing abstract words with concrete ones and omitting unnecessary weak words. Begin with a forceful subject and an active verb. Sometimes you will need to invent material to complete the sentence. The first one has been done for you.

A.   1. Another favorite place to go was to concerts.

   EXAMPLE *We also enjoyed going to concerts.* _____

2. The way I got my apartment was really quickly.

3. There has to be knowledge of how to combine the foods.

4. At the end of the day, the review of notes is essential.

5. Another aspect that distracts me is a good movie.

6. The problem is that he tries too hard.

7. The plans I have for this Thanksgiving are to go to my aunt's house.

8. Some of the ways that this large amount of money was spent was for dinners, press conferences, and traveling.

9. The chance of winning a medal is what the athletes go to the Olympics for.

10. Riding mopeds was one experience that will be remembered by us all.

B.

1. The reason I like to go to parties is that I enjoy dancing.

2. These questions are problems faced by the working student.

3. The first thing I hope to make a reality is excelling in my career.

4. All this is done very naturally by her without any awkwardness or embarrassment.

5. The worst thing I hate about riding the bus is when it is crowded.

6. The main thing is that I must feel good about what I'm doing.

7. The reason I like Sam's is because they have a lot of dishes I can choose from.

8. A nice home is something that everyone doesn't have.

9. The reason I call her generous is because she lets me have things of hers that I need.

10. In my first term in college my biggest problem was the lack of ability to concentrate on my studies.

C.

1. Therefore cooperation of the countries is needed.

2. In conclusion, the reason I like Magic is that he's successful at the age of twenty.

3. Another reason for the winter being the worst season of the year is the rain.

4. The reason is because the dealer, whom everyone plays against, always has a card showing.

5. Another important aspect to the saving of lives is a driver's reaction time decreases at 55 mph.

6. Especially in skiing, the equipment is a factor in the performance of the athlete.

7. Another example is when I was in junior high school when I hung around with people who didn't like school.

8. What I hope to achieve through my job is to help others keep balanced business books.

9. The major effect gasoline prices will have on me will be when I attend the University of Michigan.

10. Another effect of my job was when I was too tired to get up for class.

D.   Fear is a paralyzing emotion. It immobilizes the mind. There is difficulty concentrating, creativity is lost, and all the imagination can do is give impressions of doom. Fear colors everything black and has a limiting effect on our abilities. Self-confidence has the opposite effect upon us. The results are freeing. No longer do we have to limit our abilities to protect ourselves. Self-confidence gives us the courage to accept challenges, to be secure enough to risk failure in some undertakings but achieve success in others.

III. A. *The following poem uses concrete language to discuss an abstract subject. Study the poem closely, and answer the questions that follow it.*

Go by Brooks

Go by brooks, love,
Where fish stare,
Go by brooks,
I will pass there.

Go by rivers,
Where eels throng,
Rivers, love,
I won't be long.

Go by oceans,
Where whales sail,
Oceans, love,
I will not fail.

—Leonard Cohen

1. *The three stanzas of this poem have similar form. What happens in the first line of each stanza?*

2. *What happens in the second line of each stanza?*

3. *What happens in the third line of each stanza?*

4. *What happens in the fourth line of each stanza?*

5. *Compare the first lines of all three stanzas. Is there any progression?*

6. *Compare the nouns in the second lines. Is there any progression?*

7. *Compare the verbs in the second lines. Is there any progression?*

8. *Compare the last lines of each stanza. Is there any progression?*

9. *Generalize about the progression from stanza to stanza in this poem. What does it seem to show?*

10. *Is this just a poem about fish and water?*

B. Write an essay about this poem. Start with a thesis that answers question 9 or 10 above and back that up with supports that answer questions 5, 6, 7, and 8. Be sure that your supports prove your thesis. Then check your outline with your teacher. Finally, write an essay on this outline, supporting your argument with words from the poem and explanations of their use.

C. In the following paragraph, E. B. White uses concrete language to talk about writing by comparing it to a balloon flight.

> I have always felt that the first duty of a writer was to ascend—to make flights, carrying others along if he could manage it. To do this takes courage, even a certain conceit. My favorite aeronaut was not a writer at all, he was Dr. Piccard, the balloonist, who once, in an experimental moment, made an ascension borne aloft by two thousand small balloons, hoping that the Law of Probability would serve him well and that when he reached the rarefied air of the stratosphere some (but not all) of the balloons would burst and thus lower him gently to earth. But when the doctor reached the heights to which he had aspired, he whipped out a pistol and killed about a dozen of the balloons. He descended in flames, and the papers reported that when he jumped from the basket he was choked with laughter. Flights of this sort are the dream of every good writer: the ascent, the surrender to probability, finally the flaming denouement, wracked with laughter—or with tears.

D. Put one line under all subjects and two lines under all parts of all verbs in the above paragraph. Then circle any subjects and verbs that are abstract instead of concrete.

E. Write a paragraph that gives concrete details about something by comparing it to something else. You might compare a challenge at school–registration, an exam, an in-class essay–to an athletic experience–a skateboard ride, a baseball game, a boxing match.

F. Write an essay on one of the following topics. Whenever possible, use concrete words, especially subjects and verbs.

something you miss from your childhood	ROTC
something you're fed up with	tennis
something you do well	marriage

INDEPENDENT STUDY: *Concrete Subjects and Verbs* (answers in the back)

IV. A. Rewrite any abstract sentences into concrete language, paying special attention to subjects and verbs. Invent any necessary details.

1. Puck darted around the meadow, his yellow hair flashing.

2. One such example of the penny's power is when I was ten years old.

3. One more negative aspect is the effect it has on the soldiers when they go home.

4. As she rode along the narrow winding roads, she saw the sun's rays trying to squeeze between the lacy branches of the trees.

5. The noise that makes me disappear is when I hear people yelling obscenities and fighting.

6. Now that I'm in college the best thing is we don't have a curfew.

7. One example of our inflation problem is food.

8. What's encouraging me to ignore these things is when some professors say they don't care about my writing skills.

9. The first problem was when our car broke down.

10. Removing evil spirits from the body is a belief and is practiced among primitive tribes.

B.   One mistake some girls make about going to college is too many fall back on business colleges. There is nothing wrong with business, but when women think of some sort of career it tends to always be becoming a secretary. Soon there will be so many secretaries there won't be enough jobs to accommodate them. Business colleges also are very expensive. For a six-month course it's about $2000. Why pay this kind of money when it's cheaper to go to a four-year college and learn a different occupation?

9. Careful Assembly

• Sentences that flow gracefully communicate more effectively than sentences that stagger and lurch. This chapter discusses the creation of interference-free sentences that lead the reader effortlessly to the writer's conclusions.

VAGUE PRONOUN REFERENCE

Pronouns should clearly stand for particular words that have been used.

FAULTY Sharon decided not to go with Lezlee because she had to leave early.

Did Sharon or Lezlee have to leave early? The pronoun "she" could stand for either Lezlee or Sharon. Rewrite sentences whose pronouns don't clearly refer to particular words.

REVISED Because Lezlee had to leave early, Sharon decided not to go with her.

In this sentence the pronoun "her" clearly refers to "Lezlee," and the reader knows that Lezlee had to leave early.

REVISED Because Sharon had to leave early, she decided not to go with Lezlee.

Now the pronoun "she" clearly refers to "Sharon," and the reader knows that Sharon had to leave early.

The words "this," "that," "who," "which," and "it" are also pronouns and must clearly stand for particular words that have been used. In the following sentences, those pronouns are correctly used and clearly refer to particular words.

John was eager to write about junk food. This was a good topic for him because he had just finished a nutrition course which had covered the subject in detail. In fact, that had been his favorite course, and he had gotten an A in it.

Pronouns must clearly stand for particular words, not a whole general idea.

FAULTY If he ever needs something, he has a whole family that can help; this sometimes relaxes a person.

In this sentence the pronoun "this" refers to the whole idea that comes before it instead of to particular words. Rewrite such sentences to eliminate vague pronoun reference.

REVISED If he ever needs something, he has a whole family that can help; such security sometimes relaxes a person.

Here's another example of unclear pronoun reference:

FAULTY Overweight people have to go to a special store, which is very silly.

The pronoun "which" in this sentence seems to refer to "store," but it doesn't because the final clause doesn't mean that the store is silly. Sentences with unclear pronoun reference often have to be completely rewritten.

REVISED Overweight people should not have to go to a special store.

To avoid confusion, place "which" and "who" clauses as close as possible to the word that the pronoun replaces.

FAULTY Many times open invitations to concerts are posted on bulletin boards which are fun to go to.

Here the pronoun "which" seems to refer to "bulletin boards," but it should be referring to "concerts." Moving the "which" clause next to "concerts" solves this problem.

REVISED Many times open invitations to concerts which are fun to go to are posted on bulletin boards.

Also, avoid using "this" instead of "a."

FAULTY In sixth grade I had this teacher who couldn't spell.

The word "a" should be used the first time something is mentioned. "This" should only be used after something has been introduced to remind the reader of that fact. Since the teacher is being introduced in the sentence above, the word "a" is appropriate. The next reference to the teacher could use "this," however.

REVISED In sixth grade I had a teacher who couldn't spell. This teacher made more spelling errors than her students did.

English has a few idiomatic expressions that use "it" without reference to an earlier word. These are primarily expressions of weather, time, and distance.

It's snowing in Oslo.

It's two o'clock in the morning.

It's twenty-three miles to Nottingham.

Except in these expressions, "it" should always refer to particular words.

FAULTY When I do poorly on an exam, it depresses me for days.

The word "it" does not really refer to "exam," it refers to the whole clause before. This sentence can be rewritten to eliminate this vague pronoun reference.

REVISED Doing poorly on an exam depresses me for days.

CORRECTION COMMENT: Pronouns must clearly refer to particular words that have been used.

EXERCISES: *Vague Pronoun Reference*

I. *Write the sentences described below.*

    1. three sentences correctly using "which"

    2. three sentences correctly using "this"

    3. three sentences correctly using "that"

    4. three sentences correctly using "it"

    5. three sentences correctly using "who"

II. *Circle the words "this," "that," "who," "which," and "it" in the following sentences and draw lines to the words they refer to. If they don't clearly refer to particular words or those words are too far away, rewrite the sentence to eliminate that error.*

A.
1. I plan to be a computer programmer, so I am working for a degree in it.
2. The hang glider soared above the cliff, which was a beautiful sight.
3. When we arrived at the library, the door was locked. We were very disappointed about this.
4. Our television set is broken, but the repairman will fix it on Thursday.
5. I had met the lead singer at a party the night before, which made the concert especially enjoyable.
6. When we lived in Mexico, we had this nurse with one eye.
7. She wants to be a ballet dancer and studies it five hours a week.
8. Bryan got the role which he had auditioned for.
9. When we start cleaning house, Kevin always disappears. This makes us very angry.
10. I try to run every day because it greatly improves my attitude.

B.
1. My fondest memory is of a Sunday afternoon at my parents' house, which also turned out to be the most tasty and delicious meal we had all week.
2. They threw bottles into the swimming pool, which ruined the filter.

reference

3. I am glad I eat many types of foods because it makes me not biased about whom I go to dinner with.

4. The errors which he makes imply that he doesn't understand the use of articles.

5. I wish that it could be times like that for me year in and year out.

6. When she lived in Paris, she met this Frenchman that she nearly married.

7. I think it should be at least two kids to every family.

8. At the age of eight, I had a dream about this huge chicken.

9. The roads are slick, and this makes it hard on the driver.

10. When I write my essays in class, I rarely have time to eliminate my punctuation errors, so therefore it affects my grade.

C.   1. We worked out our problem without a fight. This pleased us both.

2. In the catalog it describes every possible major.

3. Doctors did not expect her to live, but she did. They attributed it to the strength of her inner resources.

4. Not too long ago, I heard of this eight-year-old boy who had broken his arm in an accident.

5. If she needs more sources, I have this book on Hopkins she can borrow.

6. Now we will continue our journey through the world of ideas which began on registration day.

7. Women with babies who do not work or do not have any other source of income can receive welfare.

8. In most countries when a person graduates from a university he will probably have a hard time finding an adequate job, and this will happen to most of the graduates.

9. I never loan money that I need, for I can't depend on anyone but myself to set me back up again. To avoid this, one should never put himself in the position of being in debt because he loaned out his money.

10. Companies are using bigger and better claims, gimmicks, and whatever else their ad writers can think of, which tells us the hard sell has hit and the public is going to pay. There will be no simple solution to this problem.

III. *Eliminate all vague pronoun references from the following sentences.*

A.   1. Whenever Dennis lets his dog inside, he leaps up in the air and wiggles all over.

2. The job took a lot out of me because it wasn't worth it.

3. I can't study well, and this has been my problem since my mother bought a television set.

4. While a passenger in my aunt's car, she ran several stop signs.

5. Carrie and Sheldon took their children to Revere Beach, but they were disappointed.

6. She loves to swim and spends two hours a day doing it.

7. We chose to visit my grandfather, which turned out to be a good thing.

8. When we visited my sister, it was a regular family reunion.

9. A lot of my friends don't enjoy going out with their older brother or sister. That would be hard to believe if they had a sister like mine.

10. In addition children like to pattern themselves after figures of authority such as policemen, soldiers, and crooks; that is how they learn about the good and bad uses of guns.

B. *Vague pronoun reference often indicates careless thinking and frequently occurs in paragraphs that are vague in other ways. Correct the vague pronouns in the following paragraph and suggest other ways to decrease its abstraction and increase its concrete detail.*

Many of the elderly are placed in institutions unnecessarily. There are many reasons for this, the main one being the fact that there is no one willing to take the time and patience to take care of them at home. True, some may need twenty-four-hour nursing, but in many cases the aged person has only lost a little of his ability to care for himself. They feel that admitting the person to a rest home is the best answer. In some cases this may be true, but in most there is a better alternative. Placing a human being, young or old, in an institution of any kind unnecessarily should be avoided. It puts limits on an individual that he or she may not be used to. This can cause irreparable damage. The strain of being in the same place day after day with no relief is sure to increase the speed of mental deterioration.

reference

IV. A. *Circle the words "this," "who," "which," and "it" in your last essay and draw lines to the words they refer to. If they don't clearly refer to particular words or if they're too far away, rewrite the sentence to eliminate that error.*

B. *Correct the errors in the following essay. Watch carefully for vague pronoun reference, dangling modifiers, abstract wording, and mixed constructions.*

My first introduction to the moped was when my family and I went to Hawaii several years ago. We were driving along and on the side of the road a teenager was desperately trying to control one of these motored marvels in some shifty gravel. Then he fell. I would have put it down to carelessness in any other situation, but he hadn't done anything dangerous and was going slowly when he had the accident. My own experience with mopeds has shown me that the braking systems are not really adequate nor is the engine output. Which leads me to the conclusion that mopeds are dangerous.

The tires used on these vehicles are too thin for the combined weight of the vehicle and the rider. Then add this to the thirty miles an hour they are capable of and you've spelled trouble. The relatively small road contact makes it easy for the moped to slide or even slip out entirely from under a rider when going around a corner at anything more than ten miles per hour. These tires are also dangerous in that they take bumps, pebbles, uneven places, and other road obstructions unpredictably. The results could be disastrous.

Another major problem is the brakes. First, they require strong hands to apply them at all. And even when brute force is used the effect is not startling, needless to say ineffective. If a person had to stop quickly to avoid an obstacle he could not readily rely on the brakes. This could present a problem on steep grades also. Combine the two situations and the result would be an accident.

The engine is worthy of concern also. The top speed of the moped is about thirty miles per hour. Since cars usually go faster even when illegal, the moped is an obstruction to them. If the car driver isn't careful the moped rider could end up in bad shape. The acceleration is insufficient to be safe also. The same problem with cars comes up here. The moped cannot accelerate swiftly enough to blend with traffic.

To be safe, these problem areas need to be redesigned. The brakes should be power-assisted with larger pads, the engine should be increased in size and the wheels and tires should be made wider. Of course the price will go up, but isn't the effect worth it?

C. Write an essay about an unusual form of transportation. Start with a good outline and flesh it out with lots of good detail. Then check your essay for weaknesses such as vague pronouns and correct them.

D. Write an essay on one of the following topics.

your college wardrobe	prisons
a cult you know about	summer school
a cheap way to have fun	a surprise

Follow the instructions in exercise C above.

INDEPENDENT STUDY: *Vague Pronoun Reference* (answers in the back)

V. Eliminate vague pronoun references from the following sentences.

A.

1. President Carter announced the United States boycott of the Olympics. This upset a lot of athletes.

2. The Moonraker is an excellent restaurant on the shore of Boston which would be a night to remember.

3. The water of the lake was very cold and the waves were very high, which was enough to make me believe that a dinosaur lived there.

4. Power from the sun must be stored and saved, and this is still an area of experimentation.

5. Now, I don't expect him to want to get up and do the three o'clock feedings, but it would be helpful.

6. The train which goes around the parkway completes its circle in about fifteen minutes.

7. He was invited to a seminar on nuclear wars which would take place in June of 1983.

8. When she left the house, it was tightly locked.

9. Some people recommend buying clothing at only the most expensive stores which are made from the best material.

10. When we had these parties, it would be about ten of us going to lunch.

B.

In these depressing times if we have available vacation time it should be used wisely and effectively. We all need time and space to do our own thing. This will give us time to relax, think out our problems, and do some of the things we enjoy. When we have to come back from our rest period and face the working world, school, or whatever it is we're doing, we'll be more aware of our abilities. We will be fresh and ready to give it our best shot. This will make us a more prosperous people.

reference

MIXED CONSTRUCTIONS

Writers of English may choose among several possible sentence constructions to express a given idea, and the best writers use many kinds of sentences. Once a sentence is begun, however, the writer is committed to that type of structure and should either complete it or begin the sentence over in a new way.

The writer of the following sentence starts out writing one type of sentence but switches to another type in the middle.

FAULTY Although I have lived in Columbus for two months, but I still haven't explored Ohio State.

This two-clause sentence starts with the word "although," so the first clause is dependent, but the second clause is connected to the first with the word "but," a word that should connect independent clauses. This sentence may be corrected so that it has one dependent clause and one independent one,

REVISED Although I have lived in Columbus for two months, I still haven't explored Ohio State.

or it may have two independent clauses.

REVISED I have lived in Columbus for two months, but I still haven't explored Ohio State.

Writing is a complex operation, and sometimes in solving one problem, a writer forgets about the beginning of the sentence. As you proofread, stand back from your sentences and be sure that their major parts fit together well. The parts of the following sentence don't go together well.

FAULTY Because Disneyland is too far away, so we'll go to Atlantic City.

The word "because" makes the first clause dependent, but the writer uses the word "so" as if both clauses were independent. The sentence could be completed as it was begun, with one dependent clause and one independent clause,

REVISED Because Disneyworld is too far away, we'll go to Atlantic City.

or the beginning could be changed to make a two-independent-clause sentence.

REVISED Disneyworld is too far away, so we'll go to Atlantic City.

The faulty sentences above resulted from the incorrect use of "fanboys" words to connect dependent clauses to independent ones.

Here's another kind of mixed construction:

FAULTY By walking up the hill strengthens my leg muscles.

In the middle of this sentence the writer switches from one type of construction to another, leaving the sentence without a subject. Either the first construction should be finished by the addition of a subject,

REVISED By walking up the hill, I strengthen my leg muscles.

or the beginning should be changed to fit the end by removing the word "by," thus releasing "walking" from the prepositional phrase so it can become the subject.

REVISED Walking up the hill strengthens my leg muscles.

Sometimes writers try to correct such sentences by adding an empty or artificial subject that further weakens the sentence.

FAULTY When planting a garden, it requires lots of bending and stooping.

Avoid such empty subjects. Either rewrite the end of the sentence to provide a good subject—an actor to do the "planting," "bending," and "stooping"—for the beginning,

REVISED When planting a garden, a person must bend and stoop a lot.

or change the beginning to fit the end by removing the word "when" so that "planting" can be the subject.

REVISED Planting a garden requires lots of bending and stooping.

mixed structure

Other kinds of mixed constructions occur within a clause, especially when it has a linking verb. Linking verbs are like equal signs: they must link logically equal things.

FAULTY Playing baseball is a popular sport.

The equation here is not quite right. *"Playing* baseball" is not a popular sport, but "baseball" is. *"Playing* baseball" is simply popular.

REVISED Baseball is a popular sport.

REVISED Playing baseball is popular.

Here's an example without a linking verb:

FAULTY The areas where the thick ashes have fallen have stopped traffic.

Here a dependent clause interrupts the independent clause, of which the subject is "area" and the verb is "have stopped." The "areas" haven't stopped traffic; the "ashes" have. The subject of the clause could be changed to "ashes,"

REVISED In some areas thick ashes have stopped traffic.

or the end of the clause could be changed.

REVISED The areas where the thick ashes have fallen have had traffic problems.

Finally, avoid repeating sentence parts for no reason.

FAULTY My sister she reads hair styling magazines.

The extra subject "she" adds nothing to this sentence.

REVISED My sister reads hair styling magazines.

Sometimes prepositions are repeated.

FAULTY I remember her putting on the clothes on me, and nothing would fit.

Only one "on" is needed in this construction.

REVISED I remember her putting the clothes on me, and nothing would fit.

CORRECTION COMMENT: Rewrite sentences that change structure in the middle so that their parts fit together into a coherent whole.

EXERCISES: *Mixed Constructions*

I. Complete the sentences that are started below.

    A. 1. By being greedy

          2. Even though we had reservations

          3. For those who prefer to travel alone

          4. Choosing a roommate

          5. By studying French

          6. When attempting to change a tire

          7. Because lions eat so much

          8. Going to the dentist

          9. In organizing a birthday party

        10. By concealing the amount of his debt

    B. 1. Although they had purchased their house twenty years before

          2. The man who won the jackpot

          3. Missing exams

          4. When speaking to his wife

          5. Buying a new Mustang

          6. Even though she had a leave of absence

          7. By tearing off the labels

          8. Feeding seven children

          9. The attention of the audience

         10. Ordering lobster

II. Correct the mixed constructions in the following sentences.

    A. 1. In wearing high-heeled shoes can ruin your ankles.

          2. Being a buyer or a consultant it takes a lot of experience.

          3. My cousin Joe he went to the Olympics.

4. In having midterms they give me headaches.

5. Since it will cost lots of money, but I know it's worth visiting.

6. Buying a pair of expensive high-heeled shoes is worth the money.

7. Even though I didn't quite understand what they were saying, but I enjoyed their conversation.

8. For those with enough money, they went to visit Bermuda.

9. We throw in our baited trap in the water, wait about five minutes, and bring up our crabs.

10. This strange encounter was an abandoned Doberman.

B. 1. For those who wanted to pay the lady to sew theirs they could do so.

2. My mother she already knew how to play, and so did I.

3. In Mexico the sound of loud trumpets, violins, guitars, and a well-uniformed group has been called a mariachi.

mixed structure

4. Although there are many famous sights around Boston, but the experience I had there cannot compare with my time in Providence.

5. On December the twenty-fifth is the day we will carol.

6. Being a pompom girl it was almost like having a job.

7. By not telling him how I felt made our relationship drift apart.

8. Veny, she has one sister and two brothers; she is the last one.

9. After my cousin's death, it brought our family closer together.

10. Musical expression is no longer the fear it was nearly two years ago.

C. 1. A common source of superstition arises from a real or imaginary resemblance between objects, persons, or events.

2. All my friends we would take turns driving to such events, but every time it came my turn I had to give a petty excuse.

3. Thus by taking care of one's body, it brings greater happiness and a whole new outlook on life.

4. As the years go on and I get out of college and the economic system growing rapidly may affect my decision.

5. Although manufacturers and designers try to push the baggy denim, but it will not do well because the heavy and coarse fabric does not match the style.

6. I disagree with this philosophy and think that after every mess you make it should be cleaned up.

7. Just by being in high school people thought that was fun.

8. Deciding to bring a small child into the home should be a well-thought-out decision.

9. For the millions of people who have no excuse I don't sympathize with.

10. In the early morning or the late afternoon was the perfect time to sit by the pool, get a good tan, and relax.

D. 1. Just by having to make my own decisions and having the freedom to do as I please is what I consider being independent.

2. My past English classes showed me that the aids to good English are going to the library and using the dictionary correctly.

3. To those who are poor know what a humbling experience poverty can be.

4. The more people Valencia gets to know like she knows me will help her to reach some of her goals she has for the future.

5. The female crab she glided out of her shell onto the gravel of the fish tank and went from shell to shell until she found the one she liked.

6. In recent magazines have had articles and charts comparing compact cars and sports cars.

7. The recording of my words, for repeated hearings by others, is an awesome thought.

8. Luckily with my friend Dave at my side helped me to understand these problems.

9. For the children they can meet Mickey Mouse, Pluto, Goofy, and other Disney characters.

10. Depending on how long our trip will be determines where we go.

E. 1. Due to this misunderstanding it caused a problem at school.

2. When a person is at home studying, and someone is in the house, the distraction that this person gives to the student that it will be very hard to concentrate.

3. Budgeting one's income it will help him decide what to buy and what not to buy.

4. I learned that by confronting a situation or problem provided me with a fuller understanding of my situation.

5. Without any skills and little education it dims their hope.

6. The fact that the glasses don't sit directly on the eyeball is very comfortable.

7. Because we had several extra gross of storm windows, so we decided to have a sale.

8. While traveling in this car, it gave me good gas mileage and a secure and comfortable ride.

9. With President Carter asking for the reinstatement of draft registration started the public talking about the draft.

10. Even through many differences will arise, by working together the relationship between sister and sister is a very strong bond.

F.   My speed enables me to be good at my favorite sport, basketball. By me being quick on my feet helps me when I am on offense. I can outrun my opponent up and down the court through the whole game with no problem. For example, in one game I played it was very tight up until the last quarter. By this time my opponent was tired and was not thinking about the game, and by his exhaustion allowed me to take advantage of him, and I finally won the game with a last second jump shot.

III. *The following body paragraph is from an essay by James Thurber, "A Discussion of Feminine Types," published in 1929 in a book he wrote with E. B. White called* Is Sex Necessary? *His thesis is that women are dangerous, and to support it he divides women into types by their behavior toward men and discusses three types in detail, showing that each type is dangerous.*

The Buttonhole-twister Type is much easier to observe. A girl of this persuasion works quite openly. She has the curious habit of insinuating a finger, usually the little finger of the right hand, unless she be left-handed, into the lapel buttonhole of a gentleman, and twisting it. Usually, she picks out a man who is taller than herself and usually she gets him quite publicly, in parks, on street corners, and the like. Often, while twisting, she will place the toe of her right shoe on the ground, with the heel elevated, and will swing the heel slowly through an arc of about thirty or thirty-five degrees, back and forth. This manifestation is generally accompanied by a wistful, faraway look on the woman's face, and she but rarely gazes straight at the man. She invariably goes in for negative statements during the course of her small writhings, such as "It is not," "I am not," "I don't believe you do," and the like. This type is demonstrative in her affections and never lies in wait with any subtlety. She is likely to be restless and discontented with the married state, largely because she will want to go somewhere that her husband does not want to go, or will not believe he has been to the places that he says he just came from. It is well to avoid this type.

Good writers often improve their sentence skills by imitating outstanding writing. Write a paragraph that describes a dangerous present-day type, either male or female, acting upon the opposite sex. Imitate Thurber's paragraph as closely as possible: sentence for sentence, even word for word.

INDEPENDENT STUDY: Mixed Constructions *(possible answers in the back)*

IV. *Correct any mixed constructions in the following sentences.*

A.
1. By being so exhausted is bad for the heart.

2. While working in the library it gave me a chance to work with people.

3. Although most of the time this system works, but at other times it is not so efficient.

4. Taking a solid stand and opposing my mother was a very trying time for both of us.

5. By having his hair cut changed his whole attitude.

6. Scheduling our hours in advance, this makes it easier to make plans.

7. I hope my children will be strong willed enough to not to have this problem.

8. For example, "Lookin' Back" it's a song about his childhood.

9. Having examinations are also some of those nervous experiences that I can never overcome.

10. By walking or looking into a store window it takes my mind off of my frustrations.

B. Giving and receiving gifts make people happy. One Christmas my mother she bought me two new pairs of pants for school. I was happy when I got them and happy evey time I wore them. That same Christmas I bought my very old and helpless uncle a present because everyone in the family had forgotten about him. By me giving him this gift made his eyes light up, and he smiled and thanked me. By me watching him be happy, made me proud and also happy.

PARALLEL STRUCTURE

Parallel structure uses similar kinds of words to express similar ideas. It can be used to reflect and even to indicate both similarities and differences among ideas. Parallel structure often adds real power to a sentence.

> Women decide the larger questions of life correctly and quickly not because they are lucky guessers, not because they are divinely inspired, not because they practice a magic inherited from savagery, but simply and solely because they have sense.
>
> — H. L. Mencken

> While there is a lower class I am in it, while there is a criminal element I am of it, while there is a soul in prison I am not free.
>
> — Eugene Debs

Whenever you list two or more items, express those items in similar grammatical forms.

FAULTY I enjoyed watching them exercise, dance, and rehearsing.

The writer of this sentence starts the list with two words without endings, "exercise" and "dance," but then breaks the pattern with the *ing* word "rehearsing." The last item should be changed to match the first two.

REVISED I enjoyed watching them exercise, dance, and rehearse.

Here's a similar example:

FAULTY Terrible food, bad service, and having to wait a half an hour for a table characterize this restaurant.

The list begins with two similar items made up of a modifier and a noun, "terrible food" and "bad service," but the third item breaks into an entirely different pattern. Rephrasing that item as "long waits" changes it to the modifier and noun pattern of the first two items.

REVISED Terrible food, bad service, and long waits characterize this restaurant.

The details about those long waits can follow in sentences describing particular experiences.

Anytime "and" connects two items, they should be expressed in parallel form.

FAULTY Both of my parents, one a school teacher and the other working in an office, spend most of their time indoors.

The parents' occupations are not expressed in similar form. The first one has an article, a modifier, and a noun, "a school teacher," but the second has an *ing* word followed by a prepositional phrase, "working in an office." The second one should be rewritten in a form similar to the first. Like "a school teacher," "an office worker" has an article, a modifier, and a noun.

REVISED Both of my parents, one a school teacher and the other an office worker, spend most of their time indoors.

Here's another example:

FAULTY My boss told me to sweep the floors and I should wash the counters.

The first thing the boss said is expressed by "to" and a verb, but the second thing is expressed in a clause. The second item should be rewritten to match the first.

REVISED My boss told me to sweep the floors and wash the counters.

Now the list has two verbs preceded by "to."

If parallel structure won't quite work, use a completely different organization instead of something that is almost parallel.

FAULTY He doesn't like seeing and wanting something and can't have it.

The last part of the sentence "can't have it" does not match the first two items "seeing" and "wanting," and it doesn't gracefully follow the material before them. Either the last part should be rewritten to parallel the first parts,

REVISED He doesn't like seeing and wanting something and not being able to have it.

or it should be written into an entirely different structure not connected by "and."

REVISED He doesn't like seeing and wanting something he can't have.

CORRECTION COMMENT: Whenever you list two or more items, express those items in similar grammatical forms.

EXERCISES: Parallel Structure

I. *Use parallel structures in the sentences assigned below.*

1. *Write three sentences with a list of nouns.*

2. *Write three sentences with a list of verbs.*

3. *Write three sentences with a list of subjects.*

4. *Write three sentences with a list of prepositional phrases.*

5. *Write three sentences with a list of "that" clauses.*

6. *Write three sentences with a list of independent clauses.*

II. *Complete each of the following sentences by adding a list of at least three items in parallel form.*

A. 1. When we went to Henry's for dinner, I had

2. The only television shows I watch are

3. On Saturday night we like to

4. Last summer we traveled

5. English teachers should

6. After failing her French course, she knew that

7. One should never

8. According to my uncle,

9. School is fun as long as

10. On Christmas, we

B. 1. Luke Skywalker

2. My son's heroes are all monsters:

3. After winning the tennis match, he

4. At six o'clock this morning,

5. She had her choice of three jobs:

6. The best parties have

7. Although he didn't like eating out,

8. The tourists

9. She testified

10. His psychiatrist advised him to

III. In each group of items below, one item is not parallel to the others. Rewrite that item to match the others.

1. addition

   subtraction

   to multiply

   division

2. French

   the language of Greece

   Spanish

   German

3. climbed from the sofa

   crawled into the bathroom

   then he hid himself behind the clothes hamper

4. cartons that eggs are sold in

   milk bottles

coffee cans

jelly jars

5. where she traveled

what she wore

how she danced

her reason for coming back

6. filling the desk drawers

under the bed

on the floor

7. that John must raise the money

that Mary must study the instructions

that Jerry must buy the parts

then the operation must be directed by Peter

8. washing the clothes

cleaning the house

planning the meals

she also bought the groceries

9. she studied French in the morning

she did her math homework during lunch

her essay was written on the bus

she went to the reading lab after class

10. he made the punch the night before

the sandwiches were prepared that morning

the fruits were cut up right before the reception

IV. *Underline any lack of parallel in the following sentences. Then rewrite them to improve the parallel.*

A. 1. People that like to see the landscape can travel by train, bus, or drive a car.

2. I walked into a room, looked around me, then I sat in the nearest chair.

3. One day I came home and couldn't find the female crab. I searched for it in the living room, in the dining room, bathroom, and kitchen.

4. They feel fed up with school, teachers, and by their parents.

5. The audience applauded along with some laughter.

6. A wife must take care of the children, paying the bills, yard work, and feeding her husband.

7. Everything around me was moving: cars passing, rain drops, and birds flying.

8. He supported me through school, gave me a nice home, bought me clothes, and always had plenty to eat.

9. The ranger explained why it is important to stay on trails and putting out campfires.

10. We enjoyed making cakes, archery, and visiting museums.

B. 1. I would much rather go to a ball game than watching it on television.

2. The French fries are big and brown and plenty on the plates.

3. I learned things like how to write, spell, count, read, and some math.

4. Here your dog is given a bath, haircut, and his toenails are cut.

5. We were surprised that she was reading in the corner and not paid attention to us.

6. In this new age of electronics, many toys are out now to test a child's memory as well as developing skills.

7. The rocket was fired at one of the kids and causing the loss of an eye.

parallel

8. Cesca was telling us stories about her grandmother: how she dressed up, her wigs, and how she acted.

9. Breaking my ankle gave me two months in a cast and without working for two and a half months.

10. He was medium-sized but strong with short hair, light complexion, and mean looks always planted on his face.

C. 1. He told me to ignore their comments and I should have more self-confidence.

2. This bill will affect our programs for those who are handicapped, sick, have mental problems, or needy.

3. When I am free, he always finds something entertaining for us to do or go.

4. A person training for the Olympics must not just work on physical ability but mentally.

5. One should study through the whole quarter and don't cram at the last minute.

6. To keep the war, fighting, and death that are all around them from getting to be too much, they do practical jokes, games, and cut down Frank.

7. I try reading one assignment and not to confuse it with another assignment.

8. I can take care of responsibilities on my own and not have to depend on my parents.

9. Is it a feeling of confidence and assurance or is it lazy, sad, a feeling that one day is enough?

10. The college grads were in a prestige position in addition to a salary gap of thousands of dollars per year.

D. If I were to drop out of college, I doubt if I could find a job to satisfy me. Most jobs I would be interested in require a person to have a college diploma, experience, to be able to type, take shorthand, file, or some kind of computer experience. I have no work skills and no experience working. One of my high school classmates decided to go to work right after high school. She didn't like any of the jobs she qualified for and was unemployed for months. Finally, she took a job at a copy center, but she doesn't make enough money to live on her own, and hating the work. If I quit school I'd probably be in the unemployment line.

V. A. *Read the following passage, underline the words you don't know, look them up in the dictionary, and write their meanings above them.*

THE DEVIL [*mortified*]: Señor Don Juan: you are uncivil to my friends.

DON JUAN: Pooh! why should I be civil to them or to you? In this Palace of Lies a truth or two will not hurt you. Your friends are all the dullest dogs I know. They are not beautiful: they are only decorated. They are not clean: they are only shaved and starched. They are not dignified: they are only fashionably dressed. They are not educated: they are only college passmen. They are not religious: they are only pewrenters. They are not moral: they are only conventional. They are not virtuous: they are only cowardly. They are not even vicious: they are only "frail." They are not artistic: they are only lascivious. They are not prosperous: they are only rich. They are not loyal, they are only servile; not dutiful, only sheepish; not public spirited, only patriotic; not courageous, only quarrelsome; not determined, only obstinate; not masterful, only domineering; not self-controlled, only obtuse; not self-respecting, only vain; not kind, only sentimental; not social, only gregarious; not considerate, only polite; not intelligent, only opinionated; not progressive, only factious; not imaginative, only superstitious; not just, only vindictive; not generous, only propitiatory; not disciplined, only cowed; and not truthful at all: liars every one of them, to the very backbone of their souls.*
— Bernard Shaw, *Man and Superman*

B. *Parallel structures can be effectively used to suggest comparison and point out differences. The passage above is based on a series of*

---

*Note: Punctuation and capitalization in this passage are unusual because of Shaw's idiosyncratic style.

contrasting pairs in parallel form. Answer the following questions about the passage.

1. *What word or words do the first elements of these pairs have in common?*

2. *What word or words do the second elements of these pairs have in common?*

3. *Write a general statement to summarize the contrast expressed in all the pairs. Exactly what is being compared to what?*

4. *What is the nature of the contrast? How do the first elements of these pairs differ from the second elements?*

5. *The thesis of this passage is not stated in so many words. What is it? What is Don Juan telling the Devil about his friends?*

C. *Many outstanding writers develop their skills by imitating writers they admire. Choose a thesis that can be supported by contrasts, and write a passage that follows the Shaw passage as closely as possible. You might want to talk about the poor quality of television shows, television heroes, movies, movie heroes, foreign cars, American cars, or fashionable clothing. Whatever topic you choose, go through the Shaw passage clause by clause, substituting words that express your contrast for the words that express his contrast.*

parallel

VI. A. *Read the following passage and notice the parallel structures.*

To every thing there is a season, and a time to every purpose
   under heaven:
A time to be born, and a time to die; a time to plant, and a
   time to pluck up that which is planted;
A time to kill, and a time to heal; a time to break down, and
   a time to build up;
A time to weep, and a time to laugh; a time to mourn, and a time to dance;
A time to cast away stones, and a time to gather stones together; a time to
   embrace, and a time to refrain from embracing;
A time to get, and a time to lose; a time to keep, and a time to cast away;
A time to rend, and a time to sew; a time to keep silence,
   and a time to speak;
A time to love, and a time to hate; a time of war, and a time of peace.
   — Ecclesiastes, 3:1–8, King James translation of the Bible

B. *The passage above is based on pairs of pairs. Answer the following questions about it. For clarity the items have been referred to by these letters, which represent the elements in each line.*

A   and   B   ;   C   and   D

1. *What is the relationship between all the A items and all the B items? Are they similar or different?*

2. *What is the relationship between all the C items and all the D items? Are they similar or different?*

3. *What is the relationship between all the A items and all the C items? Are they similar or different?*

4. *What is the relationship between all the B items and all the D items? Are they similar or different?*

5. *What is the relationship between the A-B contrasts and the C-D contrasts?*

6. *Go through the passage line by line and generalize about what the A and C units are contrasting with the B and D units.*

7. *What is the thesis of this passage?*

C. Copying good writing is an effective way to improve one's own writing. Choose a thesis that could be proven by pairs of contrasting details, and write a passage that expresses that contrast in the same way the passage above does. You might want to talk about the way someone budgets time: you, students, athletes, someone you know, or someone in a particular job. As you write, follow the original passage word by word and substitute words that describe your contrast for words that describe the original contrast.

D. Write an essay on one of the following topics. Use parallel structure whenever possible.

horror films	a teacher
being good-looking	your friends
things that make you cry	going to a ball game

INDEPENDENT STUDY: *Parallel Structure* (possible answers in the back)

VII. A. Rewrite the following sentences to improve the parallel.

1. My friends did everything together like play baseball, riding bikes, and climb trees.

2. Jonny thought he'd use his friend by letting Susan help him in his homework, by helping with his job, and helping him with his personal problems.

3. When I approached the cross street, I saw the traffic light was yellow and realizing it would turn red soon.

4. You could spend a few minutes in a boat getting sloshed around in a narrow canal only to be thrown down a waterfall and splashing into a beautiful harbor.

5. Have you ever thought whether or not a pair of shoes is harmful to you while trying them on and purchased them?

6. All of their friends entertained them very lavishly and elegant.

7. She wanted to work as a dancer and don't be on welfare.

8. Having a best friend like Dave made times a lot easier and getting a better grip on life.

9. They bought a new car, took a trip to Tokyo, and then they moved into a new house.

10. He can also check if your gums are in good condition and tell you if you need braces or have your wisdom teeth removed.

B. *Improve the following conclusion by rewriting any sentences with faulty parallelism.*

The increase in gas prices will affect me greatly. I hope that there will be a new discovery which will replace gasoline. For the time being, we must be careful how we use our cars and not to take for granted that everything available will be with us forever. We must appreciate what we have and not wasting it. If we don't, we'll find ourselves all dressed to go and no way of getting there.

parallel

DANGLING AND MISPLACED MODIFIERS

Good writers often change verbs to modifiers to add action and details to a sentence without adding a whole clause. Modifiers may be made from verbs ending in *ing*, verbs ending in *ed*, and verbs with "to" before them. Even though these words are not working as verbs, however, they come from verbs and imply action, so the doer of the action should always be clearly stated.

FAULTY Starting out as a file clerk, a high school diploma was sufficient.

In this sentence the person who started out is not mentioned, and so the modifier is left dangling with no word to modify. A reader assumes that a modifier modifies the closest noun or pronoun, but surely a high school diploma did not start out as a file clerk. This sentence must be rewritten with a word near the modifier to indicate the person who started out.

REVISED Starting out as a file clerk, he needed only a high school diploma.

Now the *ing* phrase modifies "he," and the sentence is clear. The sentence could also be corrected by changing "starting" back to a verb and making the doer of the action its subject.

REVISED Because he started out as a file clerk, a high school diploma was sufficient.

Here's another example:

FAULTY After registering for three classes, my college days began.

The doer of the action is not stated in this sentence. The word "my" implies that it's the writer, but the word "my" just describes "college days" and can't be modified. The sentence must be rewritten with a word for the person who registered, a word that can be modified.

REVISED After registering for three classes, I began my college days.

This is an excellent revision because now the *ing* phrase has a word to modify and the independent clause has a more active subject. The *ing* phrase could also be changed back to a verb with the doer of the action as its subject.

REVISED After I registered for three classes, my college days began.

Some dangling modifiers come at the end of a sentence.

FAULTY Once my heel came off while going down a flight of stairs.

This sentence leaves the word "going" dangling without a word to modify. The heel seems to be going down a flight of stairs by itself. Because the person who lost the heel is the same person who went down the stairs, a good revision of this sentence makes that person the subject of the sentence.

REVISED Once I lost a heel while going down a flight of stairs.

Another possible revision changes "going" back to a verb by adding the helping verb "was" and makes "I" its subject.

REVISED Once my heel came off while I was going down a flight of stairs.

Sometimes modifiers that don't come from verbs may be left dangling.

FAULTY At the age of three, my mother enrolled me in nursery school.

As the sentence is now written, the word "mother" is next to the words "at the age of three," and so the sentence seems to say that the mother was three years old. Like the other modifiers, "at the age of three" can be expanded into a clause,

REVISED When I was three, my mother enrolled me in nursery school.

or the independent clause can be written with a word for the three-year-old as its subject.

REVISED At the age of three, I started nursery school.

The modifier should also be as close as possible to the word it modifies to prevent confusion.

FAULTY Crawling under the fence, the old lady watched the little boy.

modification

If the old lady was crawling under the fence, this sentence is correct. If the little boy was crawling under the fence, however, the modifier "crawling under the fence" should be moved away from "the old lady" and next to "the little boy," the word it modifies.

REVISED The old lady watched the little boy crawling under the fence.

CORRECTION COMMENT: Every modifier should have a word to modify and be as near that word as possible.

EXERCISES: *Dangling and Misplaced Modifiers*

I. *Using the following phrases as introductory modifiers, write complete sentences. Be careful because some of these phrases might also work as sentence subjects.*

A. 1. **EXAMPLE** Shaking with fear, *Sue felt her way down the damp, dark corridor.*

    2. Scurrying to the top of the oak tree, _____

    3. Before pulling away from the curb, _____

    4. When faced with a writing assignment, _____

    5. Waiting patiently outside the door, _____

    6. After staring at his feet for a few seconds, _____

    7. Conscious of a figure at my side, _____

    8. Striding from the courtroom, _____

    9. Disturbed by his answer, _____

    10. Waving their hats and handkerchiefs, _____

B. 1. Turning to the last page of the book, _____

    2. Snatching the phone from his hand, _____

    3. Exhausted from her trip, _____

    4. To fasten the necklace around her throat, _____

    5. Roaring angrily, _____

    6. Hurling his body against the door, _____

    7. Dragging herself out of the water, _____

    8. After carefully placing the beaver hat on his thick hair, _____

    9. Having mastered the formula, _____

    10. To sympathize with their plight, _____

II. *Correct any dangling or misplaced modifiers in the following sentences. Invent any additional details you need.*

    A. 1. Reading in bed, cashew nuts were nibbled.

    2. After finishing the inventory, the bookkeeping was next.

    3. While driving home from work, my aunt ran several stop signs.

    4. Pecking daintily on the lawn, we stared at the robin.

    5. At the age of five, my father joined the army.

    6. Slamming my foot on the brake, the car stopped abruptly.

    7. After making the football team, his hard work began.

    8. Having worked hard during the school year, her summer vacation was welcome.

    9. Distraught by her failure, she quit her job.

    10. Crossing the border, his birth certificate was needed.

    B. 1. By getting married, their social security benefits will be cut.

    2. Using fresh ingredients, the cookies are fluffy, chewy, and plump.

    3. Filing carefully, she stood by the drawer for three hours.

    4. Being a native of New York, it is my favorite city.

    5. Thinking carefully, he came up with three possible solutions to our problem.

    6. The runner crossed the finish line dripping with sweat.

    7. As a military retiree, this cost is absorbed by the federal government.

    8. Rain causes terrifying blindness when driving to or from work.

    9. After finishing the morning routine, cooking and baby-sitting come next.

10. Reading in the library, he finished his history and philosophy assignments.

C. 1. By sharing the work, the whole process only takes a half an hour.

2. Stepping back to look at the painting, he absent-mindedly picked up a donut and took a bite.

3. Watching people skate every day, they were bruising their feet.

4. Once my dress got dirty while going to a job interview on a bus.

5. After being thoroughly scrubbed, I hose down the floor one more time and sweep the excess water out.

6. After saving up every nickel and dime, Hawaii is a place to spend it easily.

7. Using all my resources, I still didn't have enough money for a down payment.

8. After receiving the first plastic card, there is a sudden deluge of credit applications in the mail.

modification

9. Planted firmly on the ground, the gardener stared at his feet.

10. By watching my father work, I learned to refinish skis so that they were better than new.

D. 1. Once while watching a play-off game between the Philadelphia 76ers and the Washington Bullets, the 76ers were bringing the ball down and calling the play.

2. Hawaii was a beautiful sight, watching the sun rise and the colors appear as it hit the water.

3. Leaving a pool of water on the bathroom floor, soap on the mirror, towels scattered around, John's task was not really done after all.

4. Once while watching a television movie, the movie was cut into every time some part of the voting results would change.

5. After making sure I had said good-by to everyone and making sure I had enough money for two weeks, my vacation was off and running, and I do mean running.

6. Like any hobby or sport, I am competitive with myself because I know I can write better than I have been.

7. After a few weeks, I felt very comfortable in my new school and my problems seemed to diminish with my parents.

8. People start investing in gold and silver because they distrust paper money and know that by investing in precious metals their investments are sound and climb along with or faster than inflation.

9. After cats have had a satisfying meal, they usually clean and groom themselves. After feeding my cat, she sits herself in a comfortable spot and begins her little ritual.

10. I loved it so much, I tried to do it in all the games I played, but like a child's new Christmas toy, I soon became disenchanted with dunking and only did it occasionally.

E.   A malfunction of my car frightens me. Occasionally while driving somewhere, the Duster would break down leaving me stranded. One night after a party, I was driving home on the freeway at about two-thirty in the morning. While holding the steering wheel firmly, foot gently on the accelerator, eyes directly on the road, my car began to shift back and forth on the freeway. My heart beating rapidly, I quickly pulled over into the emergency lane and got out of my car to see what had happened. I discovered that I had lost my steering control and became afraid that I wouldn't be able to get home. Luckily, a highway patrolman stopped. After telling him what had happened, he decided to take me home.

III. A. *The author of the following story, John Galsworthy, uses vivid, careful, and significant modification. Read the story, paying particular attention to the modification. Circle each introductory modifier and draw a line to the word it modifies.*

The Japanese Quince

As Mr. Nilson, well known in the City, opened the window of his dressing room on Campden Hill, he experienced a peculiar sweetish sensation in the back of his throat, and a feeling of emptiness just under his fifth rib. Hooking the window back, he noticed that a little tree in the Square Gardens had come out in blossom, and that the thermometer stood at sixty. "Perfect morning," he thought; "spring at last!"

Resuming some meditations on the price of Tintos, he took up an ivory-backed handglass and scrutinised his face. His firm, well-coloured cheeks, with their neat brown moustaches, and his round, well-opened, clear grey eyes, wore a reassuring appearance of good health. Putting on his black frock coat, he went downstairs.

In the dining room his morning paper was laid out on the sideboard. Mr. Nilson had scarcely taken it in his hand when he again became aware of that queer feeling. Somewhat concerned, he went to the French window and descended the scrolled iron steps into the fresh air. A cuckoo clock struck eight.

"Half an hour to breakfast," he thought; "I'll take a turn in the Gardens."

He had them to himself, and proceeded to pace the circular path with his morning paper clasped behind him. He had scarcely made two revolutions, however, when it was borne in on him that, instead of going away in the fresh air, the feeling had increased. He drew several deep breaths, having heard deep breathing recommended by his wife's doctor; but they augmented rather than diminished the sensation—as of some sweetish liquor in course within him, together with a faint aching just above his heart.

Running over what he had eaten the night before, he could recollect no unusual dish, and it occurred to him that it might possibly be some smell affecting him. But he could detect nothing except a faint sweet lemony scent, rather agreeable than otherwise, which evidently emanated from the bushes budding in the sunshine. He was on the point of resuming his promenade, when a blackbird close by burst into song, and looking up, Mr. Nilson saw at a distance of perhaps five yards a little tree, in the heart of whose branches the bird was perched. He stood staring curiously at this tree, recognising it for that which he had noticed from his window. It was covered with young blossoms, pink and white, and little bright green leaves both round and spiky; and on all this blossom and these leaves the sunlight glistened. Mr. Nilson smiled; the little tree was so alive and pretty! And instead of passing on, he stayed there smiling at the tree.

"Morning like this!" he thought; "and here I am the only person in the Square who has the———to come out and———!" But he had no sooner conceived this thought than he saw quite near him a man with his hands behind him, who was also staring up and smiling at the little tree. Rather taken aback, Mr. Nilson ceased to smile, and looked furtively at the stranger. It was his next-door neighbour, Mr. Tandram, well known in the City, who had occupied the adjoining house for some five years. Mr. Nilson perceived at once the awkwardness of his position, for, being married, they had not yet had occasion to speak to one another. Doubtful as to his proper conduct, he decided at last to murmur: "Fine morning!" and was passing on, when Mr. Tandram answered: "Beautiful, for the time of year!" Detecting a slight nervousness in his neighbour's voice, Mr. Nilson was emboldened to regard him openly. He was of about Mr. Nilson's own height, with firm, well-coloured cheeks, neat brown moustaches, and round, well-opened, clear grey eyes; and he was wearing a black frock coat. Mr. Nilson noticed that he had his morning paper clasped behind him as he looked up at the little tree. And, visited somehow by the feeling that he had been caught out, he said abruptly: "Er—can you give me the name of that tree?"

Mr. Tandram answered: "I was about to ask you that," and stepped towards it. Mr. Nilson also approached the tree.

"Sure to have its name on, I should think," he said.

Mr. Tandram was the first to see the little label, close to where the blackbird had been sitting. He read it out. "Japanese quince!"

"Ah!" said Mr. Nilson, "thought so. Early flowerers."

"Very," assented Mr. Tandram, and added: "Quite a feelin' in the air today."

Mr. Nilson nodded. "It was a blackbird singin'," he said.

"Blackbirds," answered Mr. Tandram. "I prefer them to thrushes myself; more body in the note." And he looked at Mr. Nilson in an almost friendly way.

"Quite," murmured Mr. Nilson. "These exotics, they don't bear fruit. Pretty blossom!" and he again glanced up at the blossom, thinking: "Nice fellow, this, I rather like him."

Mr. Tandram also gazed at the blossom. And the little tree, as if appreciating their attention, quivered and glowed. From a distance the blackbird gave a loud, clear call. Mr. Nilson dropped his eyes. It struck him suddenly that Mr. Tandram looked a little foolish; and, as if he had seen himself, he said: "I must be going in. Good morning!"

A shade passed over Mr. Tandram's face, as if he, too, had suddenly noticed something about Mr. Nilson. "Good morning," he replied, and clasping their journals to their backs they separated.

Mr. Nilson retraced his steps toward his garden window, walking slowly so as to avoid arriving at the same time as his neighbour. Having seen Mr. Tandram mount his scrolled iron steps, he ascended his own in turn. On the top step he paused.

With the slanting spring sunlight darting and quivering into it, the Japanese quince seemed more living than a tree. The blackbird had returned to it, and was chanting out his heart.

Mr. Nilson sighed; again he felt that queer sensation, that choky feeling in his throat.

The sound of a cough or sigh attracted his attention. There, in the shadow of his French window, stood Mr. Tandram, also looking forth across the Gardens at the little quince tree.

Unaccountably upset, Mr. Nilson turned abruptly into the house, and opened his morning paper.

B. Answer the following questions about "The Japanese Quince."

1. *What is the story about?*

2. *What kind of house does Mr. Nilson live in?*

3. *What social class does he belong to?*

4. *What kind of life does he lead?*

5. *Compare Mr. Nilson and Mr. Tandram. Consider their looks, actions, and situations.*

6. *What do the similarities between these men suggest about their lives?*

7. *Underline all the characteristics of the tree that are mentioned. Mark everything about its appearance and smell plus the qualities and other things associated with it.*

8. *Review the words you've underlined and write a sentence that summarizes the appearance of the tree and the qualities associated with it.*

9. *How is Mr. Nilson's life different from the tree's life?*

10. *What unusual things happen because of the tree?*

11. *Why is Mr. Nilson upset by his encounter with the tree?*

C. Write an essay about "The Japanese Quince." Your thesis might answer question 11, and your supports might come from your answers to the other questions. Check your outline with your teacher. Then build it into an essay, using exact words from the story as evidence.

IV. *Correct any dangling or misplaced modifiers in the sentences below. Invent any additional details you need.*

A.
1. Not doing my homework, my grades in my math class dropped.

2. Returning late from a party, I fell onto my bed and went to sleep in my clothes.

3. After spending a long hot day in Atlantic City, night had fallen, and it was time to go home.

4. Being thirty years old, society would wonder about my mental capacity if people saw me playing with toys.

5. Grabbing his briefcase, he ran out the door.

6. Turning in all my work on time, my teacher gives me a good grade in the course.

7. Sinking slowly behind the trees, we gazed at the moon.

8. I like to see where I'm going while riding from all angles.

9. Whether big, tall, small, fat, thin, black, or white, skiing can be enjoyable.

10. Turning to the Lord, my prayer was answered.

B.   My father influenced me to be a generous person. Being in the ministry, my father's generosity is well known. He's very generous with his time. I can remember him getting a call at three in the morning from a young lady whose father had just passed away. After talking to him for a few minutes, he went to her house to comfort her in person. Also my father is generous with his car, driving fifty miles a day going various places for people. First he takes my sister to work in the morning. Then driving all the way to Tacoma, he picks up my uncle and drives him to work in Seattle. He even pays all the expenses of these trips. One day I asked him why he did that. He replied, "Alfred, you should be generous with all valuable things." After telling me this, I started being generous.

DIRECT AND INDIRECT SPEECH

Direct speech gives someone's words exactly as they were spoken. Those words should be enclosed in quotation marks, and the words telling who spoke should be outside the quotation marks and set off by a comma.

The teacher said, "Your time is up."

Jerry said, "I hope you can go to France."

"We know he needs help," my mother added.

Mary said, "I studied German for two years."

Mr. Smith said, "You didn't try."

The first word of a direct quotation should be capitalized.

Indirect speech changes the quotation into a "that" clause. In contrast to direct speech, indirect speech does not give the words exactly as they were spoken. In this case, quotation marks are not used, and the original words are adjusted to fit the new context. The whole pronoun person system changes as the new stater of the words replaces the original as first person, the new reader or listener replaces the original as second person, and the new third person group includes the original speaker who is now being spoken about.

The verb tenses also change to fit the new situation. If the original words were in the present tense and the new context is in the past tense, the original words must be changed to past tense.

The teacher said that our time was up.

Jerry said that he hoped I could go to France.

My mother added that they knew he needed help.

If the original was in the past tense and the new context is in the past tense, the original must be changed to a "had" form.

Mary said that she had studied German for two years.

Mr. Smith said that I hadn't tried.

Use either direct or indirect speech but not something halfway between.

FAULTY My teacher told me that "I had passed the test."

Either the quotation marks should be removed so the quotation will be indirect,

REVISED My teacher told me that I had passed the test.

or the pronoun and verb should be returned to the exact forms used by the original speaker

REVISED My teacher told me, "You passed the test."

Use quotation marks only when the words are in the exact form originally spoken.

Here's another quotation that's halfway between direct and indirect:

FAULTY My instructor told us I will be late on Tuesday.

Either quotation marks should be added to make a direct quotation,

REVISED My instructor told us, "I will be late on Tuesday."

or the pronoun and verb should be changed to make an indirect quotation.

REVISED My instructor told us he would be late on Tuesday.

To express orders, commands, and requests in indirect form, reduce the clause to a verb with "to."

The nurse said, "Call back later."

becomes

The nurse told me to call back later.

Larry said, "Don't wait for me."

becomes

Larry said not to wait for him.

direct/indirect

Most direct questions are formed by moving the verb or part of the verb to the beginning of the clause and adding a question mark.

Dr. Wiley is his economics professor.

becomes

Is Dr. Wiley his economics professor?

There are extra books.

becomes

Are there extra books?

He will sell those paintings.

becomes

Will he sell those paintings?

Where will he sell those paintings?

Why will he sell those paintings?

When will he sell those paintings?

How will he sell those paintings?

With verbs other than "to be," if there is no helping verb, the "do" form of the verb is used, and the helping verb is moved to the beginning of the clause. For example,

He types quickly.

is changed to

He does type quickly.

and then the helping verb is put first to form the question.

Does he type quickly?

He borrowed Audrey's typewriter.

is changed to

He did borrow Audrey's typewriter.

and then the helping verb is put first.

Did he borrow Audrey's typewriter?

To change questions from direct to indirect, move the verb or helping verb back to its normal sentence position after the subject and omit the question mark.

When will he sell those paintings?

becomes

I wonder when he will sell those paintings.

If the direct question does not begin with a question word like "when," "where," "how," "why," etc., the indirect question must be introduced by "whether" or "if."

Will he sell those paintings?

becomes

I wonder if he will sell those paintings.

or

I wondered if he would sell those paintings.

or

She asked if he would sell those paintings.

If "do," "does," or "did" was added to form the question, change the verb back to its original form.

Does he type quickly?

becomes

I wonder if he types quickly.

and

Did he borrow Audrey's typewriter?

changes to

I wonder if he borrowed Audrey's typewriter.

Use direct questions or indirect questions but not something halfway between them.

FAULTY I wondered what could I wear.

This could be changed to an indirect question by returning the helping verb to its normal sentence position.

REVISED I wondered what I could wear.

The sentence could also be changed to direct speech by changing the verb to the present tense and adding question and quotation marks.

REVISED I wondered, "What can I wear?"

direct/indirect

Sometimes sentences like this one can't easily be changed to direct speech.

FAULTY I don't know when will he return.

The "when" clause should be expressed in indirect speech, but the helping verb "will" comes before the subject "he." Put the helping verb before the subject only when you are directly asking someone a question.

REVISED I don't know when he will return.

Here's another sentence that's neither direct nor indirect:

FAULTY We hope to discover where does he study.

This indirect question should not have the helping verb "does" before the subject "he."

REVISED We hope to discover where he studies.

CORRECTION COMMENT: Use either direct or indirect speech but not something halfway between.

EXERCISES: *Direct and Indirect Speech*

I. *Paraphrase the following direct quotations into indirect ones. You may have to add details.*

   A.   1. She said, "Many of the exercise answers are incorrect."

       2. The boy said, "The Tennyson bus just left."

       3. My father said, "Be home by midnight or plan to stay home next weekend."

       4. The teacher said, "Write the introduction and conclusion before Monday's class."

       5. "Bring a warm jacket," she advised.

       6. Michael said, "Her advice never helped me."

7. "Watch out for extra commas," he said.

8. "Cotton is cooler than nylon," she explained.

9. "Trespassers will be violated," the sign warned.

10. "I'm looking for the man that shot my paw," drawled the dog in the cowboy hat.

B.
1. A character in a George Bernard Shaw play says, "I'm only a beer teetotaler, not a champagne teetotaler."

2. H. L. Mencken said, "It took me fifteen years to discover that I had no talent for writing, but I couldn't give it up because by that time I was too famous."

3. James Thurber says, "Early to rise and early to bed makes a man healthy and wealthy and dead."

4. An Oscar Wilde character says, "I can resist everything but temptation."

5. "I wanted you to have the best possible education," my father explained later.

6. "When did you leave the party?" the policeman asked Russell.

7. My mother said, "Your father wants to take us to the ball game on Saturday."

8. "I was sure you were responsible," muttered the teacher.

9. My adviser said, "A senior will get more job offers if he's had a computer course."

10. "Where did you put the tickets?" asked the manager.

II. Paraphrase the following direct questions into indirect ones. You will have to add details as in the example.

A.
1. **EXAMPLE** Where are you going? *Mr. Brown asked where she was going.*

2. When will he get back from Boston?

3. Did you find the invoice?

4. May I help you choose a dress?

5. Why did you visit Panama?

6. Where is the telephone?

7. Is it too late to register for this class?

8. Why is the Turkish government worried about mustaches?

9. Will the meeting last until noon?

10. Are supplies provided free of charge?

B. 1. Would you be able to donate time or money?

2. What was John Travolta's first movie?

3. How can we reduce our electricity bill?

4. Would you prefer salmon or steak?

5. Have they borrowed all the fencing books?

6. Should a single person consider adopting a child?

7. Would this jack work well on a Honda?

8. Shall we rest under this bridge for a few minutes?

direct/indirect

9. Where are my notes on apostrophes?

10. Are you prepared for a shock?

III. *Correct all errors in the use of direct or indirect questions and quotations in the following sentences. They should be direct or indirect but not something halfway between.*

A. 1. He asked me how long had I been skating.

2. I asked her "what was she looking at?"

3. I wonder what will I look like at the age of thirty-five.

4. She understood perfectly well. I was surprised because she asked me "Why didn't I say something a long time ago."

5. The guy beside me asked me did I want to switch cars.

6. My brother approached me by asking what's wrong.

7. That was the day I really started to notice what was an apple.

8. When I went outside and saw the disaster I said, what happened.

9. One should find out does it cover dental bills.

10. "She said, budgeting one's income makes life easier."

B. 1. Did you know that wife-beating is the number one crime in this country?

2. I can already imagine what will I do there.

3. I would ask my mother could I go out to a party, and she would say yes.

4. As I hung up I remember hearing the operator's voice asking was anything wrong.

5. One time my instructor said there's a new dance you're going to learn.

6. I told Anthony that "we shouldn't and couldn't be together anymore."

7. Without even looking in his wallet, he said I could have whatever I needed.

8. Just then the lady hung up the phone and asked could she help Myron.

9. I asked them aren't there any things you like to do that happen the same day you find out about them?

10. The next day he might wonder where is he going to get the money he needs to feed his family.

C.
1. I took a deep breath and said to myself, "this is going to be a long day for me."

2. Every year, the seniors talk about the prom months before it arrives wondering who will they be going with and whether or not they'll have a good time.

3. One bad thing about leaving a concert is trying to find the car.

4. My friend next to me kept laughing until she finally said you have your hat on backwards.

5. I would look at them and wonder what were they doing that I wasn't doing.

6. My mother said, "She didn't like the girl's appearance, and I wasn't allowed to bring her home again.

7. My great great grandmother said "when one goes outside, his life is in his hands. Be nice to everyone, especially maniacs.

8. I suggest that anyone considering college sit down and ask himself, is college really the best thing for me?

9. I asked him what he really felt about his sadness? why he felt sad? I even asked him what it would take for him not to be sad?

10. One time after my brother had returned from jail, I noticed that some of my personal goods were missing. It was easy to figure out what had happened to them. I asked my brother "did he take them" and he replied "if I did, then it was your fault for leaving them around."

D.
When I was a child, I was afraid of an old house down the street from my cousin's house. My cousin told me a lady had lived there and after a while she disappeared. Some people said, "She died in the house." All of the children on the block said, "the house was haunted," and I believed them. When we walked down the street, we always crossed before coming to the house, and we never played nearby after dark. The children used to tell tales about the house. Some said, "If you walked by the house, you could hear the woman crying inside." I stayed as far away from the house as possible. Today I realize these were just tales, but they frightened me when I was little.

IV. *The following conversation from Bernard Shaw's* Arms and the Man *takes place between a young lady and a soldier who has taken refuge in her bedroom.*

RAINA [*staring at him rather superciliously as she conceives a poorer and poorer opinion of him, and feels proportionately more and more at her ease*]: I am sorry I frightened you. [*She takes up the pistol and hands it to him*]. Pray take it to protect yourself against me.

THE MAN [*grinning wearily at the sarcasm as he takes the pistol*]: No use, dear young lady: theres nothing in it. It's not loaded. [*He makes a grimace at it, and drops it disparagingly into his revolver case*].

direct/indirect

RAINA: Load it by all means.

THE MAN: Ive no ammunition. What use are cartridges in battle? I always carry chocolate instead; and I finished the last cake of that hours ago.

RAINA [*outraged in her most cherished ideals of manhood*]: Chocolate! Do you stuff your pockets with sweets—like a schoolboy—even in the field?

THE MAN [*grinning*]: Yes: isnt it contemptible? [*Hungrily*] I wish I had some now.

RAINA: Allow me. [*She sails away scornfully to the chest of drawers, and returns with the box of confectionery in her hand*]. I am sorry I have eaten them all except these. [*She offers him the box*].

THE MAN [*ravenously*]: Youre an angel! [*He gobbles the contents*]. Creams! Delicious! [*He looks anxiously to see whether there are any more. There are none: he can only scrape the box with his fingers and suck them. When that nourishment is exhausted he accepts the inevitable with pathetic goodhumor, and says, with grateful emotion*] Bless you, dear lady! You can always tell an old soldier by the inside of his holsters and cartridge boxes. The young ones carry pistols and cartridges: the old ones, grub. Thank you.*

Because the passage is from a play, the characters' words are labeled with their names, and their actions and attitudes are described in fragments within parentheses. Rewrite this passage as if it were evidence to prove a point in an essay. Use indirect questions and quotations when possible, and combine them with the material in the parentheses into complete sentences. You might choose to prove that soldiers take war far less seriously than other people do. If so, you would begin the paragraph with that point. Then you could go on to prove that point by describing something that happened to a girl named Raina.

---

*Note: Punctuation and capitalization in this passage are unusual because of Shaw's idiosyncratic style.

INDEPENDENT STUDY: *Direct and Indirect Speech* (answers in the back)

V. **A.** *Paraphrase the following direct questions and quotations into indirect ones. You may have to add details.*

1. "How long would you like to stay in Venice?" asked the travel agent.

2. "Please go to the health service about that cough," my roommate urged.

3. The professor said, "Turn to the illustration on page ninety-three."

4. "What does rock-and-roll have to do with Sisyphus?" she asked quietly.

5. "Why is remedial spelling being taught in the philosophy department?" he wondered.

6. "May I get a refund on this book?" she asked.

7. Lynn pointed into the night sky and said, "The sparks from the fire go into the sky and become stars."

8. He said, "You won't really understand Plato if you read translations."

9. She said, "Please tell me all about industrial solvents."

10. She said, "I think that Alexander the Great was an alcoholic."

B. *Correct errors in the use of direct or indirect questions or quotations in the following sentences.*

1. They always ask if there is anything else they can get me and am I enjoying my meal.

2. People sometimes ask me why am I going to college.

3. President Reagan is doing what exactly should a president do.

4. The following year they approached me and asked me how I was doing and how good is the team this year.

5. She said Kathy don't you try to send any clothes through the wringer.

6. She moved around the tank, making sounds as though asking the male crab did he like her new dress.

7. Sometimes as I go up and down three flights of stairs to the washroom, I wonder do I have four children instead of one.

8. When I was in the tenth grade, I asked my biology teacher why do most plants lose their leaves in the fall.

9. When I see a bird fly through the skies, I often ask myself where is he coming from.

10. In response I asked him, why did he water just one plant and not the rest when they all needed it.

IDIOM

In every language some words are used together and others are not; some words sound right together and others don't. These commonly used phrases are called idioms.

Sometimes they are groups of words that mean more than the sum of their words would suggest. The difference between "make up," "make out," and "make off" cannot be explained by defining each word or citing a rule. People pick up idioms by hearing and reading English, and sometimes people who haven't been exposed to English very long will use a group of words that doesn't sound right to people more familiar with the language.

FAULTY After several minutes he cried again, so I decided to carry him in my arms until he made a sound sleep.

REVISED After several minutes, he cried again, so I decided to carry him in my arms until he slept soundly.

If you make mistakes like this there are a number of things you can do.

1. Read and listen to as much English as possible. Read books, magazines, and newspapers; listen to people in person and on tapes, records, radio, and television.

2. Notice idioms, think about them, and jot them down. Carry a small notebook just for idioms.

3. Get a good dictionary and perhaps also a dictionary of idioms. Study them regularly, browse through them in spare moments, and consult them when writing.

4. When proofreading, watch for combinations of words that seem unusual, awkward, or complicated, and try to find more common or simple ways to say the same thing.

The meaning-carrying words, like verbs and adjectives, often determine which functional words, like prepositions, should be used. If you are ever uncertain about which words go together, check the dictionary entry for the most important word, usually a verb or an adjective. For example, if you aren't sure whether a word should be followed by a "to" form of a verb or an *ing* word, check the dictionary entry for that word.

FAULTY I enjoy to go to the movies.

The following entry for the word "enjoy" includes the sentence "I've enjoyed talking to you," so that "enjoy" should be followed by an *ing* word.

> **en·joy** /ɪnˈdʒɔɪ/ *vt* [VP6A,C] **1** get pleasure from; take delight in: ∼ *one's dinner. I've* ∼*ed talking to you about old times.* **2** have as an advantage or benefit: ∼ *good health/a good income.* **3** ∼ *oneself,* experience pleasure; be happy. ∼**·able** /-əbl/ *adj* giving joy; pleasant. ∼**·ably** /-əblɪ/ *adv*

REVISED I enjoy going to movies.

Most idiom errors are wrong prepositions. Even native speakers of English make mistakes with prepositions because they are not emphasized in speech. If you aren't sure whether a preposition is needed or which one to use in a particular situation, consult the dictionary entry for the main word of the phrase.

FAULTY Cooking irritates me because I can't concentrate my other jobs.

The following entry for "concentrate" includes the sentence, "You should concentrate on your work," and so the preposition "on" should be added to the sentence above.

> **con·cen·trate** /ˈkɒnsntreɪt/ *vt,vi* **1** [VP6A,14,2A] bring or come together at one point: *to ~ soldiers in a town. The troops were ordered to scatter and then ~ twenty miles to the south.* **2** [VP14,3A] *~ on/upon,* focus one's attention on: *You should ~ (your attention) (up)on your work. You'll solve the problem if you ~ upon it,* give all your attention to it. **3** [VP6A] increase the strength of (a solution) by reducing its volume (e g by boiling it). □ *n* product made by concentrating(3). **con·cen·trated** *adj* **1** intense: *~d hate; ~d fire,* the firing of guns all aimed at one point. **2** increased in strength or value by evaporation of liquid: *a ~d solution; ~d food.*

REVISED Cooking irritates me because I can't concentrate on my other jobs.

Here's another example of a wrong preposition:

FAULTY One time my cousins invited me at dinner.

The following dictionary entry for "invite" includes the example "invite a friend to dinner," and so "to" should replace "at" in the original sentence.

> **in·vite** /ɪnˈvaɪt/ *vt* **1** [VP15A,B,17] ask (sb to do sth, come somewhere, etc): *~ a friend to dinner/ to one's house. He didn't ~ me in. We are old now, and seldom get ~d out.* **2** [VP6A] ask for: *~ questions/opinions/confidences.* **3** [VP6A,17] encourage: *The cool water of the lake ~d us to swim. Don't leave the windows open—it's inviting thieves to enter.* □ *n* /ˈɪnvaɪt/ (sl) = invitation(2).

REVISED One time my cousins invited me to dinner.

Sometimes people ruin a whole sentence by adding a preposition that doesn't belong.

FAULTY I read a novel in which I really enjoyed.

In this sentence "which" replaces "novel" in the last clause. However English idiom demands "I really enjoyed the novel," not "I really enjoyed in the novel," and so the word "in" should be omitted.

REVISED I read a novel which I really enjoyed.

Paying particular attention to prepositions, check your idioms by consulting the dictionary entries for their key words.

EXERCISES: Idiom

I. *Write sentences correctly using the following idioms in any tense. Consult a dictionary if you aren't sure about their exact use.*

A.
1. similar to
2. plan to do
3. prevent from
4. agree with
5. agree to

6. agree on
7. preferable to
8. differ with
9. differ from
10. differ about

B.
1. prohibit from
2. independent of
3. bored with
4. conform to
5. respect for

6. respect to
7. derived from
8. superior to
9. accused of
10. angry with

II. *Correctly complete the idioms in the following sentences. Check a dictionary if you aren't sure about their exact use.*

1. He has no respect _____ education.

2. Her grades have always been superior _____ mine.

3. She feels the need _____ help _____ English idioms.

4. The police accused him _____ assault.

5. My lecture will center _____ cost accounting.

6. She works _____ Western Savings Bank _____ 26 Colorado Avenue _____ Scranton.

7. You should apologize _____ your conduct last night.

8. I disagree _____ the teacher _____ the subject _____ oil exploration.

9. Then he ran off _____ search _____ a tire iron.

10. Connecticut is twice the size _____ Rhode Island.

III. *Correct errors in idiom in the following sentences. Pay particular attention to prepositions.*

A.
1. He expected his friend coming on time.
2. When I was twelve, my aunt left to Egypt.
3. We have fun in tea time every day.
4. I wish my mom would set me to better-looking guys.
5. This lake is a beautiful place to be at.
6. His diplomatic papers are in order.
7. I think everyone has time to spare enough to have a hobby.
8. I bought my books at a bookstore in which I know in Keene.
9. I did get to go to my first date before I turned nineteen.
10. I can always picture on my mind the composition of the sand, water, and rocks.

B.
1. Long Beach enriched me in becoming an adult.
2. I was frightened and confused of how to answer the question.
3. A person like Rosa is worth the time to spend with.
4. She wore the dress in which she had copied from a magazine.
5. This is the house that I loved so much and hated to move.
6. Many people enjoy skating out in the open public on the sidewalks.
7. My brother teases me to what I can't do and to what he's good at.
8. Soon I got bored of studying there.
9. I consulted a dictionary in which I have confidence.
10. It was fun to cook at the table, and everyone enjoyed to cook his own way.

C.
1. I did not want to buy the car on credit and pay a lot of interest, so I had to determine my mind not to spend.
2. After he finished my hair, I took a look in the mirror, and I almost had a heart attack.
3. A rookie player could earn at a minimum of $40,000 a year to $153,600 for a six-year man.
4. Politics are depressed because of the sensitive situation.
5. In high school English classes I didn't have to write essays.
6. On the weekends I always have to go washing or grocery shopping.

7. The strength of the vinegar applied with a hot grill produces a most intense odor.

8. Today Japan's television popularization rate is the highest in the world.

9. My mother reacted as either she or my father had to accompany me while I went to court.

10. Everything started coming at me when our electricity was turned off.

D.
1. Therefore, children acquired how to get along with the older or younger people.

2. I stayed there almost half of the trip, camping there for ten days and staying in a Scottish family for a week.

3. The cherry blossoms seem to be doing the way of lives that people want—short but meaningful life.

4. In our travels I observed the ways and means people earned for a living.

5. Also, at the age of 70's, can he stand the pressure that a professor has to go through?

6. Sales of new autos in May rose only 7.2 percent above last year's figures.

7. People who choose to go to work hold the short run ends over those who choose to go to college.

8. When I was growing up, I had no trouble out of my parents misunderstanding me.

9. People who steal, kill, and hurt others purposely never have any luck but bad luck, in which they'll eventually end up in jail over long periods of time.

10. She always asks what is the matter, in which I can turn and be completely open with her.

E. Due to the fact of how my tennis game has progressed from scratch, it seems that all the other tennis players I know are quite more experienced than I and being such do not want to play with me. There is another group of players below my experience level, but when I play with them they feel intimidated. Despite the fact of I often must play and practice alone, I am trying to perfect my tennis game.

IV. A. *The following passage is from James Thurber's essay on the dangers of women, introduced on page 307. Because his essay is longer than those previously considered in this text, this passage extends to several paragraphs though it provides evidence for only one support. Referring to the list of prepositions on page 48, complete the idioms in* *this passage by putting the correct prepositions into the blanks. Consult a dictionary when necessary.*

The element _____ menace _____ the Quiet Type is commonly considered very great. Yet if one asks a man who professes knowledge _____ the type why one should look out _____ it, one gets but a vague answer. "Just look out, that's all," he usually says. When I began my researches I was, _____ spite _____ myself, somewhat inhibited _____ an involuntary subscription _____ this legendary fear. I found it difficult to fight off a baseless alarm _____ the presence _____ a lady _____ subdued manner. Believing, however, that the best defense is an offense, I determined to carry the war, as it were, _____ the enemy's country. The first Quiet Type, or Q.T., that I isolated was a young woman whom I encountered _____ a Sunday tea party. She sat a little apart _____ the rest _____ the group _____ a great glazed chintz, I believe it was, chair. Her hands rested quietly _____ the chair arms. She kept her chin rather down than up, and had a way _____ lifting her gaze slowly, _____ disturbing the set _____ her chin. She moved but twice, once to put _____ a cup _____ tea and once to push back a stray lock _____ her forehead. I stole glances _____ her _____ time _____ time, trying to make them appear ingenuous and friendly rather than bold or suggestive, an achievement rendered somewhat troublesome _____ an unfortunate involuntary winking _____ the left eyelid _____ which I am unhappily subject.

I noted that her eyes, which were brown, had a demure light _____ them. She was dressed simply and was quite pretty. She spoke but once or twice, and then only when spoken _____. _____ a chance shifting _____ the guests _____ an adjacent room to examine, I believe, some water colors, I was left quite alone _____ her. Steeling myself _____ an ordeal _____ which I am unused—or was _____ the time—I moved directly _____ her side and grasped her hand. "Hallo, baby! Some fun— hah?" I said—a method _____ attack which I had devised _____ advance. She was obviously shocked, and instantly rose _____ her chair and followed the others _____ the next room. I never saw her again, nor have I been invited _____ that little home since. Now _____ some conclusions.

Patently, this particular Q.T., probably due _____ an individual variation, was not immediately dangerous _____ the sense that she would seize an opportunity, such as I offered her, to break up the home _____, or _____ least commit some indiscretion _____, a man who was obviously—I believe I may say—a dependable family man _____ the average offhand attractions. Dr. White has criticized my methodology _____ this particular case, a criticism which I may say now, _____ all good humor, since the danger is past, once threatened to interpose insuperable obstacles, _____ a temperamental nature, _____ the way _____ this collaboration. It was his feeling that I might just as well have removed one _____ the type's shoes as approach her the way I did. I cannot hold _____ him there. Neither, I am gratified to say, can Zaner, but _____ fairness _____ White it is only just to add that Tithridge can.

However, the next Q.T. that I encountered I placed under observation more gradually. I used to see her riding _____ a Fifth Avenue bus, always _____ a certain hour. I took _____ riding _____ this bus also, and discreetly managed to sit next her _____ several occasions. She eventually noticed that I appeared to be cultivating her and eyed me quite candidly, _____ a look I could not _____ once decipher. I could now, but _____ that time I couldn't. I resolved to put the matter _____ her quite frankly, to tell her, _____ fine, that I was studying her type and that I wished to place her _____ closer observation. Therefore, one evening, I doffed my hat and began.

"Madam," I said, "I would greatly appreciate making a leisurely examination _____ you, _____ your convenience." She struck me _____ the palm _____ her open hand, got up _____ her seat, and descended _____ the next even-numbered street—Thirty-sixth, I believe it was.

I may as well admit here and now that personally I enjoyed _____ no time any great success _____ Q.T.'s. I think one may go as far as to say that any scientific examination _____ the Quiet Type, as such, is out _____ the question. I know _____ no psychologist who has ever got one alone long enough to get anywhere. (Tithridge has averred that he began too late _____ life; Zaner that he does not concur _____ the major premise.) The Quiet Type is not amenable _____ the advances _____ scientific men when the advances are _____ a scientific nature, and also when they are _____ any other nature. Indeed, it is one _____ the unfortunate handicaps to psychological experimentation that many types _____ women do not lend themselves readily _____ purposeful study. As one woman said _____ me. "It all seems so mapped out, kind _____. . . ."

_____ my very failures I made, I believe, certain significant findings _____ regard _____ the Quiet Type. It is not dangerous _____ men, but _____ a particular man. Apparently it lies _____ wait _____ some one individual and gets him. Being got _____ his special type, or even being laid _____ wait _____, would seem _____ me _____ some cases not _____ its pleasurable compensations. Wherein, exactly, the menace lies, I have no means _____ knowing. I have my moments when I think I see what it is, but I have other moments when I think I don't.

B. *Write an essay on one of these topics.*

studying the opposite sex	a relative
a book	a boss
a television show	a newspaper

INDEPENDENT STUDY: *Idiom (answers in the back)*

V. **A.** *Correctly complete the idioms in the following sentences. Check a dictionary if you aren't sure.*

1. His blessing absolved her _____ responsibility for the results.

2. They agreed _____ a much larger price than we had expected.

3. No one could comply _____ all his demands.

4. Any job would be preferable _____ this one.

5. These results differ _____ those of the other members of the committee.

6. I must differ _____ you _____ this subject.

7. We hated to part _____ each other.

8. She hated to part _____ that car.

9. Please wait _____ me _____ the front door.

10. Warren is always preoccupied _____ money.

B. *Correct errors in idiom in the following sentences.*

1. One day my friend Barbara and I were practicing for a cheerleading routine.

2. He told me the great difference of teenagers of his time and girls of today.

3. There are techniques in which a person could use to get a good job.

4. While my mom and dad were enjoying their sight-seeing, my brothers and I wandered at the nearby woods.

5. One morning my brother and I decided that we were quitting from school, and we advised her to quit from her job.

6. At the corner of the room, there was an empty table.

7. I advise for everyone to look around before accepting a job.

8. It has been more than five years ago since I read the novel *Gone with the Wind*.

9. She gave me the cookbook in which I found my recipe for corn bread.

10. They also were very jealous because our girl classmates preferred our company than theirs.

idiom

10. Distinctive Designs

• A good paragraph is not just a list of good sentences. Each sentence must be precisely constructed to fit its particular spot, to complement its neighbors in both content and form. This chapter tells how to construct sentences that fit together into a tight system that is better than the sum of its parts.

CONCISE WORDING

Good writing is tight, direct, and densely packed with vivid detail. Wordy writing is sprawling, long-winded, and full of vague words. Good writing sparkles with life, but wordy writing is like Coke with water in it, so diluted the sparkles pass unnoticed. Which of the following paragraphs sparkles and which is wordy?

> When snow accumulates week after week, month after month, it works curious miracles. Many things that used to be in our vicinity seem to disappear. Instead there are huge piles of snow. Everywhere we look we just see snow instead of the things that we saw before the snow fell. Many objects that we are used to seeing simply disappear out of our sight. For example, the house that I made that we keep the pigs in and the top of the well that is located near the door to the barn just disappeared. After a while one tends to forget that they are still there under all that snow. We have a hedge. This hedge is made of cedars. It is about five feet from top to bottom. The hedge disappeared about four or perhaps five months ago. We also have some fences. These fences are pink. We had set out these fences because they would hold back the drifts of snow. These fences also completely disappeared from view. I have two dogs that are small that my wife named Jones and Susy. These dogs guard the farm. They really enjoy climbing up to the top of the drifts which are much higher than they usually can get. They also enjoy the excitement that they can get when they watch out for strangers from the pile of snow that is crusted on top and covers the hedge of cedar. Never before have they been able to be way up there. They have posts that they can look out from and see far away. These posts are made from the piles of snow that the plow has thrown high up in the air. These posts give them a chance so that they can view things that are very far away.

When snow accumulates week after week, month after month, it works curious miracles. Familiar objects simply disappear, like my pig house and the welltop near the barn door, and one tends to forget that they are there. Our cedar hedge (about five feet high) disappeared months ago, along with the pink snow fences that are set to hold the drifts. My two small guard dogs, Jones and Susy, enjoy the change in elevation and the excitement of patrol duty along the crusted top of the hedge, where they had never been before. They have lookout posts made of snow that the plow has thrown high in the air, giving them a chance to take the long view of things. For a while, the barnyard fence was buried under the magnificent drift. This delighted the geese, who promptly walked to freedom on their orange-colored snowshoes. They then took off into the air, snowshoes and all, freedom having gone to their heads, and visited the trout pond, where they spent an enjoyable morning on the ice. On several occasions this winter, we had to shovel a path for the geese, to make it possible for them to get from their pen in the barn to their favorite loitering spot in the barn cellar. Imagine a man's shoveling a path for a goose! So the goose can loiter!

The first paragraph is wordy, but the second one is sharp and lively. The second paragraph, written by E. B. White, gives all the details of the first paragraph in half the space and has plenty of room left for the details on the geese. Before turning in an essay, eliminate wordy passages by following these instructions:

1. Omit repetition

A. Cut out extra sentences. Don't say the same thing over and over. Say it once, then show the reader it's true by describing the experiences that convinced you. The first sentence of the wordy paragraph states that accumulated snow works curious miracles, but the next four sentences just say over and over in different words that familiar things disappeared.

When snow accumulates week after week, month after month, it works curious miracles. Many things that used to be in our vicinity seem to disappear. Instead there are huge piles of snow. Everywhere we look we just see snow instead of the things that we saw before the snow fell. Many objects that we are used to seeing simply disappear out of our sight.

In contrast, the good paragraph says it once and gives evidence that convinced the writer.

Familiar objects simply disappear, like my pig house and the welltop near the barn door, and one tends to forget that they are there.

B. Cut out extra words.

WORDY	GOOD
that is located near the barn	near the barn
disappeared out of our sight	disappeared
about four or perhaps five months ago	months ago
still there under all that snow	still there

wordy

2. Condense everything. Reduce sentences and independent clauses to dependent clauses, *ing* phrases, modifiers, or verbs—the shorter the better.

   A. Reduce prepositional phrases to modifiers.

WORDY	GOOD
top of the well	welltop
door of the barn	barn door
hedge of cedar	cedar hedge

   B. Reduce sentences and clauses to modifiers.

WORDY	GOOD
objects that we are used to seeing	many familiar objects
house that I made to keep the pigs in	my pig house
excitement that they get when they watch out for strangers	excitement of patrol duty
snow that is crusted on top and covers the hedge	crusted top of the hedge
posts that they can look out from and see far away	lookout posts
We have a hedge. This hedge is made of cedars.	our cedar hedge
We also have some fences. These fences are pink.	the pink fences
dogs that are small	small dogs
that my wife named Jones and Susy	Jones and Susy
these dogs guard the farm	guard dogs

   C. Reduce sentences and clauses to ing *phrases and verbs.*

WORDY	GOOD
because they would hold back the drifts	to hold back the drifts of snow
these posts gave them a chance so that they can view things that are very far away	giving them a chance to take the long view of things

   D. Combine sentences. The techniques above can be used to reduce eight sentences from the faulty paragraph to one. First, these four sentences

> We have a hedge. This hedge is made of cedars. It is about five feet from top to bottom. The hedge disappeared about four or perhaps five months ago.

can be reduced to one.

> Our cedar hedge (about five feet high) disappeared months ago.

Then the next four sentences

We also have some fences. These fences are pink. We had set out these fences because they would hold back the drifts of snow. These fences also completely disappeared from view.

can be reduced to one.

The pink snow fences that are set to hold the drifts also disappeared.

Finally, those two rewritten sentences can be combined into one dense, meaty sentence.

Our cedar hedge (about five feet high) disappeared months ago, along with the pink snow fences that are set to hold the drifts.

All that wordy material about the dogs

I have two dogs that are small that my wife named Jones and Susy. These dogs guard the farm. They really enjoy climbing up to the top of the drifts which are much higher than they usually can get. They also enjoy the excitement that they can get when they watch out for strangers from the pile of snow that is crusted on top and covers the hedge of cedar. Never before have they been able to be way up there.

can be reduced to two sentences.

My two small guard dogs, Jones and Susy, enjoy the change in elevation. They also enjoy the excitement of patrol duty along the crusted top of the hedge where they have never been before.

Then those two sentences can be combined into one concise sentence.

My two small guard dogs, Jones and Susy, enjoy the change in elevation and the excitement of patrol duty along the crusted top of the hedge where they have never been before.

Study the following edited version showing how the wordy paragraph could be revised into the concise one.

When snow accumulates week after week, month after month, it works curious miracles. ~~Many things that used to be in our vicinity seem to disappear. Instead there are huge piles of snow. Everywhere we look we just see snow instead of the things that we saw before the snow fell.~~ Many *Familiar* objects ~~that we are used to seeing~~ simply disappear ~~out of our sight. For~~ *like* ~~example,~~ *My* ~~the~~ house ~~that I made that we keep the~~ (pigs) ~~in~~ and the top ~~of the~~ (well) ~~that is located~~ near the door ~~to the~~ (barn) ~~just disappeared. After a while~~ *, and* ~~one tends to forget that they are~~ *Our* there ~~still~~ ~~under all that snow.~~ ~~We have a~~ hedge. ~~This hedge is made of~~ (cedars). ~~It is~~ *high* (about five feet ~~from top to bottom).~~ ~~The hedge~~ disappeared ~~about four or perhaps five~~ months ago. ~~We~~ *along* *with the* ~~also have some~~ fences. ~~These fences are~~ (pink). ~~We had~~ *that are* set out ~~these fences~~ (snow)

wordy

because they would hold back the drifts of (snow.) These fences also
~~completely disappeared from view.~~ I have two ^My^ dogs that are (small) that my
wife named Jones and Susy. These dogs (guard) the farm. They really enjoy
^the change in^
climbing up to the top of the drifts which are much higher than they usually
~~can get.~~ They also enjoy ^and^ the excitement that they can get when they watch
^of patrol duty^ ^along the^ ^of^
out for strangers from the pile of snow that is crusted on top and covers the
^where they have never been before.^
hedge of cedar. Never before have they been able to be way up there. They
have ^,^ posts that they can (look)(out) from and see far away. These posts are
made from the piles of snow that the plow has thrown high up in the air ^x^
^giving^ ^to take the^ ^of^
These posts give them a chance so that they can view things that are very
(long)
far away.

Whenever possible, prevent wordiness in the first draft by avoiding repetition and by writing concise sentences, dense with concrete evidence. Then before turning in an essay, reread it and correct wordy passages by omitting repetitious words and sentences, condensing everything else, combining the condensed sentences, and writing additional densely detailed sentences.

> **CORRECTION COMMENT:** Correct wordy passages by omitting repetitious words and sentences, condensing everything else, combining the condensed sentences, and writing additional densely detailed sentences.

EXERCISES: Concise Wording

I. A. *Without looking back to the text, eliminate the wordiness from this paragraph.*

> When snow accumulates week after week, month after month, it works curious miracles. Many things that used to be in our vicinity seem to disappear. Instead there are huge piles of snow. Everywhere we look we just see snow instead of the things that we saw before the snow fell. Many objects that we are used to seeing simply disappear out of our sight. For example, the house that I made that we keep the pigs in and the top of the well that is located near the door to the barn just disappeared. After a while one tends to forget that they are still there under all that snow. We have a hedge. This hedge is made of cedars. It is about five feet from top to bottom. The hedge disappeared about four or perhaps five months ago. We

also have some fences. These fences are pink. We had set out these fences because they would hold back the drifts of snow. These fences also completely disappeared from view. I have two dogs that are small that my wife named Jones and Susy. These dogs guard the farm. They really enjoy climbing up to the top of the drifts which are much higher than they usually can get. They also enjoy the excitement that they can get when they watch out for strangers from the pile of snow that is crusted on top and covers the hedge of cedar. Never before have they been able to be way up there. They have posts that they can look out from and see far away. These posts are made from the piles of snow that the plow has thrown high up in the air. These posts give them a chance so that they can view things that are very far away.

B. Compare your finished paragraph with the original by White, find the weaknesses in your paragraph, and correct them. Reward yourself if you find any places where you've improved upon the original.

II. *Condense the following sentences by reducing the clauses.*

A.   1. We would put curtains in the front. Then we would hang a star from the curtains.

   2. After he read the paper, he turned on the television.

   3. When I was little, I used to play house with my friends. We used to play in the garage.

   4. Be sure to add the bleach after you have filled the machine.

   5. The dishes which were in the sink were dirty.

   6. Before I get married I have to test that person. I have to see if I really want him.

   7. When my brother left the kitchen, he slammed the door.

   8. Jonny turned on the television so that he would watch "Mork and Mindy."

   9. My brother, who is a medical doctor, lives in a huge house in Atlanta.

   10. My son prefers bananas that are green.

B.   1. I want the family to do things together. I want the family to get along together.

   2. Another short boot which is very nice is one that has a gold strap around the ankle.

wordy

3. If you want to pass basic writing, you must do all the assignments conscientiously.

4. The book that was written by Jackson is the main text of the course.

5. My grandfather came into the toolshed. He picked up the hammer.

6. My car, which is a Duster, has been giving me a lot of trouble.

7. Another time we raised some money for the Children's Hospital. We obtained the money by giving a dance.

8. The other place is a lake. It is a foggy lake.

9. She discovered the cake had been cut, and she accused me.

10. I've just learned that they've recaptured ten of the prisoners. They had escaped from the prison in Attica.

C. 1. Mrs. James, who was the best teacher in the school, was happy to stay after class and help anyone who needed help.

2. We had a very big picnic area. We had lots of chairs, tables, and benches.

3. As we approached the cottage, we could see the lake through the trees.

4. My friend and I, who were just coming out of the water, ducked down behind the boat.

5. In the future I recommend that all family members share in doing the housework. I recommend that all families take turns cleaning up after one another.

6. I enjoyed all my subjects, but most of all I liked reading.

7. His back ached because he had slept on the floor all night.

8. For example, he has ordered cuts in government spending. He has also met with other top officials in Washington to curtail credit.

9. There was no way that she could get in so that she could get her clothes.

10. We were fifteen girls and fifteen boys. We were living in a big dorm.

III. *Rewrite the following sentences so that they express the same idea sharply and directly.*

A. 1. My English classes did not give me enough of the right kind of writing practice that I needed.

2. I worked at the Kensington Library. The location is on Arlington Street in Kensington.

3. You don't have to look far to have fun, and you don't have to be rich to have fun.

4. This is a problem I have which is not really liking who I am.

5. Watching my nephew trying to walk was fun for me to see.

6. High school will give a person a lot of good old memories of the past.

7. Being a mother myself I've noticed how my child can find a thousand and one things to do.

8. Disco dancing is one dance a lot of different people get involved in sometimes.

9. The same way most roads are available to everyone, the same should be done with health.

10. I want to make a cheerful home. I think this is important thing for me. Family affects me greatly. I think family is the place which I can live in peace.

B.

1. Sometimes I know there will be sadness and misunderstanding at times, but the good will hopefully overrule the bad.

2. There are always police coming to our house to see my dad. The reason for this is my father is a reserve for the Albany Police Department.

3. Crab, like shrimp, is a dish that a person can let his imagination go wild when preparing the dish of crab.

4. My boy friend developed an attitude as if he didn't care about our relationship one way or another.

5. Their height and size are considerably enormous, and they unbelievably move like real animals and men.

6. My work was done very well to my knowledge.

7. I don't know if everyone's summer will be like mine, but I know my summer will be fun, exciting, and full of adventure.

8. In the third grade, a girl named Susan was a bully. She most definitely bullied me. I was the soft-hearted, shy little girl.

9. I think it is important to know that every day of our lives won't be happy. Days are sometimes happy, but they are sometimes boring.

10. I find going to a public park to be an inexpensive way of having fun.

C.

1. They had no evidence of their birth. Even though they didn't have any evidence of their birth, they would not furnish information willingly.

2. The real reason could or may be that the phone has been disconnected because of an unpaid bill.

3. The reason was because the big bullies of our classroom would try in many ways to break our friendship, and they thought that by us being opponents in sports they would get us mad with each other, but this never worked out because we were just a little bit more smarter.

`wordy`

4. It took almost over an hour to find all the things she needed. Even if she doesn't bring me anything back, I know I did something, a job well done.

5. My faith in God played a major part in my survival because of the odds. The odds were 90 to 10 against me.

6. Being in high school was very exciting. Being on campus with other students was very exciting. I found it to be very challenging.

7. Being alone gives me the freedom of not having to be a meticulous house cleaner. I have freedom with cooking when I want, coming home at any time, going out to dinner with anyone, washing clothes, and many other things.

8. Many times a lot of people find themselves having to buy new cars every other year simply because they refuse to take their cars in for regular service repairs.

9. Now that I am older, one of my goals in life is to conquer this fear of not being able to share my innermost feelings.

10. For the adults Disneyland provides a show for them.

IV. Following the guidelines in this unit, eliminate the wordiness from the passages below. Consult a dictionary if there are any words you don't understand, and write their meanings above them. Compare your finished passage with the originals in the back of the book. Find the weaknesses in yours and correct them. Reward yourself if you find any places where you've improved upon the original.

A.   My costume for traveling was utilitarian if a trifle bizarre. I had boots on my feet. These boots were of the half-Wellington type, and they were made out of rubber. They also had inner soles inside them. These inner soles were made out of cork. These boots kept my feet warm. They also kept them dry. In addition, my shanks were covered by trousers. These trousers were made out of cotton. The material of these trousers was khaki. I had bought these trousers in a store that sold things that had originally been made for the army. I also wore a coat. This coat felt good over my chest, arms, and shoulders. This coat was made for hunting. It had cuffs and a collar that had been made from corduroy cloth. It also had a pocket in the rear. This pocket was intended as a place for hunters to put small game they had killed. This pocket was very big. I could have smuggled the princess of an Indian tribe into a Y.M.C.A. in that pocket. I also wore a cap that I had worn for many years. This cap was blue, and it was made from serge. This cap was designed for sailors in the British navy, and it had a short visor and a peak. On its peak was an emblem with the royal lion and unicorn. These animals were fighting for the crown of England as they always do.

B.   A girl stood before him in midstream. She was all alone and still, and she gazed out to sea. No one was anywhere near her. She seemed like she had been changed by magic and turned into the likeness of a bird of the sea. This bird was strange and beautiful. She had long legs. Her legs were bare. They were delicate as a crane's legs are, and they were pure save the place where there was seaweed on them. This seaweed had fashioned itself as if it were a sign upon her flesh. Outside of that seaweed, her legs looked pure. Her thighs were fuller than her legs were. They were also soft-hued as ivory is. Her thighs were bared almost all the way up to her hips. There the fringes of her drawers showed. They were white. They were very much like feathering on a bird. They looked like down that was soft and white. She had on skirts. These skirts were blue like slate, and they were tied about her waist boldly. They looked like a kilt. Her skirts also stuck out behind her like the tail of a dove. Her bosom was also as a bird's. It was soft, and it was like the breast of a dove. Of course, the dove had plumage that was dark. She also had hair. Her hair was long, and it was fair, and it was girlish. Her face was girlish too. Her face was touched with a wonder. That wonder was of beauty which was mortal.

C.   I became increasingly frustrated. In fact, I was quite upset. I was not able to express the things that I wanted to convey when I wrote letters. I was especially upset about this failure because I wrote letters to Mr. Elijah Muhammad, and I wanted to hear from him very much. When I had been out in the street I had been a hustler. I was also articulate. In fact, I was the most articulate hustler that there was anywhere out there on the streets. I commanded attention. When I said something everyone listened to me. Now, however, I was trying to write. I wanted to write in English. I wanted to write in simple language, but I was not articulate. In fact, I wasn't even functional. I couldn't really say anything in writing. I knew how to talk but not to write. How would my writing sound if I wrote in slang the way I would say it? If I said it I would say something like this. "Look here, O masculine parent. I would very much like it if you would allow me to pull on your overcoat. I want to talk about some type of feline, Elijah Muhammad—"

D.   The exact time was fifteen minutes past eight. This was Japanese time. It was in the morning. The month was August, the day was the sixth, and the year was 1945. That was the moment when it happened. The bomb flashed above Hiroshima. The bomb was atomic. At that very moment, Miss Toshiko Sasaki had just sat down. She was a clerk. She worked in the department that took care of the needs of the personnel. She worked at the East Asia Tin Works. She sat at her place in the office of the plant. She was turning her head. She wanted to speak to a girl. This girl sat at a desk. This desk was next to hers.

V. *Eliminate the wordiness in your last essay. You'll probably be surprised how much there is even if no one noticed it. Eliminate wordiness from your future essays before turning them in.*

wordy

INDEPENDENT STUDY: *Concise Wording* (possible answers in the back)

VI. A. *Condense the following sentences by reducing the clauses.*

1. When I went away from the center of town, there was nothing but the endlessly wide land where there are many houses.

2. He was rich enough so that he could hire several employees in his store.

3. When the program showed a festival in my home town, I could see landscape which was familiar.

4. I want to learn how to fix my car because the cost of fixing it at a garage is always high, and sometimes it takes longer than I had expected.

5. When there is a holiday like Christmas, children are divided in two groups.

6. Police officers in the area where I live stop drivers and give them tickets.

7. Many cars in my town are low riders, and the police officers don't like the cars or the people who drive them.

8. I use English when I am at work and at school.

9. On the first day of the festival, I went to Japan Town in the morning so that I could see the parade which is held before the festival.

10. I like the food which my mother cooks best.

B. *Rewrite the following wordy sentences so that they express the same idea sharply and directly.*

1. This is the kind of situation I often face every time I go out on a date.

2. One nice result of cooking my own food is that I get to eat as much as I want. When I cook I can have the quantity that I want.

3. I do not believe that death is the end of life; however, I do believe it is the beginning of a new life.

4. I believe that luck is one of the greatest gifts known to man, although many don't consider luck a gift. I believe that luck is a gift.

5. During the childhood of my children, I will teach them how to speak the Filipino language, how to respect each other, and how to respect other people.

6. By knowing an instrument one can help another person to play the instrument, and together they can realize the joy and beauty of playing an instrument.

7. In the future I recommend that all family members share in doing the housework. I recommend that all families take turns cleaning up after one another.

8. When I was a little girl, I had a problem of not being able to share my feelings with people around me.

9. To my knowledge I have noticed that most advisers recommend that the students they are advising take several courses that are designed to teach writing.

10. I love it very much that my boy friend and I are very compatible. It makes me feel really good to have someone who is so compatible with me.

C. Following the guidelines in this unit, eliminate the wordiness from the passage below. Compare your finished passage with the original in the back of the book. Find the weaknesses in yours and correct them. Reward yourself if you find any places where you've improved from the original.

On a night after dark the wind came to the house. The wind loosened a shingle. Then it flipped that shingle to the ground below the house. The next night another wind came. It blew at the house, and it pried into the hole that had been made by the other wind that blew off the first shingle. This second wind lifted off more shingles. In fact, it lifted off three shingles. Then another wind came, and this wind blew off twelve more shingles. After that the sun came through that hole. The sun burned in the sky. It threw a spot on the floor. That spot glared. Soon cats crept in. They were wild cats. They came from the fields, and they came at night. These cats did not mew at the steps to the door. They didn't ask if they could come in. They moved like shadows. They were like shadows of a cloud. They were like shadows moving across the moon. They came into the room. They wanted to hunt mice. And when it was night and when it was windy, the doors banged. The curtains were ragged, and they fluttered. These curtains were in the windows. The windows were broken.

wordy

SENTENCE VARIETY

Beginning writers are often hesitant to try new types of sentences, and so they use too many single independent clause sentences. Consequently, their writing seems immature, like the writing in a first-grade reading book. The excellent detail of the following paragraph is hidden by choppy monotonous sentences that seem to jump around and keep starting over.

MONOTONOUS

The strangers on Hudson Street are many. They are our allies. Their eyes help us natives. We keep the peace of the street. They always seem to be different people from one day to the next. That does not matter. One day Jimmy Rogan fell. He fell through a window. The window was plate glass. He was separating some friends. The friends were scuffling. He almost lost his arm. A stranger emerged from the Ideal bar. He was wearing a T-shirt. The T-shirt was old. He applied a tourniquet. The tourniquet was expert. He applied it swiftly. The staff says something. They say he saved a life. The life was Jimmy's. This staff works at the hospital. They work in the emergency room. Nobody remembered seeing the man before. No one has seen him since. The hospital was called in this way. A woman was sitting on the steps. The steps were next to the accident. She ran over to the bus stop. She didn't say anything. She snatched a dime from a stranger. It was in his hand. He was waiting with his fare ready. The fare was fifteen cents. She raced into the Ideal's bar. She raced to the phone booth. The stranger raced after her. He wanted to offer the nickel too. Nobody remembered seeing him before. No one has seen him since. Sometimes we see the same stranger three or four times on Hudson Street. Then we begin to nod. This is almost getting to be an acquaintance. This is a public acquaintance, of course.

The best writing uses sentences of varying lengths and types, as does the following paragraph by Jane Jacobs.

GOOD

The strangers on Hudson Street, the allies whose eyes help us natives keep the peace of the street, are so many that they always seem to be different people from one day to the next. That does not matter. When Jimmy Rogan fell through a plate-glass window (he was separating some scuffling friends) and almost lost his arm, a stranger in an old T-shirt emerged from the Ideal bar, swiftly applied an expert tourniquet and, according to the hospital's emergency staff, saved Jimmy's life. Nobody remembered seeing the man before, and no one has seen him since. The hospital was called in this way: a woman sitting on the steps next to the accident ran over to the bus stop, wordlessly snatched the dime from the hand of a stranger who was waiting with his fifteen-cent fare ready, and raced into the Ideal's phone booth. The stranger raced after her to offer the nickel too. Nobody remembered seeing him before, and no one has seen him since. When we see the same stranger three or four times on Hudson Street, we begin to nod. This is almost getting to be an acquaintance, a public acquaintance, of course.

This paragraph is much more interesting and coherent than the earlier one.

Single independent clause sentences can be eliminated and others fattened by combining several. Each detail does not need its own clause. Eliminate sentences by adding their details to other sentences in the following ways.

1. Change key words in one sentence to modifiers in another.

MONOTONOUS	GOOD
Jimmy Rogan fell through a window. The window was plate glass.	Jimmy Rogan fell through a plate-glass window.
He was separating some friends. The friends were scuffling.	He was separating some scuffling friends.
A stranger emerged from the Ideal bar. He was wearing a T-shirt. The T-shirt was old.	A stranger in an old T-shirt emerged from the Ideal bar.
He applied a tourniquet. The tourniquet was expert. He applied it swiftly.	He swiftly applied an expert tourniquet.
The staff says something. They say he saved a life. The life was Jimmy's. This staff works at the hospital. They work in the emergency room.	according to the hospital's emergency staff he saved Jimmy's life
A woman was sitting on the steps.	a woman sitting on the steps
She didn't say anything.	wordlessly
He was waiting with his fare ready. The fare was fifteen cents.	He was waiting with his fifteen-cent fare ready.
They are our allies.	the allies
This acquaintance is public, of course.	a public acquaintance, of course

2. Change clauses to phrases, and move those phrases into other sentences.

MONOTONOUS	GOOD
They help us natives. We keep the peace of the street.	They help us natives keep the peace of the street.
One day Jimmy Rogan fell. He fell through a window.	One day Jimmy Rogan fell through a window.
A woman was sitting on the steps. The steps were next to the accident. She ran over to the bus stop.	A woman sitting on the steps next to the accident ran over to the bus stop.

She snatched a dime from a stranger. It was in his hand.	She snatched a dime from the hand of a stranger.
She raced into the Ideal bar. She raced to the phone booth.	She raced to the Ideal's phone booth.
The stranger raced after her. He wanted to offer the nickel too.	The stranger raced after her to offer the nickel too.
The hospital's emergency staff says something. They say he saved Jimmy's life.	according to the hospital's emergency staff, he saved Jimmy's life.

3. Change independent clauses to dependent ones.

MONOTONOUS	GOOD
Their eyes help us natives.	whose eyes help us natives
They always seem to be different people.	that they always seem to be different people
One day Jimmy Rogan fell.	when Jimmy Rogan fell
He was waiting with his fare ready.	who was waiting with his fare ready
Sometimes we see the same stranger three or four times on Hudson Street.	when we see the same stranger three or four times on Hudson Street

4. Combine clauses with the same subject into one clause with several verbs.

MONOTONOUS	GOOD
One day Jimmy Rogan fell. He almost lost his arm.	One day Jimmy Rogan fell and almost lost his arm.
A stranger emerged from the Ideal bar. He applied a tourniquet. He saved Jimmy's life.	A stranger emerged from the Ideal bar, applied a tourniquet, and saved Jimmy's life.
She ran over to the bus stop. She snatched a dime from a stranger. She raced into the phone booth.	She ran to the bus stop, snatched a dime from a stranger, and raced into the phone booth.

5. Combine independent clauses with "fanboys" words.

MONOTONOUS	GOOD
Nobody remembered seeing the man before. No one has seen him since.	Nobody remembered seeing the man before, and no one has seen him since.

These processes generate many types of sentence parts that can be combined into sentences of varying lengths and types. Notice how different the sentences from the good paragraph are from their neighbors.

1. The strangers on Hudson Street, the allies whose eyes help us natives keep the peace of the street, are so many that they always seem to be different people from one day to the next.

2. That does not matter.

3. When Jimmy Rogan fell through a plate-glass window (he was separating some scuffling friends) and almost lost his arm, a stranger in an old T-shirt emerged from the Ideal bar, swiftly applied an expert tourniquet and, according to the hospital's emergency staff, saved Jimmy's life.

4. Nobody remembered seeing the man before, and no one has seen him since.

5. The hospital was called in this way: a woman sitting on the steps next to the accident ran over to the bus stop, wordlessly snatched the dime from the hand of a stranger who was waiting with his fifteen-cent fare ready, and raced into the Ideal's phone booth.

6. The stranger raced after her to offer the nickel too.

7. Nobody remembered seeing him before, and no one has seen him since.

8. When we see the same stranger three or four times on Hudson Street, we begin to nod.

9. This is almost getting to be an acquaintance, a public acquaintance, of course.

The edited version below shows how the first paragraph was transformed into the second one.

The strangers on Hudson Street (are ~~so~~ many). ~~They are our~~ allies. ~~Their~~ eyes help us natives. ~~We~~ keep the peace of the street. ~~They~~ always seem to be different people from one day to the next. That does not matter. ~~One day~~ Jimmy Rogan fell. ~~He fell~~ through a window. ~~The window was~~ (plate glass). (He was separating some friends). ~~The friends were~~ (scuffling). ~~He~~ almost lost his arm. A stranger emerged from the Ideal bar. ~~He was wearing a~~ T-shirt). ~~The T-shirt was~~ (old). ~~He~~ applied a tourniquet. ~~The tourniquet was~~ (expert). ~~He applied it~~ (swiftly). ~~The~~ staff ~~says something~~. ~~They say~~ he saved a life. ~~The life was~~ (Jimmy's). ~~This staff~~ ~~works at~~ (the hospital's). ~~They work in the~~ (emergency) ~~room~~. Nobody remembered seeing the man before, *and n*~~No~~ one has seen him since. The hospital was called in this way: *a*~~A~~ woman ~~was~~ sitting on the steps, ~~The steps were~~ next to the accident, ~~She~~ ran over to the bus stop, ~~She didn't say anything,~~ *wordlessly* ~~She~~ snatched the dime from *of* a stranger. ~~It was in his hand.~~ *(the)* *who* ~~He~~ was waiting with his fare ready. ~~The fare was~~ (fifteen cents) *and* ~~She~~ raced into the Ideal's ~~bar,~~ ~~She raced to the~~ phone booth. The stranger raced after her, ~~He wanted~~ to offer the nickel too. Nobody remembered seeing him before, *and n*~~No~~ one has seen him since. *When* ~~Sometimes~~ we see the same stranger three or four times on Hudson Street, ~~Then~~ we begin to nod. This is almost getting to be an acquaintance, ~~This is~~ a public acquaintance, of course.

Also add variety by starting each sentence differently. Mix some of the following beginnings into your writing.

1. prepositional phrases

   In the movie theater, the eyes and ears are overwhelmed with sights and sounds.

2. *ed* modifiers

   Armed with his lance, he tiptoed awkwardly through the trees.

3. *ing* modifiers

   Staggering to his horse, he threw his arm across its back and concentrated on improving his breathing.

4. adverbs

   Slowly and patiently, the driver steers the limousine through the crowded street.

5. adjectives

   Soft and dry, the candies gave off a brown dust as they tumbled into my hand.

6. dependent clauses

   When the eager mainlanders descend from the plane, scores of scantily clad beauties rush to drop leis of cool orchids around their necks.

CORRECTION COMMENT: Use the techniques described in this unit to combine details from several single clause sentences into one to produce sentences of varying lengths and types.

EXERCISES: *Sentence Variety*

I. **A.** *Here is the monotonous paragraph from the text. Without looking back, try to rewrite it into the paragraph of varied sentences.*

The strangers on Hudson Street are many. They are our allies. Their eyes help us natives. We keep the peace of the street. They always seem to be different people from one day to the next. That does not matter. One day Jimmy Rogan fell. He fell through a window. The window was plate glass. He was separating some friends. The friends were scuffling. He almost lost his arm. A stranger emerged from the Ideal bar. He was wearing a T-shirt. The T-shirt was old. He applied a tourniquet. The tourniquet was expert. He applied it swiftly. The staff says something. They say he saved a life. The life was Jimmy's. This staff works at the hospital. They work in the emergency room. Nobody remembered seeing the man before. No one has seen him since. The hospital was called in this way. A woman was sitting on the steps. The steps were next to the accident. She ran over to the bus stop. She didn't say anything. She snatched a dime from a stranger. It was in his hand. He was waiting with his fare ready. The fare was fifteen cents. She raced into the Ideal's bar. She raced to the phone booth. The stranger raced after her. He wanted to offer the nickel too. Nobody remembered seeing him before. No one has seen him since. Sometimes we see the same stranger three or four times on Hudson Street. Then we begin to nod. This is almost getting to be an acquaintance. This is a public acquaintance, of course.

monotonous

B. *Compare your rewritten paragraph to the original. Decide which parts were better in the original and which are better in your revision. Put an exclamation point beside any that you improved.*

II. *Combine each of the following groups of sentences into as many different single sentences as possible. Then decide which one you like best and try to figure out why.*

1. The road was stone.

   The road wound up.

   The winding was to the top.

   The knoll was gray now.

   The knoll was under the night.

   The night was pale.

The top was of a knoll.

The knoll was grassy.

The night was starry.

2. I shielded my eyes.

The shielding was with my hand.

I peered.

The peering was through the
windshield.

The windshield was streaked.

I forced my eyes.

The forcing was to stay open.

3. Garin watched.

The watching was rigid.

The watching was of the horsemen.

The horsemen swept.

The sweeping was across the
meadow.

They were robed in black.

The black was swirling.

Their swords were naked.

Their swords were in their hands.

Their hands were pale.

4. Mandrill held a candle.

She stood before them.

She wished them something.

The something was a good night.

The something was a deep sleep.

Then Harold rose.

Then Duncan rose.

They climbed the steps.

The steps were to the bedroom.

The bedroom was under the eaves.

5. They mounted their ponies.

They felt their way.

Their feeling was by the rise and
fall of the ground.

They steered their way.

The way was toward the opening.

The opening was at the end.

The end was of the valley.

The valley was long.

6. Sometimes women gathered.

Sometimes men gathered.

They gathered to sit.

They gathered to listen to music.

The phonograph was great.

It played music.

The music throbbed.

The throbbing was in his stomach.

The music made pictures.

The pictures were beautiful.

The pictures were in his head.

Oscar was happy then.

7. A house was there.

The shapes lay beyond the
shoulder.

A shoulder was behind it.

The shoulder was steep.

The shoulder was of land.

The land lay there.

It was gray.

It was bare.

The shapes were dark.

They were hills.

These hills were coastal.

They rolled backward.

The backward was toward the sea.

8. He stuffed some things into a bag.

   He stuffed a book.

   He stuffed a bundle.

   He stuffed them into the top.

   The bag was heavy.

   The bag was standing there.

   The bag was already nearly full.

9. A wail came.

   The coming was down the wind.

   The wail was like a cry.

   The cry was like one from a creature.

   The creature was evil.

   The creature was lonely.

monotonous

10. He walked back to his den.

    The walking was brisk.

    He stood for a moment.

    He smiled.

    He listened to the din.

    The din was in the pavilion.

    He also listened to other sounds.

    These sounds were of merrymaking.

    This merrymaking was in other parts.

    These parts were of the field.

III. *Combine each of the following groups of sentences into a single effective sentence and fit them together into a passage. Structure each sentence differently so that the sentences in the passage are varied.*

A. 1. The faucet dripped.

   The faucet was tired.

   It dripped into the water.

   The water was in the sink.

   The water was soapy.

   The water was cold.

2. A fly crawled.

   He was newborn.

   He was heavy-winged.

   He was fat.

   The crawling was sluggish.

   The crawling was over a cover.

   The cover was for a pie.

   The cover was plastic.

3. A woman shuffled.

   The woman was in a bathrobe.

   The shuffling was into the kitchen.

   The kitchen was tiny.

   The kitchen was gray.

   She turned on the burner.

   The burner was of the stove.

4. She picked up the teakettle.

   The teakettle was speckled.

   She filled it.

   The filling was at the sink.

   She placed it on the burner.

   The burner was sputtering.

5. She pushed some dishes.

   The dishes were dirty.

   The pushing was aside.

   The pushing cleared a place.

   The place was on the table.

   The table was cluttered.

   She spread a newspaper there.

   She sat down.

   The sitting was in a chair.

   The chair was wobbly.

6. She read the newspaper.

   She didn't notice anything else.

   She didn't notice the faucet.

   The faucet dripped.

   The dripping was into the sink.

   She didn't notice the fly.

   The fly explored the dishes.

   She didn't notice the burner.

   The burner sputtered.

   The sputtering was erratic.

   She didn't notice the water.

   The water bubbled.

   The bubbling was in the teakettle.

B. 1. Her face was calm.

   It gave no hint.

2. It stood out against the light.

   It was framed in an oval.

   The oval was her bonnet.

   The bonnet had ribbons.

   The ribbons were pale.

   They were like reeds.

   The reeds were streaming.

3. Her eyes looked straight ahead.

   They had long curving lashes.

4. They were fully open.

   They seemed narrowed.

   The narrowing was little.

   The cause was the blood.

   The blood pulsed.

   The pulsing was gentle.

   It pulsed under her skin.

   The skin was fine.

   The skin was of her cheekbones.

5. She inclined her head.   The tips were pearly.

   The inclining was to one side.   The teeth were white.

   The tips of her teeth showed.   They showed between her lips.

IV. *Use the techniques outlined in this chapter to rewrite the sentences of these paragraphs so that they are varied instead of monotonous. Compare your revision to the originals in the back of the book and put an exclamation point by any portions that you feel you've improved on.*

A.   Writing is laborious. Writing is slow. These facts hold for most people. The mind travels faster than the pen. Writing becomes a question of learning. One must learn to make shots. These shots are from the wing. These shots are occasional. One must bring down the bird. This is the bird of thought. It flashes by. A writer is a gunner. Sometimes he waits in his blind. He waits for something to come in. Sometimes he roams the countryside. He hopes to scare something up. He must be like other gunners. He must cultivate patience. He may have to work many covers. Then he might bring down one partridge.

B.   The writer will be drawn at every turn. The writer is young. He will be drawn toward eccentricities. These are eccentricities in language. He will hear a beat. This is the beat of vocabularies. These vocabularies are new. He will hear rhythms. These rhythms are exciting. They belong to segments of society. These segments are special. Each segment speaks a language. Each segment has its own language. All of us have this problem. We all come under this spell. This is the spell of these drums. These drums are unsettling. The problem is for the beginner. He must listen to them. He must learn the words. He must feel the excitement. He must not be carried away.

monotonous

V. *Write an essay on one of these topics.*

writing	playing an instrument
reading	eating out
dancing	racing
skiing	babysitting

INDEPENDENT STUDY: *Sentence Variety* (originals in the back)

VI. *A. Use the techniques described in this unit to combine the following groups of sentences into one and fit them into a paragraph. Then compare your paragraph with the original in the back. Decide where yours is better and where the original is better.*

   1. Snoopy is a commentator.   He wants man to see his errors.

     In fact he is very much a commentator.   He wants man to return to the path.

He speaks from atop his doghouse.

His doghouse is like a mock-pulpit.

From there he calls man.

This path is straight.

This path is narrow.

2. One episode has birds.

There are four.

They are homeless.

Snoopy lets them use his dog-house.

They use it as a refuge.

This refuge is temporary.

3. They are playing a game.

The game is bridge.

They become noisy.

Snoopy has to drive them away.

One bird carries a table away.

This is the last bird.

The table is for bridge.

The table is on his head.

4. Snoopy then comments.

He says this.

A Friend does not take advantage.

The advantage is of you.

5. Being on things does something.

These things are doghouses.

These things are pulpits.

These things are soapboxes.

It brings out the moralist.

The moralist is in man.

It is even in dogs.

Some dogs are like Snoopy.

B. *Use the techniques outlined in this chapter to rewrite the sentences of the following paragraph so that they are varied instead of monotonous. Compare your paragraph with the original and decide where the original is better and where yours is better.*

I have always felt that the duty of a writer was to ascend. This duty was first. This duty was to make flights. This duty was to carry others along. He could manage it. To do this takes courage. It even takes conceit. This is a certain conceit. One aeronaut was not a writer at all. He was my favorite. He was Dr. Piccard. He was the balloonist. Once he made an ascension. He was borne aloft by balloons. There were 2000 balloons. They were small. This was an experimental moment. He hoped the law would serve him well. This law was of probability. He hoped he would reach the air of the stratosphere. This air is rarefied. He hoped the balloons would burst. He hoped some balloons would burst. He hoped he would thus be lowered. He wanted to be lowered gently. He hoped to be lowered to earth. The doctor reached the heights. He had aspired to these heights. He whipped out a pistol. He killed some balloons. He killed about a dozen. He descended. The descent was in flames. The papers reported he jumped from the basket. He was choked with laughter. Flights of this sort are the dream. This dream is of every writer. The writer is good. He dreams of the ascent. He dreams of the surrender to probability. He dreams of the dénouement. This dénouement is flaming. He may be wracked with laughter. He may be wracked with tears. This is his final dream.

monotonous

Independent Study Answers

When only a few words are changed, only those words and a few of their neighbors are given. No answer is listed if a sentence is already correct. When a sentence must be rewritten, one possible answer is given although other answers may also be correct.

From Subject to Thesis *(page 13)*

A.
1. Faulty (too broad)
2. Faulty (question)
3. Good
4. Faulty (fact)
5. Faulty (question)
6. Good
7. Faulty (fact)
8. Faulty (too many ideas)
9. Good
10. Faulty (question)

B.
1. Good
2. Faulty (too many ideas)
3. Good
4. Faulty (fact)
5. Faulty (incomplete)
6. Good
7. Faulty (incomplete)
8. Faulty (fact)
9. Faulty (question)
10. Good

Building an Outline *(pages 22–23)*

A.
1. good
2. A thesis with too many ideas destroys this whole outline. A whole new outline must be written.
3. good
4. good
5. The third support doesn't prove the thesis.
   3. I learned teamwork in my home economics study group.
6. The first and third supports are the same.
   1. I like to wear the latest fashions.
7. None of the supports proves the thesis.
   1. They pinch my feet.
   2. They strain my legs.
   3. They hurt my back.
8. An incomplete thesis destroys this whole outline. A whole different outline should be written.
9. good
10. good

Writing Body Paragraphs (pages 32–34)

VII.
1. evidence needed—too general
2. good
3. evidence needed—wrong details
4. evidence needed—too general
5. good
6. evidence needed—too general
7. evidence needed—wrong details
8. good
9. evidence needed—too general
10. good

Writing Introductions (pages 40–41)

IV.
1. good
2. faulty—thesis at the beginning instead of the end
3. good
4. faulty—more details needed, breaks awkwardly before the thesis
5. good
6. faulty—limps along, too many different ideas
7. faulty—not developed
8. good
9. faulty—includes material that proves the thesis
10. good

Writing Conclusions (pages 45–46)

IV.
1. faulty—doesn't answer "so what?" or "what next?"; just repeats the thesis
2. faulty—doesn't answer "so what?"
3. faulty—doesn't answer "what next?"
4. faulty—doesn't answer "so what?"
5. faulty—doesn't answer "so what?"
6. faulty—gives material that proves the thesis
7. faulty—neither "so what?" nor "what next?" is answered well
8. good
9. faulty—gives material that proves the thesis
10. faulty—doesn't answer "so what?"

The Elements (page 53)

III. *A.*
1. (In the winter) my father took me (to school) (by bus).
2. I really loved that delicious cabbage.
3. A tiny girl (with stiff pigtails and a freckled face) softly asked the ice cream seller (for a rocky road ice cream cone) (with sprinkles) (on it).
4. Two (of my sister's friends) went (to Reed College).
5. Larry has a bad attitude (toward personal property).
6. (After fifteen minutes), the bored campers banged their knives and forks (on the bottoms) (of their tin plates).

7. Some (of the tastiest fruit) looks very ugly.

8. A young goatherd lived (near this wild girl) (in the same snowy country) (with the same mountains) (over his head).

9. Most (of the citizens) (of Washington, D.C.,) ignored George Washington (on his 250th birthday).

10. (Without a word) she ran (up the stairs) and (into her room).

B.

1. The press distorted the meaning (of the supervisor's letter) (to the accused congressman).

2. The short cooking process retains the nutrition (of the seafood and vegetables) (in most Japanese dishes).

3. One (of the ladies) (from the convention) left her hat (on the front steps) (of the hotel).

4. The play opens Friday (at 8:00 P.M.) (at the Community Theater).

5. Stoves (with porcelain tops) are not very popular (on the West Coast).

6. Several (of my favorite teachers) left the school last year.

7. Chicago's etiquette adviser resigned (from her $35,000-a-year post) only twelve days (after her appointment).

8. I mailed the bill and my check (to the main office) (in Topeka).

9. (After a brief delay), the countdown (for the test firing) (of the space shuttle's engines) began.

10. (In three seconds), she finished a hamburger and a milk shake.

Combinations (pages 58–59)

V.   A.

1. Some (of the best hunting and fresh water fishing areas) are located (in New Mexico).

2. A person can drive (through my neighborhood) and identify the rented houses.

3. (By night) these cats sit (on fences) and whine and yowl.

4. The prices (for food, clothing, services, transportation, and housing) have been steadily moving upward (with no sign) (of stopping).

5. Bad reading habits and low grades (on exams) are related.

6. Guns can be used (for hunting, target practice, or self-protection).

7. I will never forget my senior year (at Thomas Jefferson High School).

8. This country is faced (with both foreign and domestic problems).

9. The cats travel (in small groups) and chase the little dogs all (around the block).

10. (Since the rise) (in popularity) (of tennis), better equipment and facilities have been developed.

B.

This year, natural fabrics and blends are being shown. The sheerness and softness (of silk) attract a lot (of attention). Its high cost, however, and the necessity (of dry cleaning) keep it out (of reach) (for a lot) (of people). Cotton and terry are also nice natural fabrics and should be very popular this year. (For busy women), natural fabrics are blended (with synthetic ones) (for easy care). Pure artificial fabrics will never replace the natural ones.

Some Important Distinctions *(page 65)*

IV. *A.*

1. There was no traffic (on the road) (except for me and the nine other bike riders).

2. Has anyone been hired to replace Mrs. Brown?

3. (For example), he did not hear me start the car.

4. There's a lot (of vandalism) (in my neighborhood).

5. (On the bottom) (of the leaf) was a tiny snail.

6. My sister and I watched my father shoveling the heavy snow.

7. Frowning slightly, she folded her arms and began to speak.

8. There is no spicy sauce to cover up the freshness (of the meat and vegetables).

9. Cleaning the yard took up most (of my day off).

10. (From the kitchen) came the welcome odor (of stew).

B.

Japanese food is simple to cook. Once I broke my cooking record (by preparing a dish) (for twelve people) (in thirty minutes). (After a hard day) (of skiing), everyone was tired and reluctant to go out (for dinner). I decided to prepare a sukiyaki. I got everything out (of the refrigerator) and asked everyone to help. Soon everyone was chopping vegetables and slicing meat. (Within half an hour), there were an electric skillet, plates (of meat), and bowls (of vegetables) (on the table). Everyone enjoyed cooking his own way (at the table).

Connecting Clauses *(pages 73–74)*

IV. *A.*

1. I started kindergarten when I was four years old.

2. Since I had to be (at school) (at eight o'clock) (in the morning), I had to get up (at seven).

3. As I stepped out (of the house), I heard my father snoring.

4. Locking the door (behind me), I could smell the fresh air and the delicious odor (from the ribs stand) (at the corner) (of the street).

5. When I reached the end (of the street), I had to climb forty steps.

6. Those steps were so high that I almost had to claw my way up.

7. I didn't dare look back because I was afraid that I might fall down.

8. After I reached the top, I had to walk (for another two blocks) (through dirty, smelly streets).

9. I was always afraid that I would see a rat.

10. When I did, I would feel sick all day.

B. (In those days) when Japan was still poor and oppressed (by the memory) (of the lost war), many heroes came (from television). Rikidah-zan was a professional wrestler who defeated rascal white wrestlers (with his karate chop) as if he were driving out the war-beaten Japanese people's inferiority complex. Tetsuwan was a boy robot cartoon character who always defeated villains. All the heroes fought (against those) who teased the weak. These heroes helped Japan recover (from her war-beaten condition).

Inserting Clauses *(pages 81–82)*

V. *A.*

1. The forms that were (on the table) have disappeared.

2. The answer I expected was much simpler.

3. The woman who found the body saw no other person (in the room).

4. They rush me (through the line) so fast I don't even know what I bought.

5. The U.S. Secretary (of Education) said the federal role (in enforcing laws) (against discrimination) (in education) should be trimmed.

6. It seems we go (from month) (to month) anticipating the holiday that each month brings.

7. The house I remember was huge and had a round stained-glass window (in the front).

8. Whenever she opened that door, she expected to see her uncle sitting (in the heavy chair) (by the window).

9. He sat there wondering why he had come, what he would say, and how he would get away.

10. The lady who brought the eggs always wore a low flat-brimmed hat.

B.

1. Because <u>he was</u> originally a priest, Vivaldi's long-term <u>friendship</u> (with the French prima donna Anna Girand), <u>who accompanied</u> him (on his travels), eventually <u>generated</u> awkward questions, and <u>Vivaldi lived</u> out his last days (in rejection and poverty).

2. The <u>topics Brown addressed</u> then <u>are</u> still very much (in the news), so <u>we decided</u> to publish his remarks (in fuller form).

3. <u>Gordon Jackson</u>, <u>who played</u> Mr. Hudson, <u>was</u> recently <u>stopped</u> (in Piccadilly) (by an American woman) <u>who wanted</u> him to become her butler.

4. Over (at Bloom's), <u>customers who entered</u> (through the main door) <u>found</u> themselves (in the middle) (of a Southeast Asian jungle), where camouflage-print <u>clothing was displayed</u> (amid large cloth palms).

5. The <u>town was founded</u> (at the turn) (of the century) and <u>settled</u> (by workers) (for the Santa Fe Railroad) <u>who filled</u> the marshes separating the island (from the mainland).

Sentence Fragments *(pages 90–91)* *(Sentences that need no correction are omitted)*

VI. A.

2. on all medicine, Especially those new higher-strength aspirins.

3. an early age, That gravity is a powerful force.

4. narrow and winding streets, Stalling on every hill I came to and grinding gears along the way.

6. When I was a senior high school student in Korea, I had three

7. and make a profit, Like our famous oil companies.

9. in a special sauce, So that the shrimp absorbs the sauce and becomes tender.

10. father's company, Of course, as an employee.

B.

legislative bodies that consider the policies, *and the laws* of the country. ~~Also the laws.~~

solve the energy problem, Bills appropriating money for research and development of breeder reactors, fusion reactors, solar energy, and coal exploitation.

of special interest groups, ~~Groups~~ whose members were voting constituents of the representatives.

Run-Together Sentences *(pages 100–101)*

VI. A.

1. coming down lightly, then it began to come down hard. *RTS*
2. seventies still remain. however, they appear in prints now. *RTS*
3. picnics, dances, and volleyball, once they rented a party boat. *RTS*
4. of employment. if we can slow down inflation we might be able to solve some of our employment problems. *RTS*
5. Her ancestry is Korean, her radiant smile points to large, dark, expressive eyes. *RTS*
7. from the safety officer, then we went to get our ammunition. *RTS*
8. Cities began to emerge, and with them came pollution. *RTS*
9. My nephew would begin to walk, then all of a sudden I could hear a clump, he had fallen again. *RTS*
10. i went upstairs for a few minutes, when I returned to the kitchen, I looked in the oven and saw that his chocolate chip cookies were burned. *RTS*

B.

Chess Championship. two days after school
site of the tournament. the tournament lasted six days as a team
of thirty-two schools. Individually out of
got third place, and I was next with seventeenth place. Although the
the sights around Houston. We saw the Astro
and NASA. We all had a great time

Nouns *(pages 108–109)*

VI. A.

1. buildings
2. parents
3. colors   fashions
4. favorites
5. brakes
6. types
7. teenagers
8. games
9. nuisances
10. lives

B.

transporting astronauts to
Apollo rockets were
send astronauts to
  Scientists and engineers
several years to

Pronouns

Pronouns: Number *(page 115)*

A.

1. with him or her
2. saying they were
4. sadness they bring
5. remembers his or her fear.
6. telling the prisoners that
7. Working students don't have
9. People who want . . . apartments
10. All young people need

B.

in their respective

scheduled workouts, these people went over

Pronouns: Person *(pages 121–122)*

V. *A.*

1. with our best
2. behind them when
3. to help me with my work
4. on my own . . . being my own boss
5. that I enjoy . . . when I do
6. learned I have . . . what I want
7. room we could
9. having my own
10. especially when she has

B.

dates I had	that I didn't
made me sick to my stomach	after I'd studied
reading I had	that I was half

Pronouns: Form

III. *two pronouns (page 126)*

1. She and
3. when my friend and I were
4. brother and I
5. Once a couple of friends and I

6. weekend, my sister and I may
8. gave him and me the
9. Some friends and I
10. times he and I have

F. who and whom (pages 129–130)

3. Whom
8. to whomever
10. whom

B. than and as (page 131)

1. as they
3. than he
4. than I
5. than he

6. than I
8. than I
9. as I
10. than she

Noun and Pronoun Review *(pages 133–134)*

A.

1. and I hear my mother yelling at my
2. but they are
4. When overweight people step
5. She's supposed to spoil him or her.
6. My sister and I . . . than he
7. made me wonder if she and I were
8. and I talk to them so I don't
9. that they were right
10. whatever their minds want them to do. If they just . . . in the way of them and their goals, they can become whatever they want.

B.

1. smokers who are
2. dirty their clothes because they would
3. when I'm in
4. these people at times are not sure whether they have a place to stay . . . the trouble they have to go through.
5. All people have . . . they are children.
6. All young adults should get summer jobs . . . a car. They can also buy themselves some school clothes so that their parents . . . for them.
7. school. They provide . . . to let myself loose.
8. People may think . . . but find out that the scale is so high they end. . . . hard people study. If their grades match . . . if they end up . . . Grades to teachers are just letters, but to students they are their futures.
9. smaller than I.
10. of things . . . for example snakes, poison oak

Verbs

Verbs: Present Tense (page 145)

VII. A.

1. Although <u>ballet</u> and African <u>dance</u> <u>are</u> different, the <u>spirit</u> required (for these dances) <u>are</u> the same.
2. The <u>top</u> and the <u>bottom</u> (of this fruit) <u>is</u> not smooth (like the rim) (of a glass cup).
3. This <u>game</u> <u>consists</u> (of nine innings), and when there <u>is</u> a <u>tie</u>, the <u>innings</u> <u>continue</u> until the <u>game</u> <u>is</u> <u>untied</u>.
4. The <u>refrigerator</u> <u>allows</u> people to have a large variety (of food) (at any time) (of the day).
5. <u>Learning</u> to write essays <u>are</u> very important (to a student).
6. My family's <u>teeth</u> <u>is</u> always (in good shape).
7. There <u>is</u> also the <u>fights</u> (between the pitchers and players) <u>that</u> <u>has</u> just <u>been</u> <u>hit</u> with the ball).
8. Although our <u>bodies</u> <u>are</u> not alive (after death), our <u>spirits</u> <u>remain</u>.
9. If I ever <u>has</u> to go again now, <u>I</u> <u>don't</u> <u>think</u> it <u>will</u> <u>be</u> as bad because (of the new cross-harbor tunnel).
10. When the <u>pitcher</u> <u>is</u> not <u>doing</u> well, the <u>manager</u> <u>comes</u> (into the field) and <u>talks</u> (to him) (for a couple) (of minutes).

B.

James and Lewis hate each
we are only
they seem to misunderstand
one comes over and gets upset
other one is there

Verbs: Past Tenses *(page 158)*

V.   A.

1. then spread all
2. I had seen some
4. and were off
6. there were movies

7. We sang,
8. We were
9. I found
10. you've driven

B.

gone, James came up
either was coming
I kissed him
I saw James

Verbs: Combinations *(page 166)*

V.   A.

1. still be faced
2. She will be moving
3. was hospitalized quite
4. Don't American

5. not very crowded.
6. I wasn't finished.
8. programs are needed to improve our
9. my teeth are going
10. very relaxed.

B.

could travel billions
have acquired a lot
could pass on

Verbs: Tense Shifts *(pages 173–174)*

V.   A.

2. floor was mopped
3. that frightened me.
4. I do not remember
6. if I didn't have

7. He came . . . and changed the channel.
8. it was time
9. They conquered many
10. medicine was . . . it was supposed to do.

B.

The police pulled up and started asking
officers grabbed me and threw me
I asked him what I was being
he told me
that he had the
car pulled up, and the officer said that
they had

Verb Review *(pages 175–176)*

A.

1. man looks down
2. trips cost them
4. dentists always do a
6. there were any casts

7. the person wants to
8. He told Michael
9. never noticed before.
10. We have used up

B.

1. money I have saved.
2. manufacturer was subsequently
3. realized I had learned many
4. he scored forty-two points and led the Lakers
5. something I had always wanted to do.
6. stores have been
7. Have you ever gone into
8. alone contributed over
9. meal cost me . . . I paid for it.
10. there was not enough space

C.

1. and goes faster.
2. used to pull me . . . and introduce me
3. She knows that if she keeps on
4. cheese is melted
5. were forced to make
6. can be solved
7. could not stand up.
8. brother doesn't want to . . . the others want to
9. I haven't received my . . . I will just forget about
10. There are one female and two males, so I am again wakened

D.

1. is supposed to be a place to prepare for
2. My head, my looks, and my future are being
3. so scared that
4. thinks she is supposed to come
5. She was such
6. airplane has a set
7. There are so
8. be prejudiced
9. Datsuns were
10. mother got back . . . mother came back . . . to hide my valuables

Modifiers

Modifiers: *Past Participles As Modifiers* (pages 182–183)

VI. *A.*

1. A balanced diet
2. Overcooked meat
3. and handicapped people.
4. single-spaced and typed.
5. lady named Connie
6. audiences amused and
7. a long-sleeved blouse
8. barbecued potato
9. high-heeled shoes
10. show called "M*A*S*H."

B.

Yvette helped me	she overpowered me
girl named Velna	boy named
than Yvette and I	to pay. He
powerful and seemed	Yvette jumped
I grabbed her	fight him. I'll

Modifiers: *Adjectives and Adverbs* (pages 189–190)

IV. *A.*

1. very well in
2. took school seriously.
4. dress casually, and
5. out well sometimes,
6. It is really entertaining
8. screamed really loudly, and
9. ride it well enough.

B.

as quickly as
dressed distastefully or bizarrely
dressed similarly

Modifiers: Comparisons *(pages 200–201)*

VI. *A.*

1. b. flatter
   c. flatter
   d. the flattest
2. b. wealthier
   c. wealthier
   d. the wealthiest
3. b. more helpful
   c. more helpful
   d. the most helpful

4. b. more easily
   c. more easily
   d. the most easily
5. b. better
   c. better
   d. the best

B.

1. The president has more experience with inflation problems than the other candidate does.
3. I write much better since
4. much bigger and more powerful
5. is the wisest thing to do.
6. problems more easily.
7. lower than the view of the average person.
9. much happier
10. much fairer person

Wrong Word Form *(pages 207–208)*

IV. *A.*

1. a big difference between
2. some tragic and some comic stories.
3. famous natural wonders
4. Overpopulation began to appear gradually
5. for her friendliness during

6. flower dominates it.
7. the interruption.
8. feel a loss when
9. so dependent on
10. students participated in

B.

I am scared, afraid of failure
getting a disastrous hair style
see a psychiatrist

Comma Rules 1, 2, and 3 *(pages 215–216)*

V. *A.*

1. driver,³ but
2. together,² buy . . . blouses,² and
3. there,¹ I
4. cooking,¹ I
5. Calgary,² Canada,² named

7. going[3] so
8. girls,[1] I . . . way[3] but . . . guys,[1] they
10. listen,[1] I

B.

The Rex,[2] Eden,[2] and Casino were big ones,[3] and they

During weekends,[1] many

were expensive,[1] people

Romeo and Juliet,[2] *Doctor Zhivago*,[2] and *Gone with the Wind*

C.

Nguyen Hue Avenues,[1] there were department stores,[2] flower stores,[2] and television stores. On weekends,[1] people

restaurants,[2] stores,[2] and theaters were full,[3] and people

Comma Rule 4 *(pages 224–225)*

V. A.

1. sister,[4] who . . . I,[4] helps
2. Disney,[4] the . . . Mouse,[4] is
3. set,[4] each
6. Lee,[4] who . . . China,[4] married

7. Jackson,[4] my best friend,[4] rides
9. Anthony,[4] who lived in Georgia,[4] died
10. store,[4] amazingly . . . stores,[4] was

B.

busgirl,[2] hostess,[2] and
yet,[3] so
Liz,[4] the head waitress,[4] would
done,[1] she
Barbara,[4] the cook,[4] lived

us,[3] and she
Evelyn,[4] the owner,[4] was
around,[1] it
business,[3] but
pleasant,[3] and

Comma Review *(pages 226–227)*

A.

On the tables,[1] there
beef,[2] cheese,[2] and
beans,[2] rice,[2] lettuce,[2] and
Steak picado,[2] enchiladas verdes,[2]
choices,[3] but
favorite,[4] I must admit,[4] was
chile relleno,[2] two enchiladas,[2] a taco,[2] and

B.

country,[1] I
here,[1] my mother
frozen,[3] and she

crab stew,[2] octopus stew,[2] fresh meat,[2] and
while,[3] and when she does,[1]
hamburgers,[2] TV dinners,[2] and

C.

tied,[3] and there were
sudden,[1]
forward,[4] who quickly

the game,[3] and I
on,[1] the coach
up,[3] and I

D.

1. War II! a man,⁴ especially a father,⁴ was
2. States³ and
3. appetite! the Piper's⁴ located in San Leandro,⁴ offers
4. sunrise? breathe the fresh air? or see
5. college! Magic . . . Clyde's⁴ a disco in Lansing.
6. money! I
7. friends⁴ on the other hand,⁴ never . . . trouble³ and . . . promised! he
8. book? read . . . pages? and
9. Reagan,⁴ who . . . problems⁴ is
10. Cars? money? diamonds? and

Semicolons and Colons *(pages 234–235)*

V. A.

2. of steak
3. State, I
5. example, the

7. targets, it
8. as pinball
9. diploma, I

B.

include Pink Floyd
include Yes
uses more

Yes, for
of guitars

Articles *(page 242)*

IV. A.

1. have an hour
2. just a wide
3. is an escape
4. maybe an unfriendly
5. Health

6. is another
7. heard an extensive
8. and a half
9. is an Oriental
10. has a deep

B.

During the cleaning
edge of the lens
lost a soft

it the next day
in a folded

Contractions *(pages 248–249)*

IV. A.

1. she can't . . . because it's stuck.
2. Monday's over and I'm
3. Don't
4. I didn't have
5. problems; they're

6. find you're on
7. student doesn't
9. That's
10. I've

B.

like you'll be thrown
die, you'll be sued
and you'll lose

I'm willing
I'm starting
that's Hawaiian

Possessives *(pages 258–259)*

VI. *A.*
1. father's face
2. mother's decisions.
4. one's next month's budget
6. workers' wage

7. my mother's clothes . . . older sister's
8. the reader's mind.
9. boy friend's loud

B.

Colonel Potter's grandson
B. J. Honeycutt's family

B. J.'s kids

Capitals *(page 265)*

IV. *A.*
1. liberated
2. President
3. A doctor
4. this Saturday and Sunday
5. our government

7. carols every Saturday
8. holidays . . . Memorial Day.
9. Halloween
10. strong bell boy . . . weak bell boy

B.

to Fremont to
to McDonald's to
from Bellows Falls

Marlboro, Winchester, Dublin,
and Bellows Falls

Spelling *(page 278)*

V. *A.*
1. achieve
2. besiege
3. leisure
4. mischievous
5. receive

6. reign
7. retrieve
8. freight
9. fiend
10. reindeer

B.
1. angrily
2. marriage
3. destroyer
4. losing
5. receivable

6. goddess
7. transmitting
8. interesting
9. dignified
10. busily

C.
1. Everyone knows . . . important to us.
2. and their enjoyment
3. I knew . . . to lose ten pounds
4. good restaurant, I expect everything to be nice.
5. In the past, . . . more oppressive than it
6. I worked during my last two summers . . . I accepted
7. I would advise . . . that reprieve.
8. my adviser can be quite a task.
9. hang clothes, . . . to help our customers
10. in their early stages, before too

IV. *A.*

1. the <u>number</u> of
2. try <u>to</u> usher.
3. hardly <u>anything</u> in
5. or <u>any</u> other
6. experiences <u>when</u>
8. be <u>fewer</u> people
9. job <u>more</u>
10. large <u>number</u> of

B.

People who live	believe people could
must have forgotten	They could have easily
saw a lot of paper	

Concrete Subjects and Verbs (pages 293–294)

IV. *A.* *(there are other possible revisions)*

2. I discovered the penny's power when I was ten years old.
3. It also has a negative effect on the soldiers when they go home.
5. I disappear when I hear people yelling obscenities and fighting.
6. Best of all, in college we don't have a curfew.
7. For example, food prices have risen dramatically.
8. Professors who say they don't care about my writing skills encourage me to ignore these things.
9. First, our car broke down.
10. Primitive tribes believe in evil spirits and practice rites to remove them from the body.

B. *(there are other possible revisions)*

When going to college, too many girls make the mistake of falling back on business colleges. Business offers many opportunities, but women should consider becoming something other than secretaries. Soon there will be more secretaries than jobs. Business colleges are also very expensive. A six-month course costs about $2,000. Why pay so much money when it's cheaper to go to a four-year college and become an accountant, an engineer, or a teacher?

Vague Pronoun Reference (pages 300–301)

V. *A.* *(other solutions possible)*

1. This announcement upset a lot of athletes.
2. An evening at The Moonraker, an excellent restaurant on the shore of Boston, would be memorable.
3. The cold water and the high waves were enough to make me believe that a dinosaur lived there.
4. Scientists are still experimenting with ways to store and save power from the sun.
5. Now, I don't expect him to want to get up and do the three o'clock feedings, but he would help me if he did.
7. He was invited to a seminar in June 1983 on the subject of nuclear wars.
9. Some people recommend buying only the most expensive clothing made from the best material.
10. When we had these parties, about ten of us would go to lunch.

B.

Vacations give us time	give everything our best
whatever we're doing	Good vacations will make

Mixed Constructions *(page 308)*

IV. **A.** *(there may be other possible corrections)*
1. Being so exhausted is bad
2. Working in the library gave me
3. Although most of the time this system works, at other times
4. When I took a solid stand and opposed my mother, we both had a very trying time.
5. Having his haircut changed
6. Scheduling our hours in advance makes it
7. enough not to have this problem.
8. For example, "Lookin' Back" is a song
9. I can never overcome my nervousness during examinations.
10. Walking or looking into a store window takes my

B.

my mother bought me two
forgotten about him. My gift made his
thanked me. Watching him be happy made me

Parallel Structure *(pages 316–317)*

VII. **A.** *(other answers are possible)*
1. baseball, ride bikes
2. help him with his homework, his job, and his personal problems.
3. and realized it would
4. sloshed around in a narrow canal, thrown down a waterfall, and splashed into a beautiful harbor.
5. and purchasing them?
6. and elegantly.
7. and not be on welfare.
8. and helped me get a better grip on life.
9. and moved into a new house.
10. check your gums, your bite, and your wisdom teeth.

B.

careful how we use our cars and our resources.

appreciate what we have and not waste it

with no way to get there

Dangling and Misplaced Modifiers *(page 325)*

IV. **A.**
1. Not doing my homework, I got lower grades in my math class.
3. Atlantic City, I found that night had fallen
4. Because I am thirty years old, society would wonder about my
6. When I turn in all my work on time, my teacher gives
7. We gazed at the moon, sinking slowly behind the trees.
8. I like to see where I'm going from all angles while riding.
9. Whether big, tall, small, fat, thin, black, or white, everyone can enjoy skiing.
10. When I turned to the Lord, my prayer was answered.

B.

        generous person. Because he is in the ministry

        After talking to her for a few

        valuable things." After he told me this, I

Direct and Indirect Speech (page 334)

V. *A.*

1. The travel agent asked how long we would like to stay in Venice.
2. My roommate urged me to go to the health service about my cough.
3. The professor told us to turn to the illustration on page ninety-three.
4. Quietly she asked what rock-and-roll had to do with Sisyphus.
5. He wondered why remedial spelling was being taught in the philosophy department.
6. She asked if she might get a refund on that book.
7. Lynn pointed into the night sky and said that the sparks from the fire went into the sky and became stars.
8. He said I really wouldn't understand Plato if I read translations.
9. She asked him to tell her all about industrial solvents.
10. She said she thought that Alexander the Great was an alcoholic.

B.

1. if I am enjoying my meal.
2. why I am going to college.
3. doing exactly what a president should do.
4. and how good the team was that year.
5. She said, "Kathy, don't . . . wringer."
6. crab if he liked her new dress.
7. I wonder if I have four children instead of one.
8. teacher why most plants lose their
9. myself where he is coming from.
10. him why he watered just

Idiom (pages 342–343)

V. *A.*

1. from	6. with . . . on
2. on	7. from
3. with	8. with
4. to	9. for . . . at
5. from	10. with

B.

1. practicing a cheerleading	5. quitting school, . . . quit her job.
2. He told me about the great difference between	6. In the corner
3. techniques which	7. I advise everyone
4. wandered in the nearby woods.	8. five years since
	10. company to theirs.

x

IV.   *A.*

   My costume for traveling was utilitarian if a trifle bizarre. Half-Wellington rubber boots with cork inner soles kept my feet warm and dry. Khaki cotton trousers, bought in an army-surplus store, covered my shanks, while my upper regions rejoiced in a hunting coat with corduroy cuffs and collar and a game pocket in the rear big enough to smuggle an Indian princess into a Y.M.C.A. My cap was one I have worn for many years, a blue serge British naval cap with a short visor and on its peak the royal lion and unicorn, as always fighting for the crown of England.

—John Steinbeck

   B.

   A girl stood before him in midstream, alone and still, gazing out to sea. She seemed like one whom magic had changed into the likeness of a strange and beautiful seabird. Her long slender bare legs were delicate as a crane's and pure save where an emerald trail of seaweed had fashioned itself as a sign upon the flesh. Her thighs, fuller and soft-hued as ivory, were bared almost to the hips, where the white fringes of her drawers were like feathering of soft white down. Her slate-blue skirts were kilted boldly about her waist and dovetailed behind her. Her bosom was as a bird's, soft and slight, slight and soft as the breast of some dark-plumaged dove. But her long fair hair was girlish: and girlish, and touched with the wonder of mortal beauty, her face.

—James Joyce

   C.

   I became increasingly frustrated at not being able to express what I wanted to convey in letters that I wrote, especially those to Mr. Elijah Muhammad. In the street, I had been the most articulate hustler out there—I had commanded attention when I said something. But now, trying to write simple English, I not only wasn't articulate, I wasn't even functional. How would I sound writing in slang, the way I would say it, something such as, "Look, daddy, let me pull your coat about a cat, Elijah Muhammad—"

—Malcolm X

   D.

   At exactly fifteen minutes past eight in the morning, on August 6, 1945, Japanese time, at the moment when the atomic bomb flashed above Hiroshima, Miss Toshiko Sasaki, a clerk in the personnel department of the East Asia Tin Works, had just sat down at her place in the plant office and was turning her head to speak to the girl at the next desk.

—John Hersey

VI.   *A.   (possible answers)*

1. Going away from the center of town, I saw nothing but endlessly wide land with many houses.
2. He was rich enough to hire several employees.
3. ..., I could see familiar landscape.
4. I want to learn how to fix my car to save money and time.
5. On holidays like Christmas, ...
6. Police officers in my neighborhood stop drivers and give them tickets.
7. ... don't like the cars or their drivers.
8. I use English at work and school.
9. On the first day of the festival, I went to Japan Town in the morning to see the parade before the festival.
10. I like my mother's cooking best.

B. *(possible answers)*

1. I often face such situations on dates.
2. I like cooking for myself because I can eat as much as I want.
3. Death is not the end of life but rather the beginning of a new life.
4. Luck is one of man's greatest gifts.
5. I will teach my children to speak Filipino and respect others.
6. A person who plays an instrument can share that joy and beauty with another.
7. All family members should share the house work and take turns cleaning up after each other.
8. As a little girl, I had trouble sharing my feelings with others.
9. Most advisers recommend that students take several writing courses.
10. I enjoy having a compatible boyfriend.

C.

On a night the wind loosened a shingle and flipped it to the ground. The next wind pried into the hole where the shingle had been, lifted off three, and the next, a dozen. The midday sun burned through the hole and threw a glaring spot on the floor. The wild cats crept in from the fields at night, but they did not mew at the doorstep any more. They moved like shadows of a cloud across the moon, into the rooms to hunt the mice. And on windy nights the doors banged, and the ragged curtains fluttered in the broken windows.

—John Steinbeck

Sentence Variety *(pages 365–367)*

IV. *A.*

Writing is, for most, laborious and slow. The mind travels faster than the pen; consequently, writing becomes a question of learning to make occasional wing shots, bringing down the bird of thought as it flashes by. A writer is a gunner, sometimes waiting in his blind for something to come in, sometimes roaming the countryside hoping to scare something up. Like other gunners, he must cultivate patience: he may have to work many covers to bring down one partridge.

—E. B. White

B.

The young writer will be drawn at every turn toward eccentricities in language. He will hear the beat of new vocabularies, the exciting rhythms of special segments of his society, each speaking a language of its own. All of us come under the spell of these unsettling drums; the problem, for the beginner, is to listen to them, learn the words, feel the excitement, and not be carried away.

—E. B.White

VI. *A.*

Snoopy, from atop his doghouse, is very much a commentator from a mock-pulpit, calling man to see his errors and return to the straight and narrow path. In one episode, Snoopy has allowed four homeless birds to use his doghouse as a temporary refuge. They become so noisy playing bridge that Snoopy has to drive them away (the last one carrying a little bridge table on his head). Snoopy then comments: "A Friend is NOT someone who takes advantage of you!" There is something about being on doghouses, pulpits, or even soapboxes that brings out the moralist in man—and dogs like Snoopy.

—Arthur Asa Berger

B.

   I have always felt that the first duty of a writer was to ascend—to make flights, carrying others along if he could manage it. To do this takes courage, even a certain conceit. My favorite aeronaut was not a writer at all, he was Dr. Piccard, the balloonist, who once, in an experimental moment, made an ascension borne aloft by two thousand small balloons, hoping that the Law of Probability would serve him well and that when he reached the rarefied air of the stratosphere some (but not all) of the balloons would burst and thus lower him gently to earth. But when the doctor reached the heights to which he had aspired, he whipped out a pistol and killed about a dozen of the balloons. He descended in flames, and the papers reported that when he jumped from the basket he was choked with laughter. Flights of this sort are the dream of every good writer: the ascent, the surrender to probability, finally the flaming denouement, wracked with laughter—or with tears.

—E. B. White

Index

"A, an," 236–238
Abstract, 287–289
"Accept, except," 268
Adjective endings, 202–203
Adjectives, 184–186
Adverb endings, 202–203
Adverbs, 184–186
"Advice, advise," 268
"Affect, effect," 268–269
"All ready, already," 269
"All right," 269
"A lot," 269
"Amount, number," 280
"An, a," 236–238
Anderson, Sherwood, 283–285
Apostrophes
    contractions, 243–245
    possessives, 250–252
"Are," *See* "Be"
"Are, or, our," 269
Articles, 236–238

"Be"
    mixed constructions with, 303
    modifier forms after, 186
    past participle of, 148
    past tense of, 149
    present tense of, 136–137
    verb forms after, 160
    weakness of, 288–289
"Board, bored," 269
Body paragraphs, 24–27

"Can, could," 167
Capitals, 260–261
"Choose, chose," 269
Choppiness, 356-59

Clauses
    commas with, 209–211, 217–219
    defined, 66
    dependent, independent, 66–68, 75–76
    and fragments, 83–85
    inserting, 75–76
    punctuating, 95
    and run-togethers, 92–96
    words making dependent, 66, 95
"Clothes, cloths," 270
Cohen, Leonard, "Go by Brooks," 292
Colon, 229
Comma
    before an independent clause, 209
    between independent clauses, 210–211
    with interrupters, 217
    in list or series, 209
    with modifiers, 217–219
    review exercises, 226–227
    rule 1, 209
    rule 2, 209
    rule 3, 210–211
    rule 4, 217–219
    with "that" clauses, 218
Comma splice, 92–96
Comparisons, 191–194
"Complement, compliment," 270
Concise wording, 344–348
Conclusions, 42–43
Concrete words, 287–289
Condensing sentences, 93, 177, 344–348
"Conscience, conscious," 270
Contractions, 243–245
Coordinate conjunctions. *See* "Fanboys"
    words
"Could, can," 167

Dependent clauses. *See* Clauses

Details, 25–26
Direct, indirect speech, 326–329
"Do"
  helping verb, 54, 159–160
  past forms, 147
  present forms, 135
  in questions, 327–329
"Does, dose," 270
Double negative, 279–280

Ecclesiastes 3:1–8, 315
"Effect, affect," 268–269
Essay
  assignments, 64, 81, 100, 121, 144, 145,
    173, 199, 207, 234, 258, 285, 286,
    293, 300, 316, 324, 342, 365
  examples by students, 4, 12, 21–22,
    31–32, 39–40, 45, 63–64, 72–73,
    80–81, 89–90, 99–100, 107–108,
    114–115, 120–121, 143–144, 156–158,
    165, 172–173, 181–182, 188–189,
    198–199, 206–207, 214–215, 223–224,
    233–234, 241, 247–248, 257–258,
    264–265, 276–277, 299–300
  organization, 1–46
"Except, accept," 268
Evidence, 24–27

Facts, 7, 25–27
"Fanboys" words
  commas with, 209–211
  connecting clauses with, 68
  to correct run-togethers, 92–96
  in mixed constructions, 302
"Fewer, less," 280
Fragments, 83–85

Galsworthy, John, "The Japanese
  Quince," 322–324
General, specific, 24–27
"Go," 135–136, 147
"Go by Brooks," (Cohen), 292
"Good, well," 184–185

"Have"
  in combinations, 159–162
  helping verb, 54
  with past participles, 146–150
  present tense of, 136
  tense shifts with, 167–169
Helping verbs, 54
  in combinations, 159–162
  in questions, 327–329

Idea, fact, 7
"Idea, ideal," 270
Idiom, 335–337
Independent clauses. See Clauses
-ing words
  dangling, 318–319
  need helping verb, 160–161
  not working as verbs, 61–62
Introductions, 35–38
"Is." See "Be"
"It," 295–297
"Its, it's," 243–245, 170

Jacobs, Jane, 356
"Japanese Quince, The" (Galsworthy),
  322–324

"Knew, new," 271
"Know, no, now," 271

"Lead, led," 271
"Less, fewer," 280
Linking verbs, 47–48,
  mixed constructions with, 303
  modifier form after, 186
"Loose, lose," 271

"Many, much," 280
Mixed constructions, 302–304
Mixed structures, 302–304
Modification problems, 318–319
Modifier endings, 177–178
Modifiers
  adjective and adverb forms, 184–186
  comparisons, 191–194
  dangling, 318–319
  misplaced, 319
  past participles as, 177–178
  punctuation of, 217–219
Monotonous sentences, 356–360
"Much, many," 280

Names
  articles with, 237
  capitals with, 260–261
  as possessives, 250–252
"New, knew," 271
"No, now, know," 271
Noun and pronoun review exercises,
  133–134
Noun determiners, 237
Noun endings, 202–203

Nouns
  count, non-count, 102–103, 236, 280
  defined, 102
  in prepositional phrases, 48
  plurals of, 102–104
  possessives, 250–252
"Number, amount," 280

"Of, have," 281
"Or, our, are," 269
Outline, 14–16

Paragraphs
  body, 24–27
  concluding, 42–43
  in essays, 1–4
  introductory, 35–38
Paragraph writing assignments, 107, 119,
    120, 132, 158, 165, 181, 293, 307, 315,
    316, 333
Parallel structure, 309–310
"Passed, past," 271
Past participles. See also Verbs
  forms, 146–148
  as modifiers, 177–178
Past verbs, 146–150. See also Verbs
Plurals, 102–104, 250–252
Possessive pronouns, 243, 250
Possessives, 250–252
Prepositional phrases, 48
Prepositions,
  choosing, 335–337
  extra, 336
  list of, 48
  repeated, 303–304
Present tense verbs, 135–139. See also
    Verbs
Pronouns
  definition of, 110
  form, 123–124, 126–127, 130
  non-standard, 110
  number, 110–111
  person, 116–117
  possessive, 243, 250
  review exercises, 133–134
  sex, 11–111
  singular and plural, 110–111
  vague reference, 295–297
Punctuation, 228–229

Questions, 60, 327–329
Quotations, 326–327

"Raise, rise," 271–272
Readings, professional
  Anderson, Sherwood, 283–285
  Cohen, Leonard, 292
  Ecclesiastes, 315
  Galsworthy, John, 322–324
  Shaw, Bernard, 314, 332–333
  Thurber, James, 307, 339–342
  White, E. B., 293
"Real, really," 185–186
Reference problems, 295–297
"Rise, raise," 271–272
Run-on sentences, 92–96
Run-together sentences, 92–96

Semicolons, 228–229
Sentences
  analyzing, 66–68, 75–76
  beginning, 288, 360
  fragments, 83–85
  run-together, 92–96
  variety, 356–360
Shaw, Bernard, 314, 332–333
Specific, general, 24–27
Spelling, 260–273
Structures
  mixed, 302–304
  parallel, 309–310
Subject of paper, narrowing, 5–6
Subjects and verbs
  agreement of, 135–139
  concrete, 287–289
  recognizing, 49–50, 54, 60–62
Subjects of sentences
  active, 287
  in advice, requests, commands, 60
  concrete, 287
  empty, 303
  extra, 303
  more than one, 54
  recognizing, 47–50, 54, 60–61
  after verbs, 60
Supports, 2–4, 14–16

Tense shift, 167–169
"Than, then," 272
"That"
  indefinite pronoun, 295–297
  may be singular or plural, 138–139
  may be subject, 75
"That" clauses, punctuation of, 218
"The," 236–237

"Their," 250
"Their, they're, there," 243–245, 272
"Then, than," 272
"There," subjects after, 60
"There, they're, their," 243–245, 272
Thesis
    in introduction, 35–38
    writing, 5–9
"They're, there, their," 243–245, 272
"This, a," 296
"This," indefinite pronoun, 295–297
"Thorough, though, thought, through,
        threw, thru," 272
Thurber, James, 307, 339–342
Titles, capitals in, 260
"To" plus a verb
    no ending, 161–162
    not working as verb, 61–62
"Too, to, two," 272–273
Topic, narrowing, 5–6
"Two, too, to," 272–273

"Used to," 160–161

Verb endings, 202–203
Verbs
    action, 47
    active, 287
    combinations, 159–162
    in contractions, 61
    helping 54, 159–162, 327–329
    linking, 47–48, 186, 303
    many words in, 54
    more than one, 54
    past participles, 146–149, 160

past tenses, 146–150
present tense, 135–139
in questions, 162
recognizing, 47–50, 54, 60–62
review exercises, 175–176
tense shifts, 167–169

"Wander, wonder," 273
"Was." See "Be"
"Wear, we're, were, where," 273
"Well, good," 184–185
"Were." See "Be"
"Were, where, we're, wear," 273
"Where," 280–281
"Which"
    indefinite pronoun, 295–297
    singular or plural, 138–139
    who and, 281
White, E. B., 293, 345
"Who"
    singular or plural, 138–139
    which and, 281
    whom and, 126–127
"Whoever, whomever," 127
"Whose, who's," 243–245
"Will, would," 167
"Wonder, wander," 273
"Would, will," 167
Word form, 202–203
Wordiness, 93, 177, 344–348
Wrong word, 279–281
Wrong word form, 202–203

"Your, you're," 243–245